Social and Behavioural Macroeconomics

Christopher Tsoukis · Frédéric Tournemaine ·
Edward John Driffill

Social and Behavioural Macroeconomics

Theoretical and Policy Perspectives

palgrave
macmillan

Christopher Tsoukis
Keele Business School
Keele University
Staffordshire, UK

Frédéric Tournemaine
Faculty of Economics
Chulalongkorn University
Bangkok, Thailand

Edward John Driffill
Yale-NUS College
Singapore, Singapore

ISBN 978-3-031-77747-9 ISBN 978-3-031-77748-6 (eBook)
https://doi.org/10.1007/978-3-031-77748-6

This Palgrave Macmillan imprint is published by the registered company Springer Nature Switzerland AG
The registered company address is: Gewerbestrasse 11, 6330 Cham, Switzerland

To Chryssa (CT)
To Juntip (FT)
To Naoko (EJD)

Preface

This book reviews, unifies, and extends the significant but currently fragmented advancements in social and behavioural macroeconomics. It aims to more closely integrate macroeconomics with related fields such as behavioural economics, economic and analytical sociology, and social psychology. The motivation behind this effort stems from the understanding that societal and psychological factors significantly influence the behaviours that drive macroeconomic activity. Despite substantial contributions to this literature, there remains a notable disconnection among these works. Although there have been significant theoretical developments, comprehensive reviews in behavioural macroeconomics are still rare, with notable exceptions including Akerlof (2002), Akerlof and Shiller (2009), De Grauwe and Ji (2019), Baddeley (2017), and Hirshleifer (2020). Similarly, social macroeconomics has seen even fewer synthesis attempts, although growing interest is evident, as highlighted by the 2020 Third Annual Conference of the ESRC-funded "Rebuilding Macroeconomics" Group, titled "Understanding Social Macroeconomics", and the associated "Social Macroeconomics" research programme at the University of Oxford. In both social and behavioural macroeconomics, there is increasing awareness and interest, a growing body of literature, but still limited systematic synthesis.

The primary objective of this volume is to address this gap by providing a synthesis and offering rigorous, yet accessible, extensions to guide future research. The existing literature has not been sufficiently integrated either within itself or with the broader macroeconomic field or translated into teaching textbooks (though some progress has been made by Tsoukis, 2020). Thus, it remains largely unknown outside specialised academic circles. Finally, it seems that policy implications have not permeated broader discourse. This book is designed to address these deficiencies.

The departing point of the book is that the "homo economicus" paradigm, dominant in economics at large and in macroeconomics, needs to be abandoned, as so much evidence has been amassed that comprehensively rejects its foundational assumptions of rationality and atomistic agents. The book reviews this evidence and the related literatures of behavioural economics and psychology, and socio-economics and economic sociology. It also surveys at length the considerable efforts that have been made so far to introduce socio-behavioural insights into macroeconomics. Apart from literature reviews, in the middle chapters, the book takes some themes further than existing literature has done, so there is also some original analysis. As such, the book contains a mixture of discursive and analytical material. Throughout, we examine the relevance of socio-behavioural factors for traditional topics like macroeconomic policy effectiveness, the design of stabilisation (mainly monetary) policy, growth, saving, labour supply, and welfare. Furthermore, we explore whether the most relevant socio-behavioural traits can offer useful perspectives on issues old and new of enduring importance, such as (rising) inequality, factor shares or the structure of welfare state (through the provision of public versus private education). More open-ended themes include the investigation of the nature of "individual economic rationality" versus "socio-behavioural economic rationality" or even "collective rationality"; how empirically relevant socio-behavioural traits might hinder societies from achieving socially efficient outcomes; and whether these traits could provide a new foundation for (New) Keynesian macroeconomics.

The book is structured as follows: Chapter 1 presents a brief, critical overview of the history of macroeconomics and examines whether aspects of bounded rationality, largely ignored in standard literature, hold promise to enrich the sub-discipline. Chapter 2 reviews the literature on behavioural economics, questioning the fundamental assumption of rational behaviour in economics, which is often discarded in other social sciences. Chapter 3 explores how socio-economic factors, such as social aspirations or status-seeking driven by traits like envy, greed, or jealousy, can be incorporated into economic models. Chapter 4 demonstrates how these ideas can be integrated into various models of endogenous growth, discussing the key differences and implications compared to traditional approaches. Chapter 5 and Chapter 6 add the concepts of short-termism and dynamic inconsistency by combining hyperbolic discounting with status-seeking to analyse their effects on growth and income and wealth distribution (Chapter 5) and monetary policy (Chapter 6). Chapter 7 reviews the implications of socio-behavioural macroeconomic models for inequality. Finally, Chapter 8 concludes with a discussion on how social interactions impact atomistic agents, including potential effects on financial markets, and offers a review of recent developments in bio-economics to provide a deeper perspective on the issues discussed.

Thanks are due to Sugata Ghosh, George Kapetanios, George Perendia, and Avichai Snir for encouraging and stimulating discussions; and Pongsak Luangaram and an anonymous referee for helpful comments. In the writing-up stage, Chris visited John at the Yale-NUS (National University of Singapore) College, for a brief but productive and enjoyable stay; he gratefully acknowledges the hospitality and financial assistance of the Yale-NUS College. Everyone at Palgrave Macmillan has been very helpful and efficient; we thank particularly Ellie Duncan and Supraja Yegnaraman for their help in bringing this book to light. We dedicate the book to our wives with love and gratitude for their unwavering support and encouragement.

CONTENTS

List of Figures

List of Tables

CHAPTER 1

Introduction: The Social and Behavioural Turn in Macroeconomics

1 Introduction

In recent decades, there has been increasing disquiet among many economists and practitioners about the rigid theoretical underpinnings of the discipline. Critics argue that the pursuit of mathematical rigour tramples any other objective such as realism. The foundational assumptions and methodology of economics (methodological individualism, rationality) are simply chosen because they lend themselves to mathematical modelling (optimisation), and not because they bear any relevance to the real world. In the words of Nobel-winning behavioural economist Richard Thaler, the theory postulates an "econ" as its key individual, whereas the world is populated by humans (Thaler, 2016). The mathematical underpinnings and other foundational assumptions have been motivated by the need to provide an "objective" core of the discipline, with reference to which all controversies could be potentially resolved; but this edifice became gradually divorced from reality. The rigid assumptions coupled with ever-greater mathematical sophistication, the criticism continues, make the subject increasingly sterile.

Macroeconomics is subject to the same line of criticism about the relevance of its assumptions. The criticism assumes perhaps added force as the stylised assumptions of the currently dominant paradigm blur the distinction between micro and macro; with the potential loss of explanatory power for a whole raft of aggregate (macroeconomic) phenomena.

C. Tsoukis et al., *Social and Behavioural Macroeconomics*,
https://doi.org/10.1007/978-3-031-77748-6_1

This line of criticism is not new. A long line of founding fathers of economics and macroeconomics, most notably Keynes, have given prominent position in their analyses of assumptions and features that modern theory-making does not recognise.[1] Following the crisis of 2007-9, particularly the failure of economics to predict it and provide convincing cures, there is talk of a "crisis of (macro)economic theory" in some quarters, attributable to the rigidity of the assumptions and methodology of the discipline.

In the same spirit is the criticism that economics has abandoned the dialogue with neighbouring social sciences, such as sociology, politics, or psychology. It must be said that there have been remarkable forays of economics into such areas as politics (political economy) and sociology (economics of crime or family); but these have been on the terms dictated by economics, so to speak, that is, using the methodology and assumptions of economics.[2]

In contrast, behavioural economics draws on research in psychology, sociology, anthropology, and other fields to describe and model people's behaviour with descriptive realism, and it generally stands in contrast to the notion of individual-centred, rational behaviour that dominates mainstream economics. In other words, there is a dialogue with other disciplines, but the new element is that the paramount aim is the realism of the assumptions and the setups, not mathematical rigour. This has developed into a separate field, namely behavioural economics; it is situated within economics but borrows from psychology, sociology, and other disciplines. Some of these insights and models have been integrated within macroeconomics, forming an already voluminous, and growing, literature. However, it may be true to say that these features have not been integrated organically into core economic theory in their totality. One key reason is a lack of a clear way of how to proceed—what the key concepts that need to be kept are and how.

The aim of this book is to review this strand of work as it relates to macroeconomics. In this chapter, we briefly provide a brief history of

[1] Backhouse and Fontaine (2018), Colander (2005), and Kirman (2010), among others remind us that a long list of foundational names have theorised that individuals reason in a limited, non-strictly rational way, and have taken account of social interactions; the list of names includes Veblen, Pareto, Simon, Keynes, Hayek, Galbraith, Duesenberry, Frank, Hirschman, Olson, Scitovsky.

[2] This has given rise to criticisms of "economic imperialism"; see Chapter 8.

macroeconomics together with criticisms that have been directed against it, whether from a behavioural or other, more methodological, perspectives. We then proceed in subsequent chapters to review some key insights from behavioural and sociological economics and show how (some) have been integrated into macro theory. As not everything is incorporated into macroeconomics, we also explore some ideas that may be at the forefront of research and that may hold great potential for the near future. We also more suggestively consider the place that yet more insights might find in macroeconomics, in years to come. Thus, the book is a mixture of informal reviews of literature (mainly, this chapter and Chapters 2, 7 and 8), more formal accounts of how various ideas have been modelled in macroeconomics (Chapters 3 and 4), and more formal, original analyses about how yet other insights (mainly: present-bias) has and can be further incorporated into the main body of macroeconomics. Original formal analyses are contained mainly in Chapters 5 and 6, but also in Chapters 4 and 7. We also informally and briefly discuss our current research on identity in Chapter 8.

Without stealing our thunder (much), we can give a foretaste here. These are some examples:

- As Chapter 2 reviews in detail, fallacies, biases, heuristics, and rules of thumb are ubiquitous: All represent some kind of deviation from ("full") rationality. "Anchoring" effects, framing, mental accounting, confirmation bias, overconfidence, gambler's fallacy, and many more, hold the potential to explain behaviour in many areas, not least in financial markets. Recognition of these traits has found practical policy application.
- People plan for the future but do so imperfectly. They tend to save too little and regret it later. One reason for that is present-bias. More on this in Chapters 5 and 6.
- Similarly, people, on the whole, are not good at dealing with risk and uncertainty. Low probability events are often treated as if they will not happen at all. Other risks are magnified. Such considerations may hold a potential to explain the "equity premium puzzle":, a long-standing puzzle in macroeconomics. Chapters 2 and 7 elaborate.
- Investors in financial markets (and in auctions) appear to be given to "irrational exuberance" or "animal spirits" (a self-sustaining sense of optimism), bidding up prices beyond reason. Uninformed investors may follow the herd, expecting more price increases. Expert investors

may then invest in the belief that uninformed traders will continue to bid up the price. Again, behavioural traits in financial markets are reviewed in Chapter 8.

- People's behaviour is affected by the stories (accounts, narratives) they exchange concerning the economy. The pioneering behavioural finance theorist Robert Shiller talks of "narrative economics" (Shiller 2017). See Chapter 8.
- Consumers' spending is affected by advertising, and fads and fashions. Forecasts and rumours influence spending patterns. The disappearance of toilet paper and canned food at the start of the Covid pandemic is a good example; more in Chapters 2 and 7.
- Too much economics ignores altruistic behaviour, actions driven by ethical and social concerns, and concern for the welfare of others; see again Chapter 8.

The title of the book reflects our belief that the social element is equally important as the behavioural, for at least two reasons. It is now increasingly clear that individuals are not acting alone, independently of others.[3] Economics has started considering issues such as social comparisons and peer pressure, identity, social norms, trust, cooperation, social capital, altruism, networks, and herding behaviour to name but a few; all these directly refute methodological individualism. In addition, social interactions of all kinds exacerbate the behavioural traits that the behavioural part emphasises; if those behavioural traits are construed as deviations from rationality, if they occurred independently across agents, they might cancel out on aggregate. But the connection among individuals coordinates and exacerbates such "imperfections".[4]

Again, here are some examples that will be considered in Chapters 2 and 8 and elsewhere:

[3] This is something that other social disciplines (e.g. sociology, psychology, and others) have known all along.

[4] We use the term "imperfections" only once, and without agreeing with it. It implies that an ideal (here: rationality) is the benchmark and features such as cognitive limitations, biases, heuristics, are deviations from it, the connotation being that they are temporary and insignificant deviations. But in fact, we argue, such behavioural features are the essence of human behaviour.

- Phenomena such as fashion, positional concerns, charity, or contagion could not occur if individuals acted in isolation (see also Chapters 3 and 4).
- People are concerned about fairness. In laboratory experiments, when people are required to play the "ultimatum game", where player A has a sum of money, and has to offer some of it to player B. If B accepts the offer, they both get to keep the money: A keeps what is left over after giving B his share, B gets what he was offered. But if B refuses the offer, they each get nothing. It is repeatedly found that offers below 50% of the total are refused—even though the person refusing the offer loses, in violation of strict, individualistic rationality.
- On the other hand, people cooperate in games even when strictly rational play rules cooperation out. This happens in the repeated prisoner dilemma game and in the centipede game.
- People follow social norms of behaviour—in hours of work, holidays, spending.
- Altruistic behaviour, actions driven by ethical and social concerns, and concern for the welfare of others are important; they drive, e.g. charity, which is against strict individualism (the giver only enjoys a "warm glow" from giving—see Andreoni 1990).

At this point, it is tempting but also enlightening to consider the possibilities for macroeconomics arising from introducing such considerations. To this end, we turn to George Akerlof, who has been among the most forceful and early proponents of this intellectual project among the current generation of macroeconomists—and we draw, in particular, on Akerlof (2002, 2007). Akerlof (2002) argues that such behavioural traits could explain:

(a) The existence of involuntary unemployment—via social norms of fairness or morale embodied in "efficiency wage theories", or via "insider–outsider" theories;
(b) The impact of monetary policy on output and employment—via consumption theories that posit "rule of thumb" consumers along the lines of Keynes' consumption function, or due to price stickiness arising from near rationality in price setting, or due to "rational inattention";

(c) A stable trade-off between unemployment and inflation at sufficiently high unemployment and low inflation rates—due to resistance to nominal wage cuts because of "money illusion", but no resistance to erosion in real wages by inflation (at low levels of inflation);
(d) The prevalence of under-saving for retirement—due to hyperbolic discounting and time inconsistency of optimal plans, as mentioned;
(e) The excessive volatility of stock prices relative to their fundamentals—due to plain irrationality of market participants;
(f) The stubborn persistence of a self-destructive underclass, along class and ethnic lines—due to some extent to "identity", a topic that will be reviewed in Chapter 7.

In addition, reciprocity, loss aversion, herding, and many other socio-behavioural traits and "irrationalities" arguably have a great relevance for macroeconomic outcomes. In the same vein, Akerlof (2007) argues that such socio-behavioural traits hold a promise in breaking down the "five neutralities" that characterise modern macroeconomics: the independence of consumption and current income (the life-cycle permanent income hypothesis); the irrelevance of current profits to investment spending (the Modigliani–Miller theorem); the long-run independence of inflation and unemployment (natural rate theory); the inability of monetary policy to stabilise output (the rational expectations hypothesis or else "The Policy Ineffectiveness Proposition"); and the irrelevance of taxes and budget deficits to consumption (Ricardian equivalence), see Akerlof (2007, p. 6). Additionally, such traits may explain the "excess sensitivity" of consumption to current income, one of the long-standing puzzles in macroeconomics—see Conlisk (1996, p. 672).

The plan of this introductory chapter is as follows: It first contains a brief, critical review of macroeconomics from Keynes onwards (Sect. 2); the focus is on criticising the foundational assumptions of the discipline. Sections 3–5 contain reflections on bounded rationality and socio-behavioural economics and their implications, from a wide angle. Section 6 contains other methodological criticisms of macroeconomics which, though not strictly speaking emphasising the socio-behavioural aspects (or their omission), are broadly in line with that as a methodological critique. Throughout, we provide references to the sweeping critical remarks that opened the chapter. Finally, Sect. 7 contains a plan of the rest of the book.

2 A Brief History of Macroeconomics

Keynes and the Beginnings of the Discipline

Macroeconomics is the area of economics that tries to understand the economy as whole: the growth of output and living standards, economic fluctuations, the ups and downs of the rate of unemployment, the rate of inflation, movements of interest rates, exchange rates, the amount of imports and exports, the balance of payments, government spending and tax revenues, public borrowing and debt, and so on. It is contrasted with microeconomics which examines the behaviour of individual persons, or households, firms small and large, and markets. Microeconomics leads to a bottom-up approach to economic questions, starting by looking at small units and working up to bigger ones, whereas macroeconomics is (or at least, it was in the early days of the subject) more top-down, starting with the aggregate.

There is a consensus that macroeconomics came into being in 1936 with the publication by the British economist, John Maynard Keynes, of his book, *The General Theory of Employment, Interest, and Money* (or "*General Theory*" for short, Keynes 1936). What disparate analyses existed before Keynes (developed by the "Classics"—Keynes' term) evolved around simple but powerful ideas such as the following: Output grows because of the "supply-side" forces of investment and capital accumulation, technical progress, willingness and quality of the workforce, and the like. ("Say's law": supply creates its own demand.) There is a limited role that the public sector and "government" should play in the economy, namely to ensure the maintenance of the "rule of law", and maintain "sound" (i.e. non-inflationary) money through adherence to the Gold Standard of exchange rate determination and ensure that public finances are in order without deficits and debts.

The *General Theory* was a response to the Great Depression of the 1930s, a decade of unprecedented turmoil and chaos. 25% of the work force of the US were unemployed, many businesses went bust, thousands and thousands of banks collapsed, there was widespread poverty and destitution. The UK and continental European countries were similarly ravaged. Official understanding of the causes of the depression and the required policy response was based on the conventional wisdom of the time, which was permeated by "Classical" thinking: For instance, Andrew Mellon, US Treasury Secretary at the time was opposed to government intervention. He believed that recessions were a necessary part of the business cycle because they purged the economy. He advocated that firms should "...liquidate labour, liquidate stocks, liquidate the farmers, liquidate real estate. Purge the rottenness out of the system. High costs of living and high living will come down. ... enterprising people will pick up the wrecks from less competent people". The British Treasury believed that higher public spending (paid for by the government borrowing money) would only cause lower investment by firms and have no beneficial effect on the economy. Consequently, they advocated balanced budgets and letting the recession run its course. One interpretation of all this thinking may be that, no matter what its immediate cause(s) were, the recession presented an opportunity (however painful) for the economic system to renew itself. All governments had to do was hold their nerve, and the situation would improve in due course.

Against all this, the key point of the *General Theory* was that the Great Depression was due to a lack of aggregate demand; there was not enough custom for the growing supply of goods. Government intervention aiming to prop up demand was critical, as without it, the economy could be stuck in a low-output, high-unemployment equilibrium for a prolonged period of time. In Keynes' view, the policies of fiscal and monetary rectitude espoused by public officials in the US and UK (and other countries) would have made the situation worse, not better. In sharp contrast, Keynes provided theoretical underpinnings for policies of public spending, tax cuts, and government borrowing to increase total spending in the economy and bring down unemployment. Thus, Keynes' arguments turned several key preconceptions upside down. It was a radical assault on conventional economic wisdom, and it met with determined opposition. So, macroeconomics has been from the start a contested field.

Keynes argued that the conventional economics of the time might be appropriate in the long run, after the effects of shocks to the economy had dissipated and the economy had returned to a long-run equilibrium state. He wanted an analysis that had something useful to say about the short run as well. In the Tract on Monetary Reform of 1923, he had written: "Economists set themselves too easy, too useless a task if in tempestuous seasons they can only tell us that when the storm is past the ocean is flat again". He also, perhaps more famously, said, in the long run we are all dead.

In time, the General Theory became widely accepted, becoming the conventional wisdom in its turn. It dominated macroeconomics in the 1950s and 1960s, when policies of public spending and taxation based on it appeared to deliver stable growth, low unemployment, and low inflation. They were decades of prosperity and development. The French speak of Les Trentes Glorieuses, the thirty glorious years between 1945 and 1975. "You've never had it so good", said British prime minister Harold MacMillan in 1957.

Behavioural Elements of the General Theory

Keynes had achieved this remarkable turnaround in thinking by making some key assumptions that in retrospect might be considered as behavioural models, installing them in his analysis in place of cherished tenets of "Classical" economics (see, e.g. Akerlof 2002).

- He proposed that aggregate consumer spending was related to disposable income. His "fundamental psychological law" was that of a chunk of additional income, people would save some but spend a large fraction of it, and this fraction he called the marginal propensity to consume. This principle gets away from the microeconomic analysis of spending and saving based on maximising utility and looking at such factor the effects of interest rates (as the opportunity cost of consumption), inflation and intertemporal resources, on the optimal allocation of spending over time.
- He argued that cutting wages, even in an economy where many workers were unemployed, was very difficult, because it injured their sense of fairness. It would be a slow and painful process, running into stiff opposition. As each firm cut wages, and the workers involved would see their wages being cut relative to those of other workers in other firms. Cutting real wages, should it be necessary, could be done more equitably and more easily by allowing the price level to rise while money wages stayed the same; as workers would not be aware of the real value of wages, an instance of "money illusion".
- He regarded the stock market as a kind of casino, where the prices of stocks were not determined by fundamentals (the capitalised value of a firm's stream of expected future earnings) but by the values that investors thought that other investors were setting on firms. He wrote that it was like one of the beauty contests advertised in the newspapers of the time, in which: "It is not a case of choosing those [faces] that, to the best of one's judgment, are really the prettiest, nor even those that average opinion genuinely thinks the prettiest.

We have reached the third degree where we devote our intelligences to anticipating what average opinion expects the average opinion to be. And there are some, I believe, who practice the fourth, fifth and higher degrees" (Keynes, *General Theory of Employment, Interest and Money*, 1936).

- He argued that investment is driven by the "animal spirits" of the entrepreneurs.

> Even apart from the instability due to speculation, there is the instability due to the characteristic of human nature that a large proportion of our positive activities depend on spontaneous optimism rather than on a mathematical expectation, whether moral or hedonistic or economic. Most, probably, of our decisions to do something positive, the full consequences of which will be drawn out over many days to come, can only be taken as a result of animal spirits – of a spontaneous urge to action rather than inaction, and not as the outcome of a weighted average of quantitative benefits multiplied by quantitative probabilities. (Keynes, from *The General Theory*, 1936)

From the present vantage point, these ideas look remarkably prescient. But in the 1950s and 1960s, there was a gradual pushback against them, and they were gradually dismissed as being "ad hoc", not based on sound microeconomic foundations. However, such ideas have been revived and further elaborated upon in modern behavioural economics and psychology, as will be discussed in Chapter 2.

The "Keynesian Neoclassical Synthesis" and the Monetarist Counter-Attack

During the first post-WW II decades, the dominant school of academic macroeconomics was the "Keynesian Neoclassical Synthesis", a school that aimed to combine Keynes' insights with the microeconomic analysis ("Neoclassical economics") that was taught in the rest of the economics curricula. The analysis aimed to combine the demand-side analysis of Keynes with the supply side (that Keynes largely ignored) and to bring the general price level into the frame. The celebrated IS-LM model, the fiscal multiplier, the analysis of consumption, money demand, and investment, all were among the lasting contributions of this time; as was a drive to let statistical offices generate better aggregate data (National Income

Accounting) and a drive to test theory against data through the gradual development of econometrics.

Though the Keynesian Neoclassical Synthesis purported to be "Keynesian" in key respects, Keynes' message was gradually undermined, subtly in the beginning, more openly later. Milton Friedman and the "Monetarist" school led the way in the 1950s and 1960s. His permanent income hypothesis of consumer spending (along with the life-cycle hypothesis of Brumberg and Modigliani) moved away from Keynes' simple model and introduced the idea that consumers planned when deciding how much to spend, to smooth consumption over the years ahead. People receiving an increase in income now might be likely to save the bulk of it and spend little. Friedman criticised Keynes' neglect of the long-run consequences of public borrowing, noting that persistent borrowing increases the size of the national debt, raising the cost of paying the interest on it, and increasing the temptation to monetise the debt, eventually causing higher inflation.

Keynes did not pay much attention to inflation in the General Theory, but it became an issue in the 1950s after years of full employment. The Phillips curve, an empirical relation between the rate of inflation (in terms of the rate of growth of money wages) and the unemployment rate, had been added to the Keynesian model in 1958. It seemed to provide a menu of choice for governments, between lower unemployment accompanied by slightly higher inflation, or higher unemployment with lower inflation. Friedman argued that this could only be a short-run choice, and that in the long run inflation would either grow ever higher if the unemployment rate was kept too low or would progressively fall if unemployment was kept too high. At only one rate would inflation remain constant in the long run, and Friedman called this the "natural rate of unemployment". With the gradual acceptance of the notion of the "natural rate" and the associated notion of a vertical Phillips Curve by mainstream macroeconomics, the emphasis shifted, from the Keynesian objective of eliminating unemployment (the objective of the *General Theory* and of the early generations of post-WW II macroeconomists), to the more limited objective of stabilising unemployment (around the "natural rate").

Friedman was sceptical of government intervention in the economy. Fiscal "fine tuning" was likely to fail, and was maybe counterproductive, because the time taken to diagnose the economic situation, to devise policies to restore full employment, to implement those policies, and for them to have an effect on output and employment was so long that by that time the original problem might have gone away or been reversed. A policy aimed at restraining a boom might end up making a recession deeper. Because of this, he argued that the best policy for maintaining steady growth with low inflation was to get the money supply to grow at a steady rate—his k per cent rule—where k should be the trend growth rate of real GDP plus the target rate of inflation.

The broad thrust of Freidman's arguments was that government intervention in the economy was a bad thing, and that the economy would adjust itself and move back to equilibrium without assistance. Basically, it was a re-assertion of the pre-General Theory state of economics.

The Rational Expectations Hypothesis and the "New Classicals"

The reaction against Keynes' macroeconomics continued when the rational expectations revolution swept through the discipline and culminated in the 1970s with the ascendancy of the "New Classical" school of thought. The Rational Expectations Hypothesis (REH), that was developed in the 1960s and 1970s, postulated that forecasts—of things like future inflation rates, returns on financial assets, exchange rates, interest rates, and so on—should be modelled as if based on all available information including knowledge of how the economy works. As a result, there is no systematic forecast error (there are of course errors but they are entirely random); agents have learnt from any systematic pattern in their past mistakes, and in doing so, have eliminated that pattern.

The REH is essentially an application of (extreme) rationality in forecasting (cf. Chapter 2). A large subsequent literature has questioned the basic premises of the theory, whether, e.g. it arises out of learning, whether it is likely to hold when information acquisition is costly or when some market participants are not as (formally) rational. The general message is that the REH does not arise as the end result when such "frictions" have been cleared. Its main appeal is conceptual (if not operational) clarity and the lack of a clear alternative.

The REH is one key pillar (among three) of the "New Classical" macroeconomics (NC). The school owes its appeal to the wide perception of both conceptual and empirical shortcoming in the hitherto dominant Keynesian Neoclassical Synthesis. It completed the critique of Keynesianism initiated by Friedman and the Monetarists, but it went much further, being a radical departure from all previous schools. Firstly, the NCs emphasise that agents optimise along the lines suggested by microeconomics, so any macro theory must be based on sound "microfoundations" rather than on plausible looking but arbitrary assumptions, such as those propagated by Keynes. Behaviour must be explained by appeal to deep fundamentals such as utility or profit maximisation. For instance, the modelling of consumption should be based on maximisation of intertemporal utility subject to budget and borrowing constraints, uncertainty, etc. Any behavioural assumptions not derived in this manner are liable to break down when the external environment (e.g. government policy) changes.

Secondly, they espouse price and wage flexibility, so that markets clear. Firms and individuals are always on their demand and supply curves, meaning that they are doing the best for themselves, given the circumstances they face (productivity and wages, competition, price of raw materials, etc.). This implies that all market outcomes are "Pareto efficient" (in the absence of monopoly power, public goods, externalities, informational asymmetries and other "market imperfections"). This implies that important aspects of the market mechanism like business cycles or unemployment are the best response of the private sector to exogenous developments like productivity shocks (due to technology, training and skills, or organisational changes) and other various real shocks (due to taxation, energy and raw materials prices, or simply climate changes). Both business cycles and unemployment are painful, but they do reflect the best agents can do given circumstances beyond their control. If so, then there is a very limited role that government can do to either stabilise the economy or alleviate unemployment. In other words, this is the Smithian "invisible hand" all over again, or the application of the "folk theorems" of microeconomics in the sphere of macroeconomics.

The NCs articulate the results in a series of important results (see, e.g. Tsoukis 2020): The "policy ineffectiveness proposition" shows that stabilisation policy may produce more instability than stability; monetary policy, in particular is ineffective, a re-incarnation of the Classical notion that money is a "veil"; the "Lucas critique" shows that standard policy-making practice may fail as the system may change when the policy regime changes; the "dynamic inconsistency" of optimal policy shows why even well-meaning discretionary policy may fail to be implemented; the "Ricardian equivalence proposition" shows why tax cuts now may fail to stimulate the economy. These theorems have by now become standard fare in macroeconomics. Everybody knows numerous reasons why each of them can fail, yet they do serve to sharpen our thinking (a smart policy ought to be designed in such a way as not to be prone to these theorems). Nevertheless, despite this service that friend and foe alike acknowledge, these theorems serve also to shift the default position to one of policy ineffectiveness; it is incumbent upon the proponents of policy to show why and how policy can work, than on a critic to argue that it may not.

As with the REH, the optimisation postulate imbues individuals and firms with an extreme form of rationality. As Chapter 2 reviews, there are many number of reasons why agents do not have the cognitive or self-disciplining capabilities to become the mathematically optimising automata that the theory postulates. The issue is not one of realism only, it is a matter of implications, too. The supposed optimisation is crucial behind the result of Pareto optimality and the concomitant absence of a government role. If agents are prone to various cognitive limitations and "biases" like those reviewed in Chapter 2, and if those are socially combined along the lines that Keynes suggested (beauty contests, animal spirits, and the like) or in a way that socio-economics emphasises (see Chapters 2 and 7), then we may well be away from Pareto optimality, permanently, and not only transitorily. The economic role of government is then in principle re-instated.

REH and the principle of optimisation held by NCs are also in line with their beliefs about the "efficiency" of financial markets, i.e. the belief that they can quantify and price risk accurately and handle it in mutually beneficial ways (as in insurance markets). Furthermore, asset prices reflect "fundamentals" (preferences of investors about risk and return, productivity and technology by firms) and there are therefore no wild gyrations. As with policy ineffectiveness, financial market efficiency would imply a limited role in government regulation in financial markets. Since risk is priced accurately and asset prices are anchored to fundamentals, fluctuations in financial markets reflect the best responses of market participants to exogenous shocks; there is thus in principle no scope for the government to improve on market outcomes. Financial market efficiency will be reviewed in Chapter 7. It will be seen that, as with the REH and individual optimisation, the limitations to individual rationality, when combined, invalidate the efficiency claims and open the door to a government role.

Real Business Cycles

In 1982, Finn Kydland and Edward Prescott published their paper Time to Build and Aggregate Fluctuations (Kydland and Prescott, 1982) in which they modelled business cycles in the US as the consequences of random shocks to productivity hitting the economy, with the economy itself modelled as a perfectly competitive market economy populated by rational, well-informed households who maximise their utility by choosing hours of work and spending on goods and services. This initiated the "Real Business Cycle" school or programme of research, which is an application of the NC school to macroeconomic fluctuations. With it, the reaction against Keynesian analysis reached its peak. The model assumes a world in which money is purely a veil: It does not affect the real economy and makes no appearance in the model at all. As the title suggests, the model is entirely real. The fluctuations in this economy are Pareto efficient. No public policy can make someone better off without making someone else worse off. There is no reason for any government intervention at all. Implicitly, wages and prices are perfectly flexible in this world. Supply equals demand everywhere, all the time. Any unemployment that exists is voluntary. People choose not to work or work fewer hours because real wages are temporarily low. In the background are sophisticated financial markets in which all risks can be traded.

The RBC models in fact turn macroeconomics completely on its head. Instead of business cycles driven by aggregate demand, as argued by Keynes happened in the Great Depression, with swathes of the economy, capital, and labour lying idle for want of demand, the real business cycle models portray booms and recessions as being due to changes in aggregate supply—the productive potential of the economy. This paper unleashed an enormous research programme that involved building RBC models of successively greater refinement, aimed at giving a better account of actual fluctuations in the US economy. Being an offshoot of NC, from a behavioural point of view, this school can be criticised along similar lines as the NCs, particularly about the rationality assumption that permeates their entire thinking.

New Keynesian Macroeconomics and DSGE Modelling

The New Keynesian (NK) school aims to maintain some of the insights of Keynes on the role of aggregate demand for the determination of output and on the scope of stabilisation policy, while maintaining what were regarded by then as key methodological advances of rigorous micro-foundations (individual agent optimisation) and rational expectations.[5] These models have some Keynesian features, as the name implies. They typically embody slowly adjusting wages and prices, so that supply does not always equal demand in all markets in the economy. Unemployed resources can emerge. Monetary policy can have real effects and can be used to mitigate fluctuations. But in contrast to old Keynesian models, the departures from perfectly functioning competitive markets are based on what are regarded as firm microeconomic foundations. Assumptions of the kind made by Keynes in the General Theory are dismissed as being ad hoc. These models still assume, typically, that consumers are rational agents who maximise their utility. Preferences are assumed to be fixed and unchanging. A frequently used simplifying assumption is that all households in the economy are the same. There is a "representative household".

In line with NK thinking, the dominant trend in business cycle research has subsequently stepped back from the extreme positions of the NCs and the RBC school on the causes and effects of business cycles and has re-introduced some "imperfections" into the model, such as sticky wages and prices, and imperfect competition. Fluctuations in the economy arise from random shocks hitting it, but such shocks now include demand shocks in addition to the supply (productivity, technology, demographics) shocks allowed by the RBC school. Now, government and central bank actions can yield modest improvements in well-being. The Central Bank's use of interest rates can influence the inflation rate. But in other key respects, the methodology is that of RBC models. Such models, known as DSGE Models—Dynamic Stochastic General Equilibrium models—have come to dominate macroeconomic modelling in many central banks and have become a leading approach in academic macroeconomics research.

The remarkable resilience and appeal of the New Keynesian DSGE model is that it provides a conceptual framework for macroeconomic analysis that can be stripped down to three equations:

[5] Michael Woodford (2003) book *Interest and Prices* is often cited as a definitive statement of New Keynesian modelling (Woodford 2003). Jordi Gali, 2008, *Monetary Policy, Inflation and the Business Cycle: An Introduction to the New Keynesian Framework* (Gali 2015, 2nd ed.) provides a more concise statement.

- An aggregate demand curve, that explains demand in terms of past demand, expected future demand, and real interest rates;
- A Philips curve, that explains inflation as depending on past inflation, expected future inflation, and a measure of aggregate demand;
- A monetary policy rule, that explains how interest rates are set depending on aggregate demand and inflation (the "Taylor rule").

These can be derived from microeconomic foundations: optimising households who choose consumption optimally and plan for the future; firms who set prices optimally at random intervals; and a Central Bank that sets interest rates to keep inflation under control. Its appeal may also derive from providing a quantitative model, that can be estimated statistically and in principle tested against data.

While the DSGE model (or family of models) contains much that is broadly true, and has attractive features, it provides a highly idealised account. The dominant practice of using these models for policy evaluation in both academia and in central banks has elicited a big debate on their usefulness, with views both supportive and critical; see, e.g. the contributions by leading macroeconomists in Gürkaynak and Tille (2017). Critics focus mainly on these models' growing air of unrealism. For instance, Olivier Blanchard writes of DSGE models that "they are based on unappealing assumptions. Not just simplifying assumptions, as is necessary in any model, but assumptions profoundly at odds with what we know about consumers and firms" (Blanchard 2017, p. 94). Furthermore, he assesses the methods by which they are estimated—a mixture of calibration and Bayesian estimation—as unconvincing (see also Colander 2016). This state of affairs maybe a legacy of Milton Friedman's prescriptions in his highly influential 1953 paper on "The Methodology of Positive Economics" in which he argued that the value of a theory should be judged by the truth of its predictions, not by the descriptive realism of its assumptions. The present authors share Blanchard's (2017) assessment that much macro theorising (such as DSGE) may have gone too far in building elaborate models on highly implausible assumptions. Among the most glaring omissions, or indeed dead-ends, may be the omission to account for the key socio-behavioural characteristics that we review and emphasise in this book. Individuals are neither the calculating machines of DSGE theory nor do they live in isolation; the individual cognitive limitations or behavioural traits are combined and amplified through social interactions, to produce aggregate developments that differ fundamentally for random number-generating processes.[6,7] See Stiglitz (2018) for more critical perspectives on DSGE models.

Another line of criticism laid against DSGE models at the time of the financial crisis of 2007-9 was that they did not allow for speculative bubbles in stock markets or house prices to emerge. Asset price bubbles—price rises that occur only because people believe prices will carry on rising, regardless of the profits of the company in question—pose a problem for models based on fully rational, well-informed optimising agents. In theory these should not exist. Rational agents can work out that at some point in the future the bubble is bound to collapse. But then by a process of backward induction, no one should be willing to pay an inflated price for the asset. In practice, "bubbles" seem to occur frequently, and a bubble in property prices in the US was a key ingredient in the "Great Recession" of 2007-9.

Responses to the "Problems" with Macroeconomics

Since the Global Financial Crisis, several initiatives have been taken to shift the agenda, including:

- The CORE project aims to revitalise the teaching of introductory economics, by putting issues and practical questions ahead of developing a body of theory, and by introducing more of the descriptive realism into the analysis. Sam Bowles and Wendy Carlin, who lead

[6] Computational models (e.g. Tesfatsion 2006; Lebaron and Tesfatsion 2008; Commendatore et al. 2018) can incorporate such elements, but at the cost of great complexity.

[7] There have been efforts to incorporate cognitive limitations in NK-style work, e.g. the models of "rational inattention" (Sims 2003), "sticky information" (Mankiw and Reis 2002, 2007), or general myopia (Gabaix 2020; see also Chapter 6). The general idea is that of cognitive limitations or complex signals ("sticky" information) the require costly processing, therefore calling for intermittent processing (inattention or myopia). Interestingly, in some of this work, such features are used to motivate price stickiness. This replaces earlier work in which price stickiness was motivated by clear-cut costs of changing prices ("menu costs"). Another strand of behavioural work related to price stickiness is associated with the study of 9-ending prices. Such prices purport to fall below the psychological barrier of 0-ending (rounded) prices, thereby giving the illusion of being low (a kind of money illusion); see Snir et al. (2017). Such prices are shown to be associated with asymmetric price rigidity (more up than down—Levy et al. 2020).

this project, set out their views in a paper "What students learn in Economics 101: Time for a Change" in the Journal of Economic Literature, 2020.

- The Institute for New Economic Thinking, set up in 2009/10 with $50 million from George Soros attempts to put research on a different track, with more interdisciplinary work, aiming to challenge conventional wisdom in economics.
- A large research programme in the UK, Rebuilding Macroeconomics, was funded by the UK's Economic and Social Research Council from 2017 until around 2021. Its aim was to consider a broad range of approaches to macroeconomics, drawing on many disciplines, and put forward a road map for future research.

3 Reflections on Bounded Rationality, Behavioural Economics, and Macroeconomics

There is a gathering body of research, reviewed in Chapter 2, showing that people do not behave like "homo economicus". This is a fictitious creation, the archetypal rational economic man—or person—whose choices of work, leisure, and all activities—consumption of goods and services, savings, investments, and so on—can be understood as the solution of a problem: the problem of how to maximise the value of a utility function, taking into account the constraints, i.e. the limits of what this person can achieve. Many strands of research in behavioural economics show that the assumptions of "homo economicus" are not valid. An area in which behavioural ideas have made important and widely accepted contributions is in how people make decisions when faced with risk and uncertainty. Dealing with (unquantifiable) uncertainty is a particular challenge.

The utility functions widely used in economics assume that a person's utility depends only on his or her own actions. They are fixed, and do not evolve over time, or because of a person's experiences or interactions with other people. No one believes that this is literally true, only that it is a useful working assumption for economic analysis, i.e. that changes in preferences that take place as time passes do not significantly affect the analysis. Therefore, they can be ignored.

Economics is unusual among the social sciences in treating preferences in this way. One peculiarity is that there is no discussion in economics of where preferences come from. The question of how preferences are formed is generally viewed as not being economics. It is regarded as a subject for psychology or sociology or some other social sciences discipline.

A "representative household" underpins much modelling of economic fluctuations; although, agent heterogeneity is now allowed for, at the cost of extra complexity.[8] But much research has shown that a bunch of people with differing tastes do not behave as if they were a single rational utility maximising household (see Kirman 1992; Stiglitz 2015). Furthermore, an economy populated by one person cannot be subject to key phenomena such as imperfect information, trade, or indeed the existence of markets. It follows that in the one-person world, it would be impossible to have market failures such as externalities or incomplete markets, inequality, coordination failures, networks and social interactions. Therefore, the explanatory power of such a model for phenomena like unemployment and business cycles (among others) will be very limited. Arguably, the "representative agent" paradigm blurs the distinction between the micro- and the macroeconomy (Colander 2016).

The discipline of economics may cling to fixed and unchanging preferences because it is the basis of "welfare economics"—normative economics. If preferences are constant, a change in the maximum value of the utility function that a rational person can achieve, because of some change in circumstances, or a change in activities, like a reduction in hours of work, or less spending and more saving for the future, or some intervention by a government (a change in tax rates or public spending for example) can be used to judge whether the change is for the better, or for the worse, and by how much. But if preferences evolve over time, or reflect a person's position in the social hierarchy, or other influences, or if behaviour is such that it cannot be represented by a function that is being maximised at all, then the basis for normative economics is swept away. It becomes much more difficult or impossible to say whether some change or other is an improvement or not.

A striking instance of this is the notorious fact that people are bad at planning for the future. Instant pleasures are hard to resist; deferred gratification is hard to practice. People systematically do not save enough for old age and regret it when it is too late. This issue is so old and

[8] See, e.g. Heathcote et al. (2009) and the "HANK" (Heterogeneous Agent New Keynesian) model of Kaplan et al. (2018).

well known, and such a massive potential problem that governments routinely intervene with social insurance schemes that force people to save minimally, whether through public pensions or forced saving.[9]

This phenomenon can be understood in a variety of ways. One of them is by assuming people do not discount the future at a constant proportional rate—exponential discounting—but discount future events relative to the present more than they discount more distant-future events relative to events in the nearer future, so-called "hyperbolic discounting". This means, in effect, that the person is not the same person at different points in their life. People plan imperfectly for the future: an optimal decision now (e.g. to save or exercise) fails to be implemented later ("time inconsistency"). The young person who puts off saving for old age is different from the old person who regrets youthful profligacy. Whose utility is then the appropriate judge of the effects of public policy and other changes, the young person who discounts old age heavily, or the old person who does not?

There are other ways this phenomenon might be understood. It may be that people do not optimise, but adopt conventional behaviour, or follow simple rules of thumb about saving and spending. They may be "satisficing"—making decisions that achieve a satisfactory outcome, without worrying whether it is optimal or not. This idea goes back to Herbert Simon, the University of Chicago multi-disciplinary scientist, who coined the word in 1956, as part of his theory of bounded rationality. This element of behavioural economics is not exactly a new thing.

Social conventions and norms of behaviour may influence people, and norms might tend not to change despite changing underlying circumstances. Patterns of spending and tastes for particular goods may also be affected by the desire to be seen as a member of a group or a person of taste and fashion. Fads and fashions affect demand for particular goods. Advertising plays a big part in this. John Kenneth Galbraith, in *The Affluent Society* (Galbraith 1958), said of American industry and consumer society that "wants are increasingly created by the process by which they are satisfied". De Vries (2008, Chapter 2) writes that the

[9] Such as Singapore's Central Provident Fund. Under provision for old age may be a bigger problem in Western societies where people seem to be less thrifty than in Asian economies, where personal savings rates have been much higher.

Frankfurt School of social theory, viewing critically the emerging materialism of the post-World War II era, argued that the meaningless work of industrial capitalism led to alienation—of workers from their true selves, their traditions and their cultural bearings. In these conditions, workers are incapable of distinguishing use value from exchange value, objective needs from subjective wants. The alienated worker loses all self-control and develops a voracious appetite for goods and an insatiable need for fantasy, distraction, and ostentatious display. Max Weber's "heartless hedonist" and Herbert Marcuse's "one-dimensional man" were born in this environment. The ensuing mass-consumption behaviour supported the developing and increasingly affluent mass-production economy of the post-war years. Viewed in a positive light, this state of affairs supported a widely diffused prosperity—through what some have called the "Fordic model" where corporate profits are partly disseminated to workers, who in turn plough them back in through their consumption. What the criticism of the Frankfurt School highlights, apart from the alienation, is that behaviour is socially determined—in sharp contrast to the neoclassical postulates.

Another example may be hours of work, where there are conventional patterns of full-time work. We speak of "normal working hours" or "normal office hours". Some people have to—or choose to—work "unsocial hours", in the evenings, overnight, or at weekends or public holidays. There are normal patterns of holidays and travel. One of many questions that are asked about working hours is why they differ between countries in ways that are not associated with differences in wealth, income, or wage rates, the economic factors that might be expected to influence them. Another question is: why have they not fallen as much as incomes have grown? The US is generally thought of as a high work economy, with longer hours and shorter holidays, while Germany is a high leisure economy, with longer holidays and shorter working hours. Such differences might be attributable to differences in taxation, as Prescott (2004) has argued. But not everyone takes this view. It may be at least in part a consequence of different preferences for work and leisure.

Keynes, writing in 1930 in his "Economic Prospects for our Grandchildren" (Keynes 1930) observed that with 2% real growth per person each year, real incomes would have increased eight-fold in a hundred years, and wondered how long people might be working. He guessed that 15 hours of work per week would be enough to satisfy most needs.

How would they spend the extra leisure? And yet in 2024 hours of work remain much higher than that throughout the developed world.

In his book *The Industrious Society* (de Vries 2008), de Vries has written of the "Industrious Revolution" that led to greater hours of work in the eighteenth century, and the possibility of a New Industrious Revolution that keeps working hours high despite higher incomes. He views preferences as subject to change and social influence. The book explores the role of the household in economic development as it gradually changed from doing a lot of production and consumption within the household towards more work outside, in the market economy, and correspondingly buying more goods and services from outside. He argues that these changes in household behaviour played a significant role in the Industrial Revolution, which was not, in his view, driven only by advances in technology and growth in the supply of goods and services. But he wonders why, as societies have become more prosperous and productive, they have focused more on money and goods (i.e. consumption time rather than cultural time, cultural time being time devoted to cultivation of the mind and spirit and to governance and charity).

An alternative—complementary—view as to why hours of work remain so high is that people are concerned partly about status and their position in the social and economic hierarchy. They are concerned about relative income or spending. To the extent this is true, it leads to people generally working too hard. Everyone could be made better off by working less hard and earning less. The idea that relative income and or consumption matters to people goes back a long way. Thorstein Veblen's set out the idea in his 1899 *Theory of the Leisure Class* (Veblen 1899), and similarly James Duesenberry proposed his "relative income hypothesis" (Duesenberry 1949). This may be important for both the choice of working hours and the pattern and level of consumption spending.

The view that relative income matters rather than absolute income for people's happiness is supported by findings that reported happiness does not increase as much as income as populations grow more prosperous. But happiness does increase with relative income. This finding, the Easterlin Paradox (Easterlin 1974), goes back to 1974. It reinforces the idea that, to the extent that utility can be inferred from statements about happiness, utility depends on the consumption or incomes of other people, not just the individual concerned. It undermines the practice of "methodological individualism". In a similar spirit, Gomes (2021) argues that a move to a four-day working week could bring about widespread benefits, noting that the length of the working week is a social norm. We may be stuck at five days, even though a shorter week would benefit (almost) everyone.

Prospect theory (Kahneman and Tversky 1979) was based on findings that people generally find a loss of income or wealth much more painful that gaining the same amount. They have what is known as "loss aversion". People evaluate gains and losses relative to a benchmark, often their own recent income, or that of people in a reference group. It implies that over time, people adjust to circumstances.

As a partial summary, there is mounting evidence that people have preferences that change over time under social influences, do not optimise consistently, or even they do not optimise at all, but "satisfice". All serve to undermine normative economics. They make it much harder to judge among different economic situations. Prospect theory also implies that utility is something changeable, depending on a changeable benchmark. The same level of income gives different amounts of utility depending on the circumstances. The social influences on preferences, and the fact that the well-being of other people enters into one's own preferences is also another key theory underlying behavioural economics. It, too, has radical implications about how individual utility may be understood.

4 Further Effects of Bounded Rationality

People may value things according to their relative status. The attractiveness of a house may depend on how it compares to other houses. People may want a bigger house, or a faster car than their neighbours. These are long-established ideas. Gilles Saint-Paul refers in his book, The Tyranny of Utility (Saint-Paul 2011), to Duesenberry's (1949) relative income hypothesis mentioned above. Similar insights, he notes, are also an element in Keynes' arguments explaining the existence of nominal wage rigidity. More broadly, the utility someone derives from income or wealth may depend on their ranking in the distribution of income or wealth within the relevant reference group. A person might take their own prior income as the relevant point of reference. There is much analysis of this kind of *habituation*, and we consider it in detail in Chapter 3. Among other things, it implies that people feel more keenly the loss of income than an equal gain, relative to their present position. In our work (e.g. Tournemaine and Tsoukis 2009, 2010; Tsoukis and Tournemaine 2013), we refer to this as "pain from the loss of status", and it is akin to the idea of loss aversion that behavioural psychology has highlighted (see Chapter 2).

As Saint-Paul (2011) observes, the model of the "unitary individual", a rational utility maximising person, provides a rationale for only limited government intervention in people's lives. But the loss of the unitary person because of time inconsistency, may lead to a loss of liberty, a tyranny. Once people are not rational utility maximisers and may do things which are not in their own best interests, as measured by the utility function, the social objective of maximising utility invites illiberal government interventions, restricting their freedom of action, to protect people from themselves. Behavioural economics may not be a totally welcome development.

Saint-Paul argues that "instead of constructing its theory of consumers' behaviour on the basis of some empirical description of how individuals do behave in reality, economics postulates that individuals rationally pursue consistent goals...it has developed theoretical constructs aimed at aggregating this notion of individual preferences and behaviour into collective ones that can be used for policy analysis". So economic model of consumers' behaviour is a methodological as opposed to an empirical construct. It has the advantage that the assumptions are minimal (the fewest needed to get the result), but the disadvantage that they are liable to be invalidated empirically. The many and varied instances in which the predictions of rational behaviour have turned out to be inconsistent with data have spurred the growth of behavioural economics.

It might be noted that not only does Saint-Paul deplore the effect of behavioural economics on public policy (at least when embedded in a utilitarian framework), but also he regards it as a hodgepodge of results of unverified importance. "To date, behavioural economics is a catalog of empirically documented phenomena, each of them being a particular deviation from the unitary view. There is no attempt at bringing them together in a synthetic theory nor of imposing restrictions on their frequency in the population". "Behavioural economics is disturbingly silent on how general these tendencies are".

Support for the idea that preferences are socially influenced and liable to change comes from the maybe unlikely quarter of Friedrich Hayek. Dold and Lewis (2022) provide a detailed account. Hayek remarked at one point that "the tastes of man, as is also true of his opinions and beliefs and indeed much of his personality, are shaped in a great measure by his cultural environment". He argued that there is a bidirectional relationship between purposeful human agency and social structures. "Individuals generate and/or transform social structures through their actions, whilst those structures in turn shape the cognitive processes and therefore the actions of the individuals in question". Dold and Lewis summarise his views under four headings. (1) Hayek commented on the dependence effect, set out by Galbraith in The Affluent Society, according to which wants are created by the process of satisfying them by advertising by large firms. Hayek agreed with Galbraith that this is a real phenomenon, but unlike Galbraith, Hayek argued that these wants may be important rather than trivial. He asserted that many wants result from social processes of emulation, imitation, and so on. But Hayek includes acquired tastes for music, painting, and literature among them, tastes which he argues are highly valuable. (2) Hayek argued that employment in large corporations may affect attitudes to risk, inducing greater risk aversion, and also influencing behaviour by rewarding salaried employees for conforming to organisational rules, and making them feel less responsible for the outcomes of their own actions, a negative development in Hayek's view as likely to undermine entrepreneurship and the competitive market economy. (3) Hayek subscribed to the doux commerce thesis, whereby taking part in market transactions contributes to people's moral development: "social virtues...which smooth social contacts and which make control from above less necessary...flourish wherever the individualist and commercial type of society has prevailed". (4) Hayek gives an evolutionary account of social institutions. "Groups that have adapted rules conducive to a more effective order of actions will tend to prevail over other groups with a less effective order." These views emerge from Hayek's work on theoretical psychology.

Relative to current strands of thought in behavioural economics and political economy, Dold and Lewis infer that Hayek would be sceptical of what they call strand one, in which situational influences impact individual decision-making and lead to markedly different behaviour from that predicted by rational choice theory (Kahneman and Tversky). He doubts the ability of the "nudge" arguments and the paternalistic policy prescriptions that are derived from it to achieve their ends. A second strand in behavioural economics examines the effect of socio-cultural cues which affect who people are and goes beyond mere situational framing. This strand connects with research on "social economy". In this line, Storr (2014) remarks that "economists should be in the business of explaining the cultural origins of preferences and specifically should highlight how culture shapes and colours economic activity rather than rejecting preference-based explanations".[10]

For Hayek, then, preferences are the result of classificatory mental processes, shaped by an individual's cognitive history and evolving social circumstances. It is no good for economists to use general rationality axioms assuming context independence and rank stability. An evaluative strand of political economy based on Hayek's insights might criticise existing normative orders and defend institutions such as investigative journalism, a pluralist academia, and a provocative art world, that foster debate, reflecting on and learning about what preferences people want to hold. This would not involve "nudge" policies; it would instead focus on the nature of social rules which would constrain and cultivate individual decision-making capabilities. Dold and Lewis argue in favour of moving away from outcome-oriented thinking of the nudge agenda and instead looking at capabilities and a process-oriented institutional analysis.

5 Policy Responses to Global Warming and Their Effects on Utility and Happiness

The fluidity of preferences, and the social element in their determination, may undermine some cherished results in economics. And Saint-Paul (2011) argues that the rise of behavioural economics combined with a utilitarian approach to public policy is a danger to freedom, indeed, a path towards tyranny, as governments impose laws, regulations, and taxes to manipulate behaviour and protect people from themselves. But as global warming imposes a need for lower consumption, the adaptation of preferences, people's tendency to habituate to circumstances, to derive happiness from their relative standing in society rather than absolute income levels, will soften the blow.

[10] Hayek's analysis of preferences speaks to the distinction drawn by Hargreaves-Heap between providential and prudential approaches to political economy. The providential uses rational choice theory and assumes fixed and exogenous preferences. The prudential goes back to Hume, Smith, and John Stuart Mill, for whom rules and norms were not only constraints but also constitutive, shaping the perceptions and preferences of economic actors. One example of this is the way that a punitive regime may encourage the behaviour it is intended to deter. A constitution for knaves may induce knavish behaviour.

What has all this got to do with global warming? The need to cut carbon emissions to zero within the next few years to limit the global temperature rise to 1.5 or 2.0 degrees centigrade, and the need to reduce other forms of pollution to protect biodiversity, will require many changes to economic activity. Renewable energy will replace fossil fuels. Advances in technology are making renewables relatively cheaper. We are told that lower production and consumption of beef and dairy products can (and should) make a substantial contribution to lower methane emissions. Agriculture will have to change. Something needs to be done about waste plastic which ends up in the oceans damaging marine life, and indeed ends up in the form of microscopic particles in human organs with long-term effects that are so far unknown. There is some blaming of individual consumers for their wastefulness and extravagance and attempts by big corporations to greenwash their image by making environmental gestures of various kinds, advertising the fuel efficiency of their new aeroplanes, selling their passengers carbon-offset schemes, and so on. The predominant view is that producers will need to greatly reduce their carbon emissions and polluting activities. Small gestures by individual consumers, like recycling, walking, and cycling more and driving less, are going to have essentially no effect. Nevertheless, lower consumption and less production overall may well be a useful contribution to lower pressure on the planet, in a portfolio of measures. Carbon taxes and Pigovian taxes on other polluting activities, and the switch to renewable energy sources will, it is argued, not be enough. Technology alone will not do it.

There is a view among environmental scholars that consumption will need to be cut to reduce the pressure on the planet. This appears to be a quite widely held and reputable view. If a person's happiness depends to a large extent on relative standing in society, in terms of income or wealth, then a general reduction in incomes would not have as great an impact on welfare as in the case of purely individualistic utility (utility that depends on the individual's consumption alone and not on anyone else's). If people experience loss aversion, then a fall in income would be felt keenly in the short term, but as habituation to generally lower incomes sets in, the welfare cost would fade.

An example of the arguments made for lower consumption as a response to the climate crisis is provided by the proposals for consumption corridors put forward by Fuchs et al. (2021). They make a familiar criticism of the consumer society, writing of the problem of too much consumption, pursuit of variety and fleeting pleasures, which "compounded by social norms and structural forces, can lead to status competition, stressful choices, time pressures, and endless debt, to name but a few ailments". It leads to social and ecological exploitation, in their view. Low-cost goods are a product of under-paid workers, unfair working conditions, and environmental costs, such as loss of rainforests and greenhouse gas emissions. After a point, they assert, further wealth does not increase well-being. While many people on the planet need greatly improved quality of life, there are many in the developed world whose standards of living are, in the view of these authors, too high.

"In an increasingly inequitable and ecologically full world, living well within limits thus becomes the core challenge of our time". They propose corridors between the minimum consumption needed for a good life and a maximum to prevent some people from harming the chances of others doing the same. The minimum is dictated by considerations of justice, and the maximum by environmental and social sustainability. The question they try to address is how to reconcile this with freedom. They argue that people have empathy with others and a desire for justice. They devote a lot of space to defining what is meant by a good life, in terms of quality of life, well-being and human flourishing, drawing on the Aristotelian concept of eudaimonia. They want to avoid paternalism: what people think must matter; avoid standardisation and coercion, acknowledge autonomy and freedom.

They contrast a hedonistic approach to well-being with a eudemonic approach. The hedonistic focuses on happiness and life satisfaction, while the eudemonic focuses on needs and capabilities. They distinguish between needs and desires. Whereas desires are endless, untrammelled, subjective, and are not a condition for human flourishing, needs are limited, universal, irreducible, and are a condition for human flourishing. An example of a desire might be to drive at unlimited speed, climb Mount Everest, or to live in huge houses. Needs can be satisfied through various means, which they refer to as satisfiers. Among the satisfiers are consumer goods, and societal institutions, which serve the need to participate in society, for example via democracy. Needs, as said, they believe to be universal in nature. Examples of needs might be participation, belonging, freedom, and autonomy. As examples of satisfiers, they offer water, energy, money, food, bike lanes, a legal system, and housing. They divide satisfiers into five categories. Violators or destroyers might be something like the weapons industry. Pseudo-satisfiers, for example, a work-credit-spend cycle. Inhibiting satisfiers meet one need but curtail satisfaction of others. Singular satisfiers meet only one need. Synergic satisfiers address one need and have positive spillover benefits for others.

Fuchs et al. spend a lot of time on a rather utopian discussion of how to identify the consumption corridors. "It is about starting a conversation about what should be meaningful to us and our societies, including the global one, for a good life, here and now and in the future." They dismiss technology as a sufficient solution to climate change, and are very negative about consumer sovereignty, not believing that the efforts of individual consumers actions can have strong enough effects, partly because producers package and advertise goods too cleverly. Like many in this field they draw a distinction between consumers and citizens.

Frank Trentmann (*The Empire of Things: How we became a world of consumers from the fifteenth century to the twenty-first*, 2016) examines the growth of consumption and the idea of people as consumers over this long period, emphasising the long development, and the fact that many phenomena that are thought to be new are not, in fact, but have long histories. The consumer society has been growing for a long time. In his view, "to have any chance of success, proposals the hope to create more sustainable lifestyles need to appreciate the personal and social meaning people take from their things". He is doubtful that low or zero growth would reduce consumption, views which put him at odds with Fuchs et al.

He contemplates the imagined replacement of "things" with experiences, emotions, and services, as dematerialisation and post-consumerism arrive, and concludes that it is not happening. Though he concedes that on a small scale there may be a revival of repairing and sharing taking place, enabled by the internet. But they are only small moves, if in the right direction, but none the less to be encouraged. He recommends a cut in VAT on repair services to help cobblers and bicycle repair shops, for example. He notes that leisure and communication require equipment, infrastructure and energy, and thus the shift to services does not necessarily reduce the use of resources. He doubts that ICT, the internet and sharing networks will lead to greater sustainability. They may save time and resources, but if people use the savings to buy more clothes, holidays, and electronics, there will be no reduction in resource use overall. Greater efficiency of domestic appliances has led to people buying bigger ones. "As one car sharer told the Wall Street Journal in 2014, she used the money saved to go skiing in Utah, holidaying in Bermuda, and touring Europe".

Like de Vries (2008) mentioned above, Trentmann is among those who take it as given that preferences are socially influenced and change over time, though probably slowly. “Domestic comfort, exotic holidays, eating and drinking routines, shopping hours, what it means to be clean, fit and fashionable: these and many other aspects our lifestyles are the historical product of social norms, expectations, and arrangements” (p. 688). Nevertheless, his recommendations for action are fairly conventional. Public bodies need to act if there is to be change. There needs to be proper pricing of carbon and water, but by themselves these are insufficient. “We need a more honest public debate about how standards and habits have come to be what they are”. Current standards are not permanent or to be taken for granted. “The high-flying multi-tasking consumer lifestyle in particular, which requires so much coordination and with it, mobility and resources, has been a quite recent phenomenon, driven by the highly educated middle classes, who have taken standards of productivity from the world of work and injected them into the world of leisure, radically intensifying its course. It is easy to forget that even sixty or so years ago, the same kind of people lived more sedentary, relaxed lives, and other groups continue to enjoy fewer, less hectic and less mobile pastimes”. In his view “there has to be a more general appreciation of the pleasures from a deeper and longer-lasting connection to fewer things”. His views chime with those of Fuchs et al. (2021) when he asserts that “our lifestyles should be the subject of serious public debate and policy”. Trentmann, like Fuchs et al., wants to make the distinction between consumers as citizens, rather than mere customers. He wants people to act as citizens, not customers.

6 Methodological Criticisms of Macroeconomics

Macroeconomics is obviously a very diverse field. So, there is a great deal of macroeconomics research which is not the object of any criticisms in this chapter. However, the key point of this chapter and the entire book is that there is mounting evidence for the practical relevance of many of the ideas that make up behavioural and sociological economics. Individuals and firms are not the computational automata with the exogenously immutable objective functions that theory envisages. The discipline, long captive to the Friedmanian “as if” line of thinking (it is the implications of a theory that are important, not the realism of its assumptions), has been slow to respond to this criticism. But its growing acceptance has led to numerous advances in macroeconomic theory, modelling, and estimation, but a lot more remains to be done.

This line of criticism, on the relevance of bounded rationality and behavioural hypotheses, is part of wider recent debates on the nature of macroeconomics. Much of this discussion is methodological, so strictly speaking outside the remit of this book; however, they are broadly in line with our themes, so we briefly review them here. Akerlof (2020) argues that economics as a discipline favours topics that can addressed in a "hard" way, with algebraic models, quantifiable concepts, and propositions that can be tested statistically. In macroeconomics, DSGE modelling is the prime example. Much behavioural economics is not "hard" in this sense, but soft. The "hardness" and the ever-increasing mathematical sophistication has drawn criticism from different angles.

Akerlof (2020) argues that this preference for hardness has left economics biased against new and important ideas, overspecialised, and overly obsessed with publishing in a "top five" set of journals. To this he attributes several failures of economics ("sins of omission"), including failure to predict the 2008 Global Financial Crisis, and of narratives—stories that people tell each other about the economy and the way they affect behaviour and the way the economy evolves—as an example of an important idea but one that has not been explored or integrated into the mainstream enough.

The mathematical sophistication is also misdirected, according to Caballero (2010), because we do not know the macroeconomy even approximately (as the financial crisis of 2007-9 that caught everybody by surprise). Therefore, if we do pretend to know and aim to be more precise, we risk being precisely wrong. More open-mindedness about the foundational assumptions, and sound judgement, is the only strategy that may allow us to gain even approximate knowledge. Empirical tests of alternative foundational hypotheses arguably lack power and they cannot distinguish between alternatives (Akerlof 2007; Akerlof and Michaillat 2018). Thus, the choice of the null is all-important. From an almost opposite angle, Romer (2015) argues that some economists, including growth theorists, use math to impress but in a way that obscures rather than illuminates ("mathiness").

In calling for a "Post Walrasian" macroeconomics paradigm, Colander (2006) has called for a (set of) micro-foundations that is not axiomatic or "first-principles analytical", but relies instead on empirical behavioural foundations, using whatever evidence is available, including case studies, surveys, and institutional research. Equally, Bowles and Gintis (2000) call for economics to become more behavioural and institutional; and the same goes for macroeconomics. One could add disciplines such as economic history, psychology, economic sociology, and anthropology as providing illuminating perspectives on the macroeconomy; this calls for interdisciplinarity in producing and testing theories, including macroeconomics (see also Akerlof 2002; Hoover 2016).[11]

In some quarters, there is talk of a "crisis in economic theory" (e.g. Colander et al. 2014; Kirman 2011; Stiglitz 2015; Hoover 2016).[12] The traumatic experience of the Global Financial Crisis/Great Recession of 2007-9, the failure to predict and prevent it and the failure to guide the policy response has been a great motivation for such talk. Macroeconomics and leading macroeconomists also stand accused of peddling false optimism when at various times they have claimed that depressions are now prevented, or that exchange rates, price levels, and interest rates are now stable (the "Great Moderation" thesis), or that crises are a thing of the past (see Kirman 2011, for the exact instances).

Colander (2016) argues that "the usual definition of economics"—that it is concerned with the "allocation of scarce resources"—is misleading. It reduces economics to the study of optimal decisions in well-specified choice problems". Romer (2016) perhaps goes further than most in arguing that there is a negative beauty contest (or Nash equilibrium, or in plain English, cynicism) in the way theory is produced: "The trouble is not so much that macroeconomists say things which are inconsistent

[11] Backhouse and Fontaine (2018) is an interesting study on how economic theory started as interdisciplinary, in a dialogue with neighbouring social disciplines; but this interdisciplinarity gradually withered away and mathematical rigour became the paramount objective. This rigour led to overconfidence and a sense of self-sufficiency, so the benefits of interactions with other disciplines were forgotten. Regarding macroeconomics in particular, they write (p. 29): "In macroeconomics, there was a move from treating markets as institutionally rich oligopolistic structures that were too complex to analyse rigorously, to seeing them as perfectly competitive structures in which aggregate behaviour could be modelled as essentially mimicking the behaviour of individual, rational agents".

[12] Witztum (2019a, b) presents an ambitious and bold critique of the modern state of the discipline, in which the notion of human sociality and the contention that it has been ignored by modern economics play a central role. In a similar vein, Skidelsky (2021) criticises modern economics for its rigid orthodoxy and narrow vision. Similar arguments motivate the present book. Human sociality, in its many facets, is analysed in various places, particularly in Chapters 3, 4, and 8.

with the facts. The real trouble is that other economists do not care that the macroeconomists do not care that the macroeconomists do not care about the facts. An indifferent tolerance of obvious error is even more corrosive to science than committed advocacy of error" (Romer 2016, p. 22).

Hoover and Svorenčík (2023) find that there is a bias in the leadership of the American Economic Association, the leading association of professional economists: It resembles a closely knit elite and the question remains whether it is so on merit or in a closed-shop logic. The bias of the profession for "hard science"-type of economics (though sometime illusory, if we believe Romer 2015) makes it perhaps no surprise that the leadership of the profession is biased: If the creation of economics is biased (as per Akerlof 2020), and if that gets knowingly perpetuated (Kirman 2016), then the leadership will be biased, too, favouring the dominant practice.

There are other distortions, too (to use current terminology). Colander (2016) argues that the increased mathematical sophistication of macroeconomics, in the pursuit of rigour, computational calculation and (it has to be added) complexity in order to instil a degree of realism leads to a divorce between macroeconomics research and undergraduate teaching. Macro researchers find it difficult to teach undergraduates, particularly in liberal arts programmes (in the US), as those students are generally not too technically advanced. Furthermore, in a survey of graduate students at seven top-ranking graduate economics programmes in the US, Colander (2005) generally finds that creating researchers for major universities is clearly the role that these schools see for themselves; students are concerned about the lack of relevance for the real world in what they were doing. But he noted a shift towards a more empirically driven discipline: "But compared with our previous study, the change away from theory for the sake of theory, and toward empirical and applications, is strongly apparent" (Colander 2005, p. 179). But the issue of bias emerges here, too, and is an issue of concern: Bias in who selects and is selected by top graduate programmes, and bias in favour of mathematical ability but perhaps against creativity.

7 Plan of the Book

It is by now clear that both individuals and firms do not behave in the mathematically rigorous, and rigid, way that core economic theory postulates. Both behavioural and sociological considerations and evidence argue forcefully for this conclusion. However, although these insights have been collected to form a distinct sub-discipline of economics, namely behavioural economics, it is fair to say that these features have not been integrated organically into core economic theory. As mentioned, the aim of this book is to review the body of this work that has been integrated into macroeconomics and to suggest ways in which yet more insights can be beneficially considered in the future.

We have argued in this chapter that there has been a clear cycle in macroeconomics.

- Keynes' model of the General Theory included some key behavioural features.
- Many other founding fathers of the discipline, both before and after Keynes, took the same view and pursued interdisciplinarity.
- Neo-classical reaction against it led to a restoration of microeconomic principles in macroeconomics, an attempt to re-integrate micro and macro. Macroeconomics would be distinguished from microeconomics by the questions it deals with but not by the models it uses. The high point of this movement was the prominence of real business cycle models in the 1980s.
- The later move towards re-introducing market imperfections, allowing for imperfect competition, sticky wages and prices, non-market-clearing is a cautious move back towards pragmatism, descriptive realism, albeit with what are regarded as sound microeconomic foundations.
- More radical moves, incorporating more behavioural insights, if at the expense of losing some of the "hard" focus in favour of softer elements, have already begun, but need to gather pace. In emphasising the need for this trend to continue, this book should be added to the list of other authors (including Schelling 1978; Akerlof 2002, 2007; Akerlof and Shiller 2009; De Grauwe and Ji 2019; Baddeley 2016; Zafirovski 2016) who have convincingly called for the emergence of a "socio-behavioural macroeconomics" (if not using precisely this label).

The plan of the rest of the book is as follows: In Chapter 2, we review in some detail the insights and findings of behavioural economics and psychology that challenge the notion of "rationality", that permeates economics and the associated notion of the "economic (hu)man". In Chapter 3, we review in detail some social influences on preferences, including the notion of relative position and its many re-incarnations in the literature, and how these can be modelled. This task continues in Chapter 4, where such considerations are introduced into a basic growth model. Implications for long-run growth are considered. In Chapters 5 and 6, we review some of the ways in which hyperbolic discounting and time inconsistency have been incorporated into basic models and show their implications for growth, labour supply and the "functional distribution" of income (Chapter 5) and for the optimal design of stabilisation policy (Chapter 6). Chapter 7 is a brief excursion into the socio-behavioural macroeconomics of inequality. While Chapters 3 to 4 are increasingly analytical, leading on to Chapters 5 to 6 that also contain original formal analyses, and Chapter 7 is partly analytical as well, in Chapter 8, we return to an informal review of more sociological issues (identity, social capital and others) and their implications, particularly for financial markets. We also offer some policy implications and brief conclusions.

References

Akerlof, G.A. 2002. Behavioral Macroeconomics and Macroeconomic Behavior. *American Economic Review* 92 (3): 411–433.

Akerlof, G.A. 2007. The Missing Motivation in Macroeconomics. *American Economic Review* 97 (1): 3–36.

Akerlof, G.A. 2020. Sins of Omission and the Practice of Economics. *Journal of Economic Literature* 58 (2): 405–418.

Akerlof, G.A., and R.J. Shiller. 2009. *Animal Spirits: How Human Psychology Drives the Economy and Why it Matters for Global Capitalism*. Princeton University Press: Princeton.

Akerlof, G.A., and P. Michaillat. 2018. Persistence of False Paradigms in Low-Power Sciences. *Proceedings of the National Academy of Sciences of the United States of America* 115 (52): 13228–13233.

Andreoni, J. 1990. Impure Altruism and Donations to Public Goods: A Theory of Warm-Glow Giving. *Economic Journal* 100 (401): 464–477.

Backhouse, R.E., and P. Fontaine. 2018. Economics and Other Social Sciences: A Historical Perspective, Annals of the Fondazione Luigi Einaudi: An Interdisciplinary Journal of Economics, History and Political. *Science* 52 (2): 7–44.

Baddeley, M.C. 2016. Behavioural Macroeconomics: Time, Optimism and Animal Spirits. In *Routledge Handbook of Behavioral Economics*, 266–279. Abingdon: Routledge.

Blanchard, O.J. 2017. Do DSGE Models Have a Future? Chapter 9. In *DSGE Models in the Conduct of Policy: Use as intended*. Edited by R. Gürkaynak, and C. Tille. Paris and London: CEPR Press.

Bowles, S., and H. Gintis. 2000. Walrasian Economics in Retrospect. *Quarterly Journal of Economics* 115 (4): 1411–1439.

Caballero, R.J. 2010. Macroeconomics after the Crisis: Time to Deal with the Pretense-of-Knowledge Syndrome. *Journal of Economic Perspectives* 24 (4): 85–102.

Colander, D. 2005. The Making of an Economist Redux. *Journal of Economic Perspectives* 19 (1): 175–198.

Colander, D., ed. 2006. *Post Walrasian Macroeconomics: Beyond the Dynamic Stochastic General Equilibrium Model*. Cambridge: Cambridge University Press.

Colander, D. 2016. Liberal Arts Macro Economists are Becoming an Endangered Species. *Eastern Economic Journal* 42 (1): 1–6.

Colander, D., H. Foellmer, A. Haas, M. Goldberg, K. Juselius, A. Kirman, T. Lux, and B. Sloth. 2014. The Financial Crisis and the Systemic Failure of Academic Economics, Chapter 13. In *The Economics of Economists Institutional Setting, Individual Incentives, and Future Prospects*, 344–360. Cambridge: Cambridge University Press.

Commendatore, P., Kubin, S. Bougheas, A. Kirman, M. Kopel, and G.I. Bischi. eds. 2018. *The Economy as a Complex Spatial System, Macro, Meso and Micro Perspectives*. Springer: Berlin.

Conlisk, J. 1996. Why Bounded Rationality? *Journal of Economic Literature* 34 (2): 669–700.

De Grauwe, P., and Y. Ji. 2019. *Behavioural Macroeconomics: Theory and Policy*. Oxford: Oxford University Press.

Dold, M., and P. Lewis. 2022. F.A. Hayek on the Political Economy of Endogenous Preferences: An Historical Overview and Contemporary Assessment. *Journal of Economic Behaviour and Organization* 196 (3): 104–119.

Duesenberry, J.S. 1949. *Income, Saving and the Theory of Consumer Behaviour*. Cambridge: Harvard University Press.

Easterlin, R.A. 1974. Does Economic Growth Improve the Human Lot? Some Empirical Evidence. In *Nations and Households in Economic Growth: Essays in*

Honor of Moses Abramowitz. Edited by P.A. David, and M.W. Reder. New York: Academic Press.

Fuchs, D., M. Sahakian, T. Gumbert, A. Di Giulio, M. Maniates, S. Lorek, and A. Graf. 2021. *Consumption Corridors: Living a Good Life within Sustainable Limits*. Routledge; Open Access.

Gabaix, X. 2020. A Behavioral New Keynesian Model. *American Economic Review* 110 (8): 2271–2327.

Galbraith, J.K. 1958. *The Affluent Society*. Boston: Houghton Mifflin.

Gali, J. 2015. *Monetary Policy, Inflation, and the Business Cycle: An Introduction to the New Keynesian Framework and Its Applications*, 2nd ed. Princeton: Princeton University Press.

Gomes, P. 2021. *Friday is the New Saturday: How a Four-Day Working Week Will Save the Economy*. London: Flint.

Gürkaynak, R., and C. Tille. eds. 2017. *DSGE Models in the Conduct of Policy: Use as Intended*. CEPR Press: Paris & London.

Heathcote, J., K. Storesletten, and G.L. Violante. 2009. Quantitative Macroeconomics with Heterogeneous Households. *Annual Review of Economics* 1: 319–354.

Hoover, K.D. 2016. The Crisis in Economic Theory: A Review Essay. *Journal of Economic Literature* 54 (4): 1350–1361.

Hoover, K.D., and A. Svorenčík. 2023. Who Runs the AEA? *Journal of Economic Literature* 61 (3): 1127–1171.

Kahneman, D., and A. Tversky. 1979. Prospect Theory: An Analysis of Decision Under Risk. *Econometrica* 47 (2): 263–291.

Kaplan, G., B. Moll, and G.L. Violante. 2018. Monetary Policy According to HANK. *American Economic Review* 108 (3): 697–743.

Keynes, J.M. 1930. Economic Possibilities for our Grandchildren, in J.M. Keynes. 1963: *Essays in Persuasion*. New York: W.W. Norton & Co. (pp. 358–373).

Keynes, J.M. 1936. *The General Theory of Employment, Interest and Money*. London: Macmillan.

Kirman, A.P. 1992. Whom or What Does the Representative Individual Represent? *The Journal of Economic Perspectives* 6 (2): 117–136.

Kirman, A.P. 2010. The Economic Crisis is a Crisis for Economic Theory. *Cesifo Economic Studies* 56 (4): 498–535.

Kirman, A.P. 2011. *Complex Economics: Individual and Collective Rationality*. Routledge.

Kirman, A.P. 2016. Complexity and Economic Policy: A Paradigm Shift or a Change in Perspective? *A Review Essay on David Colander and Roland Kupers's Complexity and the Art of Public Policy, Journal of Economic Literature* 54 (2): 534–572.

Kydland, F.E., and E.C. Prescott. 1982. Time to Build and Aggregate Fluctuations. *Econometrica* 50 (6): 1345–1370.
Lebaron, B., and L. Tesfatsion. 2008. Modeling Macroeconomies as Open-Ended Dynamic Systems of Interacting Agents. *American Economic Review* 98 (2): 246–250.
Levy, D., A. Snir, A. Gotler, and H. Chen. 2020. Not All Price Endings Are Created Equal: Price Points and Asymmetric Price Rigidity. Journal of Monetary Economics 110 (C): 33–49.
Mankiw, N.G., and R. Reis. 2002. Sticky Information Versus Sticky Prices: A Proposal To Replace The New Keynesian Phillips Curve. *Quarterly Journal of Economics* 117 (4): 1295–1328.
Mankiw, N.G. and R. Reis. 2007. Sticky Information in General Equilibrium. *Journal of the European Economic Association*. 5: 603–613.
Prescott, E.C. 2004. Why Do Americans Work So Much More than Europeans? Federal Reserve Bank of Minneapolis *Quarterly Review*. 28 (1): 2–14.
Romer, P. 2015. Mathiness in the Theory of Economic Growth. *American Economic Review: Papers & Proceedings* 105 (5): 89–93.
Romer, P. 2016. The Trouble with Macroeconomics, Update. https://paulromer.net/trouble-with-macroeconomics-update
Saint-Paul, G. 2011. *The Tyranny of Utility: Behavioral Social Science and the Rise of Paternalism*. Princeton University Press.
Schelling, T.C. 1978. *Micro Motives and Macro Behavior*. New York: W.W. Norton.
Shiller, R.J. 2017. Narrative Economics. *American Economic Review* 107 (4): 967–1004.
Sims, C.A. 2003. Implications of Rational Inattention. *Journal of Monetary Economics* 50 (3): 665–690.
Skidelsky, R. 2021. *What's Wrong with Economics? A Primer for the Perplexed*. New Haven: Yale University Press.
Snir, A., D. Levy, and H. Chen. 2017. End of 9-Endings, Price Recall, and Price Perceptions. *Economics Letters* 155 (C): 157–163.
Stiglitz, J.E. 2015. Reconstructing Macroeconomic Theory to Manage Economic Policy, in Laurent, E. and J. Cacheux (Eds). 2015. *Fruitful Economics: Papers in honor of and by Jean-Paul Fitoussi*, Palgrave Macmillan. Ch. 1 (pp. 20–56).
Stiglitz. J.E. 2018. Where Modern Macroeconomics Went Wrong. *Oxford Review of Economic Policy* 34 (1–2): 70–106.
Storr, V.H. 2014. Why Culture in Economics? *Review of Austrian Economics* 27 (4): 495–503.
Tesfatsion, L. 2006. Agent-Based Computational Economics: A Constructive Approach to Economic Theory, Chapter 16. In *Handbook of Computational Economics*. Edited by L. Tesfatsion, and K.L Judd, vol. 2, Part 2. Amsterdam: North-Holland.

Thaler, R.H. 2016. *Misbehaving*. London: Penguin.
Tournemaine, F., and C. Tsoukis. 2009. Status Jobs, Human Capital and Growth: The Effects of Heterogeneity. *Oxford Economic Papers* 61 (3): 467–493.
Tournemaine, F. and C. Tsoukis. 2010. Gain versus pain from status and ambition: Effects on growth and inequality. *The Journal of Socio-Economics* 39 (2): 286–294.
Trentmann, F. 2016. *Empire Of Things: How We Became a World of Consumers, from the Fifteenth Century to the Twenty-First*. Toronto, Ontario: Allen Lane.
Tsoukis, C. 2020. *Theory of Macroeconomic Policy*. Oxford: Oxford University Press.
Tsoukis, C., and F. Tournemaine. 2013. Status in a Canonical Macro Model: Status, Growth, and Inequality. *The Manchester School* 81 (S2): 65–92.
Veblen, T. 1899. *The Theory of the Leisure Class: An Economic Study of Institutions*. Macmillan.
de Vries, J. 2008. *The Industrious Revolution: Consumer Behavior and the Household Economy, 1650 to the Present*. Cambridge: Cambridge University Press.
Witztum, A. 2019a. *The Betrayal of Liberal Economics: Volume I: How Economics Betrayed Us*. London: Palgrave Macmillan.
Witztum, A. 2019b. *The Betrayal of Liberal Economics: Volume II: How We Betrayed Economics*. London: Palgrave Macmillan.
Woodford, M. 2003. *Interest and Prices: Foundations of a Theory of Monetary Policy*. Princeton: Princeton University Press.
Zafirovski, M. 2016. Toward Economic Sociology/Socio-Economics? *Sociological Components in Contemporary Economics and Implications for Sociology, American Sociologist* 47 (1): 56–80.

CHAPTER 2

Behavioural Economics: A Review

1 Introduction: The Meaning of Rationality

Economics is committed to "methodological individualism", the claim that social phenomena, including economic, result from the behaviour of agents, individuals, or firms acting in an individual capacity (they are said to be "atomistic"). Although not logically necessary, methodological individualism is usually accompanied by the rationality postulate.

Economics is unusual among the social sciences in having clung on to the assumption of rational behaviour long after it has been abandoned elsewhere, e.g. in psychology and other behavioural sciences which emphasise bounded rationality and (actual) "behaviour" as opposed to full rationality. For anyone aiming to draw the line between these concepts, the starting question is, "what is rationality?" The early seventeenth-century philosopher and mathematician Descartes is among the first to define and emphasise the importance of rationality. His position is summed up in his famous quote: "Cogito ergo sum": I think, therefore I am. The implication is, I can doubt everything else, even my own existence, but the ability to reason shows convincingly that I do exist. The essence of Descartes' approach is rationality as systematic and thorough scrutiny, taking the inquirer step by step from a starting point to a conclusion.

Aside from its intrinsic philosophical value, Descartes' philosophy resonated at two levels: Firstly, with a society that slowly but increasingly

C. Tsoukis et al., *Social and Behavioural Macroeconomics*,
https://doi.org/10.1007/978-3-031-77748-6_2

was beginning to question the antiquated and arbitrary institutions of early modern France (and elsewhere); would such institutions stand up to rational scrutiny? Secondly, this philosophy was in line with the prevailing logic of the nascent capitalism. Feudalism had traditionally been autarchic at the level of the manor, but even when it slowly started producing for the market, it was based on received norms, customs, and traditions for its production methods or for setting prices and rents. In sharp contrast, the logic of capitalism was to produce for the market and for profit; and for this, it required a rational organisation of the methods of production, and a rational calculation of prices, rents and wages based on costs, yields, and market conditions.[1]

There is a variety of meanings by which the term "rationality" is used: "instrumental" rationality is displayed insofar as the agent adopts suitable means to her ends; see Kolodny and Brunero (2023). This implies that goals are clear, encapsulated in "well-behaved" preferences, whose meaning will become clearer below. "Substantive" rationality, on the other hand, implies that actions and even preferences conform to normative reason; for instance, to gamble all one's lifetime savings in one go may be said to go against any sense of what is reasonable, normal or sensible, hence substantively irrational—Kiesewetter and Worsnip (2023)—although it may be perfectly rational in the instrumental sense, i.e. it does not violate the axioms underlying the postulated preferences.[2] The severe informational and cognitive limitations of real individuals (as opposed to theoretical constructs—on which more below) have led Simon (1978, p. 9; see also Kroes et al. 2009) to introduce "procedural rationality", i.e. the optimal choice not of outcomes, on which

[1] See Gellner (1992) for an illuminating analysis of the philosophy and sociology of "reason". Interestingly, via the scientific revolution which it engendered, the rational mindset led to an accumulation of knowledge that went in parallel with the accumulation of wealth facilitated by the nascent capitalism. Furthermore, Gellner (1992, Ch. 7) argues that the two processes of cognitive and material accumulation, giving rise to technological and industrial revolution respectively, reinforced and sustained each other and thereby avoided the lapse to stagnation.

[2] As an example, a researcher may be "instrumental" when they pursue the research that maximises their professional or pecuniary returns; and "substantive" when they pursue the research that they may find more meaningful. This parallels the distinction between "extrinsic" and "intrinsic" motivation (see, e.g. Benabou and Tirole, 2003); see below. Of course, in practice, the distinction may not be as sharp as these definitions suggest.

both instrumental and substantive rationality rest, but the optimal choice of processes, which can be revised along the way.[3]

Finally, and not least, there is the question of how to "aggregate" the individual (non-) rationalities, so to speak. Even if individuals are rational, will organisations, families, societies, states, and humankind, behave rationally?This is the question of "collective" rationality—the question whether a structured group (society) is able to arrive at collectively beneficial outcomes. The distinction between individual rationality and aggregate outcomes is the bread and butter of game theory.[4] It abounds with analyses of how rational individuals find themselves in prisoners' dilemmas, rat races, arms races, races to the bottom, and tragedies of the commons.[5] In other words, individual rationality is by no means a guarantee that the aggregate outcome will be in any way pleasant, welfare-maximising, moral or indeed, rational.

The distinction between individual and social rationality has been highlighted in a few contributions. On this, one can discern two strands: First are those who draw a sharp line between the two; e.g. Kirman (2011): "We should distinguish between collective and individual rationality. Neither implies the other". Kay and King (2021, Ch. 1) call it "social intelligence". Drawing inspiration from the study of bees, Kirman and Serletis (2016, p. 609) call the former "swarm intelligence", a situation in which a group can overcome the cognitive limitations of its members. So, in this case, social rationality is higher-order than the individual one, so to speak. In contrast, the tragedy-of-commons situations (e.g. climate change) and the privately beneficial but socially harmful

[3] To add to an already growing list of concepts, Kahneman (2012, p. 49) makes a distinction between rationality and intelligence. But we will not dwell more.

[4] Game theory analyses the interactions among rational agents and shows how they can lead to suboptimal outcomes. But what if individuals are imperfectly rational? How will they perceive and respond to others' limitations? It seems reasonable to say that the imperfection of rationality will be compounded by the interactions. Thus, there may be more complexity than can be formally analysed.

[5] At a time when climate change is putting the life on the planet as we know it in doubt, tragedy-of-the-commons arguments become acutely relevant. There are many other issues that pose similar questions, not least inequality, crises, electoral behaviour, indebtedness, behaviour in pandemics, the list goes on. Is war rational? Or the nuclear arms race (the aptly named MAD—mutually assured destruction)? Even so, Mearsheimer and Rosato (2023) argue that collective rationality generally holds in state behaviour and international relations.

financial trades that led to the 2007–9 crisis are instances of individual rationality but systemic or social irrationality (see for instance Stiglitz 2023). Second, we have approaches which argue that individual rationality is socially conditioned. Backhouse and Fontaine (2008, p. 9) remind us that the pioneer behaviourist and polymath Herbert Simon wrote that the assumption of rationality must not be "global" but informed "by the kinds of environments in which [individuals] exist" (Simon 1955, p. 99). Additionally, again drawing from Backhouse and Fontaine (2018, p. 33), the leading experimental economist Vernon Smith emphasised that to understand individual rationality, attention must be paid to the institutional context. He writes: "[…] institutions serve as social tools that reinforce, even induce, individual rationality […]" (Smith 1991, p. 881). Similarly, Simon (2001) argues that group identification (a theme to which we return in Chapter 7) prompts individuals to accept information without independent verification. Thus, "rationality must be assessed in a social and historical context" (Simon 2001, p. 12,782). In a similar vein, economic sociologists (see, e.g. Linderberg 1990, 2006, 2013; Frerichs 2019) argue that the effectiveness or indeed meaning of individual actions cannot be judged outside of social context. Mearsheimer and Rosato (2023), in analysing state rationality, argue that collective rationality presupposes individual rationality and then thorough deliberation. Despite the great relevance of all these lines of inquiry, in this chapter, we shall put the question of collective rationality to one side, focusing solely on the question of individual rationality.

Economists generally use the term in the sense provided by Pinker (2021, ch. 2) who defines rationality as "the ability to use knowledge to attain goals".[6] This is closest in spirit to instrumental rationality.[7] A growing body of theory, encapsulated in the now established field of behavioural economics, and drawing from experimental economics, psychology, socio-biologists, and other disciplines, challenges the notion

[6] This views rationality as a prerequisite to action. Gellner (1992, e.g. Ch. 7), on the other hand, views "reason" and rationality as a "path that … leads to the discovery of truth…".

[7] It may be fair to say that economists seem to be in more-or-less agreement among themselves about the meaning of the term more than, say, the philosophers. This is not to imply that debates between economists are non-existent; see, e.g. Caldwell (1982, Ch. 7).

of individual rationality and associated methodological assumptions traditionally used in economics. This chapter reviews these findings and the numerous instances where individual behaviour deviates from the (full) rationality postulate.[8]

2 Methodological Individualism, Rational Choice, and the "Economic (Hu)Man"

Methodological Individualism and "Rational Choice" Theory

Economics is committed to "methodological individualism", the claim that social phenomena, including economic, result from the behaviour of agents, whether individuals or firms, acting in an individual capacity (they are said to be "atomistic"), to pursue their best interest as they perceive them (Blaug 1992, Ch. 15; Blume and Easley 2007). Methodological individualism is usually accompanied by the rationality postulate. Taking Pinker's definition (2021), mentioned above, a little further, we may define rationality as the ability to devise and follow a course of action that leads to the best possible attainment of given goals. To do so, the individual utilises their knowledge, as per Pinker, but may also choose to further this knowledge through learning or (re)searching. All this presupposes (a) well-defined goals or objectives, (b) full utilisation of all available information and prior knowledge, and costly upgrading thereof, (c) purposeful action consistent with the objectives, and (d) flexibility and adaptation to revise the knowledge and action plan when information or the extraneous environment changes.

More concretely, individuals maximise utility subject to the constraints of endowments and technology. The objectives of the individual are encapsulated in ordinal utility functions, typically with consumption and leisure as their main arguments. The dominant tradition views utility as entirely "selfish" (based on individual variables only); but a growing

[8] The discussion below presupposes (how rationally?) that there is a clear demarcating line between rationality and irrationality; and people are said to be non-fully or boundedly rational if they make elementary cognitive mistakes or are prone to repeated biases. But a point can be made that the line between rationality and irrationality is fuzzy in the first instance (see Pinker, 2021, ch. 2). Can voluntary ignorance be rational?—e.g. when future parents choose not to know the sex of their as-yet-unborn child; or the "prepared for everything" attitude of someone involved in conflict, designed to intimidate an opponent; which may lead to either victory or (self-)destruction.

literature has emphasised the relevance of "other-regarding preferences" (whereby the utility or consumption of others is an argument in individual utility)—a theme to which we return below and in Chapters 2 and 7, and which motivates much of this book. It is a moot point whether the latter are consistent with rationality; and the motivation for such extensions is subject to debate. In the case of risk (i.e. quantifiable uncertainty), rationality takes the form of expected utility theory based on cardinal utility (unique up to additive transformations, therefore interpersonal comparisons are not allowed). Action is guided by optimisation, i.e. maximisation of said utility subject to all relevant constraints. The optimal path is characterised by the mathematically derived first-order conditions. In a similar spirit, firms are assumed to maximise profits, again subject to all the relevant constraints (such as technology, market conditions, and so on).

Psychologists, behavioural economists, and others have noticed numerous instances where behaviour does not conform to the above postulates. Such findings, dubbed "anomalies", are most obvious in financial markets, but they are by no means unique there. They are often waived away by a combination of two arguments, either that deviations from rational behaviour are random and therefore disappear on average, or that competitive markets eliminate such behaviour because those that exhibit limited rationality (presumably) make losses and therefore disappear over time (see Blaug 1992, Ch. 15).[9] As Blaug (Ch. 4) reminds us, the "Darwinian" argument that any agent who does not optimise will be handicapped and ultimately eliminated goes back a long way; it has been used by Friedman and others as a way of justifying optimisation a priori, discouraging testing of it or serious consideration of non-optimising, alternative models of behaviour. Thus, as briefly mentioned in Chapter 1, optimisation and rationality may be called "as if" hypotheses, used not for their realism but because they deliver (arguably) useful predictions. Conlisk (1996) discusses extensively the nature of the "as if" argument: Is rationality useful as an approximation to how real people think or behave? Or because the same people learn over time to behave smartly? Or do the

[9] Thaler (2016) calls such arguments the "invisible hand-waive", as they are often (he says) not explicitly spelt out but, in conversation, left unfinished and completed by a gesture that means "you know ..., it's obvious ...., we don't need to elaborate...". The parallel with Adam Smith's "invisible hand" is both informative and amusing: One bridges individual behaviour with desirable aggregate outcomes, the other bridges bounded individual rationality with the desired aggregate rationality. Arrow (1991), reviewed next, reminds us how uncertain this latter bridge is even when individual rationality is full.

dumb ones get eliminated, so that only the smart ones survive? Another argument is definiteness and tractability—the optimal solution is one, but deviations from it can be of any number; which ones are the prevailing ones? These are open questions and dwelling more on them would take us too far. The interested reader can consult Conlisk (1996).

Another argument for rationality is pragmatic: Based on it, economics has shown tremendous intellectual progress and empirical success in explaining data. Against that, one may counter that macroeconomics, in particular, has failed in recent years to predict several crises such as the Asian crisis of 1997 and the "Great Recession" of 2007–9; see Chapter 1 about the (putative) "crisis of economic theory". It is also unable to offer widely accepted, general explanations of developments such as the rising inequality (or inequalities) and global imbalances. In any case, any successes, whatever those might be, are not arguments against striving for more realism in the foundational hypotheses.

In one view, the powerful implications of rationality are mostly due to the other accompanying concepts of neoclassical theory—auxiliary assumptions such as agent homogeneity, full information, perfect competition, and complete markets.[10] Agent homogeneity simplifies things enormously but it is very restrictive; as both Arrow (1991) and Kirman (1991) emphasise, if agents have identical tastes, endowments, and information, then there is no point of trading. If agent heterogeneity is allowed in either of these respects, as recent work allows (as mentioned in Chapter 1), then the computational difficulties of calculating the general equilibrium are very large. Furthermore, rationality implies acting based on all available information. Yet, there is a paradox, as pointed out in the debates on the Rational Expectations Hypothesis (an extension of rationality to information, as mentioned in Chapter 1 and discussed further below): If information is costly to acquire, then for someone to produce this information, there must be an informational differential that confers an advantage; hence, not all information can be available to everybody. In other words, there must be some heterogeneity at least in this respect. This puts into question the key premise of the "efficient market hypothesis", the extension of rationality to financial markets, namely that

[10] Indeed, Conlisk (1996) argues that it is not clear whether various "anomalies" (e.g. the "excess sensitivity" of consumption to transitory income, or the various ways by which the efficiency hypothesis fails in financial markets) are due to erroneous basic theory or the limited rationality of agents.

prices reflect accurately all available information. In fact, they cannot reflect all the information if not all information is available to everybody (Arrow 1991, p. 208). Recent models allow for imperfect information, at great computational cost. The difficulties are compounded under market power. Under perfect competition, all that is required to know is the market price; instead, under monopolistic competition, the informational requirement is much higher: demand curves must be known for optimal behaviour to be calculated. Therefore, firm A must know the behaviour of firm B, and B that of A, giving rise to the problem of "infinite regress": A must know that B is rational, and that B knows that A knows that B is rational, and so on. In other words, rationality must be common knowledge. As with the Rational Expectations Hypothesis, agents are assumed to know the "true" model of the economy, shared with the economic theorist. As Arrow (1991) remarks, this is one key sense in which rationality is a social, not an individual, requirement. Finally, market incompleteness, a very pervasive phenomenon at least as far as the future is concerned, only compounds the problem. If any of these assumptions fail, even the concept of rationality and certainly the likelihood that it prevails become very problematic (Arrow 1991). At the very least, computing the general equilibrium is very taxing for the specialist—which then sends the ball back to square zero, to ask how this can be shared and agreed upon by any private agent.

However, the problem of "infinite regress" and the question of common knowledge or not can be turned on its head, to provide a defence of rationality—by arguing that the problems become infinitely more complicated in the absence of it. If agent A assumes that B is not rational, then what is s/he? Irrational? And how exactly? And what is A assuming about how B views A? In the absence of rationality, there is nothing to anchor these higher-order beliefs. The problem is much more involved than with rationality, as the latter is well defined, but irrationality is not—an answer can be wrong in infinite ways. So, rationality becomes a coordinating mechanism of beliefs. Such arguments have led Mearsheimer and Rosato (2023) to argue that without rationality, there would be no theory of international relations; and the same can be argued of economics. So, the way forward may be to use the standard analyses but introduce more realism in the underlying assumptions in a focused way; and this is the spirit that permeates this book.

Foley (2004) places the methodological individualism-cum-rationality framework of modern economics in line with the political philosophy of Hobbes and Locke, which explains the emergence of modern political institutions as the agreement of rational individuals. Recognising the perils of anarchy and all-out conflict, such individuals are said to agree to democratic institutions of government combined with respect for individual freedom and property. Modern economics parallels this agenda with Adam Smith's invisible hand and the striking two Welfare Theorems that connect market competition with aggregate welfare: a competitive market economy is Pareto efficient, and any Pareto efficient allocation of resources can be sustained as a competitive market equilibrium with a suitable distribution of endowments. Thus, desirable aggregate outcomes are linked to individual motivations and actions and that is arguably one appeal of rationality.

The fundamental problems Foley (2004) sees with all "rational choice" theories, in economics and other social sciences, are two: Firstly, that individual preferences are not ultimately reconciled: They cannot be aggregated into a social welfare function, as the Arrow Impossibility Theorem tells us, hence no agreement on institutions can result. Secondly, and even more importantly, in contrast to the abstract individual of economic theory, real individuals are as much a product of society as society is a product of them: Real individuals have socially constituted motivations and preferences, as well as endowments. They are influenced by, among others, fashion, group identity (community, class, nationality, gender), norms, morals, religion, or culture, all of which affect motivations and require placing individual(s) in a social context, not to treat them in the abstract. (We dwell more on these themes in Chapters 2 and 7.) In other words, Arrow (1991) and Foley (2004) agree that rationality must be placed in a social context, as reviewed above. The "microfoundations" agenda of modern economics, including macroeconomics, fails to account for the two-way interaction between the individual and society. Various of the difficulties identified by Arrow (1991), Foley (2004) argues, are ultimately due to the failure to recognise this.

"Economic (hu)man" and Robinson Crusoe

The combination of rationality and atomism, which is often assumed, even implicitly (though not necessary) has been termed "economic (hu)man" (or "*homo economicus*"). This fictitious agent pursues his/her perceived interests as best they can, as mentioned. Practically, they utilise their endowment of resources efficiently (see below) and they respond to incentives (the firm turns to the most profitable activity and employs the most cost-effective combination of inputs, or the individual chooses optimally). Often labelled choice under constraints, this (postulated) behaviour is synonymous with an efficient allocation of scarce resources, which is a leading definition of economics (Robbins 1935).[11] This "rational choice" methodology has been applied to topics such as electoral behaviour, and the economics of family or crime, that traditionally belonged to neighbouring disciplines such as political economy and sociology (see Hardin 2015).[12]

The approach of economic theory to economic decision-making and behaviour is well illustrated by the Robinson Crusoe parable. The "economic man" maximises "utility" that reflects preferences, subject to all relevant constraints. These may be of different types. Firstly, resources: e.g. income, if that is exogenous; or resources received as endowments or by inheritance; or time, or exogenous skill; secondly, the available technology; thirdly, market conditions, e.g. the wage for a given level of skill or the prices of goods.[13] Starting from these constraints, and guided by their preferences, individuals allocate their spending between various goods or services so as to maximise utility; allocate their income between (current) consumption and savings (which is consumption tomorrow); allocate their time between work (which will provide income), leisure

[11] An alternative, broader definition may be that economics is concerned with all the decisions and activities related to production, exchange, and distribution of material goods and services.

[12] It is sometimes said that one key difference between economics and other social sciences (or at least those strands that are not based on "rational choice") is that the former emphasises the choice aspect of "choice under constraints" while the latter emphasise more the constraints. An example is provided by the economics of education. In standard economic models, the individual exercises choice (e.g. of the amount of education) to maximise their life-chances subject to the relevant constraints. In doing so, they respond to incentives such as the return to education (the "college" or skills premium over the lifetime) and the (opportunity) cost of education. Sociologists would emphasise more the social influences and expectations the individual is under when they make decisions, as well as any constraints due to birth or class. Similar distinction in outlook may be evident in considering, e.g. international trade. Thus, although economics considers both choice and constraints, it has a flavour that the individual has considerable leeway in decision-making and that they are ultimately master of their own destiny. The arguments on the socially constituted preferences or constraints point out that the individual is not as "sovereign" as economic theory postulates.

[13] As is standard, prices or wages may not be exogenous if the individual or firm has monopoli(psoni)stic power.

(and all the activities that go with it, creative as well as pleasurable), or education—which is investment in human capital and will enable them to acquire better skills and higher income in the future.

The story of Robinson Crusoe summarises it all. Robinson aims to maximise "utility", which is his chances of survival on an uninhabited island. He faces a binding time constraint; he must make clever use of his time between work and leisure: He needs to be active enough in order not to die of hunger, yet also to allow enough rest, else he will die of exhaustion.[14] His innate ability (skill or "productivity"), willingness to work (or rest), and resources of the island all play a key role in determining Robinson's choices. In allocating his time of work into fishing or hunting, he takes his preferences into account (does he like fish or meat more?) and technology (abundance of fish or hares and implicit relative price). Finally, once he can comfortably secure survival, he can spend some time building nets or traps, which is physical investment—building physical capital, which involves partly abstaining from consumption now, in order to enjoy more consumption tomorrow. (The other side of the same coin is saving). So, Robinson makes similar economic decisions to those all individuals and societies make. The key determinants of his decisions (preferences, resources) are an example of the (much wider) set of factors that shape economic life. The story illustrates the approach of all economic theory; in macroeconomics, the "real business cycle" model of economic fluctuations is the closest in spirit (starting with the celebrated article of Kydland and Prescott 1982, and followed up by a voluminous literature—see Chapter 1). On this basis, a powerful set of "predictions" follow, i.e. a set of empirically testable propositions that summarises all aspects of economic behaviour.

In terms of macroeconomics, such stylisation helps to build macroeconomics from "micro-foundations" by embedding such preferences into the standard macroeconomic model as in fact a cornerstone of it. The New Classical and its successor, the Real Business Cycle programme took preferences and technology as the fixed, policy-invariant parameters and asked to what extent business cycles can be explained by shocks hitting a competitive market economy. While things are changing in economics,

[14] Any "constraint" is binding, strictly speaking, otherwise it is not a constraint. The binding nature of time is often missed, particularly at a young age, but as life goes on (at least), individuals become more acutely aware of the competing uses of time which a mere 24-hour day must accommodate.

as acceptance grows of the idea that preferences are socially influenced, change over time, and are not consistent, it is striking how commonplace these views are in other disciplines. The fluidity of preferences, and the social element in their determination, may undermine some cherished results in economics.

Key Concepts in Neoclassical Economics: Equilibrium and Preferences

As Manski (2000) emphasises, the approach of economics is remarkably parsimonious in terms of concepts (in contrast to other social sciences, it is argued, with their plethora of concepts): Economic analysis is based on four main concepts: Preferences, expectations, constraints, and equilibrium. To these, one may add another two aspects of traditional theory that are not there so much by definition as by custom: the "selfishness" of the individual (his/her preferences are entirely self-centred); and, in a similar spirit, the absence of social interactions outside the market. A wealth of recent literature, drawing on neighbouring social sciences such as sociology, psychology, behavioural theory, and others, challenges the (presumed) narrow focus of economics on these concepts and associated assumptions; on this, see Chapters 3 and 7. We comment here on the meaning of equilibrium as there have been calls for theory to be developed to analyse situations "out of equilibrium".[15]

There may be four senses (at least) in which the term "equilibrium" is used. In everyday parlance, "in equilibrium" may be taken to mean a state of affairs (or even mind) that is balanced, calm, therefore by implication good; as Schelling (2006, p. 27) remarks, the word is sometimes taken to signify "approval". More technically, equilibrium may be used as synonymous to "market clearing", though that is not necessary. Equilibrium may be static, as is often assumed to be the case (see, e.g. Nelson and Winter 1995). Finally, most closely to physics where the term originates, equilibrium is the state to which the forces that apply at a certain moment lead. It may be a static one, or it may lead to steady-state motion such as a constant growth rate, or even in a motion that involves perpetual oscillations or cycles. We would argue that equilibrium in the first two senses must be dispensed with (if it is used in that way). But the last

[15] See, e.g. remarks made at the Symposium on Alan Kirman, on 16–17 March 2023, by the Rebuilding Macro group, hosted by the Bank of England; https://www.rebuildingmacroeconomics.ac.uk/_files/ugd/1a4a52_1f851a5b627d4719b59275c615c8d7c8.pdf.

sense cannot be dispensed with; after all, physical bodies move under the influence of forces, and so do economic entities. What is important is to account properly for all the relevant economic "forces".[16] In macroeconomics, steady-state balanced growth is the norm, while models of perpetual cycles are at the fringe, but we would argue that the discipline would benefit from a further development and a closer integration of the latter class of models with standard theory. About market-clearing, this is often assumed, but this is one notion of equilibrium that can be shed: Indeed, models of excess demand could provide insights about crises, in the spirit of Keynesian economics. Finally, economists do not suppose that equilibria are in any sense "good"; game theory and the existence of multiple, Pareto-ranked Nash equilibria provide ample reminder of this.

In economics, preferences have been treated with a degree of reverence not shared in other social sciences. Preferences are usually defined over some variable of material well-being—consumption, wealth, or leisure.[17] Elaborating on component (a) of rationality above, preferences are assumed: (i) exogenous (encapsulated in "consumer sovereignty", giving rise to critique such as that of Foley 2004); (ii) clear and unambiguously known to the individual (so that, e.g. when I am shown on the menu of a restaurant with dishes and prices, I know—after perhaps a little time for processing the information—what I want, there is no dithering or procrastination; and the utility that I anticipate from a given consumption turns out to be true, the "decision utility" is the same as the "experienced utility"[18]; or the *ex ante* and the *ex post* utility, see Kahneman 2012; Rabin 1998); (iii) measurable (Hammond 1997); (iv) constant over time (no changing of mind without any information or circumstances having

[16] In the symposium, an example was given for someone who wanted to go to a place in central London, but because of technical fault, the GPS guided them to drive round M25 (the London orbital) forever. In this case, the equilibrium path, considering all the forces such as the information provided by the GPS, is perpetual cycles along the M25.

[17] One criticism of rationality as employed by economists is that it is too narrowly defined over "economic" variables (e.g. Steele, 2004)—we may derive utility from feelings, identity, sociality, morality, creativity, aesthetics, or memory; in other words, by everything that generates a sense of self. This bears on the distinction between instrumental and substantive rationality, mentioned above.

[18] This is a strong assumption: Many goods—new electronic devices, for example—are complex. Their attractiveness or benefits are not immediately apparent; they must be experienced in order for people to assess the value they set on them, so decision and experienced utility are unlikely to coincide.

changed); internally, logically consistent, therefore (v) complete,[19] (vi) transitive, and (vii) reflexive.[20] The enormous appeal of "well-behaved" preferences in the above sense is that they can then be represented by a utility function, subjective, unobservable, and ordinal, to be maximised subject to the relevant constraints. This is the broad approach of standard economic theory, often labelled "neoclassical".

Furthermore, part (b) of the rationality postulate implies (viii) a view of the constraints, current and expected future variables, and beliefs about the behaviour or beliefs of other actors (including the government). (ix) Outcomes are given (subjective) probabilities that should obey basic laws of probability and Bayesian inference. Furthermore, (x) agents synthesise disparate information and build views or theories (rudimentary or not) that are logically consistent (internal validity), involve sensible ideas about causality and are congruent with evidence (external validity). They also (xi) engage in costly acquisition or systematisation (via theoretical or empirical enquiry) of new information, an endeavour that itself will be the subject of optimisation (i.e. one of the decisions to take is on how much research to do). All this imposes heavy information requirements, which can be criticised, as mentioned. In addition, though often this is not explicitly stated, the purposeful action implied by part (c) of rationality presupposes (xii) considerable cognitive and analytical ability to calculate the optimal plan, and (xiii) self-control and discipline to follow that plan. As Simon (2001) remarks, the informational requirements and the processing ability imply that optimisation over all real-world alternatives is impossible. This difficulty and the requirement (d) to adapt and revise the plan as required leads to the notion that rationality cannot be outcome-based but procedure-based (the "procedural

[19] Completeness may seem innocuous: Between A and B, I prefer one or the other or I am indifferent; logically, there is no other possibility. But the real, and not so innocuous, claim is that A and B (and all pairs) be commensurate and comparable. But what about a comparison between (say) a body organ and a sum of money? For most people, this comparison is impossible, as organ sale is considered taboo (immoral as well as illegal). Sandel (2012) shows lots of spheres (friendship, justice, civic life, and many more) where "price" comparisons are (or, used to be) impossible.

[20] Formally, the axioms of rational choice are (following Pinker, 2021): reflexivity, completeness, transitivity, closure, consolidation, independence of irrelevant alternatives, consistency, and interchangeability. These theoretical axioms presuppose the exogeneity, clarity, and stability of preferences mentioned in the text. See Koundouri, Pittis, and Samartzis (2023) for a more in-depth discussion of rationality from the point of view of philosophy of science.

rationality" remarked above).[21] In this view, rationality is not concerned with "what" but with "how".[22]

All the difficulties with rationality are compounded if we take uncertainty into account, as opposed to (quantifiable) risk, or when outcomes cannot be put on a well-defined, continuous scale.[23] Gigerenzer (2021, p. 3549) contends that rationality is a normative concept and it should be limited to "small worlds": "A small world consists of a set S of mutually exclusive and exhaustive future states of the world and a set C of mutually exclusive and exhaustive consequences of one's actions if a particular state occurs". (Gigerenzer 2021, p. 3549) In this case, actions map clearly into consequences. But the small-world concept is very restrictive; for instance, excludes two everyday activities: planning a picnic: simple, but open-ended, uncertain and fuzzy; and chess: precise but with uncountably large states (sequences of moves). If we cannot think through these relatively simple activities, we can imagine the difficulty with other situations. Arguably, as Gigerenzer (2021) implies, all interesting real-world problems belong to the "large world", where full rationality is simply impossible.[24]

[21] In relation to (bounded) rationality and related matters, the name of Herbert Simon deserves a special mention. A true polymath, recipient of the both the Nobel Prize in Economics and the Turing award in computing, he was an early forerunner of various ideas discussed in this chapter. But closer engagement with his multi-faceted work is beyond our scope.

[22] Arguably, another important dimension of decision-making concerns the "when", including when to decide. On this, there is a theory of rational choice of timing (of irreversible investment decisions), see, e.g. McDonald and Siegel (1986). Recent research (O'Donoghue and Rabin, 1999, 2001a, 2001b; Schade and Snir, 2020) finds that waiting to decide is often longer than any rational approach could justify, so it is procrastination, for which behavioural traits may be the explanation. We touch on these themes below and in Chapters 5 and 6 when we discuss "present-bias".

[23] The distinction between risk and uncertainty is well known: the first is quantifiable, where probabilities can be assigned to potential outcomes; it is the "known unknowns" case of everyday language. In contrast, uncertainty is not quantifiable, the "unknown unknowns" case. Kay and King (2021) call it "radical uncertainty" for added emphasis, but it could be argued that the "radical" adjective is strictly speaking superfluous.

[24] A small-world decision space includes for instance utility maximisation: the objective (utility) maps on a well-defined, continuous scale, marginal changes are considered, and predictions are reasonably clear; for instance, when the relative price of a good rises, the rational response is to buy less of it. But things are different with more open-ended goals, for instance maximisation of intertemporal profits or lifetime satisfaction, or with binary choices. What is "the" rational business plan in the face (e.g.) of geopolitical uncertainty

Uncertainty, "Ecological Rationality", and the Emotion-Reason Nexus

Time now to take partial stock: The rationality postulate can be criticised along many dimensions. Individual and collective rationality are distinct concepts, and the former does not guarantee the latter. One line of criticism is the problem of "infinite regress" and the requirement for common knowledge of rationality; but we have argued that this can be turned into a defence of the concept. In its totality, the concept presupposes an exorbitant amount of cognitive power and willpower.[25] Behavioural economics, reviewed below, provides numerous instances, when particular aspects of rationality fail. Before proceeding to review those in the next Section, we consider two further points, namely (the question of) rationality as an evolutionarily successful strategy; and the relation between rationality and emotions. These are less well researched points, so the discussion below is more exploratory in nature.

We may ask, is it really optimal to be (fully) rational, in the way outlined above? Is there a higher-order rationality that might dictate whether we should perhaps not be rational or be rational with limitations, i.e. boundedly rational as outlined in the next section? Where might that higher-order rationality and imperative come from? In international relations theory, Mearsheimer and Rosato (2023) argue that the ultimate objective of states is survival. As evolutionary biology emphasises, the same could be said of human individuals, as indeed of all sentient beings. The point therefore can be made that animals use their cognitive powers to the extent that they lead to greater chances of survival. Now, psychologists tell us of the "fight or flight" mode of thinking: at a critical moment (say, after a sound in the forest), the animal has the option to stay and analyse the situation or to run fast. The sound may be an innocent fall of a branch of a tree, or it may be a lion approaching. Here is the cost–benefit calculus: if the animal flees, if it is a branch falling, it will have made a tiring run; if it is the lion, the quick escape will be lifesaving. If the animal takes time to think, it will have saved the pointless run when the branch is falling; but in the case of the lion, the delay

or AI? Or, what is my "optimal" career path? Foreign policy and international relations are other activities or decisions that do not fit the small-world concept, because of uncertainty and intractability; see Mearsheimer and Rosato (2023).

[25] Thaler and Sunstein (2009, p. 6) argue that rationality requires "unlimited" cognitive power and "total" self-control. Rabin (2013b) concurs about the former.

will be fatal. All said, immediate flight is the best strategy. Long experience ingrained through selection and evolution will then be encoded in instinctive decision-making, a "heuristic" (see the next Section) which says, "in the case of the sound, flee without thinking". The bottom line is that a heuristic or mental template, such as "flee!", may be critical for survival; even though, on occasion, it may lead to waste.

The same can apply to humans, only at a higher level, dictated by their higher cognitive powers. Surely, all the decisions we need to make do not all require the same cognitive effort; some require more effort than others. As the law of diminishing returns suggests, the effort that the tasks or decisions require are characterised by some frequency distribution. Using hypothetical numbers, if I can correctly answer two thirds of the questions or decisions with one third of the cognitive effort that would be required to achieve 100% "correct" answers (i.e. rationality), that might be a winning strategy; considering that all effort, both mental and physical, draws on the same, finite, pool of psychological resources (see below). Heuristics and all the devices associated with what Kahneman calls "System 1" (see below) may save mental energy and lead to an outcome-effort balance that may be more conducive to survival. Artinger et al. (2022, Sect. 4.1) review work that explores how humans trade-off the costs and benefits of cognitive effort. Of course, the winning strategy will depend on what others do. It would indeed be fascinating to explore "how much" rationality an evolutionarily stable Nash equilibrium would involve; but we are not aware of such an analysis.

Such a thinking is formalised in the concept of "ecological rationality" (Gigerenzer 2021; Artinger et al. 2022; Smith 2003). The argument starts from the premise that full logical rationality is only applicable to "small worlds" and inapplicable to the real world-interesting "large worlds", as mentioned. Furthermore, Gigerenzer (2021) surveys a literature that shows that, despite the widespread violations of (full) rationality, there exists little empirical evidence that these violations would incur substantial costs such as diminished health, wealth, or happiness. In this world, heuristics (comparative simple decision rules based on analogies, rules of thumb, or intuitive reasoning) may offer a way of thinking that, despite being short of the "correct" answer or theory, can be faster, more frugal (requiring less information or research) and, not least, may improve the accuracy of judgement (Gigerenzer and Brighton 2009; Gigerenzer

2021). In this light, heuristics are imperfect but efficient mental techniques that can serve until a better one becomes available[26]; they are not synonymous with "biases" and other shortcomings of reasoning, as much of the literature on behavioural economics (reviewed below) implies. Examples of heuristics in macroeconomics are the "rational inattention" that may be the cause of price stickiness (see Chapter 1); simple indexing rules related to the same issue; the approximate optimisation ("near rationality") of Akerlof and Yellen (1985); and even the well-known Adaptive Expectations mechanism which is a much simpler, "good enough" alternative to Rational Expectations.[27] The Taylor rule of monetary policy-making (Taylor 1993) is a widely used heuristic to model the art of monetary policy-making. Seen in this light, full rationality is a straw man; tests should be between heuristics, not between a heuristic and the (presumed) null of full rationality.

All this sounds plausible enough; what may be more debatable is some implications of "ecological rationality" regarding (the absence of) an accuracy-effort trade-off and a (presumed) "less-is-more" effect. Gigerenzer (2021) argues that this trade-off (see Kahneman 2012) applies only to "small-world" problems. The accuracy-effort trade-off disappears in "large worlds" and is replaced by an inverted U-shaped relation: Up to a point, more effort improves accuracy, but beyond a certain point, more effort worsens accuracy, presumably because it confuses matters.[28]

[26] It was exactly in this spirit that Einstein titled his 1905 paper: "On a heuristic point of view concerning the generation and transformation of light" (Einstein, 1905). See Artinger et al. (2022) on the different interpretation of "heuristics" in the behavioural economics and the Ecological Rationality literatures.

[27] There is an ironical twist here. In their analysis of state rationality in international relations, Mearsheimer and Rosato (2023) argue that (i) states are rational on the whole, and (ii) that in any case, without rationality, we could not build any theory of international relations, as we would not know on what premise to base it on. Rationality is a necessary assumption, until we have a more realistic theory of state behaviour. The same argument has been made of the Rational Expectations Hypothesis. In other words, the assumption of rationality itself becomes a heuristic (for the theorist)! This is the spirit of Friedman's (1953, p. 15) famous phrase: "...the relevant question to ask about the assumptions of a theory is not whether they are descriptively realistic, for they never are, but whether they are *sufficiently good approximations* for the purpose in hand". Note the emphasised words (by us), implying that assumptions and theories are heuristics.

[28] This is reminiscent of the fabled Laffer curve in macroeconomics, of which everybody has heard but without coming up with any analysis or evidence for it.

This implies that in the region beyond the apex of the curve, "less-is-more", i.e. less mental effort, relying on more frugal heuristics, improves matters. In all, "ecological rationality" seems to hold promise, compared to the straw man of (full) rationality. It is quite plausible that complex algorithms and parameter-rich models, used to emulate full rationality in "large worlds", impose heavy informational requirements, while simple routines may greatly economise on cost by not sacrificing accuracy much (and arguably by improving accuracy—see Gigerenzer 2021; Artinger et al. 2022). But perhaps more work is needed before various implications of the theory become widely accepted.

A thinly explored area is the relation of rationality to emotion. The relevance of the latter is of course emphasised by psychology (and politics and sociology, as well as literature, music, and art) but not by economics. In fact, if anything, emotion will be considered antithetical to rationality, "passion" tramples "reason", giving rise to phenomena such as herding, contagion, bubbles, panic, "irrational exuberance" (Shiller 2005) and the like. In fact, the issue is a whole lot more complicated than that, as Smith (2022) outlines. In the sequel, we draw on this article to highlight some of the links. In fact, a big argument can be made that emotions and the recognition and awareness of them ("emotional intelligence") are important for rationality: They help us be clear about what we want and what we don't; not only in a narrow sense (what makes me selfishly happy) but also, if I am in any way altruistic (others' utility enters my own utility function), then emotional intelligence helps me understand better what others want and this indirectly clarifies my own utility function. Emotional intelligence makes me clearer about my own capabilities and limitations and better able to address these; and clearer about those of the world around me, since I am better able to understand others' thinking and reactions. In a nutshell, if rationality is roughly synonymous to optimisation, choice under constraints, then emotional intelligence potentially helps to clarify both the objective and the constraints; as would be expected, as, at a basic level, emotional awareness is akin to more information. As a result, optimisation will require less mental effort and will be more effective (with less blockage and going in circles). Smith (2022) quotes experimental results that show that people with emotional skills perform better in intelligence and rationality tests. Furthermore, articulated expression of feelings such as love, joy, anger, sadness, or anxiety may ease communication with others and help in numerous ways; equally, inarticulate or exaggerated expression of the same may be harmful. Repressed feelings and emotions often are the source of problems, mental and physical.

So, is the conventional wisdom that emotion runs contrary to reason entirely wrong then? Perhaps, such a conclusion may be rash. In Chapters 5 and 6 we highlight a tension between longer-term objectives (e.g. good health) and the incentives for immediate gratification (such as the urges to indulge in food, drink, alcohol, and to avoid effort). It can be argued that long objectives are favoured by a cool state of mind, while a "hot" state gives way to immediate gratification. It is a small step then to argue that various emotions, such as anger, frustration, or depression, create the hot state associated with short-termist decision-making. The fear, panic or groundless euphoria that underlie the financial crises or instances of "irrational exuberance" mentioned above also belong to the same category—emotions that lead to hot-headed thinking. So, not all emotions lend themselves to a rational state of mind. In fact, an important distinction can be made (we would argue) between emotions and our awareness of them. Not all emotions lead to clear thinking (some do); but in all cases, our recognition and awareness of emotions and feelings of ourselves and others always helps, by clarification, communication, and better management.

3 Challenges to the Rationality Paradigm: Behavioural Economics

Heuristics and Biases

Situated at the interface between psychology and economics, behavioural economics is a relatively young branch of economics (well, maybe middle-aged, having originated in the mid-70s). Based on extensive experimental evidence, this interdisciplinary field points out a wide range of ways in which the requirements for rationality as expounded above fail. There now exist two brilliant, accessible compendia of behavioural economics by Kahneman (2012), Thaler (2016) and at least two equally good survey articles by Conlisk (1996) and Rabin (1998). To this, we should add the nice and succinct review of Baddeley (2017). A pioneering, Nobel-prize-winning economist, Daniel Kahneman summarises the field, including his own joint research with Amos Tversky, who would no doubt have shared the Nobel if it were not for his premature death. Being originally a psychologist (as was Tversky), Kahneman emphasises the psychological foundations of this area of work relatively more. Along the same wavelength, Thaler, who has also won the economics Nobel, emphasises more the economics end of this work, in reviewing his own contributions as well as the wider literature. We draw on these sources quite extensively in this section and we refer the reader to them for more explanation or discussion, as well as for references to the underlying original research.

Kahneman (2012) begins by analysing two modes of thinking which he calls Systems 1 and 2. Their features and limitations greatly help to make sense of the psychology-based criticisms of rationality in behavioural economics.[29] System 1 is like an automatic reflex, quick and impulsive; because of its limited resources, it is unable to make complex or nuanced calculations and judgements. Instead, it often uses intuition and mental shortcuts such as heuristics, rules of thumb, analogies, and metaphors, which may or may not be misleading. System 2 is our conscious, deliberative self (Kahneman 2012, p. 75): thorough, attentive, and focused, it arrives at a solution (or opinion, or judgement) only after careful consideration of all the available information on the problem at hand. It is used in deliberate memory search, complex computations, comparisons, planning and choice. The downside is that System 2 is slow and effortful. Therefore, our minds try to make sparing use of it, relying on System 1 as much as possible. But in doing so, they risk making mistakes. To use a metaphor, System 1 is a lightly armed sentinel; it can defend if the "enemy" (the problem at hand) is not a serious one; but it can be defeated (i.e. to provide a wrong answer) if it erroneously takes up a serious task on its own. So, here is the trade-off (as economists call it): Reliance on System 1 is fast and requires less resource, but it can lead to error, potentially serious; System 2 gives better answers at higher cost. The question is to get it right. Of course, nothing is immutable, and circumstances change with individuals as well as the nature of the task: Time pressure, skill, experience, self-control, emotional and physical state, all play a role in what each System is able to accomplish, and which one is it is appropriate to use.

In its intuitive, light-touch and quick approach, System 1 is prone to several common fallacies, that a dormant System 2 may fail to correct.

[29] The distinction between these "systems" is itself a heuristic, our own rough-and-ready way of understanding how our minds function. There is no evidence linking the different "systems" to separate brain segments or processes.

It does not like what psychologists call "cognitive dissonance", contradictory information that requires careful processing. Many of the biases outlined below occur as the mind (System 1 in particular) pays selective attention to information. For instance, it processes information in such a way as to validate past choices, paying more attention to information that supports them and downplaying information that contradicts those choices. As a result, it places too much confidence in its judgements ("overconfidence") and tends to suppress doubt. When effort has been expended on one task, "ego depletion" occurs in the next task, which leads to reluctance to use System 2; this is because all mental (as well as physical and emotional) tasks rely on the same pool of mental energy (as evidence shows, Kahneman 2012, p. 41). As a result, both fatigue and hunger (because of lack of glucose) can lead to intuitive errors.

Furthermore, System 1 is impatient and demands immediate gratification. It proceeds by "associative activation", evoking concepts, images, words, or memories that appear associated on instant reflection but may actually be unrelated. Apparent resemblance (often unconscious) connects concepts and ideas in ways that can be misleading—this is the "priming effect". (A good example is money: in a culture where we are bombarded with messages about money, we are "primed" to think of individualism and of money as an end in itself—Kahneman 2012,p. 56). Such associations can also give rise to false ideas about causality, programmed as we are by evolution to seek causation. The trap there is that we rely on such perceptions and avoid the careful statistical thinking that would clear the confusion. The emotional state influences System 1. Being in a state of "cognitive ease", having a sense that the cognitive tasks can be comfortably met, promotes over-reliance on System 1 and bias to accepting intuitions or beliefs without proper scrutiny. Mood plays a role—a good mood is both a cause and an effect of cognitive ease.

System 1 tends to (over)simplify and think of the world as more coherent than it is—black and white, rather than all the hues and tonalities in between. As a result, it is prone to a "halo effect", a tendency to "like the president's voice and style of dress if you happen to like his/her politics" (p. 82). And conversely, dislike him/her thoroughly if his politics does not feel right. There surely exists an ugly/attractive president but with good/bad politics, but the mind finds it difficult to process such apparent incongruity and tends to oversimplify, to suppress ambiguity. This leads to the importance of first impressions, as any contrary evidence that may appear subsequently tends to be ignored. Hence, the sequence by which, for instance, evidence is presented in court may be important. Another limitation of System 1 goes by the fancy name of "what you see is all there is" (WYSIATI), or, in plain English, jumping to conclusions on the basis of limited information, making rushed judgements; which may be due to the wish to avoid the possible incongruence that may arise among the various pieces of information, so we act on a subset of it. Related is the "confirmation bias", where we selectively pay attention to evidence that is in line with preconceived ideas. Moreover, we often engage in "substitution": if the answer to a difficult problem is not available, we may (subconsciously) replace the problem with a simpler, seemingly related, but different one, to which an answer is more easily available (the "availability bias"). Other common fallacies that psychologists have uncovered include illusions, false associations, and "intensity matching" (translating emotion to a numerical scale and allowing that to cloud judgement)—see Kahneman (2012) for more discussion.

Such limitations of System 1 and its interface with System 2 give rise to various common biases and "heuristics"—i.e. procedures that help produce adequate, though often imperfect, answers to difficult questions (using the definition of Kahneman 2012, p. 98); in plain language, mental shortcuts that allow more intuitive, faster, simpler, less expensive thinking. Among these, the "judgment heuristic", WYSIATI and "halo effects" make voters prefer good-looking candidates—because, surely, those cannot be wrong in their political views, can they? The same limitations give rise to "framing effects". The way the problem or question is presented may influence the answer or judgement, if different facets of it are emphasised (even though the substance is identical). Shared biases may lead to (what may be called) "group think" or "conformity bias" if many individuals are called upon to make a judgement but not independently, so one influences the others. This bias may underlie Keynes' "beauty contest" effect to which we return below. The "affect heuristic" is an instance of substitution where the answer to a difficult question is guided by the answer to a simpler or more readily available one: Thus, my political preferences (readily available) may affect my position on a debate, the details of which are more difficult to examine. Therefore, if I am conservative (progressive), I may be prone to finding the arguments against (for) public services more compelling. Or emotion may cloud judgement: The opinion towards a political candidate, which should be based on political views and possibly character, may be inordinately affected by whether they are a warm personality or not (thus, the "emotional tail wags the rational dog", p. 140). WYSIATI, overconfidence, false association and similar effects give rise to intuitive, but wrong, statistical inferences, often due to the inability to infer that extreme outcomes may be due to small samples; and due to the erroneous attribution of causal links to chance events; or due to failure to understand simple laws of probability. We return to this point below when we discuss "Galton's fallacy". Priming and similar effects (such as "insufficient adjustment") give rise to "anchoring", whereby background ideas unrelated to a certain problem may influence (often again subconsciously) the answer to this problem.

The availability heuristic and substitution effect may give rise to judgement by stereotypes, preconceived ideas that are easily available. Furthermore, there is evidence of (what an economist would call) failure of Bayesian updating, when we fail to consider new information because perhaps it conflicts with previous ideas, which would require careful rethinking, or because of overconfidence in initial judgement. Failure to appreciate basic statistical laws is demonstrated in "Galton's fallacy" and the failure to appreciate "mean reversal". Extreme outcomes, such as a very good or bad performance in a task, may be due to a combination of innate skill and (good or bad) luck on the day.[30] More often than not, luck plays a bigger role in individual performance. (It plays a smaller role in groups, as the individual "lucks" average out, the more so as the size of the group is getting greater due to the law of large numbers.) Future performance therefore tends to "revert (or regress) to the mean", as the effect of luck wears out; extreme outcomes do not normally repeat themselves. Failure to appreciate that leads to "Galton's fallacy" (e.g. to think that the sons of tall fathers are all tall). In (macro)economics, this effect features in discussion concerning income distribution and the (possible) convergence of living standards across countries.

Kahneman (2012) discusses a whole array of biases, heuristics, fallacies and illusions that are at once amusing and, when you realise how prone you are to them, annoying, too! There is the "hindsight bias" ("I knew it all along"), "an almost unlimited ability to ignore our ignorance" (p. 201) or failure to allow for "unknown unknowns", the important "outcome bias" (e.g. whatever the coach did was good if the team won—we

[30] Economists, following engineers, would call the former the "signal" and the latter the "noise".

return to this below). Close to the illusion of understanding perfectly the past, and because of it, is the overconfidence in forecasting the future. Both Kahneman (2012) and Thaler (2016) discuss the relevance (and prevalence!) of this in financial markets. There are cognitive illusions of all kinds (such as the "illusion of validity", failure to revise our method of prediction when it demonstrably is not valid, or an illusion of skill in financial markets, a belief that we can beat the market—to which we also return below), a "planning fallacy" (failure to plan even approximately even in activities that have taken place in the past, e.g. writing a book; the experience of the HS2 rail project in the UK which has been scaled back, delayed and gone over budget many times over, is another painful reminder). Following on from WYSIATI and the confirmation bias is the "optimism bias", overconfidence and an illusion of control, all evidenced in financial markets, among others.

Prospect Theory, Loss Aversion, Reference Points, and the "Endowment Effect"

One celebrated part of behavioural economics is "Prospect Theory", originally proposed by Kahneman and Tversky (1979) and now outlined in every book on behavioural economics, including the ones we have mentioned. The traditional economic theory of choice under uncertainty was based on "expected utility theory": under the axioms mentioned above, the utility of a lottery is the weighted average of the utilities of the possible outcomes, each weighted by its probability of occurrence. The theory is familiar to even undergraduates; a quick refresher is given in Fig. 1.

Let x be wealth and U(x) the utility derived from it. Because $x > 0$, standard theory concentrates in the north-eastern quadrant of Fig. 1. Due to diminishing marginal utility, U(x) is concave. Wealth levels x_1 and x_2 are the outcomes of a lottery either in the literal sense (where x_1 is my normal wealth and x_2 is the one after I have won a lottery) or in a figurative sense (e.g. x_2 is the normal value of my house and x_1 is its value after a burglary). Assume that x_1 occurs with probability $0 < p < 1$ and x_2 with probability (1-p). E(x) is average wealth ($=px_1 + (1\text{-}p)x_2$)) and the value of the lottery is $pU(x_1) + (1\text{-}p)U(x_2)$. As shown, the utility of the average is higher than the average of the utilities (point A). Formally: $E(U(x)) < U(E(x))$, which is due to concavity. Put otherwise, the utility of the "sure thing" E(x) (i.e. if we were to have E(x)) for sure) is higher

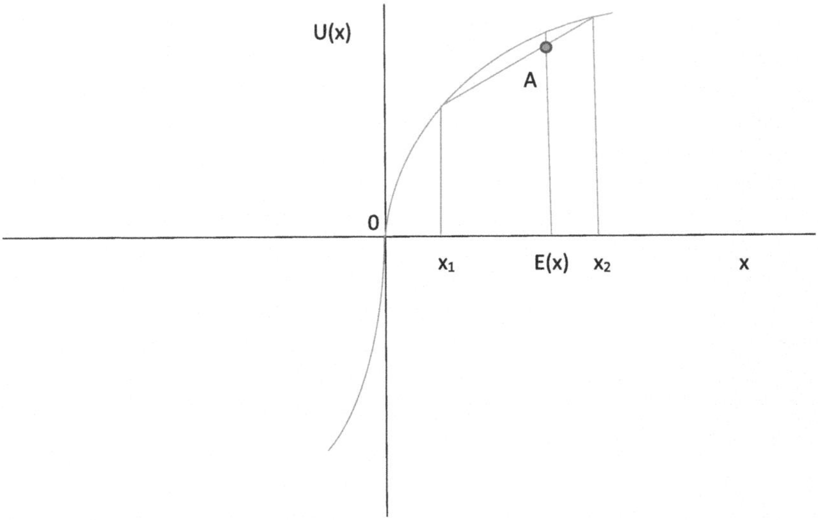

Fig. 1 Expected utility theory versus prospect theory

than the value of the lottery. This is due to risk aversion and the basis on which we are prepared to buy insurance: We are prepared to pay a risk premium so as to be guaranteed the sure thing through compensation.

Prospect theory takes this framework but changes it in a number of ways. Firstly, x is interpreted not as the level of wealth but as the change from a reference point, denoted by the origin. It is argued that this is how subjective evaluations occur, by comparison to a reference point, which becomes crucial in this theory. Therefore, secondly, the south-western quadrant also becomes relevant, as there can be loss as well as gain from the reference point. Thirdly, there is "loss aversion": losses hurt more than equally sized gains give pleasure by an order that could be 1.5 to 2.5, the "loss aversion ratio". Thus, the curve shows a kink at the reference point (the origin), with $MU_0^- > MU_0^+$, the marginal utility (slope) being steeper in the south-western quadrant (going down from point 0). Lastly, the curve changes curvature at the reference point, giving rise to diminishing sensitivity to both gains and losses (marginal utility is rising in the south-western quadrant). As a result, there may be risk aversion in terms of gains but risk-seeking for losses, which intuitively happens as individuals value more strongly the possibility of staying closer to the reference point and thus the pain to going to more extreme losses is relatively low. In contrast, in the standard expected utility model, the "pain" (loss of utility) associated with lower wealth is sharper. Such features contradict the standard model of expected utility, as will be demonstrated in the context of the related "endowment effect" below. In sum, prospect theory introduces a reference point and treats losses from it differently than gains. Often, this reference point is the status quo. Both Kahneman (2012) and Thaler (2016) point out that these key features are in line with the psychology of decision-making, and these are the key advantages of this theory—its realism and more nuanced possibilities. The weakness of the theory is that the reference point is treated as exogenous and context-specific. With a reference point in every possible decision, it is hard to build a general theory of decision-making, both at the micro and most certainly at the macro level.

Aside from the kink at the reference point, prospect theory also makes the assumption that the weights which utilities receive (p and 1-p above) are subjective weights that reflect probabilities but also the vividness of the outcomes. In this, prospect theory differs sharply from the standard expected utility model which posits that these weights are the objective probabilities of the possible outcomes. The celebrated "Allais paradox" warns of pitfalls in this assumption as a theory of actual behaviour. But it was only thanks to psychological research and the formulation of prospect theory by Kahneman and Tversky (1979) that all this was taken into account by economists. In particular, evidence from psychology suggests extreme events tend to be over-represented. Such extreme, very rare outcomes, dubbed "black-swan" events (Taleb 2008), tend to get subjective weights that are multiples of the actual probabilities.[31] Various cognitive limitations are at work here: Emotion may make extreme, often dramatic events, vivid and over-represented in our imagination. Cognitive ease discourages a careful consideration of objective probabilities. The results of such behaviour depend on whether the potential outcomes are considered as gains or losses from a reference point (hence, the two aspects of prospect theory interact). Though fascinating, a discussion of the resulting possibilities would take us too far; the interested reader is referred to Chapter 29 of Kahneman (2012) for a discussion of a 2

[31] More formally, the subjective probabilities or "decision weights" may be a sigmoid function of actual probabilities—with both extremes over-represented.

× 2 grid of possibilities (gains/losses x high/low probabilities) and the resulting behaviour (risk aversion/seeking).

For macroeconomists, this analysis offers interesting insights on financial panics. The theory suggests that a rare possibility (a "black swan" with probability 1%) that the individual ignores receives a zero weight in their preferences and therefore does not influence behaviour. If the possible outcome now comes "into the radar", while still having the same low probability (1%), the individual will now put a weight on it that, though low, will be markedly different than zero (e.g. 5%). Such behaviour may lead to emotional reaction and "overreaction"—Thaler (2016, ch. 22), as exhibited, e.g. in financial panics and bank runs.

Another implication of loss aversion and the overweighting of extreme events is the rejection of strategies, that in their totality, would be beneficial. E.g. an individual project (in the case of a firm) or a financial investment strategy (for an individual) that offers a positive expected return but is risky may not be appealing in one-off cases. But, taken in large bundles, when their riskiness is reduced (because of the law of large numbers), the reduced risk-(same) return configuration, makes the strategy more appealing. Thaler (2016) points out that, because of the traits emphasised by prospect theory, an investor or manager will likely reject "broad framing" and thereby will miss out on opportunities that seem risky in the small but beneficial in the large.

One feature of loss aversion is that it applies not only at literal gains or losses from a reference point, or the status quo; it also applies to potential losses or gains from a target (Kahneman 2012, ch. 28). An example is provided by the behaviour of New York taxi drivers who seem to behave in a paradoxical way—at least from the point of view of traditional economic theory. It was noticed that they tend to work fewer (longer) hours in rainy (sunny) days. The paradox is that clients are easier to find on rainy days, so, effectively, the real wage per hour rises. As that is the opportunity cost of leisure, standard theory predicts that on rainy days, drivers should work more; conversely, they should enjoy more leisure on sunny days. But this is the opposite of what actually happens.

Behavioural economics explains this behaviour by assuming that cab drivers have a target income that they aim to earn each day; when they reach this income, they stop. On rainy days with the greater demand for their services, they reach the target income earlier, so they work less. The target works as a reference point, and cab drivers care more not to fall behind the target than to go above it. As such, they display loss aversion, a common behaviour: "Animals, including people, fight harder to prevent losses than to achieve gains" (Kahneman 2012, p. 305). The notion of a target as a reference point is very useful in macroeconomics when one aims to incorporate these insights. The obvious reference point is average consumption, as a voluminous literature that goes by various names (relative consumption, "keeping up with the Joneses, status-seeking behaviour) has emphasised; we review this literature and its extensions that emphasise loss aversion in Chapters 3 and 4.

Related to the reference point of Prospect theory is the "endowment effect". This is best illustrated with the (real) example of someone who owned some expensive bottles of wine. (They were bought at lower prices in the past and had appreciated over the years.) The key point is that this person was neither willing to sell them at the current price nor buy any other at this price. Theory tells us that, in equilibrium, price equals marginal utility, P = MU.[32] At this price, the individual is indifferent between buying or selling one more unit. There are two other possibilities: P > MU, in which case an extra unit is worth more in the market than in terms of the utility it provides, so the individual will be prepared to sell; and P < MU, where, conversely, the individual will be prepared to buy one more unit. What standard theory does not allow is both P > MU and P < MU (which would be a logical impossibility, anyway). But things change if the status quo is a reference point with a kink in utility at it, as before, and if it happens that $MU_0^- > P > MU_0^+$. . In this case, the (absolute) utility loss from selling one unit (MU_0^-) is greater than the price, so the individual will not be prepared to sell; at the same time, the price is greater than the extra utility from acquiring one more unit (MU_0^+), so the individual will not buy, either. In other words, the status quo is a reference point that the individual considers normal, an "endowment", from which they are reluctant to move in either direction—neither by buying nor selling. In this way, the "endowment effect" is seen to be formally equivalent to the status quo as a reference point. Both notions present the same challenge to standard theory.

[32] We ignore the shadow price of wealth, the "λ" of constrained optimisation.

Intertemporal Choice, the "Present Bias" and Time Inconsistency

A rejection of rationality that is receiving increasing attention in macroeconomics is time inconsistency of optimal plans, resulting from an in-built "present-bias" in preferences (see Thaler 2016, ch. 12; and Chapters 5 and 6). Standard theory models intertemporal planning via the existence of current and future consumption as two separate arguments in utility; the latter is discounted, leading to impatience. The optimal intertemporal plan weighs this impatience against the (opportunity) cost of earlier consumption, i.e. the interest rate (via foregone saving or via borrowing). To this, the assumption of exponential discounting (in continuous time) or geometrical discounting (in discrete time) is usually added, leading to time consistency of plans: The optimal plan is the same, no matter when you do the planning. Recent psychological research, however, suggests that behaviour both of humans and animals is characterised by present-bias: The discount rate applying to the near future is higher than that applying in the far future: impatience is higher right now. This builds in a tendency for immediate gratification that makes optimal plans time-inconsistent: I plan for the future with my long-term interest in mind (e.g. to eat healthily); but when time comes to implement the plan, when the future has arrived so to speak, I succumb to the temptation for immediate gratification (e.g. by indulging on delicious but unhealthy stuff). Thus, a change of plans occurs without any external change forcing it: The optimal plan simply does not stand the test of time ("time-inconsistency of the optimal plan"). This may also be a source of regret, when the impulsive decision is later put in perspective. The key point is that, without an external commitment, the short-term goal will dominate at the expense of the long-term one. The parable of Ulysses who was torn between the long-term goal (to return home) versus the short-term one (to listen to the Sirens) is well known. In order not to be lured away from his long-term objective of returning home, Ulysses asked his mates to tie him (commitment). The story puts in sharp relief the question of (the lack of) self-control in enforcing the long-term plan.

Similar dilemmas arise in more real contexts such as: saving for the future, with the failure to save adequately for old age; or other financial planning, with the failure to insure adequately against risks. As this behaviour is likely followed by regret, a corollary is that this kind of behaviour undermines the notion of a unitary utility function. In contrast to what traditional theory assumes, both concerns (for current and future gratification) are real and there seems to be tension between the two. The conflict within the self is evident in the change of plans, but its nature is not entirely clear: it may be explained by reference to the tension between Systems 1 and 2, as discussed, or perhaps by reference to Freudian ideas about conscious and unconscious. This lack of clarity has led to a variety of approaches in modelling intertemporal choice with this feature (see Thaler 2016, ch. 12): One approach (Thaler and Shefrin 1981) emphasises the contrast between the "planner" and the "doer" selves, taking a principal-agent approach. Another approach (Laibson 1997; see also the literature mentioned above on "procrastination") models intertemporal choice as a game between two selves, the current one, seeking immediate gratification, and the future one, caring for long-term utility. In addition to undermining the notion of "nice", unitary preferences, this set of phenomena show that the self-discipline required for the individual to enforce what is optimal for themselves, i.e. to pursue their own good, is often lacking.

Further Topics: Mental Accounting, Preference Reversals, Context, Anchoring, and Framing

Mental accounting is the phenomenon of people treating income received from different sources differently; e.g. using gambling winnings or winnings on the national lottery for treats and holidays, while using salary for regular spending on food and heating. It is a form of narrow framing which only the Humans do, not the Econs. The latter construct a unified budget constraint encompassing all sources of income and outlays and engage in various types of activity up to the point where the marginal utility of each divided by its price equals the marginal utility of wealth (to recall elementary microeconomics). This is however a very complex calculation, involving myriads of ratios. Humans, therefore, construct truncated budget constraints as rules of thumb ('I'll go to a fancy holiday if I get a bonus'), thus avoiding challenging calculations about which they cannot be confident.[33,34,35]

A further challenge to received theory is presented by the contrast between "intrinsic" and "extrinsic" motivation (Benabou and Tirole 2003). Intrinsic motivation is the idea that there are some activities that people would carry out for the pleasure of doing them, for the sense of achievement or for their social value. Once the activity is paid for, people's attitude to it changes. The most striking example may be that of the nursery that required parents to pick up their children by a certain time of day when it closes, out of consideration for the staff. To reduce lateness, they introduced a fine for late pick-ups, expecting this to provide a disincentive and reduce the number of parents who came late to collect their children. At least this is what theory would predict and how rational individuals ("Econs") would respond. In fact, they found that lateness became more common: Once parents had to pay for being late, they regarded it differently than when it was a moral obligation to be on time. The monetary incentives crowded out the intrinsic motivation. This has been called the motivation-transfer effect by Frey and Jegen (2001). This challenges traditional theory in a number of ways. Obviously, individuals

[33] In technical language, Thaler (2016) explains, money (as a metaphor for income) is *fungible*, it can be turned to any use (unlike material, e.g. food cannot be used for housebuilding). This implies that in theory, there should be a single, unified budget constraint, but in practice we construct a series of partial budget constraints.

[34] It must be said that theory does allow for behaviour that resembles mental accounting in a restricted way, through "two-stage budgeting". Under some restrictions on the utility function and if the relative price is constant, two goods may be treated as a single bundle, e.g. "food" (rather than meat and veg separately). We can then have a budget for food (allocated at the first stage) and then apportion that to individual components of the bundle without regards to other items in the utility function (at the second stage). This is like mental accounting, albeit standard theory allows for that only to a very limited degree.

[35] At the aggregate level, too, something akin to partial budgeting also happens, and standard theory plays insufficient attention to it. Like money or income, output or resources are treated as fungible, able to be turned at once to private consumption, or investment, or public services. That may be true in the long run, but in the short run, there are restrictions on how much can be obtained of each due to their nature. A practical reminder of this is provided at every instance when humanitarian aid is needed (alas, too frequently). While general resources may be more plentiful, through donations, there is urgent need of specific items (food or medical material or equipment) which are readily available in limited quantities. This slows down the aid—and money is slow to be taken up. Macroeconomists speak of "bottlenecks" in this case.

are not cold calculators of incentives; associated with lateness are norms and morals (shame, guilt). Monetary disincentives alter preferences by normalising lateness and reducing the negative emotions associated with it. Thus, preferences are not independent of the context of the activities in question, which here is the reward structure.

Psychology research has uncovered lots of instances of "preference reversals", instances where A is preferred over B at one point, later on for the rank to be reversed—B preferred over A (see Thaler 2016, Ch. 6; Rabin 1998). Obviously, such results have caused consternation among economists, but the psychology research and its findings appear robust. Preference reversals are not entirely random or chaotic; they appear to be subject to some patterns. In much of the research, both A and B are lotteries (each offering gains and losses under different probabilities); it appears that preferences are constructed by some "salient" feature in mind, e.g. if the chooser values losses/gains more, they may prefer the lottery that has this characteristic as salient. The preponderance of System 1 in much thinking implies that at every instance, we only take one such salient feature into account (technically: we make a "single evaluation").[36] The choice can then be reversed if at some other point we take another salient characteristic into account. If, on the other hand, the more resource-demanding System 2 were in control, we would consider all characteristics all the time, arriving at a more balanced choice that would not be reversed later. Regret is a form of preference reversal; its dynamics involve various effects among those discussed, but the key point is that it is not allowed in standard theory (where the individual is doing their best *ex ante*, and they know that *ex post*—after a shock has occurred or the lottery turned, even if the outcome turns out not to be favourable).

In other words, System 1 being in control implies that comparisons are partial, giving rise to other phenomena like preference reversals. E.g. individuals are known to be prepared to contribute more to the rescue of dolphins than to medical check-ups for humans in risk of cancer; or compensation to bank fraud can be higher than compensation to a victim

[36] One example is the famous "bank teller" fallacy (discussed by both Kahneman and Thaler and others). In an experiment, participants are told by a fictitious character, Linda, whose profile suggests that she is a feminist. Participants are then asked to choose what is more probable, (a) that Linda is a bank teller, or (b) that she is a bank teller and a feminist. They mostly choose (b), against the elementary laws of probability. The likely explanation is that the feminist feature is salient, and they fail to make a full evaluation of the two possibilities they are given.

of fire due to neglect (all examples from Kahneman 2012, Ch. 33). A key detail is that the various questions were posed to separate sets of individuals, who placed more emphasis on different particulars. Various characteristics of System 1 played a role, such as a salient monetary feature, emotional intensity, or context; the key is the absence of System 2 (by the construction of experiments), which would have compared outcomes holistically, thus arriving at more consistent choices. The public policy implication is that compensations may be consistent within categories (e.g. cases of human casualty receive compensation according to severity) but inconsistent across categories (e.g. compensation for animal welfare may be more than compensation for human casualty).

Context effects cover a much broader range of phenomena. They refer to environmental or situational information that guides perception and interpretation of signals; a good example being the symbol being read in different ways in different words, guided by the word themselves. Framing refers to similar effects, whereby the way a problem is posed guides the answer, and the same problem can be answered in different ways. The anchoring effect arises because of the ubiquitous nature of reference points in our thinking and calculations. The number 9-ending price effect mentioned in Chapter 1 is a case in point; it arises because such prices appear just short of a 0-ending number, hence they are perceived as low (and 10 or 100 are natural references because of our familiarity with the decimal system). Plenty of examples of context, anchoring, and framing effects are given in Kahneman (2012) and Thaler (2016). All challenge the rationality postulate because they all imply, in different ways, that information that is (supposedly) "background", but which is in fact irrelevant, affects perception and decision.[37] They have had also numerous and powerful policy applications, some of which are reviewed below; we first discuss the approaches available to macroeconomics in order to incorporate "bounded rationality".

[37] Context, anchoring, framing, and similar effects (including endowment) violate the "independence of irrelevant alternatives" axiom of rational preferences (see Rabin, 1998, p. 37).

4 Bounded Rationality and Implications for Macroeconomics

The evidence for reasoning errors, fallacies, and general failures to conform to the assumptions of received theory is overwhelming and the catalogue of such imperfections is very extensive indeed. It is also clear (Conlisk 1996; Selten 2001) that cognitive imperfections and fallacies do not "wash out" in the aggregate; they are systematic deviations from what full rationality would imply, so that the line of defence that the latter is approximately valid cannot be sustained. But it should also be clear that all these shortcomings do not make humans "irrational"; they are boundedly rational (emphasis on both words), smart but with important limitations, finite minds, not the super-efficient human computers postulated by economic theory (see, e.g. Selten 2001). As Conlisk (1996) emphasises, one reason underlying these limitations is the deliberation cost involved in information-processing and decision-making. The rationality postulate implicitly assumes that this cost is zero, so agents reach the mathematically derived optima. But, consistently with the Systems heuristic of Kahneman (2012), the deliberation cost is non-zero and this implies a trade-off between deliberation effort and judgemental accuracy (Conlisk 1996, p. 671).[38] Explicit recognition of the deliberation cost implies that agents are required to solve an even more complex problem than that implied by full rationality (see Selten 2001).[39] The same is true of learning models.

Models that take bounded rationality explicitly into account are the "transactions costs" theory of the firm (see Williamson 2000), which suggests that firms arise as a way of economising various transactions

[38] It is a moot point whether cognitive limitations, captured by deliberation costs, are the *only* source of the limits to rationality; Rabin (2013b) suggests not, but the Systems heuristic suggests, ultimately yes. Recall that System 2 provides correct answers, but it is costly to use.

[39] Explicit recognition of deliberation costs in optimisation also leads potentially into logical difficulties, namely the problem of "infinite regress" (see Conlisk, 1996, p. 687n.). Let the optimal solution under full rationality be X* and the best solution with a limited amount of deliberation be X**. In deciding how much to deliberate, the agent then faces a trade-off: the benefit of a better solution (X*-X**) versus the deliberation cost. What is the optimal amount of deliberation? Determining that involves an extra layer of cost (deliberate on how much to deliberate) and leads to a second-round optimisation. And what is the optimal amount of deliberation on how much to deliberate? This leads to an yet another layer of cost and additional round of optimisation; and so on.

costs. The "X-inefficiency" (Leibenstein 1966) whereby a firm's production lies at the wrong side (inside) the efficient production frontier is arguably due to various imperfections, including information and deliberation inefficiencies, which fall in the domain of bounded rationality. The early pioneer of bounded rationality, Simon (1955, and much else since) has suggested that instead of maximising utility subject to some kind of global opportunity set, individuals perform limited searches and decide on the first solution that is "good enough"—the "satisficing" hypothesis (see Artinger et al. 2022). "Hierarchical decision" models (Ermini 1991) suggest that individuals arbitrarily structure the calculation into a decision tree (e.g. I first decide my employment and then, subject to the solution, I select the optimal place of residence—or vice versa, but the important element is that the dimension of the decision space is reduced arbitrarily).[40] Adaptive expectations and partial adjustments are also rules of thumb that arbitrarily cut through analytical complexity, hence they fall under the same fold. The "near rationality" of Akerlof and Yellen (1985) and the "rational inattention" literature mentioned in Chapter 1, that both help explain the infrequent price adjustment, are also models of bounded rationality. Complexity, self-organising markets, multiple equilibria, and path dependence may be some of the implications of such behaviour (Conlisk 1996). But it is not entirely clear whether such outcomes are the result of reasoning errors and cognitive limitations or other features of the models. So, does bounded rationality alter market outcomes? Maybe, suggests Conlisk (1996, p. 680), adding, "bounded rationality matters but not in a simple way".

All this implies that there is no single theory of bounded rationality as yet. The various results of behavioural economics and psychology do not lead to any framework that holds with any degree of generality. For instance, Conlisk (1996, p. 692) argues: "The evidence and models surveyed suggest that a sensible rationality assumption will vary by context, depending on such conditions as deliberation cost, complexity, incentives, experience, and market discipline". Thus, the (macro)economic theorist must select the feature of bounded rationality that is most salient for the task at hand. There cannot be any general

[40] Hierarchical decision-making together with narrow framing or partial comparisons can be seen to violate the "transitivity" axiom of rational preferences; see Pinker (2021, Ch. 6).

theory. However, one thing seems clear: Any instance of bounded rationality or behavioural model must rely on some heuristic or short-cut from full rationality.[41] The evidence is often consistent with "rough" optimality but inconsistent with "finer" optimality (Conlisk 1996, p. 675). This approach offers the advantage of utilising standard theory up to a point, while building deviations from it that have significant effects and implications.[42] An alternative approach, namely that of equating bounded rationality with explicitly non-optimising procedures (Selten 2001) may be exciting but requires building theory essentially from scratch. Improving the realism of preferences while retaining a core of accepted macroeconomics based on optimisation is in line with many recent contributions that introduce behavioural elements into economics (Rabin 2013a, b).

In view of the above, there are three possible routes on how to proceed: First, ditch the rational-actor programme in its entirety (advocated by Foley 2004, among others). For macroeconomics, in particular, this would suggest building theory on postulated aggregate behaviour; something entirely at odds with the micro-foundations programme. A second approach (Selten 2001) suggests building theory on an entirely non-optimising basis. One difficulty with these first two approaches is to select an alternative; there is also the pragmatic difficulty that theory needs to be developed from scratch. Hence, these two approaches, despite potential merits, have not been followed up by the literature and are outside our scope. The last approach, to be followed in this book, is that of Rabin (2013a, b), namely, to proceed with standard models but with alterations to the utility function, aiming to capture some of the most salient features of the "Humans".

The general approach of bounded rationality as "near rationality" informs the rest of this book: For instance, much of the analysis in Chapters 3 and 4 is based on the notion of "status" (or "keeping up with the Joneses") built into preferences and utility. This implies that consumption comparisons (usually, with average consumption as a reference point)

[41] We can illustrate the point by using the arts-vs.-science heuristic: Cognitive limitations cannot be addressed by more science (yet more math) but instead require some art (using intuition to suggest prominent instances where optimisation is incomplete or takes short-cuts).

[42] Rabin (2013a, b) calls these realism-improving extensions to core theory "portable extensions of existing models (PEEMs)".

enter the individual utility function and impart a negative consumption externality. The explanation that is usually offered for that is envy, but it is often offered in passing, without much analysis. It is not explained why envy prevails over altruism, which is emphasised by the research on socio-economics (see below). If altruism prevailed, then relative consumption (or any other reference point) should also enter individual utility, but with the opposite sign—inducing a positive externality instead.

An alternative justification that may be offered for the negative externality in consumption may be more in line with the arguments on bounded rationality: Comparisons and relative position may be an indicator of how well I am doing in optimisation: All the arguments surveyed above, primarily cognitive limitations, imply that "maximisation of my life chances under the applicable constraints" is a fuzzy and complex task to the point of being almost meaningless. Hence, I cannot be sure of the answer. Comparisons and relative standing may offer a rough indication of how well I have done—imperfect monitoring of whether I am on course to hit the target; assuming of course that that (the lifetime optimum) is well defined. Ideally, comparisons should be done over the subset of individuals with similar exogenous characteristics or initial endowments (the "Joneses") but, once again, we are not in an ideal world. Selecting this sample and monitoring it involves cost—not worth it. Hence, instead, I compare myself with the average.[43]

Rabin (1998) offers a typology of behavioural effects in terms of what they imply for theory: One category (reference levels, status quo bias, endowment effects, norms, loss aversion) can be treated by alterations in the utility function. This insight has guided much of the related research in macroeconomics. As mentioned, reference points and the like are context-specific, so a key challenge is in providing a general model of reference points or the status quo. The approach that much macroeconomics has taken is dual: Firstly, references and norms are provided by social comparisons; often, a key reference point is average consumption or wealth, which should enter the utility function alongside the individual consumption or wealth. This strand of the literature goes by various labels such as "keeping up with the Joneses", "status" or "external habits". It

[43] In Chapter 3, we call the question "Have I attained my lifetime's potential?" the "Kazantzakis question" and argue that, under full rationality, the question is void: By the definition of rationality, the answer is yes. Therefore, the above reasoning would suggest that comparisons in utility are a behavioural trait.

will inform much of the book from Chapter 3 onwards. Second, reference points and norms evolve adaptively from past behaviour. The strand of the literature on (internal) "habits" emphasises this fact. It points out that past individual consumption or wealth should enter the utility function alongside the current one(s). This approach, too, will be surveyed and its implications will be discussed in Chapter 3. A further, broader category is "other-regarding preferences". Aside from social comparisons, this includes effects such as social norms, including fairness norms, altruism, envy, identity, and the like. This category, overlapping with the first one, will be discussed in Chapters 3 and 7. Another extension to the standard theory informed by psychological research is the modelling of present-bias and preference reversal ("time inconsistency"), mentioned above. We shall review this in Chapters 5 and 6.

A further, quite disparate category is all the heuristics, fallacies, and biases that were mentioned above. Differences between decision and experience utility, difficulties of recollection, as well as misperceptions of all kinds and preference reversals belong here (Rabin 1998; Kahneman 2012). All these challenge core assumptions of rationality. It is difficult to know whether/when/under what conditions the individual errors produce systematic patterns of behaviour at the aggregate level. Chapter 1 has reviewed work by George Akerlof and others who have suggested that some of these behavioural traits hold the potential to resolve long-standing questions in macroeconomics. We saw how "rational inattention" has been invoked to explain price stickiness. But it is probably fair to say that such attempts have not produced clear-cut theories of any generality. A separate category may be socially minded behaviour such as public-spiritedness and conditional or reciprocal altruism and punishment (Conlisk 1996; Rabin 1998), which calls for game-theoretic approaches, so it has not (yet?) entered mainstream macroeconomics.[44] Hence, we shall not have much more to say about these approaches in this book.

[44] Conlisk (1996, p. 674) suggests that it is unclear whether the failure of the optimal selfish strategy of free-riding is due to altruism or a reasoning error. Our reading of the literature (see Chapter 7) suggests that the most widely accepted interpretation of the evidence is that it this failure is due to altruism.

5 Summary and Policy Implications

Summary: Humans vs. "Econs"

The list goes on. The main point is that all the various biases and fallacies undermine the agency, autonomy and rationality with which individuals are supposed to be endowed by neoclassical theory ("consumer sovereignty"). This is of course most obvious in preference reversals and regret that undermine the postulate of "nice" preferences (particularly stability); anchoring, framing, and herd effects also imply that both preferences are not exogenous and sacred but malleable and susceptible to outside influences; prospect theory and the endowment effect both undermine the assumption of "rational" thinking in various ways. The very reluctance to invoke (what Kahneman and other psychologists call) System 2 and the over-reliance on System 1 bears testament to the limited cognitive powers that Humans (as opposed to Econs) possess. Of course, nobody, not even the most-die-hard of the neoclassical economists, would argue for the realism of the pure theoretical model. A proponent of standard theory would put forward an "as if" argument, namely (a) what matters in a theory is not its realism but its predictions (of the type: when price goes up, the quantity demanded will go down according to a certain formula), and (b) that economic agents exhibit a behaviour that embodies the predictions of the theory even if subconsciously—"as if" they followed the model. So, the demand will decline following the price rise in the same way a footballer can send the ball across without knowing the laws of physics. This is the real issue of contention: whether the standard theory can predict behaviour "as if" agents possessed the assumed properties. And no one would look for behaviour exactly in accordance with predictions; the issue is whether standard theory is a useful approximation. To these questions, behavioural economists would answer "no and no"—actual behaviour is not in agreement with standard theory, not even approximately.

We may summarise partially by returning to a theme mentioned above. Both Kahneman (2012) and particularly Thaler (2016, e.g. p. 258) draw a sharp distinction between the economic agent postulated by economic theory, possessing the well-behaved preferences described above, rationality in the sense of efficient collection and analysis of information, and cognitive ability to work out how to maximise whatever is to be maximised. They dub this, arguably fictitious agent, an "Econ". The Econ knows clearly their preferences and goals without ambiguity, dithering, or regret (except if there is new information that makes them recalculate). They respond efficiently to economic incentives (rewards and punishment, but also more subtle changes in underlying "technology", e.g. if hares become somehow easier to catch, Robinson will turn more to hunting and away from fishing) and they are able to focus on what really matters by ignoring irrelevant bits of information—so, there is no context, or framing. Resembling more real human beings is another type of agent, aptly labelled a "Human". Humans are subject to all the cognitive shortcomings highlighted above. They are characterised by one or more of inconsistent or blurred preferences, bounded cognitive power (inability to work out complex problems), bounded willpower to see through any solution that they have calculated. Humans often fail to respond to incentives (they may not even recognise them) and/or respond to supposedly irrelevant factors. Their thinking is characterised by ubiquitous "heuristics" (rules of thumb or thinking by inappropriate analogies) and biases (tendencies to make common mistakes) that lead them away from the fully optimal solution. To take one example, an Econ taxi driver will work more hours when the pay (or implicit pay) is higher, as is the case on rainy days. In contrast, the New York taxi drivers (and many others, no doubt) are Humans, guided more by heuristics such as target income for a day, mental accounting, and the like.

In sum, the literature on behavioural economics has led to a much better understanding of how real people, not theoretical constructs, behave. This realisation has found important practical policy applications; we finish the chapter with a brief review of these.

Policy Applications and Other Implications

Richard Thaler and Cass Sunstein devote their book *Nudge* (Thaler and Sunstein 2009) to policy applications of behavioural traits; similar ideas are also present throughout both Kahneman (2012) and Thaler (2016). Such insights have become so mainstream and influential that the British government have for some years had a "nudge unit" which has used its insights to tweak government policy. One element of behaviour that has led to numerous applications concerns the framing of choices, for instance, whether one is required to opt in or opt out of a scheme. For instance, when considering whether to subscribe to a pension scheme when one starts work, an Econ will consider their preferences for consumption now as opposed to the future (as a subscription transfers resources from now to the future), the terms of the scheme, and whether it might be preferable to do that transfer of resources themselves via the market (by saving in some way). They then choose "yes" or "no", irrespective of what the default option is (opt in or out). A Human, however, may, firstly, be unable to engage in such complex financial calculations, and secondly, because perhaps s/he does not form strong views, s/he is susceptible to influence from the seemingly irrelevant default option. Usually, s/he will accept the default option. Behavioural economists talk of a "status quo bias" (analogous to neither buying nor selling those bottles of wine). The status quo is a strong reference point and individuals are often reluctant to change it. Context, framing, and other effects are also at play. Since the take-up of pension, or insurance, depends on how the choice is framed, governments that want to encourage this behaviour have made opt-in the default option. Opt-out requires action and is on the whole avoided. More generally, "choice architects" present alternatives to people with a view to steering them to their (the choice architects') preferred choice.

Both Kahneman (2012) and, in particular, Thaler (2016) emphasise the economic implications of such behaviour—some already mentioned. Leading on from the "illusion of skill"—the question mark over the possibility of close knowledge of behaviour—are a whole raft of issues or indeed open questions (see Kahneman 2012, chs. 21 and 22): the value of expertise or indeed presumed "expertise", e.g. managerial expertise, around which there is vested interest (Thaler 2016, p. 216); the optimal combination of leadership (with its putative expertise) with ability to listen to the outside view so as to avoid group think; and whether predictions of ability and future behaviour can be made on the basis of detailed assessment of character or on the basis of algorithmic calculations based on simple questionnaires (the "intuition versus algorithms" question).

In Chapter 1, we highlighted some intriguing implications of this agenda, though (Saint-Paul 2011). With intertemporal choice and the conflict of the two selves, how should the state intervene to bring about the desired result? Because the individual has at least two, that of the younger profligate and another of the older, sadder and wiser saver, whose utility is to be maximised? In fact, of course, states often intervene by forcing saving to ensure at least a low level of income in old age. States themselves also suffer from cognitive biases and cannot commit themselves to letting people bear the consequences of their earlier decisions, risking the emergence of a population of destitute seniors. Therefore, they impose restrictions on people's ability to spend their income freely, by imposing social insurance schemes or forced saving.

Keynes (1936) has highlighted the "animal spirits" of financial investors, i.e. sudden changes in their behaviour or strategy, and the expressions have entered the standard vocabulary of both commentators and macroeconomists. It is a moot point whether such changes are entirely exogenous, whimsical and abrupt changes of sentiment, or exaggerated responses to shocks or pieces of information. Behavioural economics offers ample explanation of either (particularly the latter, it may be added), such as overreaction, emotional reaction due to inability to engage in detailed thinking, panic due to loss aversion, exaggerated attention to a possibility that has just "entered the radar" (but is still small), herd behaviour, loss of nerve due to narrow framing (focusing on an individual episode), and many other lines of explanation. All such behaviours are on display in financial crises such as the Great Depression, the various bubbles (including the "dot.com" bubble of 2000/1 and house price bubbles), and the Great Recession (the crisis of 2007–9 and its aftermath). The then US Fed Chair Alan Greenspan has coined the memorable term "irrational exuberance" to describe the bullish, euphoric side of this type of behaviour, an expression that Shiller (2005) used as a title and has subsequently entered the popular lexicon. Akerlof and Shiller (2009) offer a catalogue of instances where such animal spirits hold the key to explanation; we return to them in Chapter 7.

Related to animal spirits is another expression, or parable, of Keynes', that of the "beauty contest". To appreciate its importance, we should note that much economic behaviour, in financial markets and elsewhere, depends on prediction of future outcomes (e.g. share prices). Such outcomes depend on how the market treats (buy/sell) those shares, which in turn depends on what other investors are thinking and predicting. In other words, each investor is trying to predict other investors' predictions, thereby "beating the market" (buy/sell before everybody buys/sells). Now, we have seen above ample warning against such type of behaviour (illusion of skill, overconfidence, excessive optimism), but the key point is that behaviour often depends not on a simple guess about the value of something, but on guessing the guesses of others about that. Keynes described essentially this behaviour as a "beauty contest", the winner of which is someone whose judgement is closer to the judgement of others—i.e. to something subjective. As Thaler (2016, ch. 21) discusses, the solution is a Nash equilibrium of forecasts (the game being of the type, "I forecast your forecast and you forecast mine"). Even in simple, well-defined contests, the Nash equilibrium is rather surprising (to the untrained eye), being away from anything objective. One can easily extend this reasoning to situations where measurement is ambiguous to begin with (e.g. the fundamental value of the stock market index), to see how much room for subjective reasoning there is, and for scope for all the traits discussed above to influence thinking and behaviour. One can also think of equilibria (if they exist) that are not stable, allowing for gyrations of behaviour and therefore of the market. We leave the matter for the moment but return to implications for financial markets in Chapter 8.

References

Akerlof, G.A., and J. Yellen. 1985. A Near-Rational Model of the Business Cycle, with Wage and Price Inertia. *Quarterly Journal of Economics* 100 (Supplement): 823–838.

Akerlof, G.A., and R.J. Shiller. 2009. *Animal Spirits: How Human Psychology Drives the Economy and Why it Matters for Global Capitalism.* Princeton University Press: Princeton.

Arrow, K.J. 1991. Economic Theory and the Hypothesis of Rationality. In The New Palgrave: The World of Economics. Edited by J. Eatwell, M. Millgate, and P. Newman. New Yok: Macmillan.

Artinger, F.M., G. Gigerenzer, and P. Jacobs. 2022. Satisficing: Integrating Two Traditions. *Journal of Economic Literature* 60 (2): 598–635.

Backhouse, R.E., and P. Fontaine. 2018. Economics and Other Social Sciences: A Historical Perspective, Annals of the Fondazione Luigi Einaudi: An Interdisciplinary Journal of Economics, History and Political. *Science* 52 (2): 7–44.

Benabou, R., and J. Tirole. 2003. Intrinsic and Extrinsic Motivation. *Review of Economic Studies* 70 (3): 489–520.

Blaug, M. 1992. *The Methodology of Economics, or How Economists Explain*, 2nd ed. Cambridge: Cambridge University Press.

Blume, L., and D. Easley. 2007. *Rationality, New Palgrave Dictionary of Economics*. Edited by S. Durlauf, and L. Blume, 2nd ed.

Caldwell, B.J. 1982. *Beyond Positivism: Economic Methodology in the Twentieth Century*. London: Routledge.

Conlisk, J. 1996. Why Bounded Rationality? *Journal of Economic Literature* 34 (2): 669–700.

Ermini, L. 1991. Hierarchical Decomposition in Economic Analysis. In *Behavioral Decision Making: Handbook of Behavioral Economics*, vol. 2B, 547–62. Edited by R. Frantz, H. Singh, and J. Gerber. Greenwich, CT: JAI Press.

Foley, D.K. 2004. Rationality and Ideology. *Social Research* 71 (2): 329–342.

Frey, B.S., and R. Jegen. 2001. Motivational Interactions: Effects on Behaviour. *Annales D'économie Et De Statistique* 63 (64): 131–153.

Friedman, M. 1953. *The Methodology of Positive Economics, in His: Introduction: Essays In Positive Economics*, 3–16. Chicago: University of Chicago Press.

Gellner, E. 1992. *Reason and Culture*. Blackwell.

Gigerenzer, G. 2021. Axiomatic Rationality and Ecological Rationality. *Synthese* 198 (4): 3547–3564.

Gigerenzer, G., and H. Brighton. 2009. Homo Heuristicus: Why Biased Minds Make Better Inferences. *Topics in Cognitive Science* 1 (1): 107–143.

Hammond, P.J. 1997. Rationality in Economics. *Rivista Internazionale di Scienze Sociali* 105 (3): 247–288.

Hardin, R. 2015. Rational Choice Explanation: Philosophical Aspects. In *The International Encyclopedia of the Social and Behavioral Sciences*. Edited by J.D. Wright, 2nd ed., 896–900. Amsterdam: Elsevier.

Kahneman, D. 2012. *Thinking, Fast and Slow*. London: Penguin.

Kahneman, D., and A. Tversky. 1979. Prospect Theory: An Analysis of Decision Under Risk. *Econometrica* 47 (2): 263–291.

Kay, J., and M. King. 2021. *Radical Uncertainty: Decision-Making Beyond the Numbers*. Norton.

Keynes, J.M. 1936. *The General Theory of Employment*. Interest and Money, London: Macmillan.

Kiesewetter, B., and A. Worsnip. 2023. Structural Rationality. In *The Stanford Encyclopedia of Philosophy (Fall 2023 Edition)*. Edited by E.N. Zalta, and U. Nodelman.

Kirman, A.P. 2011. *Complex Economics: Individual and Collective Rationality*. Routledge.

Kirman, A.P., and A. Serletis. 2016. Ants and Nonoptimal Self-Organization: Lessons For Macroeconomics. *Macroeconomic Dynamics* 20 (2): 601–621.

Kolodny, N., and J. Brunero. 2023. Instrumental Rationality. In *The Stanford Encyclopedia of Philosophy (Summer 2023 Edition, Online)*. Edited by E.N. Zalta, and U. Nodelman.

Koundouri, P., N. Pittis, and P. Samartzis. 2023. Conceptions of Rationality and Their Justifications, DEOS Working Paper 2322, Athens University of Economics and Business.

Kroes, P., M. Franssen, and L. Bucciarelli. 2009. Rationality in Design. In *Handbook of the Philosophy of Science, Philosophy of Technology and Engineering Sciences*. Edited by A. Meijers, 565–600. North-Holland.

Kydland, F.E., and E.C. Prescott. 1982. Time to Build and Aggregate Fluctuations. *Econometrica* 50 (6): 1345–1370.

Laibson, D. 1997. Golden Eggs and Hyperbolic Discounting. *Quarterly Journal of Economics* 112 (2): 443–477.

Leibenstein, H. 1966. Allocative Efficiency Versus "X-Efficiency". *American Economic Review* 56 (3): 392–415.

Manski, C.F. 2000. Economic Analysis of Social Interactions. *Journal of Economic Perspectives* 14 (3): 115–136.

McDonald, R., and D. Siegel. 1986. The Value of Waiting to Invest. *Quarterly Journal of Economics* 101 (4): 707–727.

Mearsheimer, J.J., and S. Rosato. 2023. *How States Think: The Rationality of Foreign Policy*. New Haven: Yale University Press.

Nelson, R.R., and S.G. Winter. 1995. Recent Evolutionary Theorizing About Economic Change. *Journal of Economic Literature* 33 (1): 48–90.

O'Donoghue, T., and M. Rabin. 1999. Incentives for Procrastination. *Quarterly Journal of Economics* 114 (3): 769–816.

O'Donoghue, T., and M. Rabin. 2001a. Choice and Procrastination. *Quarterly Journal of Economics* 116 (1): 121–160.

O'Donoghue, T., and M. Rabin. 2001b. Self Awareness and Self Control. In *Chapter in Now or Later: Economic and Psychological Perspectives on Intertemporal Choice*. Edited by R. Baumeister, G. Loewenstein, and D. Read. Russell Sage.

Saint-Paul, G. 2011. *The Tyranny of Utility: Behavioral Social Science and the Rise of Paternalism*. Princeton: Princeton University Press.

Sandel, M.J. 2012. *What Money Can't Buy: The Moral Limits of Markets*. London: Allen Lane.

Schade, C.D., and A. Snir. 2020. A Lab Test on the Decision not to Decide. *Business Research* 13 (3): 1253–2129.

Selten, R. 2001. What is Bounded Rationality? In *Bounded Rationality: The Adaptive Toolbox*, ed. G. Gigerenzer and R. Selten, 13–36. Boston: The MIT Press.

Shiller, R.J. 2005. *Irrational Exuberance*, 2nd ed. Princeton: Princeton University Press.

Simon, H.A. 1955. A Behavioral Model of Rational Choice. *The Quarterly Journal of Economics* 69 (1): 99–118.

Simon, H.A. 1978. Rationality as Process and as Product of Thought. *American Economic Review* 68 (2): 1–16.

Simon, H.A. 2001. Rationality in Society. In *International Encyclopedia of the Social and Behavioral Sciences*, ed. N.J. Smelser and P.B. Baltes, 12782–12786. Oxford: Pergamon Press.

Smith, V.L. 1991. Rational Choice: The Contrast between Economics and Psychology. *Journal of Political Economy* 99 (4): 877–897.

Smith, R. 2022. Do Emotions Help or Hinder Rational Thinking? More Rational Individuals Show Greater Emotional Awareness, Psychology Today (Online), August. https://www.psychologytoday.com/us/blog/the-neuroscience-emotion-and-decisionmaking/202208/do-emotions-help-or-hinder-rational-thinking

Smith, V.L. 2003. Constructivist and Ecological Rationality in Economics. *American Economic Review* 93 (3): 465–508.

Steele, G.R. 2004. Understanding Economic Man: Psychology, Rationality, and Values. *The American Journal of Economics and Sociology* 63 (5): 1021–1055.

Taylor, J.B. 1993. Discretion Versus Policy Rules in Practice. *Carnegie-Rochester Conference Series on Public Policy* 39 (1): 195–214.

Thaler, R.H. 2016. *Misbehaving*. London: Penguin.

Thaler, R.H., and C. Sunstein. 2009. *(Updated Edition): Nudge: Improving Decisions About Health, Wealth, and Happiness*. New York: Penguin.

Thaler, R.H., and H.M. Shefrin. 1981. An Economic Theory of Self-Control. *Journal of Political Economy* 89 (2): 392–406.

Williamson, O.E. 2000. The New Institutional Economics: Taking Stock, Looking Ahead. *Journal of Economic Literature* 38 (3): 595–613.

CHAPTER 3

Sociality and Behavioural Traits in Macroeconomics

Standard economic theory suggests that individual behaviour is determined by "fundamentals", such as preferences, endowments, and technology, all guiding independent individual choice. Much of macroeconomics has been developed on this basis; in particular, on the postulate of (full) rationality and on methodological individualism, whereby atomistic agents interact with each other only indirectly, via market prices (taken as given). But as discussed in Chapter 2, behavioural psychology and related research emphasise the role of behavioural traits, largely deviating in some way from the postulate of full rationality, and of direct social interactions such as status-related comparisons, choice of peer group, adoption of external norms of behaviour, and the like. In recent years, macroeconomics has started incorporating some of these insights. In this chapter, we discuss the key socio-behavioural insights adopted by macroeconomics and their formal representation.[1] To preamble, we begin by discussing the insights around positional concerns and comparisons, the pursuit of status and the goal of "keeping up with the Joneses"; the role of a reference standard is crucial. We then pursue extensions that incorporate loss aversion, aspirations, and the choice of a reference standard. The case where individual utility features wealth as well as consumption, said to captured

[1] See Dhami (2016) for a thorough treatment of the analytical foundations of behavioural economics.

C. Tsoukis et al., *Social and Behavioural Macroeconomics*,
https://doi.org/10.1007/978-3-031-77748-6_3

the "capitalist spirit", is reviewed next. Short-termism and "present bias are treated in Chapters 5 and 6. Endogenous group formation, adoption of the group's norms and "identity" are considered in Chapter 8 as is the issue of social capital.[2]

1 Social Status: Introduction

The social status of an individual can be defined as their relative position in society compared to others. It is a truism to suggest that individuals strive to achieve a social position in society because they care about how they are perceived by others; this age-old idea has been recognised at least as far back as Smith (1759). The fundamental reason why individuals are concerned about their social status is rooted in a basic aspect of human nature—the innate need to evaluate one's position in society compared to others. In conducting these comparisons, individuals consider certain characteristics they consider crucial (at least from their own perspective) in determining their social standing within society. This behaviour, commonly known as the "keeping up with the Joneses" hypothesis, represents a well-established trait in human behaviour (e.g., see the surveys of Frey and Stutzer 2002; Clark et al. 2008). In particular, Frey and Stutzer (2002, p. 412) write: "There is little doubt that people compare themselves to other people and do not use absolute judgements".

Attributes individuals use to compare themselves to others include wealth (e.g. housing); the goods they consume; the nature of their occupation or job; or simply their level of education. This list is not exhaustive; we leave the identification of additional examples to the reader's discretion. Depending on the context, we shall assert that any factor that may induce jealousy or envy is a potential candidate. Numerous arguments support the "keeping up with the Joneses" hypothesis. Festinger (1954) provides a seminal explanation of social comparisons, referred to as "self-concept". According to this concept, individuals evaluate themselves based on their achievements relative to others, leading to a phenomenon called "cognitive dissonance". Cognitive dissonance arises

[2] Throughout this chapter and the book, our focus is on theoretical work. Empirical work on social interactions, a topic that has not received a lot of attention, is summarised in Durlauf and Ioannides (2010). For empirical work on the "keeping up" hypothesis, see Maurer and Meier (2008).

when individuals experience a conflict between their self-perception (self-esteem) and the observed achievements of others. Aronson et al. (1994) assert that individuals typically respond to this dissonance by changing their behaviour, e.g. by trying harder or working more.

The pursuit of higher social status and the subsequent ranking of individuals within society are not determined by the individuals themselves; rather, an individual's social status is conferred by society. This is because members of society collectively recognise certain traits as "status-enhancing". Cultural or historical factors can explain why some attributes or characteristics are considered as status-enhancing in some societies and less so in others. For instance, in certain societies, honour and prestige associated with family heritage or noble titles can be highly esteemed. Individuals from aristocratic backgrounds or with prestigious family names may be accorded higher social status.[3] However, in societies with a more egalitarian or meritocratic philosophy, such historical lineage or noble titles may hold less significance. Wealth or conspicuous consumption can be regarded as status-enhancing in many societies, particularly those with a strong emphasis on consumerism, and less so in others, those that prioritise collective or spiritual values. Similarly, societies that place a high value on education and intellectual accomplishments may confer higher social status on individuals who have attained advanced degrees, pursued academic careers, or made significant contributions in intellectual or artistic fields. However, in societies that prioritise practical skills or traditional knowledge, formal education may carry less weight as a status indicator. In certain societies, the status-enhancing factor may lie in an individual's social connections, networks, or influential families. In contrast, societies that value individual achievement and self-reliance may place less emphasis on such social connections as a status determinant. Lastly, leisure can be an indicator of status; in many traditional societies (particularly, but not exclusively, in antiquity or the Middle Ages), it was not considered "gentlemanly" to engage in a practical occupation. More recently, the rule of thumb may be that it is employment, particularly in

[3] However, an aristocratic or noble status was not only inherited but often acquired either through marriage into nobility or granted in return to service or loyalty to the monarchy, or even by outright purchase. For instance, during the seventeenth century, French King Louis XIV started selling noble titles to common people, to find the necessary funds for the costly expenses of the state. The target was the rich business class who wished to obtain a title for prestige. Molière expounds this with sarcasm in his play "Le bourgeois gentilhomme".

certain high-regarded occupations, rather than leisure, that confers status. We can partially generalise by saying that, while wealth and conspicuous consumption always confer status, modern capitalist societies, guided by ideals of meritocracy, place more emphasis on individual achievement, including education, and less on social connections, accident of birth or leisure.

The bottom line is that status is a social process, based on (tacit) agreement within society about the attributes that confer social status. These attributes reflect the values, norms, and expectations prevalent within a particular social context. By conforming to these recognised status traits, individuals gain the benefits and privileges associated with status. In economics, this is formalised by including a measure of status (often the relative position or rank in income, consumption, wealth, education, and so on) as an argument in the utility function.

Status-seeking and related motives represent a social but also possibly a behavioural extension of traditional macroeconomics. Since it is an example of direct social interactions among individuals, status belongs to the "social" side of this book. But there is perhaps another aspect of status, not recognised so far. What is the ulterior motive for status-driven comparisons? One possible answer is that the individual alone decides what their utility function contains. After all, page one of the microeconomics textbook talks about "consumer sovereignty". If so, the concern about status is perfectly rational, but we cannot say anything more about what motivates it. Another line of argument, however, may cast status as a feature of bounded rationality. Consider a generic characterisation of an individual's problem—to maximise one's "life utility" subject to the constraints that apply. The traditional approach is to say that the individual decides the path that best attains that goal and follows it without any ambiguity or doubt in self-evaluation. But do I know whether I have maximised my utility or achievement? Have I used my exogenously inherited talents to my full potential? What else might have been possible? Ambiguity and doubt are integral aspects of self-evaluation.[4] One possible

[4] We can call this the "Kazantzakis question", after the novelist Nikos Kazantzakis. In his philosophical memoir *Report to Greco* (Kazantzakis, 1965), he imagines himself reporting to his compatriot, the painter known as El Greco. A burning question on which Kazantzakis is reporting is whether he has used his talents to their full potential over his lifetime. Well, if we are fully rational, the question is void—everyone attains their "potential" (considering both exogenous endowments and constraints).

reason for social comparisons, therefore, is that it informs the individual about how well s/he is doing—by looking at others. In that line of argument, which does not seem to have been pursued in the literature, status and related motives are as much a feature of "behavioural" economics as of macroeconomics.[5]

In macroeconomics, the general implications of status-driven social interactions (such as comparisons, "keeping up" and positional concerns) is that they affect individual behaviour, as will be discussed below. To preamble, often the result is more effort, motivated by the need to catch up or keep up. And often, the result is suboptimal. There will also be implications for inequality, as the extra effort may be unequal, hence the distribution of any exogenous endowments or abilities will produce a different distribution of outcomes (income, consumption, education, and so on). Furthermore, in extensions of the key idea that allow for endogenous reference standards (used to guide comparisons), the macroeconomic outcomes themselves (growth, inequality) feedback and interact with norms of comparison and reference benchmarks.

2 Status: Examples

Economists have identified a reduced set of typical factors that play pivotal roles in individuals' pursuit of social status across a majority of societies. In the subsequent discussion, we discuss the concept of social status derived from comparisons in consumption (including wealth), leisure, and education. These domains have been extensively explored by economists and are widely recognised as significant elements in shaping individuals' behaviour towards obtaining social status. All these attributes satisfy two properties:

(1) They are readily observable by others.
(2) They are scarce or possessed to a limited extent by others. Individuals place value on attributes that are scarce or exclusive characteristics, not widely shared or easily attainable by everyone.

[5] A strand of the literature analyses the relative position or status motive in open economies; see. e.g. Becchetti, Castriota, Corrado and Ricca (2013); Dai, Gao and Tian (2020); Fisher and Hof (2005). But engagement with this vast topic is beyond our scope.

Conspicuous Consumption and Positional Goods

One of the most prominent and extensively discussed factors recognised for conferring social status to individuals is the concept of "conspicuous consumption", first introduced by Veblen (1899). In the pursuit of a high social rank and the associated prestige, individuals engage in the consumption of goods or services that serve as visible indicators of their wealth. Examples include the acquisition and flaunting of high-end luxury brands such as jewellery or refined clothing; expensive houses; going on vacations to exclusive destinations and sharing pictures on social media platforms to showcase a luxurious lifestyle; dining in upscale restaurants and ordering expensive dishes to demonstrate a refined taste and social standing; driving luxury cars which not only provide transportation but also serve as status symbols. These are examples of goods or activities that are pursued as much or more for status, or to signal a taste for luxury, or by the desire to be perceived favourably by others in society, as for their intrinsic value or utility. The term "Veblen effect" is sometimes used to describe a situation in which individuals are willing to pay higher prices for goods that, in theory, are perfectly substitutable. An extreme example of this phenomenon is the consumption of "positional goods", as analysed by Hirsh (1976) and Frank (1985). These goods are primarily consumed to signal affluence and thereby confer social status.

The economic implications of conspicuous consumption are that it can lead to a suboptimal high level of consumption, particularly of positional goods. Consequently, this may result in a relatively low level of savings. As demonstrated by Tournemaine and Tsoukis (2008), the conclusion regarding the impact of conspicuous consumption on savings is, however, not straightforward. To preview the arguments discussed in Chapter 4, Corneo and Jeanne (1998) suggest that the outcome is contingent upon the specific details and timing of individuals' desires. The authors posit that the effect of conspicuous consumption on savings hinges on whether individuals aspire to display their status early or late in their lives. Other important effects of the status motive concern individuals' welfare and life satisfaction. We return to this important issue below.

Saint-Paul (2011) emphasises further implications of the status-seeking and income comparisons. He argues that such motives play a key role in Keynes's arguments about the existence of nominal wage rigidity. In particular, it has been argued that nominal wage stickiness is asymmetric, wages being sticky downwards but not upwards (Akerlof et al.

2000). In addition to the loss of income, the relative income hypothesis tells us, that wage cuts also entail a loss of relative income. So, the hypothesis provides a more powerful rationale for asymmetric wage stickiness. Akerlof, Dickens and Perry (2000) discuss the implications of such stickiness for the Phillips Curve, arguing that it implies a well-behaved Phillips Curve when inflation is at low digits (and when it helps provide downward real wage flexibility) but not when it rises to higher levels.

Conspicuous Leisure

In addition to conspicuous consumption, Veblen (1899) also introduced the concept of "conspicuous leisure" and discussed the existence of a "leisure class". He emphasised that conspicuous leisure has historical origins but allows for some evolution over time. During the Middle Ages, for example, the noble class, who owned land, was exempted from manual labour, which was typically reserved for the serfs, the lower social class. The nobility's resources were derived from various forms of direct impositions (e.g. to provide produce or work in the fields of the lord) or monetary obligations imposed on the population, ostensibly to cover expenses such as land use or protection against potential invasions.

Intuitively, the potential implication of conspicuous leisure is that individuals' labour supply will be suboptimally low, or even non-existent, as exemplified by the original noble class in the Middle Ages. Consequently, such behaviour is likely to lead to reduced income for individuals and may have significant consequences for economic development. Illustratively, Wiener (1981) argues that cultural factors, including social status, have a broader impact on economic growth through their influence on individuals' occupational choices, investment decisions, and educational pursuits. He suggests that the high social status attributed to the idle gentleman and the simultaneous disdain for entrepreneurs can help explain England's economic decline during the nineteenth century.

Education and Occupation Choice

Another significant variable that is easily observable and can potentially confer pride and social status is education. It is often observed that individuals who attain high degrees are proud to frame and prominently display diplomas or certificates in one's office or workspace. This visual representation of educational accomplishments serves to exhibit status as well as to provide proof. Similarly, including educational details in professional profiles can highlight their educational background, degrees obtained, and academic honours or awards. Interestingly, a higher level of education also provides individuals with indirect means to choose from a wider range of jobs, thereby attaining a social position in society. Certain occupations, such as physicians, lawyers, or engineers, enjoy a high level of admiration in most societies. This is significant because it implies that individuals may select their occupations and level of education not solely based on expected wages, as suggested by standard economic theory, but also considering the social status associated with the job itself. Various authors, including Fershtman et al. (1996), Boonprakaikawe and Tournemaine (2006), Tournemaine and Tsoukis (2009, 2010a, b), and Tsoukis and Tournemaine (2013) have extensively discussed these issues in diverse contexts. We provide a more detailed discussion in Chapter 7 when we tackle the topic of inequality.

The Relative Income Hypothesis and the "Demonstration Effect"

In his seminal work, Duesenberry (1949) proposed the "relative income hypothesis" to explain individuals' behavioural choice in terms of consumption and savings in comparison to that of others. The hypothesis posits that individuals' welfare depends not only on their gross level of consumption (or other variables affecting one's status), but also on their relative position in the distribution in the society. Thereby, individuals lower down in the distribution (i.e. with a lower relative consumption) will tend to consume more in relation to their income. The reason is, it is argued, that such individuals emulate those higher up the ladder (a "demonstration effect") so as to maintain their status in society (using our terminology). Duesenberry (1949) further argued that this feature implies that, with an unchanged income distribution, the long-run average propensity to consume (consumption-income ratio across the entire economy) does not fall as national income rises. This had been the subject of debates, as the evidence of a constant average propensity to consume was seen to be contradicted by a (hypothesised) diminishing marginal propensity to consume. Arguably, Duesenberry's "relative income hypothesis" helped to reconcile the two and thus settle the debate.

Empirical evidence, among others by Bowles and Park (2005), Ferrer-i-Carbonell (2005), and Senik (2009), suggests that individuals engage in consumption emulation, often referred to as the "demonstration effect", by imitating the consumption patterns of those perceived as occupying higher positions in society. This upward emulation and imitation behaviour can be explained by the notion that individuals with lower social status perceive those above them as having better knowledge of the "right" decisions to make. This is particularly relevant when individuals are imperfectly informed about the quality of available goods or the prevailing economic conditions. For example, people may imitate the lifestyle choices of successful individuals, such as their leisure activities, travel destinations, or even their educational pursuits. By adopting similar behaviours, individuals seek to align themselves with those they perceive as having higher social status. Such findings are in line with findings of the research in psychology and behavioural economics reviewed in Chapter 2; numerous cognitive biases and heuristics point to the idea of choices made under the influence of others, particularly those that are considered more successful.

The "demonstration effect" has been invoked to explain the propagation of financial or economic crises. The rationale behind this argument lies in the limited availability of information regarding the economic conditions and uncertainties individuals face. In the absence of complete knowledge, individuals often rely on the actions and decisions of others as a guide for their own behaviour ("herding behaviour"). While such behaviour is harmless or can even seem beneficial during periods of relative stability and optimism, it is likely to amplify the spread of negative sentiments and contribute to the rapid transmission of financial and economic shocks when adverse events occur.

Consumption Comparisons, Externalities, And Welfare

Many of the above hypotheses are linked by the idea that relative (as well as the own) consumption matters in utility. This has gained widespread acceptance in the literature and is supported by empirical evidence from various studies (e.g., Clark and Oswald 1996; Kapteyn et al. 1997; McBride 2001). Frey and Stutzer (2002, pp. 411–412) and Clark et al. (2008, Sects. 1, 3.1 and 3.2) show that social comparisons in individual decision-making is a long-established theme across a variety of social disciplines and subdisciplines, including economics and happiness-related research.

An important implication of the hypothesis is that, since relative position matters, the individual may experience distress from the success of others. This can be the result of observing others' more lavish lifestyles (conspicuous consumption), or their success at work, or higher wealth, all of which result in the worsening of the individual's relative position. This sense of dissatisfaction or envy for the success of others impacts negatively on an individual's utility. Indeed, Clark and Oswald (1996) demonstrate that workers' job satisfaction is negatively related to their comparison earnings levels. Similar situations and effects arise with conspicuous consumption or other status symbols. It is as if the individual finds themselves in indirect perpetual competition with the rest of society.

The fact that an individual's success confers a negative externality on everyone else has important implications for individuals' utility and life satisfaction, as well as for their choices and behaviour. In their pursuit of status, and in order not to be left behind, individuals will try harder: to work more, to consume more (and more obviously), or to publish more (like those of us in academia). And more, and more—to catch up with everyone else, who is also trying harder. The origins of the "24/7" societies (Choudhary and Levine 2006; Hamermesh and Slemrod 2008), which never sleep, may well be found here. Or the origins of "super-capitalism" (Reich 2007), in which everyone is breathing down everyone else's neck.

But eventually, as with all negative externalities, the effect cancels out: Not everyone can be better than average. As a result, the work or amount of consumption may be suboptimally high: more that would be justified by the intrinsic value of the work (monetary benefit or even inner satisfaction) or the consumption, motivated by the futile attempt to be better than others. The usual example here is of the spectators in a stadium. To see better than others, individuals start standing up (hard work). But this prompts others to also stand up, and eventually, on average, no one can see any better, but they all get sore feet: individuals end up worse off.

Economists commonly refer to this situation as a "rat race". The term "rat race" was initially introduced by Akerlof (1976) to highlight that individuals' pursuit of social status is likely to result in the inefficient allocation of resources, ultimately reducing their overall welfare. Here, the waste of resources refers to the excessive efforts exerted by individuals in their pursuit of an elusive higher position in the workplace. This is significant as it raises many issues, concerning behaviour, individuals' work-life balance, overall welfare, and of course policy.

Such comparisons and consumption externalities in utility, variously also called status-seeking and "keeping up with the Joneses" effects typically motivate effort (Choudhary and Levine 2006; Goerke and Pannenberg 2015). The status-related motive to work harder may hold the potential to explain the difference in labour supply between the US and Europe (Prescott 2004); unlike a generation ago, Europeans seem currently to work less than Americans, who may be more motivated to work in pursuit of the "American dream". Such differences might be attributable to differences in taxation, as Prescott (2004) has argued. But not everyone takes this view. It may be, at least in part, a consequence of different preferences for work and leisure. Again, the outcome will in general be suboptimal.

Frank (1985) argues that individuals, driven by status comparisons, are also likely to over-consume positional goods. There are also implications for long-term growth (Futagami and Shibata 1998; Corneo and Jeanne 1997, 2001; Carroll et al. 1997; Tournemaine 2008; Tournemaine and Tsoukis 2008; Ghosh and Wendner 2017). Alonso-Carrera et al. (2004) and Alvarez-Cuadrado et al. (2004) draw implications for macroeconomic dynamics. Since labour supply increases, so does the marginal product of capital and the real interest rate. Thus, the rate of growth will be permanently higher, possibly suboptimally so. Furthermore, such status-seeking has implications for distribution and inequality as well as growth (Tsoukis 2007; Tournemaine and Tsoukis 2009; Tsoukis and Tournemaine 2013).

As a result, in no small part due to the suboptimality of outcomes, there are profound effects on individuals' welfare. Clark et al. (2008) review an enormous literature on the role of status in self-reported satisfaction or happiness. Many empirical studies find that reported happiness does indeed depend negatively on the income or wealth of the reference group. This may help explain the so-called "Easterlin paradox" (Easterlin 1974, 2001) whereby self-reported "happiness" or life satisfaction rises much more slowly than national income. Thus, in the cross-section, income does matter for happiness (it is better to be in a rich than a poor country—see Clark et al. 2008), but in a longitudinal sense, happiness is only weakly affected by income. As an example, the study by Knight, Song, and Gunatilaka (2009) using data from China finds that, after allowing for status effects, the long-term aggregate effect on the satisfaction of an increase in income is only about 13% of the impact effect on an individual. Additionally, Clark and Senik (2010) find that income comparisons are associated with both lower levels of subjective well-being and a greater demand for income redistribution. The consensus is that such comparisons are important.

The above considerations have important policy implications. When individuals derive non-pecuniary rewards from achieving a higher social status, there are in general no specific markets for these rewards, except in certain exceptional cases discussed above. Consequently, this economic issue naturally calls for government intervention and public policy measures. Drawing from basic microeconomic theory and the objective of implementing an optimal resource allocation, it becomes necessary to introduce a tax on the factor used to establish relative standing. However, caution must be exercised when applying this simple rule. The primary reason is that, in many cases, there may also be positive externalities associated with the "status-enhancing" factor. Depending on whether the positive or negative effects dominate, a subsidy may ultimately be required (see, e.g. Arrow 1971; Corneo and Jeanne 1997). Additionally, one consequence of status-related consumption is that people may work more than is socially optimal, as mentioned. This creates a rationale for taxes on income to encourage less work and more leisure. We pursue the issue further in Chapter 4.

3 A Simple Formal Model of Social Status

A General Form

We can formalise the above considerations by assuming that individuals, denoted by i, $i = 1, \ldots, N$, have preferences represented by a utility function taking the general form:

$$U_i = U(c_i, x_i), i = 1, \ldots, N \tag{1a}$$

where c_i represents individual i's consumption and x_i is his/her perceived measure of relative standing in society. Under the plausible assumption that the level of utility of individuals is positively related to their level of consumption and relative standing in society, we have:

$$\frac{\partial U_i}{\partial c_i} > 0 \text{ and } \frac{\partial U_i}{\partial x_i} > 0. \tag{1b}$$

The generality of the formulation (1a)-(1b) allows its application to a wide spectrum of contexts.

Let us denote the observable characteristics of individual i as z_{ij}, $j = 1, \ldots, M$. Examples of such characteristics may be conspicuous consumption, education, income, wealth, occupation, or any other relevant attributes. We also recall that each individual compares themselves to others. We therefore assume that:

$$x_i = Z(z_{i1}, z_{i2}, \ldots, z_{iM}; z_{-i1}, z_{-i2}, \ldots, z_{-iM}), \tag{2a}$$

where z_{-i} is shorthand for indicating the set of all individuals s except individual *i*. The properties of the function $Z(\bullet)$ are:

$$\frac{\partial Z(\bullet)}{\partial z_{ij}} > 0, \forall j = 1, \ldots, M \text{ and } \frac{\partial Z(\bullet)}{\partial z_{sj}} < 0, \forall j = 1, \ldots, M \text{ and } \forall s \neq i. \tag{2b}$$

That is, any attribute $j = 1, \ldots, M$ belonging to individual *i* confers positive utility to that individual, while any such attribute belonging to anyone else confers disutility to individual *i*. In an economy where individuals compare themselves to others, they suffer (enjoy) utility losses (gains) from others' success (poor performance). Thus, Eqs. (1a,b and 2a,b) capture the essential features of the status-seeking or conspicuous consumption or positional goods hypotheses, and the associated negative externalities.

Function $Z(\bullet)$ can vary across individuals, reflecting their own subjective preferences, values, and societal norms. It may also involve different combinations or weights assigned to various observable characteristics, as perceived importance can differ from person to person. The specific form of $Z(\bullet)$ can in principle be determined through empirical analysis. In its generality, this formulation points out the multidimensional nature of status and relative standing. The flip side of this coin, however, is the lack of parsimony. The selection of a more parsimonious model of status or similar motives is a matter of choice and debate. Below, we present three commonly used functional forms and some extensions. These functional forms are not exhaustive and other variations and combinations may exist in the literature.

Interdependent Preferences, Envy and Altruism

A variation of Eq. (1) is:

$$U_i = U(c_i, U_{-i}), \tag{3}$$

whereby an argument in the utility function of individual i is the utility of all other individuals (the set -i). This type of utility would, therefore, introduce (directly) "interdependent preferences". It is further sub-divided into "negatively interdependent preferences" when:

$$\frac{\partial U_i}{\partial U_{-i}} < 0. \tag{4a}$$

This case incorporates the negative externality discussed above and captures the everyday notion of jealousy or envy. In contrast, the case of:

$$\frac{\partial U_i}{\partial U_{-i}} > 0, \tag{4b}$$

is that of "positive interdependence", corresponding to altruism. The literature on human sociality discussed in the previous chapter has emphasised the altruistic traits of human (and animal) behaviour. However, most literature has focused on the case of envy, or negative interdependence, as that captures the negative externality and status-seeking that seems more prevalent in consumption. We shall follow in that tradition and leave altruism out of our scope. In addition, both the negative and positive interdependence of preferences lead to more involved analytics and, therefore, do not lend themselves for incorporation into macroeconomics. Hence, as detailed below, we shall follow an approach that allows (indirect) interdependence only via outcomes.

Relative Standing

Two of the most well-known status functions are the linear and multiplicative formulations. Both cut through the multi-dimensionality of the function Z(.) in (3) by assuming that there is only one attribute that confers status. Hence, the relative position of individual *i* is simply z_i, while $\overline{z}$ is the average of all individuals with respect to this attribute. In the additive version, used by Gali (1994) and Ljungqvist and Uhlig (2000), among others, the status function in the utility function of individual i, (1), takes the form:

$$x_i = z_i - \alpha\bar{z}, i = 1, \ldots, N \tag{5}$$

where $0 < \alpha < 1$, and $\bar{z}$ is the arithmetic average level of the "status-enhancing" factor. Importantly, this is taken as given by individual i. α introduces the negative externality and envy ($\alpha < 0$ would introduce altruism which is excluded, as mentioned). We may refer to $\bar{z}$ as the reference standard or benchmark to which individuals compare themselves. An important characteristic of the presented formulation is that the term $\alpha\bar{z}$ exhibits a similar role to a subsistence level in a Geary-Stone utility function. Therefore, parameter α can be interpreted as measuring an individual's aversion to a low social status. A higher value of α indicates a greater difficulty for the individual to tolerate a decrease in social status. In other words, the parameter α reflects the individual's sensitivity and resistance to experiencing a reduction in their relative standing within society.

In the case of a multiplicative formulation, we have:

$$x_i = f\left(\frac{z_i}{\bar{z}}\right), f'(.) > 0, \tag{6}$$

where $f(\bullet)$ is a continuous and twice-differentiable function. Its first derivative is denoted by f'(), therefore, this sub-utility increases (decreases) in the own (average) status-enhancing attribute.

Both the linear and multiplicative specifications exhibit similar characteristics. However, as noted by Tsoukis (2007), the linear specification has a significant drawback. Combining (1) and (5) to get $U_i = U(c_i, z_i - \alpha\bar{z})$, if diminishing marginal utility applies to status as well as own consumption, the effect of the externality (exemplified by $\bar{z}$) as $\bar{z}$ itself grows. In other words, the relevance of status becomes less in more conspicuous societies, in contradiction to intuition and casual observation. Additionally, such an argument would rule out status as a possible resolution of the Easterly (1974, 2001) paradox and thus diminish its usefulness. Therefore, in this book, we will mainly use the multiplicative formulation (6) as our preferred approach.

Ranking

Some authors, primarily focusing on the microeconomic level, define an individual's social status as their rank in the distribution of the "status-enhancing" factor (Hopkins and Kornienko 2004). The key distinction between the linear and multiplicative formulations is that individuals do not necessarily suffer from others' improved relative standing unless someone overtakes them on the status ladder. This approach brings out the similarities between status-seeking and sports competitions. Typically, the winner is determined by the ranking of individual performances. The winner is generally unaffected by the last-minute change in the ranking between second and third. Additionally, record-breaking apart, absolute performances do not matter, and the distance between first and second (say) is of no consequence. In summary, defining social status as an individual's rank in the distribution appears more restrictive than the relative comparison formulations. Therefore, in this book, we will focus on the relative standing formulation, which aligns better with the arguments presented in Sect. 1.1.

Interested readers can refer to the insightful framework by Corneo and Jeanne (2001). The authors develop a one-sector endogenous growth model following the approach of Romer (1986), where individuals value both consumption and their rank in the wealth distribution. Remarkably, they demonstrate that the long-term per-capita growth rate is positively correlated with both the strength of individuals' preference for social status and the equality between individuals. In other words, a more equal distribution promotes economic development. The underlying intuition is that a more compressed distribution not only encourages those lower in social status to strive to catch up with those above them but also motivates the latter group to maintain and defend their position. Conversely, in a scenario with greater wealth dispersion, these incentives are weakened. Although this framework is appealing, it has two important drawbacks. As highlighted by Corneo and Jeanne (2001) themselves, the first issue stems from the definition of social status itself: since it depends on an individual's rank in the distribution, perfect forecasting of the wealth distribution is required when determining optimal saving policies. Second, the existence of a steady-state equilibrium relies on specific and tractable classes of utility functions and initial wealth distribution. In other words, the rank-based status motive is generally not conducive to tractable formal analysis.

Differential Status Effects, "Pains" vs. "Gains", and Loss Aversion

Tournemaine and Tsoukis (2009, 2010a, b) have introduced a more general status functional form represented by:

$$x_i = \frac{z_i}{\overline{z}}^{\overline{\varphi_i} + \frac{\varphi_i}{2} \ln\left(\frac{z_i}{\overline{z}}\right)}, \tag{7}$$

where $\overline{\varphi_i} > 0$ and φ_i are constant and idiosyncratic parameters. The status function (1.7) summarises several ideas. The main one is the distinction between "average" and "differential" status effects. Indeed, computing the status elasticity from Eq. (7), we obtain:

$$\frac{\partial x_i}{\partial (z_i/\overline{z})} \frac{(z_i/\overline{z})}{x_i} = \overline{\varphi_i} + \varphi_i \ln\left(\frac{z_i}{\overline{z}}\right) > 0. \tag{8}$$

In Eq. (8) the "average" status motivation is given by the portion of the elasticity of the status function that does not depend on the relative standing of the individual, $\overline{\varphi_i}$. This is the exogenous part of the elasticity. The "differential" status motivation, $\varphi_i \ln\left(\frac{z_i}{\overline{z}}\right)$, in contrast, does depend on the relative position of the individual and thus is determined in an endogenous manner by the model.

Eq. (8) shows that the status elasticity is upward-sloping. Whether it is convex or concave depends on the strength of the differential status effect measured by φ_i. In the neighbourhood of symmetry, i.e. for $z_i \approx \overline{z}$, it directly follows that the status elasticity is strictly convex (concave) if $\varphi_i > 0$ ($\varphi_i < 0$). Understanding the curvature of the status function is crucial. Futagami and Shibata (1998) emphasise that a higher curvature of the status function indicates a stronger preference for social status. This argument can be illustrated through a graphical representation. In the vicinity of symmetry, we can refer to Fig. 1.

Figure 1 shows that, whatever the value of the strength of the differential status effect, the status function passes through the coordinate (1,1) representing the symmetry case. The noteworthy, somewhat interesting, feature here is that, if $\varphi_i > 0$ ($\varphi_i < 0$) and if $z_i > \overline{z}$ ($z_i < \overline{z}$), i.e. individual i's level of "status-enhancing" factor is above (below) the average, he/she obtains increasingly more (less) utility as his/her relative standing, $z_i/\overline{z}$, , increases (decreases). In other words, if $\varphi_i > 0$, , utility rises faster as the individual's relative consumption (own-to-benchmark ratio) rises, while if $\varphi_i < 0$, utility falls faster as relative consumption falls below the

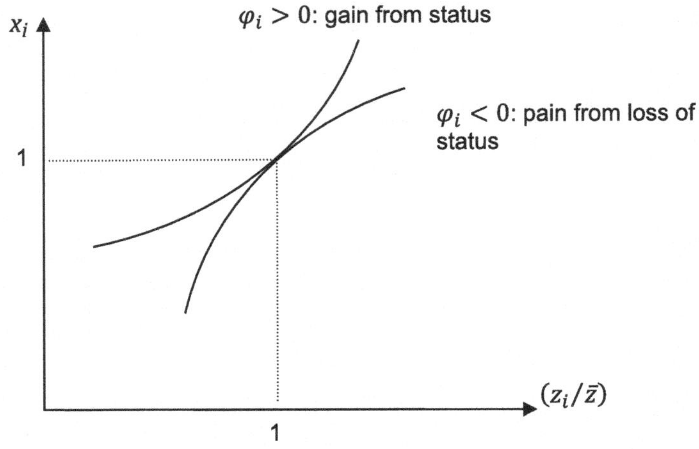

Fig. 1 The status function

benchmark. Hence, the status function (7) allows us to make the clear distinction between "gain from status" if $\varphi_i > 0$ and "pain from loss of status" ($\varphi_i < 0$): gain (pain) from status arises if the status function increases (decreases) faster than the relative position.

Despite its importance, there is no compelling empirical evidence allowing us to securely sign the differential status effect, φ_i. The notion of loss aversion,[6] according to which losses from a reference point are more highly valued than potential gains, may, however, guide us towards $\varphi_i < 0$. Similarly, if equality is a reference point, moving upwards from it may be less important than moving downwards. In this line, the recent empirical works on the asymmetry of comparisons, like that of Bowles and Park (2005) and Ferrer-i-Carbonell (2005) which show that comparisons are mostly made upwards, or Senik (2007) which shows that unfavourable comparisons are more important than favourable ones, suggest that the hypothesis $\varphi_i < 0$ seems the most plausible.

There are also good intuitive arguments underpinning this hypothesis: As Tsoukis and Tournemaine (2013) show, $\varphi_i < 0$ implies strategic complementarity (Cooper and John, 1988): As others' consumption rises, individual *i*'s consumption also rises. $\varphi_i > 0$ would instead imply strategic

[6] See Chapter 2.

substitutability, with individual's consumption falling as that of others' rises, which would be very counterintuitive. In a similar vein, Clark and Oswald (1998) show that concavity implies a follower's (or conformists) behaviour, whereas convexity implies a deviant behaviour—the individual enjoys being different; they argue in favour of the concavity case; see also Bratsiotis and Peng (2008). Clark and Oswald (1998) also emphasise the analogy between concavity and "loss aversion" (Tversky and Kahneman 1991), discussed in Chapter 2. In this, in line with psychology research, "loss" is understood metaphorically as falling short of a reference benchmark or default position (not literally as losing something). Loss aversion is a key finding in psychology and behavioural research, and thus a guiding light in helping to sign φ_i. Hence, both indirect empirical evidence and theoretical reasoning suggest taking the "pains" (from loss of status, i.e. $\varphi_i < 0$) as the plausible case.

Timing of Comparison: "Catching up with the Joneses" and Habits

An important variable, omitted so far, is time. This allows us to distinguish between two slightly different concepts: "keeping up with the Joneses" and "catching up with the Joneses". So far, we have assumed that individuals compare their current levels of characteristics, such as consumption or leisure, only to the current levels of others—the case of "keeping up". In contrast, in the case of "catching up with the Joneses", individuals may also consider past levels of observed characteristics to establish their relative standing. To capture this insight, the status function can be represented as follows:

$$x_{i,t} = Z_i(z_{i,t}; z_{i,t-1}; \bar{z}_{i,t-1}). \tag{9}$$

In the spirit of the more parsimonious Eq. (5), we would have (e.g. Gali 1994):

$$x_{i,t} = z_{i,t} - \alpha \bar{z}_{i,t-1}. \tag{10}$$

Another version of Eq. (9) emphasises a related but distinct idea, that of "habits" in consumption. This is the idea that past levels of own consumption influence current consumption:

$$x_{i,t} = z_{i,t} - \alpha z_{i,t-1}. \tag{11}$$

Note the sharp contrast with (9), where we had, $\frac{\partial x_{i,t}}{\partial z_{i,t-1}} > 0$; ; but in (11), we have $\frac{\partial x_{i,t}}{\partial z_{i,t-1}} < 0$: Past consumption affects current utility negatively. If the last period's own consumption were higher, in order to maintain the same level of utility, consumption in this period must be higher still. In other words, as again proposed by Duesenberry (1949), past consumption creates a habit that influences current behaviour; furthermore, it may be difficult to forfeit a standard of consumption (and broadly: standard of living) once it has been attained. Duesenberry (1949) argues that this may be part of the explanation why the average propensity to consume does not fall, as discussed. Fuhrer (2000) offers support for the "habits" hypothesis and discusses its implications for monetary policy.

In the remainder of the book, we will concentrate on the "keeping up with the Joneses" effect. This feature is the one most analysed in macroeconomics; it also is the one related to both the social and the behavioural side of our approach. Furthermore, in certain key respects both the "keeping up" and "catching up" hypotheses are observationally equivalent: At the steady state, balanced-growth-path with the economy-wide growth rate at g, Eq. (10) gives:

$$x_{i,t} = z_{i,t} - (1 - \alpha g)\overline{z}_{i,t-1}. \tag{12}$$

This is equivalent to (5) with the addition of the growth rate. Conceptually, this is both an advantage and a weakness. As discussed by Tsoukis (2007), the implication is that a higher level of economic growth, all else the same, will be perceived as an enhancement in social status, although in fact the relative position remains unaltered. Such a scenario is sometimes referred to as a "relative position illusion" or "status illusion". This aspect of bounded rationality gives an enhanced rationale for growth as it affects both felicity, as well as intertemporal utility. This feature may help explain why many modern societies are in such a thrall to further growth, when the available material wealth is more than enough to satisfy basic human needs and when the cost (e.g. environment) is by all accounts rising. Features such as the role of growth in the "catching up" story are surely relevant; but we consider status as more fundamental and therefore we will focus on the "keeping up" specification (1, 6)—which is also simpler.

Wealth-Based Comparisons

Comparisons based on wealth utilise the same utility function (1), coupled with the following function on relative standing:

$$x_i = f\left(\frac{k_i}{\bar{k}}\right), f'(.) > 0. \tag{13}$$

Accordingly, relative standing is indicated by the amount of physical capital (k_i) owned by individual i relative to mean wealth (with overbar). In reality, wealth may include items such as housing, jewellery, or artworks that are not productive. But more often than not, such items do not feature in models for reasons of economy; hence, relative capital is used as the sole measure of his/her wealth. As we shall see in the next chapter, wealth-based relative standing (13) entails some similarities but also some importance differences with (multiplicative) consumption-based relative standing (6) with z = c. But as a more detailed comparison depends on the analytics of optimisation, we defer the discussion till Chapter 4. Do let us note here that this case, of relative wealth and capital in utility, is different to that of the level of individual capital in utility, nicknamed the "capitalist spirit" case, which we review in Sect. 5.

4 Extensions

Heterogenous and Endogenous Reference Standards

As already emphasised, the importance of a reference standard in status-related comparisons is well established (Ferrer-i-Carbonell 2005; Maurer and Meier 2008; McBride 2001; Senik 2009). So far, for simplicity, we have taken this reference standard to be the arithmetic average in the economy. However, as argued by Tournemaine and Tsoukis (2010a, b), there is no compelling reason to believe that the reference standard should be the average or indeed the same for all individuals. Empirical evidence suggests that social comparisons tend to be made in an upward manner, meaning individuals may have different reference standards depending on their position on the social status ladder. Using subjective data on well-being ("happiness"), Clark and Senik (2010) find support for localised consumption comparisons (one compares oneself with their social milieu); Maurer and Meier (2008) and Goerke and Pannenberg (2015) also find localised effects. Building upon this insight, Tournemaine and Tsoukis

(2010a, b) propose replacing the previous common reference standard ($\bar{z}$) by the individual-specific $\bar{z}_i$, where the subscript i indicates that the reference standard can vary across individuals. Arguably, this extension can offer valuable insights into explaining differences in labour supply across countries and discussing the relationship between growth and inequality.

This insight further suggests that the reference standard is endogenous, and, in a stronger way, a matter of choice: Individuals may decide in an endogenous way the reference point or benchmark they use in comparing themselves against. For instance, researchers may compare the number and quality of their publications with their peers in the department but not necessarily with the recent Nobel laureates. Kids may compare the type of clothes they wear with their friends at school but not with other children from different institutions. In other words, individuals have various perceptions of their own and others' performances in the sense where the reference standard is not fixed or predetermined but rather influenced by various elements such as the work environment, the idiosyncratic attitude of individuals or their culture. On this issue, Diener and Fujita (1997) provide some support from the field of social psychology as they establish that individuals actively participate in selecting their reference standards.

Falk and Knell (2004) have formalised this concept theoretically and evaluated it empirically. Specifically, they argue that there exists a trade-off between two kinds of goals when individuals must decide their reference standards. First, there is a goal of "self-enhancement". In this case, individuals prefer to compare themselves to those who are lower down on the status ladder. For instance, individuals in a middle-income neighbourhood might consciously or unconsciously compare themselves to individuals in lower-income neighbourhoods. By doing so, they gain utility from a perceived (if perhaps false) sense of status. Second, the goal of "self-achievement" (or "self-improvement") whereby individuals prefer to compare themselves with high achievers to get a source of motivation. E.g. by observing the achievements and accomplishments of high achievers, a student or researcher can find inspiration and motivation to work hard, set ambitious goals, and strive for excellence.

Falk and Knell (2004) show that ambitious individuals often establish higher reference standards compared to the average person. As a result, the pursuit of social status holds the potential to affect not only the selection of a reference standard but also the level of inequality. When individuals assign greater (lower) importance to the objective of "self-achievement" in comparison to the objective of "self-enhancement", they tend to establish higher (lower) reference targets. Consequently, this leads to an increased (decreased) exertion of effort. Ultimately, it is argued that individuals tend to compare themselves with others possessing similar abilities. As a result, individuals' choice of a reference standard serves to balance the trade-off between the goals of "self-enhancement" and "self-improvement".

In a different setting, Barnett et al. (2010) analyse the choice of whether to participate or not (at all) in a status game. They conclude that this insight produces results on the distribution of income and leisure that are unattainable by more standard formulations. While this is a worthy contribution, in order to streamline the analysis and integrate it with more standard approaches, one could approximate the setup of Barnett et al (2010) by two (fixed) reference standards, a positive one and one arbitrarily close to zero, and letting individuals decide between the two. Genicot and Ray (2017, 2020) term a broad class of consumption reference standards "aspirations" (to which we return below) and discuss their features and effects. In this regard, they analyse "local income windows", what may alternatively be termed neighbourhood effects in determining the reference benchmark. But the size of the window is arbitrarily fixed. In unpublished work, Tsoukis and Tournemaine (2016) endogenise both the reference standard and the size of the neighbourhoods of comparison; they use this setup to analyse "identity", a notion to which we turn in Chapter 8.

Social Norms

A broader concept than reference standards is social norms.[7] We can define social norms as unwritten rules or shared expectations within a society that guide how individuals should behave in various situations. They are often shaped by cultural, social, and historical factors but bear on the economy. As noted by Akerlof (1980), social norms can significantly influence individual economic behaviour, market outcomes, and economic policies. In particular, they may affect behaviour by shaping preferences, choices, and actions. Individuals tend to conform to these

[7] See Elster (1989) and Festré (2010) for comprehensive discussions and surveys of the literature on the topic.

norms to gain social acceptance and avoid disapproval from their peers and communities (Bénabou and Tirole 2006). For example, norms can affect consumption patterns by dictating what goods and services are considered prestigious or appropriate within a given society. In their quest for social status, people may adjust their consumption choices to align with prevailing norms, which can lead to the adoption of specific brands, lifestyles, or consumption habits (see, e.g. Frank 1985). In a similar way, norms can influence labour market dynamics, including the type of jobs considered acceptable or prestigious. Certain occupations may be preferred due to social norms, even if they do not necessarily offer the highest monetary rewards. In this way, a norm-related motivation may be a hybrid of the "intrinsic" and "extrinsic" rewards (Benabou and Tirole 2000) mentioned in Chapter 2. Such a structure of rewards can impact the distribution of labour across different sectors and professions (see, e.g., Fersthman et al. 1996; Tournemaine and Tsoukis 2008).

The potential impacts of norms on economic development are noteworthy too as they can influence saving and investment behaviour. Societies that place a strong emphasis on saving for the future may see higher savings rates. Conversely, societies with norms that encourage conspicuous consumption might have lower savings rates. Such differentiated behaviours may lead to a very different long-term level of economic growth and development. In the same spirit, societies in which norms promote hard work, innovation, and education may have advantages in terms of economic development and prosperity. The noteworthy feature of these effects is that it naturally implies that norms have implications for public policy. Policymakers need in effect to consider existing norms when designing policies, the reason being that certain behaviours influenced by norms can be leveraged to implement effective policies (see, e.g. Chapter 4 for further discussion). Formally, the effect of norms is captured by their effect on the reference standards, i.e. in a way similar to status, and this is how we proceed in Chapter 4.

It is important to note that social norms are not fixed throughout time and can evolve over time due to changes in culture, technology, or societal values. This evolution can impact economic behaviour and outcomes. For instance, shifts in norms related to gender roles have influenced labour force participation and family dynamics potentially affecting countries' population dynamics (see, e.g., Black and Juhn 2000; Dolado et al. 2001; Balestrino and Ciardi 2008; and Chapter 4 for a formal discussion of this issue).

Similarly, the concept of time inconsistency (see Chapters 5 and 6) which refers to the tendency of individuals to make choices that are inconsistent with their long-term goals due to the influence of immediate rewards or short-term gratification can be linked to social norms. Individuals might succumb to short-term temptations or immediate rewards due to the desire to conform to prevailing norms and gain social acceptance. Thereby, conformity can lead to choices that deviate from long-term goals. In other words, if norms prioritise immediate satisfactions, individuals might be more prone to give in to peer pressure and engage in time-inconsistent behaviour. The reason is that individuals are more motivated to seek social approval by demonstrating alignment with prevailing norms, even if it means making choices that are at odds with their long-term interests (see, e.g., Rabin 1998).

Aspirations

As mentioned, the recent contribution of Genicot and Ray (2017) emphasises the role of "aspirations", how they are determined and how they affect growth and inequality. Aspirations are endogenous, influenced by both individual characteristics and the income distribution. As such, they depend both on personal and social circumstances (caste, religion, geography). The difference between aspirations and the actual outcome regarding an individual's lifetime income can either encourage or frustrate investments. An aspiration is satisfied if the chosen optimal solution exceeds the level of aspiration. In contrast, frustration occurs if the chosen optimal solution falls short compared to the level of aspiration.

For a given initial wealth, there is a unique threshold value of aspirations below which aspirations are satisfied and above which there is frustration. If aspirations are satisfied, wealth grows with aspirations. If frustration occurs, then wealth does not react with aspirations. Aspirations have a great bearing on inequality, and this relationship is analysed within two contexts. In the first one, Genicot and Ray (2017) assume that incomes are bounded (exogenous growth based on the Solow model). They show that perfect equality cannot be achieved. The reason is that, with a compressed distribution of wealth, some individuals invest to a greater extent than others, leading to a steady state in which income distribution is bimodal. The second environment is an AK model. The results are twofold: If, initially, income is distributed equally (a compressed distribution), the economy converges to a perfect equality outcome, with equal growth rates of incomes. If, on the other hand, the initial income distribution is unequal, the economy develops clusters and inequality increases.

In their follow-up study, Genicot and Ray (2020) glean a few more results from their review of the literature. Aspirations seem to present the same type of negative externality as the status-seeking motive: For example, one successful person affects the aspiration of others. Furthermore, assuming linear homogeneity (if all incomes go up by the same proportion, then aspirations rise by the same proportion), aspirations are more likely to frustrate the lower end of income distribution and more likely to satisfy the upper end.

In addition to the effects on growth and inequality, aspirations also have secondary effects. Economic inequality brings frustration and may lead to a reduction in investments. Instead of putting the effort of reducing the disparities, individuals may try to achieve a second-best source of satisfaction such as sports or social activism. A further effect may be scapegoating: One group unable to achieve its objectives can redirect its frustration and aggression towards another group that is not the causal agent of their frustration. In terms of fertility, in the case of low incomes, there may be unsuccessful aspirations. In this case, fertility levels are high with low child quality. When aspirations are fulfilled there is a drop in fertility followed by a rise of fertility thereafter if high quality children are normal goods. In terms of other behaviour, the poorest segment who are frustrated does not invest in aspiration management; instead, they may engage in excessive risk-taking (something which is in line with Prospect Theory discussed in Chapter 2—evident in the change of the curvature of utility at very low levels).

In all, Genicot and Ray (2017, 2020) put forward a forceful reminder of the multi-faceted nature and importance of aspirations. Aspirations are determined by the society individuals live in and their position in it. Social positions such as caste, ethnicity, religion, but also traditional media, social media, family, are important in shaping aspirations. The multi-faceted nature of the concept is in line with the problem of identification in estimation. For these reasons, in this book, aspirations will be captured formally by the endogenous reference standards that are used in status comparisons.

5 The "Capitalist Spirit"

One formulation of utility that is related to our discussions is the following (Zhou 1994; Francis 2009):

$$U_i = U(c_i, k_i). \tag{14}$$

This features wealth (capital) as well as consumption in utility, but in contrast to (13), it is individual and not relative capital. The rationale for this is that the "capitalist spirit" is to accumulate as an end in itself, rather than in order to enjoy a higher future consumption; this is an idea pointed out by the German sociologist-economist Max Weber (see Weber 1958 [1905]) and Schumpeter (1954). Another difference between utility with relative capital in Eq. (13) is that relative capital in that case is a proxy for relative wealth that may confer utility, e.g. housing. Instead, here it is capital itself that is the object of desire, as it were.

The insight has potentially far-reaching implications: Zou (1994) argues that it enhances long-run growth and living standards. Francis (2009) shows that a model with a "capitalist spirit" generates inequality in line with observed US inequality. Karnizova (2010) shows that, if added to a "news" model of the business cycles, this idea helps to generate business cycles with more realistic properties than would be the case without such a "capitalist spirit". Zhou (2016) shows that it can generate bubbles. He, Luo, Nie, and Zou (2023) investigate the properties for monetary economies. In all, the idea is powerful, intuitive and as mentioned, it has powerful implications. It also upends neoclassical thinking, in that now, "utility" is partly driven not by anything that can confer real utility, but by a "passion", an almost irrational urge to accumulate.

References

Akerlof, G.A. 1976. The Economics of the Caste and of the Rat Race and Other Woeful Tales. *Quarterly Journal of Economics* 90 (4): 599–617.

Akerlof, G.A., W.T. Dickens, and G. Perry. 2000. *Brookings Papers on Economic Activity* 31 (1): 1–60.

Alonso-Carrera, J., J. Caballé, and X. Raurich. 2004. Consumption Externalities, Habit Formation and Equilibrium Efficiency. *Scandinavian Journal of Economics* 106 (2): 231–251.

Alvarez-Cuadrado, F., G. Monteiro, and S. Turnovsky. 2004. Habit Formation, Catching Up with the Joneses, and Economic Growth. *Journal of Economic Growth* 9 (1): 47–80.

Aronson, E., T.D. Wilson, and R.M. Akert. 1994. *Social Psychology: The Heart and the Mind*. New York: Harper Collins.

Arrow, K.J. 1971. Political and Economic Evaluation of Social Effects and Externalities. In *Frontier of Quantitative Economics*. Edited by M. Intriligator. Amsterdam: North-Holland.

Balestrino, A., and C. Ciardi. 2008. Social Norms, Cognitive Dissonance and the Timing of Marriage. *Journal of Socio-Economics* 37 (6): 2399–2410.

Barnett, R.C., J. Bhattacharya, and H. Bunzel. 2010. Choosing to Keep up with the Joneses and Income Inequality. *Economic Theory* 45 (3): 469–496.

Becchetti, L., S. Castriota, L. Corrado, and E.G. Ricca. 2013. Beyond the Joneses: Inter-Country Income Comparisons and Happiness. *Journal of Socioeconomics* 45: 187–195.

Black, S.E., and C. Juhn. 2000. The Rise of Female Professionals: Are Women Responding to Skill Demand? *American Economic Review* 90 (2): 450–455.

Boonprakaikawe, J., and F. Tournemaine. 2006. Production and Consumption of Education in a R&D-Based Growth Model. *Scottish Journal of Political Economy* 53 (5): 565–585.

Bowles, S., and T. Park. 2005. Emulation, Inequality, and Work Hours: Was Thorsten Veblen Right? *Economic Journal* 115 (507): 397–412.

Bratsiotis, G.J., and B. Peng. 2008. Social Interaction and Effort in a Success-at-Work Augmented Utility Model. *The Journal of Socio-Economics* 37 (4): 1309–1318.

Carroll, C.D., J. Overland, and D. Weil. 1997. Comparison Utility in a Growth Model. *Journal of Economic Growth* 2 (4): 339–367.

Choudhary, M.A., and P. Levine. 2006. The 24/7 Society and Multiple Habits, Department of Economics, University of Surrey, Discussion Paper no. 0506.

Clark, A.E., and A.J. Oswald. 1996. Satisfaction and Comparison Income. *Journal of Public Economics* 3 (61): 359–381.

Clark, A.E., and A.J. Oswald. 1998. Comparison-Concave Utility and Following Behaviour in Social and Economic Settings. *Journal of Public Economics* 70 (1): 133–155.

Clark, A.E., and C. Senik. 2010. Who Compares to Whom? *The Anatomy of Income Comparisons in Europe, Economic Journal* 120 (544): 573–594.

Clark, A.E., P. Frijters, and M.A. Shields. 2008. Relative Income, Happiness, and Utility: An Explanation for the Easterlin Paradox and Other Puzzles. *Journal of Economic Literature* 46 (1): 95–144.

Cooper, R., and A. John. 1988. Coordination Failures in Keynesian Models. *Quarterly Journal of Economics* 103 (3): 441–463.

Corneo, G., and O. Jeanne. 1997. On Relative Wealth Effects and the Optimality of Growth. *Economics Letters* 54 (1): 87–92.

Corneo, G., and O. Jeanne. 1998. Social Organization, Status and Saving Behaviour. *Journal of Public Economics* 70 (1): 37–52.

Corneo, G., and O. Jeanne. 2001. Status, the Distribution of Wealth, and Growth. *Scandinavian Journal of Economics* 103 (2): 283–293.

Dai, D., W. Gao, and G. Tian. 2020. Relativity, Mobility, and Optimal Nonlinear Income Taxation in an Open Economy. *Journal of Economic Behavior and Organization* 172: 57–82.

Dhami, S. 2016. *The Foundations of Behavioral Economic Analysis*. Oxford University Press.

Diener, E., and F. Fujita. 1997. Social comparison and subjective well-being. In *Health, Coping and Well-being: Perspectives from Social Comparison Theory*. Edited by B.P. Buunk, and R. Gibbons. Lawrence Erlbaum Associates: Mahwah.

Dolado, J., F. Felgueroso, and J.F. Jimeno. 2001. Female employment and occupational changes in the 1990s: How is the EU performing relative to the US? *European Economic Review* 45 (4–6): 875–879.

Duesenberry, J.S. 1949. *Income, Saving and the Theory of Consumer Behaviour*. Cambridge: Harvard University Press.

Durlauf, S.N., and Y.M. Ioannides. 2010. Social Interactions. *Annual Review of Economics* 2 (1): 451–478.

Easterlin, R.A. 1974. Does Economic Growth Improve the Human Lot? Some Empirical Evidence. In *Nations and Households in Economic Growth: Essays in Honor of Moses Abramowitz*. Edited by P.A. David, and M.W. Reder. New York: Academic Press.

Easterlin, R.A. 2001. Income and Happiness: Towards a Unified Theory. *Economic Journal* 111 (473): 465–484.

Elster, J. 1989. Social Norms and Economic Theory. *Journal of Economic Perspectives* 3 (4): 99–117.

Falk, A., and M. Knell. 2004. Choosing the Joneses: Endogenous Goals and Reference Standards. *Scandinavian Journal of Economics* 106 (3): 417–435.

Ferrer-i-Carbonnel, A. 2005. Income and Well-Being: An Empirical Analysis of the Comparison Income Effect. *Journal of Public Economics* 89 (5–6): 997–1019.

Fershtman, C., K.M. Murphy, and Y. Weiss. 1996. Social Status, Education and Growth. *Journal of Political Economy* 104 (1): 108–132.

Festinger, L. 1954. A Theory of Social Comparison Processes. *Human Relations* 7 (2): 117–140.

Festré, A. 2010. Incentives and Social Norms: A Motivation-Based Economic Analysis of Social Norms. *Journal of Economic Surveys* 24 (3): 511–538.

Fisher, W.H., and F.X. Hof. 2005. Status Seeking in the Small Open Economy. *Journal of Macroeconomics* 27 (2): 209–232.

Francis, J.L. 2009. Wealth and the Capitalist Spirit. *Journal of Macroeconomics* 31 (3): 394–408.

Frank, R. 1985. The Demand for Non-observable and other Non-positional Goods. *American Economic Review* 75 (1): 101–116.

Frey, B.S., and A. Stutzer. 2002. What Can Economists Learn from Happiness Research? *Journal of Economic Literature* 40 (2): 402–435.

Fuhrer, J.C. 2000. Habit Formation in Consumption and Its Implications for Monetary-Policy Models. *American Economic Review* 90 (3): 367–390.

Futagami, K., and A. Shibata. 1998. Keeping One Step Ahead of the Joneses: Status, the Distribution of Wealth and Long Run Growth. *Journal of Economic Behavior and Organization* 36 (1): 109–126.

Gali, J. 1994. Keeping up with the Joneses: Consumption Externalities, Portfolio Choice, and Asset Prices. *Journal of Money, Credit and Banking* 26 (1): 1–8.

Genicot, G., and D. Ray. 2017. Aspirations and Inequality. *Econometrica* 85 (2): 489–519.

Genicot, G., and D. Ray. 2020. Aspirations and Economic Behavior. *Annual Review of Economics* 12 (1): 715–746.

Ghosh, S., and R. Wendner. 2017. Positional Preferences and Efficient Capital Accumulation when Households Exhibit a Preference for Wealth. *Oxford Economic Papers* 70 (1): 114–140.

Goerke, L., and M. Pannenberg. 2015. Direct Evidence for Income Comparisons and Subjective Well-Being Across Reference Groups. *Economics Letters* 137 (C): 95–101.

Hamermesh, D.S., and J.B. Slemrod. 2008. The Economics of Workaholism: We Should Not Have Worked on This Paper. *The B.E. Journal of Economic Analysis and Policy* 8 (1): 1793–1793.

He, Q., Y. Luo, J. Nie, and H.-F. Zou. 2023. Money, Growth, and Welfare in a Schumpeterian Model with the Spirit of Capitalism. *Review of Economic Dynamics* 47: 346–372.

Hirsch, F. 1976. *Social Limits to Growth*. Cambridge: Harvard University Press.

Hopkins, E., and T. Kornienko. 2004. Running to Keep in the Same Place: Consumer Choice as a Game of Status. *American Economic Review* 94 (4): 1085–1107.

Kapteyn, A., S. Van de Geer, H. Van de Stadt, and T. Wansbeek. 1997. Interdependent Preferences: An Econometric Analysis. *Journal of Applied Econometrics* 12 (6): 665–686.

Karnizova, L. 2010. The Spirit of Capitalism and Expectation-Driven Business Cycles. *Journal of Monetary Economics* 57 (6): 739–752.

Kazantzakis, N. 1965. *Report to Greco*. Translated by P.A. Bien. London: Faber and Faber.

Knight, J., L. Song, and R. Gunatilaka. 2009. Subjective Well-Being and Its Determinants in Rural China. *China Economic Review* 20 (4): 635–649.

Ljungqvist, L., and H. Uhlig. 2000. Tax Policy and Aggregate Demand Management Under Catching Up with the Joneses. *American Economic Review* 90 (3): 356–366.

Maurer, J., and A. Meier. 2008. Smooth it Like the 'Joneses'? *Estimating Peer-Group Effects in Intertemporal Consumption Choice, Economic Journal* 118 (527): 454–476.

McBride, M. 2001. Relative Income Effects on Subjective Well-Being in the Cross-Section. *Journal of Economic Behavior and Organization* 45 (3): 251–278.

Romer, P. 1986. Increasing Returns and Long-Run Growth. *Journal of Political Economy* 94 (5): 1002–1037.

Saint-Paul, G. 2011. *The Tyranny of Utility: Behavioral Social Science and the Rise of Paternalism*. Princeton: Princeton University Press.

Schumpeter, Joseph. 1954. *History of Economic Analysis*. London: George Allen and Unwin.

Senik, C. 2009. Direct Evidence on Income Comparisons and Their Welfare Effects. *Journal of Economic Behavior and Organization* 72 (1): 408–424.

Tournemaine, F., and C. Tsoukis. 2008. Relative Consumption, Relative Wealth and Growth. *Economics Letters* 100 (2): 314–316.

Tournemaine, F., and C. Tsoukis. 2009. Status Jobs, Human Capital and Growth: The Effects of Heterogeneity. *Oxford Economic Papers* 61 (3): 467–493.

Tournemaine, F. 2008. Social Aspirations and Choice of Fertility: Why Can Status Motive Reduce Per-Capita Growth? *Journal of Population Economics* 21 (1): 49–66.

Tournemaine, F., and C. Tsoukis. 2010a. Gain Versus Pain From Status and Ambition: Effects on Growth and Inequality. *The Journal of Socio-Economics* 39 (2): 286–294.

Tournemaine, F., and C. Tsoukis. 2010b. Status, Fertility, Growth and the Great Transition. *The Singapore Economic Review* 55 (3): 553–574.

Tsoukis, C. 2007. Keeping up with the Joneses, Growth, and Distribution. *Scottish Journal of Political Economy* 54 (4): 575–600.

Tsoukis, C., and F. Tournemaine. 2013. Status in a Canonical Macro Model: Status, Growth, and Inequality. *The Manchester School* 81 (S2): 65–92.

Tsoukis, C., and F. Tournemaine. 2016. *Status, Identity and the Macroeconomy*. New York: Mimeo.

Tversky, A., and D. Kahneman. 1991. Loss Aversion in Riskless Choice: A Reference-Dependent Model. *Journal of Economic Literature* 106 (4): 1039–1061.

Veblen, T. 1899. *The Theory of the Leisure Class: An Economic Study of Institutions*. Macmillan.

Weber, M. 1958. The Protestant Ethic and the Spirit of Capitalism, English Translation, Charles Scribners' and Sons [from the Original 1905 German Edition].

Wiener, M. 1981. *English Culture and the Decline of the Industrial Spirit, 1850–1980*. Cambridge: Cambridge University Press.

Zhou, G. 2016. The Spirit of Capitalism and Rational Bubbles. *Macroeconomic Dynamics* 20 (6): 1432–1457.

Zou, H.-F. 1994. The Spirit of Capitalism' and Long-Run Growth. *European Journal of Political Economy* 10 (2): 279–293.

CHAPTER 4

Socio-Behavioural Traits and Long-Run Growth

Having discussed conceptually the main ideas related to social comparisons, status-seeking, and adhering to norms and reference benchmarks, we now proceed in this chapter to show more formally how such insights are embedded in standard frameworks of dynamic macroeconomics. Consumption-, wealth-, and education-based comparisons are three of the most discussed and analysed factors in the socio-macroeconomics literature. In the first part of this chapter, we will essentially concentrate on the economic implications of social status comparisons based on wealth and consumption. Then, the extension of the analysis to education-based comparisons will be explored. Finally, we turn to a slightly different but related topic, that of habit formation.

1 Consumption and Wealth-Based Comparisons in a Dynamic Setting

General Overview

The study of social status comparisons based on consumption and wealth in a single framework can be justified by two primary reasons. Firstly, both types of comparisons may seem to take different perspectives to tackle a similar issue at first glance, but each formalisation may come with its list of pros and cons. For instance, criticisms of comparisons in wealth may stem from the fact that they are not easily observable, but

C. Tsoukis et al., *Social and Behavioural Macroeconomics*,
https://doi.org/10.1007/978-3-031-77748-6_4

in a dynamic setting or growth model, wealth may represent an individual's future consumption. Therefore, taking into account wealth-based comparisons can capture the notion that individuals are delaying the exposure of their social status.[1] Secondly, combining these two types of status comparisons in a single framework and analysing their interactions can enable us to distinguish between "short-term" and "long-term" comparisons, which has significant implications for the expected impact of status comparisons on the economic outcome and specifically on the long-term rate of economic growth.

The relevant literature can be categorised into two main strands: The first strand focuses on wealth-based comparisons, defining social status as the ratio/difference of an individual's level of wealth to the arithmetic average level of others in society. The works by Corneo and Jeanne (1997), Futagami and Shibata (1998), Pham (2005), and Ghosh and Wendner (2017) are examples of this strand. They show that wealth comparisons can raise individuals' incentives to invest in growth-enhancing activities, ultimately leading to higher long-term economic growth. The second strand focuses on consumption-based comparisons, defining social status as the ratio/difference of an individual's level of consumption to the arithmetic average level of others in society. Rauscher (1997) and Fisher and Hof (2000) are among the many authors who have employed this strategy. They find that consumption-based comparisons affect the level of variables but not the steady-state growth of a decentralised economy. This is because individuals are forward-looking and realise that greater current consumption, if it improves their current standing, may worsen their future relative standing. At the steady state, these two opposite effects cancel each other out leading to zero long-term impact on growth. Importantly, the authors point out that this result is robust to changes in the way we formalise the social status function (see Chapter 3). Interestingly, Tsoukis (2007) presents a challenge to this latter view. With a similar dynamic setting, he shows that, in the presence of endogenous labour supply, consumption-based comparisons can give incentives to individuals to work longer (harder), i.e. to increase their labour supply. Intuitively, the additional wage income has two major effects. First, this allows them to increase consumption and keep up with their peers in terms of status comparisons. Second, it allows individuals to

[1] Interested readers can refer to the article by Corneo and Jeanne (1998) for a discussion about this issue.

allocate part of their additional wage income in wealth accumulation. This leads to a greater accumulation of physical capital which itself translates into a higher level of long-term growth.

In a further extension, by taking into account both wealth-based and consumption-based comparisons, Tournemaine and Tsoukis (2008) establish that, not only can the previous result be mitigated, but it can even be overturned. The rationale behind this result follows from the arguments developed earlier: while consumption-based comparisons can be related to current and flow problems, wealth-based comparisons refer to future and stock issues. As we will see, the distinction between these two types of status comparison and the analysis of their interaction are the key to a clearer understanding of their impact on long-term economic growth. In a nutshell, we posit that social status comparisons focused on current and flow decisions are likely to have a detrimental effect on long-term economic growth, while those centred on future and stock decisions are likely to have a positive effect. The underlying rationale behind this outcome is based on the way in which the status comparison affects an individual's rate of time preference for the present relative to the future. This finding is critical as it can be extended to other types of social status comparisons, such as education-based comparisons, as the underlying mechanisms share similar properties.

To formalise these ideas, we choose to present a simplified version of the model developed by Tournemaine and Tsoukis (2008). The choice of this model is motivated by the fact that it provides a unified economic framework that incorporates various forms of status comparisons (based on consumption and wealth), in line with the arguments above. This facilitates the comparison of various results of the literature but also the analysis of the interplay between different forms of status comparisons and their effects. The remainder of the section is structured as follows. Firstly, we introduce a simple one-sector endogenous growth model that considers two types of status comparisons (i.e. consumption-based and wealth-based comparisons). Secondly, we characterise the equilibrium of this model. Thirdly, we discuss the welfare and policy implications of the model.

A Basic Growth Model with Two Status-Seeking Motives

The main building block of the model is taken from Tournemaine and Tsoukis (2008). We consider a closed economy in continuous time. Time, denoted by t, goes from zero to infinity. There is a single commodity, output, Υ_t, which can be consumed, C_t, or invested to give new units of physical capital, C_t. At each instant, the economy is populated by a constant unit mass of identical individuals, each endowed with $K_0 > 0$ units of physical capital (wealth) and one unit of labour-time that must be allocated between leisure-time and output production. As we assume symmetry across individuals, we shall not present any individual-specific indices. When we want to distinguish between individual and mean, we shall use an overbar for the latter.

Output is produced by a representative firm with the following constant returns to scale technology with respect to private factors of production:

$$Y_t = A(K_t)^{\alpha}(L_t\widehat{K}_t)^{1-\alpha}, \tag{1}$$

where $0 < \alpha < 1$, $A > 0$ is a constant technological parameter, K_t is the stock of privately owned physical capital, L_t is the endogenous quantity of labour-time employed by the firm, and $\widehat{K}_t$ represents the stock of technology, other technical knowledge, and the concomitant labour productivity—terms which are not mutually exclusive and will be collectively referred to as "technology". In the spirit of Arrow (1962), Frankel (1962), and Romer (1986), we assume that these intangible factors are ultimately due to K_t, which generates a positive externality in the form of a learning-by-doing (or more specifically learning-by-investing) effect. Alternatively, $\widehat{K}_t$ may capture productive public services, assumed to be proportional to private capital (K_t), as analysed by Barro (1990). (Productive public services may alternatively be proportional to national output, but the two specifications are virtually identical—the one we use here is slightly simpler.) In either the technology or productive public services cases, $\widehat{K}_t$ is proportional to K_t.

Like Bertola (1993), we assume that each unit of physical capital yields one new unit of productivity. So, in equilibrium, we have: $\widehat{K}_t = K_t$. Although the resulting technology (1) is of a "AK" type in equilibrium, it combines a number of desirable features, namely diminishing returns to private physical capital, but constant returns at the aggregate level. This setup generates constant returns to scale in the accumulated factor (capital, inclusive of the externality) combined with diminishing marginal products of the privately owned factors (labour and private capital), in turn, guaranteeing a steady state with a strictly positive and endogenous long-term economic growth.[2]

Since the stock of knowledge or productivity, $\widehat{K}_t$, and labour, L_t, enter multiplicatively in the production function (1), the effects of technology are channelled into output through the labour force. Technical progress that enters in this fashion is known as labour-augmenting or Harrod-neutral. Labour augmenting technological change means that raw labour units (the total number of aggregate hours worked) are being augmented by a coefficient of labour productivity to produce an increase in effective labour input. This happens independently of what is happening to capital. Hence, with the same equipment a worker today produces more than a worker yesterday. Other specifications are possible. Technological change can be Solow- or Hicks-neutral. For the sake of simplicity, in this chapter, we analyse the case of labour-augmenting technical progress only. It should be mentioned, however, that, as we assume a Cobb–Douglas technology of production for output, the three specifications turn out to be equivalent with the appropriate modification.

Assuming that each unit of output devoted to investments is used to either replace depreciated capital or produce new physical capital (one-for-one), we have:

$$Y_t = C_t + \dot{K}_t + \delta K_t, \tag{2}$$

where $\delta > 0$ is the depreciation rate of physical capital.

Regarding the preferences of individuals, we again favour simplicity over complexity. Formally, we assume that individuals derive utility from their per-capita level of consumption, C_t, leisure, l_t, and their social status in society which is determined by two factors: (i) the ratio of their level of wealth, K_t, to the arithmetic average level in society, $\overline{K_t}$; (ii) the ratio of their level of consumption, C_t, to the arithmetic average in society, $\overline{C_t}$. As we discussed in Chapter 3, other specifications of the status functions are

[2] "*AK*" models are sometimes criticised on the ground that they do not fit with empirical evidence (see, e.g., Jones 1995a). However, authors such as McGrattan (1998) and Li (2002) have challenged this view. As a result, we can argue that the empirical validity of a AK model probably remains an open question. From a theoretical point of view, though, and as far as this book is concerned, we argue that the extended *AK* formulation we use (1) is, as a first pass, sufficient to raise issues regarding the impact of individuals' status comparisons on growth. Later, we will extend the analysis to more refined models. We shall show that the key results derived from the AK formulation are due to mechanisms that continue to operate in more complex settings.

possible. But these are the specifications that have been employed most extensively in the literature, and none of our key results depends on this particular specification. Preferences are assumed to be represented by the following utility function:

$$U = \int_0^{\infty} \frac{\{(C_t)(l_t)^{\omega}(K_t/\overline{K_t})^{\beta}(C_t/\overline{C_t})^{\gamma}\}^{1-\theta} - 1}{1-\theta} e^{-\rho t} dt, \tag{3}$$

where $\omega > 0$ is a measure of the strength of preference for leisure, $\theta > 1$ is the inverse of the elasticity of intertemporal substitution in consumption, and $\rho > 0$ is the rate of time preference (discount rate), a measure of impatience. Parameters $\beta > 0$ and $\gamma > 0$ represent the strength of preferences for social status based on wealth and consumption, respectively. Several comments are in order here. First of all, parameter θ can also be interpreted as a coefficient of relative risk aversion. In this chapter, though, we prefer to adopt the standard view of growth models: we interpret parameter θ as a measure of the willingness of individuals to shift consumption over periods as the return to saving and/or the rate of impatience change. Notice that, as θ decreases, the marginal utility of individuals falls less when consumption increases. Hence, individuals are more responsive and ready to re-allocate consumption over time. In the limit case where $\theta = 0$, or infinite elasticity of intertemporal substitution, we obtain a linear instantaneous utility function, meaning that individuals are willing to accept infinitely large changes in consumption in response to small differences between the rate of time preference and the rate of return on savings. We shall see later in the characterisation of the equilibrium that the introduction of status comparisons will play a great role regarding individuals' preference for the present relative to the future thereby impacting their decisions to consume and save at each instant.[3]

Second, it will be important to keep in mind the interpretation of parameters $\omega > 0$, $\beta > 0$, and $\gamma > 0$ as they will help us to keep track of

[3] By using l'Hopital's rule, we can show that, if parameter θ equals one, the utility function given by Eq. (3) reduces to: $U = \int_0^{\infty}[\mathrm{Log}(C_t) + \omega \mathrm{Log} l_t + \beta \mathrm{Log}(K_t/\overline{K_t}) + \gamma \mathrm{Log}(C_t/\overline{C_t})]e^{-\rho t} dt$. On the whole, empirical studies suggest that the elasticity of intertemporal substitution is less than unity (i.e. $\theta > 1$), and we, therefore, make this assumption (see Hall 1988, and Tsoukis 2020, Ch. 1 for further discussion).

the potential effects of leisure and status comparisons. The main advantage of the simple formulation (3) is that it allows us to keep track of their effects by considering one channel at a time ($\beta = 0$ and $\gamma > 0$ or $\beta > 0$ and $\gamma = 0$) with or without leisure ($\omega > 0$ or $\omega = 0$). In this way, we are able to recover the results from the standard literature and to clarify the interaction between status comparisons and leisure.

Equilibrium Analysis

In this section, we characterise the equilibrium of a decentralised economy in which all markets (output, labour, physical capital) are perfectly competitive. We analyse how status comparisons in wealth and consumption affect growth and welfare and the key role of endogenous labour supply regarding the outcome.

We assume that individuals buy physical capital and rent it to firms. We normalise the price of output to one and denote by w_t and R_t the price of labour and the rental price of physical capital, respectively.

Efficiency Conditions

At each moment, the competitive firm of the output sector maximises instantaneous profit given by: $\pi_t = A(K_t)^\alpha(\widehat{K}_t L_t)^{1-\alpha} - R_t K_t - w_t L_t$. Equating the marginal product of inputs with their market prices leads to:

$$R_t = \alpha A(L_t)^{1-\alpha}, \tag{4}$$

and

$$w_t = (1-\alpha)AK_t(L_t)^{-\alpha}, \tag{5}$$

where we have used the equilibrium condition $K_t = \widehat{K}_t$ after differentiation (the latter is taken as given by the individual).

Firms are perfectly competitive, hence in equilibrium profits are zero. As a result, all output is remunerated as either capital income, $R_t K_t$, or labour income, $w_t L_t$. Therefore:

$$Y_t = R_t K_t + w_t L. \tag{6}$$

Each individual chooses per-capita consumption, C_t, to maximise lifetime utility (3) subject to their budget constraint given by (2) with

(6):

$$\dot{K}_t = (R_t - \delta)K_t + w_t L_t - C_t. \tag{7}$$

We also recall that the time constraint is given by: $l_t + L_t = 1$. The initial condition $K_0 > 0$ and arithmetic averages of consumption and wealth in the economy are taken as given.

After substitutions, the current-value Hamiltonian of this problem is:

$$\begin{aligned}\text{CVH} = &\frac{\{(C_t)(l_t)^{\omega}(K_t/\overline{K_t})^{\beta}(C_t/\overline{C_t})^{\gamma}\}^{1-\theta} - 1}{1-\theta} \\ &+ \lambda_t[w_t(1 - l_t) + (R_t - \delta)K_t - C_t],\end{aligned}$$

where λ_t, which can be interpreted as the shadow price of physical capital, is the co-state variable associated with the budget constraint (7). After straightforward manipulations, the first-order conditions yield:

$$\frac{\omega}{(1+\gamma)}\frac{C_t}{1-L_t} = w_t, \tag{8}$$

and

$$\frac{C_t}{K_t}\frac{\beta}{(1+\gamma)} + R_t - \delta + \frac{\dot{\lambda}_t}{\lambda_t} = \rho. \tag{9}$$

Due to the unit mass, mean and aggregate quantities coincide, and we have used: $K_t = \overline{K_t}, C_t = \overline{C_t}$, as implied by the homogeneity of individuals (but the mean quantities are taken as given in optimisation). To gain intuition, the symmetric outcome allows us to proceed without worrying about the inequality between individuals or firms, which are assumed homogeneous (identical); but the distinction between the individual and the mean allows us to build the motive to outdo all others (status-seeking) into individual behaviour. The fact of course that eventually this motive proves futile (because of symmetry), but not before it has altered individual behaviour, is a manifestation of the status motive as exerting a negative externality, as discussed.

Moreover, the transversality condition is given by: $\lim_{t\to\infty} \lambda_t K_t e^{-\rho t} = 0$. This states that the value of capital is nil at the end of the horizon: the optimising individual does not want to have any wealth left at the end of the planning horizon. Had this condition not been satisfied, it would have been possible to increase the level of utility of individuals (welfare) by transferring the capital remaining at the end of history into consumption. In that case, the individual would not optimise, which is a contradiction.

Equation (8) is an efficiency condition which must be satisfied at each instant for every individual. It says that the marginal rate of substitution between work effort and per-capita consumption equals the level of real wage (the marginal rate of transformation). This rate depends negatively on the strength of the consumption-based comparisons, γ. Ceteris paribus, as γ increases, individuals must give up a greater amount of leisure to maintain their level of utility. Note that with no preference for leisure ($\omega = 0$), Eq. (8) disappears. In this case, individuals' labour supply is inelastic, exogenously given and equal to one. It is also worth pointing out that wealth-based status-seeking does not affect labour supply (β does not appear in (8), in marked contrast to consumption-based status).

Equation (9) is a modified "Keynes-Ramsey" rule also called the Euler equation of consumption. It states that the return to wealth (physical capital accumulation) must equate the rate of time preference. The term "modified" is being used to point out that, in comparison to the "standard case" (without any status comparisons nor endogenous labour supply, i.e. $\omega = \beta = \gamma = 0$), we can clearly identify the impact of status comparisons, notably their opposite effects. Let us observe that the rate of return on physical capital comprises three main elements: (i) the marginal productivity of physical capital net of its depreciation rate, $R_t - \delta$; (ii) the growth rate of the shadow price of physical capital, $\dot{\lambda}_t / \lambda_t$; and (iii) the new element coming from the introduction of status comparisons compared to a standard model, $[\beta/(1+\gamma)] \times (C_t/K_t)$. Interestingly, we can see, via parameters $\beta > 0$ and $\gamma > 0$, that status comparisons in wealth (physical capital) and consumption interact and potentially have opposite effects on the rate of return of physical capital. We will see later, in full equilibrium, that this primary effect will be mitigated/reversed via the role played by the endogenous labour supply (see efficiency condition given by Eq. 8).

Steady State

We now characterise the steady state. Along the way, we can show that there is no transitional dynamics.[4] To proceed, we denote by $\chi_t = C_t/K_t$

[4] The analysis of the implications of status comparisons for growth and dynamics have been highlighted in different settings by Alonso-Carrera et al. (2004), and Alvarez-Cuadrado et al. (2004), among others.

the consumption-capital ratio which yields: $g_\chi = g_C - g_K$, where g_χ denotes the growth rate of any variable x. We recall that, written in growth form, the first-order conditions (8) and (9) imply: $\theta g_C + \omega(\theta - 1)g_l = -g_\lambda$ and $g_C - g_l = g_w$. With further manipulations, we can show that the amount of leisure (or equivalently individuals' labour supply) must be constant at each instant along the transitional path (if any) to the steady state. With this information in mind, the efficiency conditions (4–6) and (8–9) yield the following dynamic equation:

$$g_\chi = -\frac{(\theta - \alpha)A(L_t)^{1-\alpha} + \rho - (\theta - 1)\delta}{\theta} + \frac{\theta + \frac{\beta}{1+\gamma}}{\theta}\chi_t, \tag{10}$$

along with the relation

$$\frac{\omega \chi_t}{(1+\gamma)} = (1-\alpha)A(L_t)^{-\alpha}(1 - L_t). \tag{11}$$

The system (10) and (11) is clearly unstable. Hence, the economy jumps immediately to its unique steady state where the labour supply (leisure), L^* (l^*), is constant and output, physical capital (wealth) and consumption share a common rate of growth, g^*. Using (9)–(11), we obtain:

$$g^* = \frac{\beta\chi^*}{(1+\gamma)} + \alpha A(L^*)^{1-\alpha} - \delta - \rho, \tag{12}$$

$$\frac{\omega\chi^*}{(1+\gamma)} = (1-\alpha)A(L^*)^{-\alpha}(1 - L^*), \tag{13}$$

$$\chi^* = \frac{C_t}{K_t} = \frac{(\theta - \alpha)A(L^*)^{1-\alpha} + \rho - (\theta - 1)\delta}{\theta + \beta/(1+\gamma)}. \tag{14}$$

Equations (12)–(14) allow us to analyse how the various status motives affect growth, g^*, labour supply, L^*, and the consumption-capital ratio, χ^*. For simplicity, the results from the comparative statics are reported in Table 1.

The main result of Table 1 is probably that, from a development perspective, it is crucial to understand the kind of comparisons that individuals use to establish their ranking in society.

From Table 1, while wealth-based comparisons are growth-enhancing (denoted by β), the macroeconomic impact of consumption-based

Table 1 Effects of change in β and γ on g^*, L^*, and χ^*

	$\frac{\partial g^*}{\partial x}$	$\frac{\partial L^*}{\partial x}$	$\frac{\partial \chi^*}{\partial x}$
$x = \beta$	>0	>0	<0
$x = \gamma$	>0 or <0	>0	>0

comparisons (γ) is ambiguous. The reason is quite intuitive. Re-arranging condition (9), we obtain:

$$R_t - \delta + \frac{\dot{\lambda}_t}{\lambda_t} = \rho - \frac{C_t}{K_t} \frac{\beta}{(1+\gamma)}, \tag{15}$$

where the terms on the left-hand side represent the net return from investments in physical capital accumulation and those on the right can be interpreted as the net rate of time preference (difference between discount rate and the status comparisons effect). While the terms on the left are reminiscent of those depicted in standard theory, those on the right are key for our purposes. They basically establish that social status comparisons affect individuals' decision-making through the channel of their preference for the present relative to the future.

With this in mind, seeking greater social status in wealth (i.e. if β increases) makes individuals more patient. Then, they allocate a greater amount of their resources to wealth accumulation which, in turn, is beneficial to long-term economic growth. This is the standard result obtained in the literature (e.g. Corneo and Jeanne 1997; Futagami and Shibata 1998; Pham 2005). This is reminiscent of the argument of Corneo and Jeanne (1998) which states that competing for social status at old age or late in the life-cycle can foster the decision of individuals to save, as in our model, individuals have simply a greater willingness to postpone consumption. Interestingly, moreover, we can notice that this effect is reinforced by the positive impact of seeking greater social status in wealth on labour supply: $\partial L^*/\partial \beta > 0$. We also have $\partial \chi^*/\partial \beta < 0$, therefore, there is more saving and growth.

Consumption-based comparisons, on the other hand, make individuals more impatient. Their willingness to consume is immediately greater. We have the balance of two effects, the direct one in (15) which creates more impatience; and $\partial \chi^*/\partial g > 0$, which does the opposite. Thus, the final outcome on long-term economic growth might be of either sign: $\partial g^*/\partial \gamma < 0$ or $\partial g^*/\partial \gamma > 0$. It is worth dwelling more here, to obtain more intuition on the mechanisms at work. To start with, status-seeking from consumption makes individuals more impatient. This comes from examination of Eq. (15). Such behaviour leads them to increase their level of consumption during current periods relative to the future. As they save less, this has a negative impact on growth. This result can be emphasised by setting $\omega = 0$, i.e. when labour supply is exogenous. In this case, Eq. (13) vanishes and $L^* = 1$. From there, examination of Eqs. (12) and (14) clearly shows the negative impact of status comparisons on long-term growth and consumption-to-capital ratio. However, once we account for endogenous labour supply ($\omega > 0$), status comparisons from consumption may lead to the opposite outcome. The reason is that social status comparisons in consumption induce individuals to increase their labour supply:$\partial L^*/\partial\gamma > 0$. This means, ceteris paribus, that a greater amount of output can be produced. Thereby, individuals can increase their investments in physical capital accumulation which is beneficial to long-term economic growth. This mechanism is probably more apparent if we set$\beta = 0$. In effect, if individuals do not derive utility from status comparisons in wealth, the second term on the right-hand side of Eq. (15) vanishes. In this case, seeking greater social status from consumption comparisons unambiguously positively affects long-term per-capita growth as it acts indirectly through the channel of endogenous labour supply (see Eqs. 12–14). We then recover the basic result of Tsoukis (2007).

To close this discussion on the interplay between status comparisons and endogenous labour supply, let us note that, if individuals do not derive utility from leisure ($\omega = 0$) and wealth comparisons ($\beta = 0$), we recover the result obtained by Rauscher (1997) and Fisher and Hof (2000). In this case, status comparisons in consumption have no effect on the outcome of the decentralised economy. The intuition is that the status comparisons in consumption impact the price of current consumption, but not the relative price of future consumption in terms of present consumption. To see this, let us recall that, from the first-order conditions of the maximisation problem of individuals with respect to consumption, we have: $(1+\gamma)(C_t)^{-\theta}(l_t)^{\omega(1-\theta)} = \lambda_t$. In other words, the marginal utility from consumption (where we clearly see the role of status comparisons via the presence of parameter γ) equals, at each instant, the shadow price of physical capital. However, from Eq. (9), when we set $\beta = 0$, we recover the standard form of the Euler equation: $R_t - \delta + \dot{\lambda}_t/\lambda_t = \rho$. As a consequence, there is no steady-state effect of status comparisons in consumption. In the presence of the wealth externality (i.e. $\beta > 0$), however, there are steady-state growth effects, as explained above.

To sum up, we can then establish the following proposition which restates the results:

Proposition 1: *In a standard one-sector endogenous growth model:*

(a) *Higher wealth-based comparisons have a positive effect on growth, as both the intertemporal preferences and the labour supply effects are positive.*
(b) *The effect on growth of higher consumption-based comparisons, however, is ambiguous, as the intertemporal effect is negative (individuals are more impatient) but the labour supply effect is positive.*

In conclusion, the model presented herein, while simple, has enabled us to demonstrate the various outcomes highlighted by the literature on the topic. Additionally, the model has expanded our understanding of the important roles that status comparisons can play when they interact together but also with endogenous labour supply.

Welfare Analysis

In this section, we examine the welfare properties of the model economy outlined in Sect. "A Basic Growth Model with Two Status-Seeking Motives". Firstly, we demonstrate how a government that is perfectly informed can implement an optimal allocation of resources with the use of appropriate policy instruments.[5] Subsequently, we augment our discussion regarding the manner in which status comparisons impact the economy. To be specific, based on the work by Corneo and Jeanne (1997), who, in turn, draw on earlier ideas developed by Smith (1759), we argue that status comparisons (i.e. envy, jealousy, and greed) can, in certain scenarios, work as a market corrective mechanism.

Implementation of the Optimum

As a matter of fact, three factors contribute to the misallocation of resources of the decentralised economy as depicted in Sect. "A Basic Growth Model with Two Status-Seeking Motives": status comparisons

[5] See also Ljungqvist and Uhlig (2000) who discuss the role and impact of tax policies in economies subject to productivity shocks when individuals are status-driven.

in (i) consumption, (ii) wealth, and (iii) the learning-by-investing externality, or knowledge spillover, in the output sector. Obviously, at the optimum, the social planner considers the homogeneity of individuals and internalises the spillover effect of knowledge in the output sector. Consequently, to implement an optimal allocation of resources within the decentralised equilibrium, the policy recommendation is rather straightforward: the government ought to employ two policy instruments.[6]

Let us denote by $\tau_{C,t}$ and $\tau_{K,t}$ the policy instruments introduced to remove the distortions due to consumption and physical capital accumulation, respectively. For the sake of simplicity, we assume that, to implement such an economic policy, the government uses a lump-sum transfer, Θ_t, on individuals. In this case, the budget constraint of the government, assumed to be balanced at each moment, is given by:

$$\Theta_t = \tau_{C,t} C_t + \tau_{K,t} K_t.$$

Straightforward computations imply that, at each instant, the optimal policy levels are given by:

$$\tau_C = \gamma, \tag{16}$$

and

$$\tau_K = \beta \chi^o + (\alpha - 1)(L^o)^{1-\alpha}, \tag{17}$$

where the symbol "o" is used to denote any optimal value at the steady state. To implement the optimal allocation of resources, the government chooses a tax on consumption so as to remove the external effects it produces (see Eq. 16). On this ground, we notice that the tax on consumption exactly equals the strength of preferences for consumption-based comparisons.

On the other hand, it is interesting to note that the policy instrument used to obtain an optimal accumulation of physical capital can be a tax

[6] With respect to physical capital, let us note that despite the presence of two market distortions (namely, the knowledge spillover effect and the wealth-based comparisons effect), a single policy instrument is deemed sufficient. Although the analysis may lose in terms of clarity due to the implicit combination of these two effects in a single tool, it obviously gains in analytical simplicity. See Ghosh and Wendner (2017) for an analysis of optimal taxation when relative wealth appears in utility; in that case, two instruments are required.

if $\tau_K > 0$ or a subsidy if $\tau_K < 0$ (see Eq. 17). Whether the government should implement a tax or subsidy on physical capital depends on the relative impact of the knowledge spillover effect and the social status effect resulting from wealth-based comparisons. These two forces work effectively in opposite directions with respect to the rate of growth of physical capital accumulation. Intuitions behind this argument are the following. Recall that the knowledge spillover effect implies that firms employ a suboptimal level of physical capital, as they do not receive any compensation for the knowledge they produce. Thus, they do not entirely internalise the total social value they create. As a result, demand for physical capital is lower than the optimum. To remove this distortion, a subsidy policy should be implemented. On the other hand, status comparisons in wealth give incentives to individuals to save excessively compared to the optimum. Therefore, the amount of physical capital exceeds the one at the optimum. In this scenario, a tax policy on physical capital is more appropriate to address such a negative effect.

Status Comparison: A Possible Market Corrective Mechanism Tool

The analysis of the previous section demonstrates that social status comparisons require government intervention if we seek to implement an optimal allocation of resources. This is because the basic human traits such as envy, jealousy, or greed induce individuals to alter their behaviour which results in a misallocation of resources. In this context, at first glance, the policy recommendation is quite simple: the government should implement policy tools, such as taxes, to encourage individuals to internalise this behaviour. To be more general and expand our line of reasoning, we can assert that the government should employ a policy instrument like a tax on any factor that individuals use to compare themselves and establish a social ranking in society.

However, the story is more complex than that because various activities may induce other externalities, as well as the externality associated with status-seeking interacts. In the standard theory of growth, it is well known that some of the factors or variables that individuals may use to compare themselves are also known to have positive external effects on the economy. This was, for instance, the case in the model outlined in Sect. "A Basic Growth Model with Two Status-Seeking Motives" with the introduction of a learning-by-investing effect. The same is true of education or knowledge production from the R&D activity, which are two strong candidates to explain long-term economic growth through well-documented spillover effects. This is the reason why most of the literature (both theoretical and empirical) without social status comparisons usually prescribes a policy intervention in the form of a subsidy to education or research to implement an optimal allocation of resources.

In this sub-section, we seek to offer a different perspective. We argue that individuals' social status comparisons might influence the extent to which individuals engage in some growth-enhancing activities. In other words, social status comparisons could serve as the required corrective market mechanism tools. As noted by Corneo and Jeanne (1997), this is an old idea that we can trace back to the landmark work by Smith (1759). In pages 184–185, he wrote[7]:

> [T]he quest for social status works as an invisible hand that leads individuals to unintentionally act on behalf of the growth prospects of society as a whole.

In the same vein, Arrow (1971) discusses the role of social rewards such as social status as a tool that can be used to remove inefficiencies arising from external effects. The author explains that the behaviour of individuals which induces the production of external effects can either be appreciated or rejected by others in society depending on whether the impact is positive or negative. In the case of a positive external effect, society may reward individuals in the form of social status. For instance, they may receive a special distinction, such as a school end-of-year prize or a medal of honour. In the case of a negative external effect, on the other hand, society shall disapprove of the behaviour and eventually punish individuals via a reduction of their social status through ostracism or exclusion (see, e.g., Weiss and Fershtman 1998).

We can easily illustrate the arguments developed above by using the endogenous growth model developed in Sect. "A Basic Growth Model with Two Status-Seeking Motives". From Eq. (16) we notice that $\tau_K = 0$ if:

$$\beta = (1-\alpha)(L^o)^{1-\alpha}/\chi^o. \tag{18}$$

This equation implies that when the strength of preferences for wealth-based comparisons on the left-hand side is equal to the external effect of

[7] Taken from Corneo and Jeanne (1997, p. 87).

the knowledge spillover effect in the output sector on the right-hand side, then no policy instrument is required on physical capital accumulation to achieve an optimal allocation of resources. This implies that, in such a case, status comparisons serve as the required corrective tool: the distortions due to the learning-by-investing externality and status comparisons in wealth offset each other. The following proposition restates the result:

Proposition 2: *In a one-sector model of endogenous growth characterised by a learning-by-doing (-investing) externality, seeking greater social status in wealth can restore efficiency by adding a countervailing distortion. Social status comparisons can play the role of a corrective market mechanism tool.*

2 Extensions: Human Capital, Fertility Choice, and Status

We now expand upon the basic model presented in Sect. "A Basic Growth Model with Two Status-Seeking Motives" by exploring various extensions about the impact of social status comparisons on individuals' behaviour at the microeconomic level. Thereby, we aim to obtain a better understanding on the manner such behaviour translates at the macroeconomic level. In particular, the extensions are mostly drawn from the families of two-sector endogenous growth models. This approach is justified by at least two arguments. Firstly, while the model presented in Sect. "A Basic Growth Model with Two Status-Seeking Motives" is attractive due to its simplicity and ability to capture several interesting outcomes, it fails to provide a complete understanding of how technical progress occurs in the economy. So far, it has been assumed that technical progress is the result of external effects. This is not entirely satisfactory, particularly if we consider that the creation of knowledge is primarily the consequence of agents' conscious private decisions. For example, individuals decide to invest (or not) in schooling activities to acquire skills, a form of which is knowledge (Uzawa 1965; Lucas 1988); but also private firms choose to invest (or not) in R&D activities to produce new goods (Romer 1990) or improve the quality of existing ones (Grossman and Helpman 1991; Aghion and Howitt 1992). It then follows that adding social status comparisons to the picture will allow us to shed some new light on the channels through which social status interactions may affect individuals' decision-making, particularly with respect to these two fundamental elements.

Secondly, it is worth noting that human capital-based or R&D-based models, as they are commonly referred to, have largely contributed to a new interpretation of the determinants of technical progress. Apart from the appealing stories they bring with them, these frameworks also shine through their technical aspect. More precisely, they are characterised by a clear separation between the knowledge production sector (via human capital accumulation or R&D activities) and the output production process: so the nickname of this kind of model, namely two-sector model of endogenous growth.[8] This change, in terms of philosophy of modelling, in comparison to the one-sector formulation offers a much higher degree of flexibility and freedom to the modeller. This is probably the reason why these frameworks have become so popular outside the field of growth theory itself. For instance, among others, they are common in the fields of environmental economics and sustainable development, economics and geography, or as specified in this book, socio-macroeconomics. It then appears as a natural step forward into our analysis and review of social and behavioural macroeconomics to analyse the issue of social status comparisons within this class of framework.

To proceed, the rest of this section is structured as follows. Firstly, we will explore some extensions in relation to the "human capital approach" to endogenous growth theory. Secondly, this initial step will enable us to introduce the concept of endogenous population growth (or individuals' endogenous fertility choice).

Human Capital/Education

Definition of Human Capital

The notion that human capital is a strong candidate to favour economic development can be traced back to the seminal work of Smith (1776). However, it was not until two centuries later that this idea was formally included within an economic framework (Uzawa 1965; Lucas 1988). Though the concept appears simple at first sight, defining "human capital" could be a challenging task. The reason is that it is a broad concept that encompasses various dimensions, including an individual's level of education (knowledge), health status, motivation, and any

[8] In contrast, one-sector models combine the law of motion of physical capital (source of knowledge production) and output production in a single equation (see Eq. 2).

skills acquired through training or experience. Despite its various dimensions, most economic models have simplified the concept by considering education as a proxy for human capital. This simplification has probably been influenced by the empirical findings of Mankiw et al. (1992).[9] Consequently, human capital is commonly regarded as the amount of knowledge possessed by individuals. Here, we adopt this conventional approach.

Education and Returns from Education

The analysis of education as the primary driving force of long-term growth brings several important elements to light. The first one is that individuals' motivation for investing in educational activities extends beyond the expectation of higher future wages. More specifically, individuals also obtain rewards in a "non-pecuniary" form. For instance, Schultz (1963) identifies three distinct components in the decision to invest in education: (i) the expected future earnings as mentioned; (ii) a present consumption component, such as the pleasure derived from acquiring new knowledge; and (iii) a future consumption component. To illustrate the second and third components, consider an individual who decides to learn how to play a musical instrument. If we exclude professional musicians from the picture or any expectation to become a professional, then the question is: why do individuals take such a decision? A possible answer might be: This decision is motivated not only by the pleasure of learning and improving (component ii), but also by the pleasure of a greater ability to appreciate the next concert of classical music (component iii). To sum up, several elements contribute to the individual's overall level of satisfaction, and some come from the background knowledge acquired during the learning process. Importantly, these components are additive and may complement one another. On this theme, authors such as Schaafsma (1976) and Alstadsaeter (2011) argue that non-pecuniary returns to education come in various forms. Among other things, it can be: (i) the simple pleasure of learning something new; (ii) the joy of meeting new people or discovering a new environment and culture via a student exchange programme; (iii) the ability to consume and appreciate a wider range of goods as stated in our example. In his empirical analysis,

[9] In their analysis, Mankiw et al. (1992) use the number of years of schooling as regressors in a standard growth regression. They demonstrate that investments in schooling activities are a key determinant of long-term economic development.

Gullason (1989) even suggests that individuals may pursue higher education for reasons such as avoiding military service. He takes the example of the young Americans who wanted to avoid the draft during the Vietnam War in the 60's.

It then follows that the social status that individuals can obtain through education can also be considered a non-pecuniary return. For instance, education earns social esteem and prestige in its own right; and/or it gives individuals a choice between a wider range of jobs, thus potentially reaching a higher social position (see, e.g., Fershtman et al. 1996; Boonprakaikawe and Tournemaine 2006; Tournemaine and Tsoukis 2009). This is important as several empirical studies suggest that non-pecuniary returns are a significant factor in individuals' decision to invest in education (e.g. Dodge and Stager 1972; Oosterbeek and Ophem 2000). Haveman and Wolfe (1984) even estimate that, from an individual perspective, non-pecuniary returns from education are approximately equal to pecuniary returns. Therefore, considering sociological and psychological factors in formal economic models is necessary to understand the various forces that drive economic decision-making.

Illustration in a Basic Education-Based Model

In this section, we present a simple two-sector model of endogenous growth that incorporates human capital (education) as a crucial ingredient for sustaining long-term economic growth (see, e.g. Lucas 1988). Additionally, we assume that individuals derive utility from education-based comparisons. The key features of the model are the following (similar to those in Sect. "A Basic Growth Model with Two Status-Seeking Motives"). The economy is closed. Time, denoted by t, is continuous and goes from zero to infinity. There is a single commodity, output, Y_t, which is only used as a consumption good, C_t. There is a unit mass of individuals, each one of them endowed with $H_0 > 0$ units of human capital (innate skills) and one unit of labour-time that must be allocated between output production, $1-u_t$, and human capital accumulation,u_t. It is possible to add physical capital accumulation as in the model presented in Sect. "A Basic Growth Model with Two Status-Seeking Motives", but it would solely complicate the analysis without altering any of the results and intuitions.

Output is produced by a representative firm with the technology:

$$Y_t = A(1 - u_t)H_t, \tag{19}$$

where $A > 0$ is a constant technological parameter and H_t is the amount of human capital of an individual. This latter accumulates according to the following law of motion:

$$\dot{H}_t = \varphi u_t H_t, \tag{20}$$

where $\varphi > 0$ is a constant productivity parameter. Equations (19) and (20) illustrate the key feature of the model: the law of motion of human capital is disentangled from output production.

Regarding individuals, we assume that they derive utility from their level of consumption, C_t, and social status in society measured by the ratio of their level of human capital, H_t, to the arithmetic average level in society, $\overline{H_t}$. Preferences are represented by:

$$U = \int_0^\infty \frac{\{(C_t)(H_t/\overline{H_t})^\beta\}^{1-\theta} - 1}{1-\theta} e^{-\rho t} dt, \tag{21}$$

where $0 < \beta < 1$ is the strength of preferences for social status based on human capital comparisons, $\theta > 1$ is the inverse of the intertemporal elasticity of substitution in consumption, and ρ, with $0 < \rho < \varphi$, is the rate of time preference. Assuming that the rate of time preference is lower than the productivity parameter in the human capital accumulation sector is a non-stringent and standard practice in this kind of model. It allows us to ensure the existence of a steady state with a strictly positive level of growth in the long run.

In this simple economy, the characterisation of a perfectly competitive equilibrium is straightforward. Normalise the price of output to one and denote by w_t the wage per unit of human capital. The necessary first-order condition from profit maximisation of the competitive firm yields:

$$w_t = A. \tag{22}$$

Equation (22) implies that the level of wage is constant at each instant. This result comes from the "AK" formulation employed for output production.

Regarding individuals, we can easily demonstrate that the optimisation problem leads to:

$$\beta\varphi(1-u_t) + \varphi(1-u_t) + \frac{\dot{H}_t}{H_t} + \frac{\dot{\mu}_t}{\mu_t} = \rho, \tag{23}$$

where μ_t is the co-state variable associated with the law of motion of physical capital and, as before, we have used the property of symmetry between individuals: $H_t = \overline{H_t}$. Moreover, the transversality condition is given by: $\lim_{t\to\infty} \mu_t H_t e^{-\rho t} = 0$. Expression (23) is a kind of Euler equation reminiscent of the one derived in the model of Sect. "A Basic Growth Model with Two Status-Seeking Motives" (see Eq. 8). It essentially states that, during any transition path to the steady state, the return on investments in human capital on the left-hand side must equal the discount rate on the right-hand side. We note that this return comprises four terms. The first one, given by $\beta\varphi(1 - u_t)$, measures an individual's marginal utility gain from a higher level of education, H_t. As discussed earlier, it can be interpreted as the "non-pecuniary return" to education. In other words, this term captures the willingness of individuals to invest in schooling or learning activities because of the reward they obtain in the form of, for instance, the prestige they gain via education. We observe that in the absence of status comparison, (i.e. if $\beta = 0$), this term vanishes. Therefore, in the case $\beta > 0$, all other things being equal, as the strength of education-based comparisons increases, individuals have greater incentives to allocate more of their time in schooling/learning activities.

The three last terms on the left-hand side of (23) are more conventional. The term $\varphi(1-u_t)$ represents the consumption gain from a higher level of education: a higher level of education is synonymous with greater productivity. The growth rate of human capital, $\dot{H}_t/H_t$, shows the contribution of investments in education to the future production of human capital. To give an illustration, we could say that the current students today will become the teachers in the future. Finally, the return to human capital investments also depends on the growth rate of the shadow price of human capital, $\dot{\mu}_t/\mu_t$.

We now proceed to the characterisation of the equilibrium. Through straightforward calculations, we can demonstrate that there are no transitional dynamics. The reason is that, in the interests of simplicity, we have not introduced any physical capital accumulation sector or heterogeneity between individuals.[10] We can then show that human capital, output, and

[10] The impact of introducing heterogeneity between individuals in such a model will be discussed later in Chapter 7.

consumption grow at the same rate in the long run:

$$g^* = \frac{\varphi(\beta + 1) - \rho}{\theta + \beta}. \tag{24}$$

Moreover, the amount of time allocated to schooling activities (also constant at the steady state) is given by:

$$u^* = \frac{\varphi(\beta + 1) - \rho}{\varphi(\theta + \beta)}. \tag{25}$$

The results presented in Eqs. (24) and (25) are intuitive. When individuals put a greater weight on human capital-based comparisons (i.e. β takes larger values), they are willing to devote a greater proportion of their labour-time to human capital accumulation. Such behaviour positively impacts long-term economic growth as shown in Eq. (24). Therefore, education-based comparisons have a similar effect as wealth-based comparisons: they cause individuals to over-invest compared to the optimal level.

The question that arises from this simple static comparative exercise is whether investments in education should be taxed to eliminate the externality due to status comparisons. At first glance, given the formulation of the model, the answer is positive. Nonetheless, we can bring an argument to the table that will temper this conclusion. One crucial element was missing in our presentation, namely knowledge spillovers in education. Several authors, such as Tamura (1991), de la Croix and Doepke (2004), and Alonso-Carrera (2001) have highlighted their importance both theoretically and empirically, particularly for human capital convergence. A formulation accounting for these features could be the following:

$$\dot{H}_t = \varphi(u_t H_t)^{\zeta} \left(\overline{H}_t\right)^{1-\zeta}, \tag{26}$$

where $0 < \zeta < 1$ is a parameter measuring the direct contribution of individual knowledge relative to the arithmetic average in the society in the production of individual knowledge. The latter term, weighted by $1 - \zeta$, accounts for the knowledge spillover effect. Using such a law of motion for human capital would add the necessary opposing force to education-based comparisons possibly rendering individuals' investments in education excessive or insufficient compared to the optimum. The implication is that the policy instrument required to implement an optimal allocation of resources could be either a tax or a subsidy. In a similar way as in Sect. "Welfare Analysis", the outcome shall depend on the relative strength of status comparisons in education and the knowledge spillover effect.

Education and Fertility Choice

The objective of this section is to enrich the preceding analysis by integrating endogenous fertility choices into the analysis. The justification is twofold. Firstly, rearing children to adulthood is costly in terms of resources and time. Thus, it makes fertility choice another important decision variable in individuals' optimisation problems that is inextricably linked to educational choices. The reason is that both variables compete for the same kind of resources. Thereby, it follows that we can also infer a potential trade-off between status achievement and fertility choice.

To proceed, the remainder of this section is structured as follows. Firstly, we justify the introduction of endogenous fertility choices within an economic framework comprising a status comparison component. Secondly, we discuss the influence of such choices on the economic outcome. Thirdly, we examine how comparisons of status can impact individuals' decisions regarding education and fertility, and then how these translate to the macroeconomic outcome.

Quality-Quantity Trade-Off on Children

It is a widely acknowledged fact that there is a trade-off between education and fertility, which is commonly referred to as the quality-quantity trade-off with respect to children. This notion has been formalised and demonstrated in the seminal work of Becker et al. (1990). Essentially, this trade-off implies that, as individuals prioritise investments in education, they may simultaneously postpone or limit their fertility rate. There are several reasons that account for this outcome. Firstly, as highlighted by the aforementioned authors, a primary explanation is the increase in the opportunity cost of having children as the level of education rises. Additionally, we can note the broader range of job opportunities that become available to individuals with higher education and the resulting social status that can result from it. We will expand on this notion in the next sub-section. Lastly, but certainly not least, individuals with higher levels of education are more knowledgeable about contraceptive methods and family planning. This may contribute not only to reducing unintended pregnancies but also to a more deliberate decision-making process regarding fertility choices.

The Population Debate: Quality-Quantity Trade-Off Versus the "Mozart Effect"

The quality-quantity trade-off on children has significant implications for economic development. This is due to the varying impacts of education and fertility both at the micro- and macroeconomic levels. For instance, education is a factor affecting individual's productivity and earnings potential, while fertility may shape the size and composition of the labour force. In this context, it appears as a natural step to open a discussion on the well-known population debate in economic literature.

The least we can say is that the ongoing discussion about the relationship between individuals' living standards and population growth is fascinating. Despite decades of research, no consensus has been reached on the issue (see, for example, Kelley 1988; Ehrlich and Lui 1997; Tournemaine 2007). Then, it is interesting to study how social status comparisons may alter the different points of view shared on the issue.

From an historical perspective, the population debate in economics probably started with the seminal analysis of Malthus (1798). He argued that population growth is incompatible with long-run improvements in living standards because resources are limited. Beyond a certain level of development, increases in population size will decrease individuals' living standards, potentially leading to reduced fertility rates and the emergence of diseases, such as malnutrition. Ultimately, Malthus believed that the population should reach a constant size in the long run. Interestingly, at the same time as the publication of Malthus' work, several countries, including the UK, the US, France, and Germany, experienced the first Industrial Revolution. It led to increased living standards and population size, an outcome at odds with the prediction of the theory.

Based on the above arguments and observations, we can count three main branches regarding the impact of population growth on economic development. Firstly, building on the seminal work of Becker et al. (1990), numerous economists argue that economic development is accompanied by a simultaneous increase in the average level of education and a decrease in fertility rates (see Galor and Weil 1999; Doepke 2004). This literature implicitly suggests that population growth, through the channel of fertility, has a negative correlation with economic development. Following in Malthus's footsteps, authors such as Barro (1991) and Mankiw et al. (1992) contend that population growth is detrimental to economic development because it means sharing a limited amount of resources with a greater number of individuals.

In contrast, others belonging to a second branch, including Boserup (1965), Simon (1981), and Lee (1988), argue that the non-rival property of knowledge, or technical progress, leads to scale effects, sometimes referred to as the "Mozart effect" (Phelps 1968), or "Population Push" (Simon 1977). This means that a greater number of individuals can benefit from the production of knowledge, either through education (human capital accumulation) or R&D. In turn, it can promote economic development in the long run. The empirical work of Kremer (1993) supports this view from a historical perspective.

Finally, the third branch, comprising authors belonging to the "revisionist interpretation" of Malthusianism (see, e.g., Kelley 1988),[11] adopts a more balanced perspective. It is stated that the relationship between population growth and economic development is complex and may vary depending on the country or circumstances. For instance, population growth may act as a stimulus for economic development in low-income countries where a larger population may help overcome fixed costs of production and boost innovation (Bloom and Sachs 1998). Conversely, in high-income countries where resources are more limited, population growth may lead to a dilution of resources and will thus have a negative effect on economic growth. In this spirit, the empirical work of Crenshaw et al. (1997) and the theoretical ones of Tournemaine (2007) and Tournemaine and Luangaram (2012) show that a higher fertility rate may have: (i) short-term negative effects on economic development due to the costs of raising children to adulthood (quality-quantity trade-off on children); but also (ii) long-term positive impacts by generating a larger (educated) labour force (Mozart effect). In all, the final outcome of long-term growth depends on the relative strength of these two opposite forces.

[11] According to the revisionist interpretation of Malthusianism, population growth does not necessarily lead to overpopulation and food scarcity. This is due to the combined effect of social and economic development, as well as technological progress, which can help mitigate these risks.

The main message, then, is that a nuanced approach that takes the various mechanisms and channels through which population growth may affect economic development into account is necessary in order to draw accurate conclusions. To this end, it is crucial to consider the context and specific characteristics of each country when analysing the relationship between population growth and economic development. This is the reason social and cultural factors such as social status comparisons may play an important role in this regard.

On the Impact of Status Comparisons on Economic Development Through the Channels of Education and Fertility

As implied in the previous sections, the impact of status comparisons on economic development in societies where education (or knowledge production) and fertility play significant roles in individual decision-making depends on the transmission channel of the various effects. To illustrate this claim, in what follows, we take the view supported by Fershtman et al. (1996) and Tournemaine and Tsoukis (2009) whereby education-based comparisons also extend to the quality of jobs. We can effectively argue that education provides a means for individuals to obtain well-regarded positions in society, such as a surgeon, pilot, or engineer, among others. In addition to the pecuniary returns to education in the form of wages, individuals also obtain non-pecuniary rewards in the form of the social rank the perception of the position provides. This is important because raising children to adulthood can induce a partial sacrifice with regard to professional careers. On this point, Becker (1991) argues that women, who are the primary caregivers typically incur a considerable portion of the costs incurred in raising a child. Empirical works by Black and Juhn (2000) and Dolado et al. (2001) establish a positive correlation between women's education level and their participation in the labour force while noticing a negative relationship between fertility rates and education levels. We can then interpret this observation as a simple manifestation of the trade-off between fertility choice and professional careers at the microeconomic level.

At the macroeconomic level, it appears that the analysis of such a trade-off is more complex, or at least more dependent on the chosen formalisation. For instance, Tournemaine and Tsoukis (2010b, 2018) develop a setup "à la Becker et al. (1990)" that accounts for social interactions between individuals. They demonstrate that social status comparisons can help explain why countries that seemed stuck in poverty traps suddenly started a "great transition" to a state of perpetual development. The result occurs following a shock on individuals' preferences, leading them to allocate more resources to investments in education while reducing the number of children they bring up. In this case, social status comparisons act through the channel of the quality-quantity trade-off on children, which is beneficial to long-term economic growth because of the absence of any Mozart effect. It simply simultaneously raises the average level of education across the population and reduces the fertility rate.

However, it is also possible to obtain a very different outcome. Using a R&D-based growth model in which fertility choices are endogenous (see, e.g. Jones 2003), Tournemaine (2008) shows that social status comparisons give incentives to individuals to substitute the quantity for the quality of children. This is detrimental to long-term economic growth because, in such a formalisation, population growth stands as the ultimate engine of economic development. In other words, the Mozart effect dominates the quality-quantity trade-off on children.

In conclusion, the potential impact of status comparisons on economic development in societies where education or knowledge production and fertility play significant roles in individual decision-making depends on the transmission channel of the various effects: it can either be beneficial or detrimental to long-term economic growth as it ultimately depends on which effect between the quality-quantity trade-off on children and the Mozart effect dominates.

3 Habit Formation

We now turn to a slightly different topic that is, however, often examined in a parallel fashion to status-seeking or "keeping up with the Joneses" motives and related issues: that of "habit formation". As introduced in Chapter 3, "habits" affect the reference standard on which comparisons are made; this is the similarity with status, in which the reference standard is affected by a societal average (of consumption, wealth, or related variable). But in contrast to status, the reference now involves also past own consumption (usually), not only the societal average of the same. Clearly, status-seeking (and similar ideas) and habits occupy neighbouring positions in socio-behavioural macroeconomics, and habits, therefore, will be briefly analysed further in this section.

The Basic Concept

The notion of habit formation is often examined together with the "keeping up with the Joneses" idea because the latter exhibits significant effects in the presence of the former (see, e.g., Alonso-Carrera et al. 2004; Tsoukis 2007). Habit formation relates in effect to the concept that individuals' behaviours and preferences are shaped by their prior experiences. These habits can yield noteworthy implications for macroeconomic outcomes. In simpler terms, people tend to develop habits and routines in various aspects such as consumption, savings, and educational choices. This phenomenon is rooted in the idea that consistent repetition of a certain action over time creates an expectation of a routine; failure of that routine to continue implies a loss of utility or welfare. Consequently, established habits are difficult to break, while obtaining new habits is equally challenging, as an individual's current action is significantly influenced by their historical behaviour. This emphasises the notion that habits are typically formalised as a cumulative stock variable that accrues over time.

Following authors such as Carroll et al. (1997, 2000), Alvarez-Cuadrado et al. (2004), and Gomez (2008), the rate of change of habits per unit of time can be formalised as:

$$\dot{Q}_t = \xi\left[(X_t)^{\upsilon}\left(\overline{X}_t\right)^{1-\upsilon} - \varrho Q_t\right], \tag{27}$$

where Q_t is the current stock of habits of an individual and X_t is the corresponding current flow of actions such as consumption, savings, investments in education, and so on and $\overline{X_t}$ represents the average set of actions in the society. Parameter $0 < \nu < 1$ measures the relative influence of private and economy-wide average flows of actions in the process of habit formation. Parameter $\xi > 0$ represents the speed of adjustment of habits. It accounts for the importance of recent actions in determining the reference stock of habits: a higher value of ξ leads to a higher influence of the current individuals' actions in the determination of the future reference stock, or alternatively to a lower level of persistence in habits. Parameter $\varrho > 0$ introduces the depreciation habits rate; it stands, for instance, for the abandonment of ancient customs.

Aligned with Alvarez-Cuadrado et al. (2004), the extreme case of $\nu = 0$ can be interpreted as a scenario where individuals adopt an outward-looking perspective. In this context, the reference stock emerges as an average of economy-wide action flows, consequently condensing the reference stock's influence into an external effect. Conversely, when $\nu = 1$, individuals adopt an inward-looking stance, in which an individual's habit reference stock is rooted in their own historical action flows, a scenario where perfect information is available. In this case, individuals completely internalise the impact of their actions on the future trajectory of their habit reference stock and, by extension, on their future well-being.

Due to the formalisation of habit formation as a stock variable, incorporating habit formation into growth models presents a challenge: adding such a state variable inevitably augments the dimensionality of the dynamic problem. Despite this complexity, Gomez (2008) points out that the introduction of habit formation into growth models initially aimed to address several issues and to explain empirical observations within the confines of standard time-separable preferences. We can, for instance, cite the paper by Abel (1990) which introduces this concept to clarify the equity premium puzzle in finance.[12] Closer to growth theory, in an "AK" model, the analyses by Carroll et al. (1997, 2000) highlight the importance of habits to provide an explanation of the observed correlations between saving behaviour and long-term economic growth.[13] In the same vein, using a Ramsey-Cass-Koopmans model, Alvarez-Cuadrado et al. (2004) demonstrate that, when preferences exhibit time non-separability, the model can replicate the consumption and saving trajectories observed empirically during the initial stages of a transition following a capital stock loss. A prime example of this scenario is the capital destruction experienced by Europe and Japan during World War II (see references such as Wolf 1993; Saint-Paul 1993; Maddison 2001, for more in-depth insights).[14] Finally, in a different context, Schafer and Valente (2011) argue that economic development can impact population

[12] See, e.g. Li et al. (2021) for a recent theoretical analysis and more references on the issue related to the interplay between habit formation, consumption, and portfolio choices.

[13] See Yand and Zhang (2018) who build on the model developed by Carroll et al. (1997, 2000) to explain a variety of observed economic development configurations such as catching up, overtaking or falling behind: ultimately, the outcome depends on the relative initial endowments of economies in terms of physical capital and habits stocks.

[14] See Hiraguchi (2011) who extends the standard analyses to a two-sector model of endogenous growth to show that habit formation in consumption has a negative impact on the speed of convergence to the steady state.

dynamics through the interplay between fertility choices and consumption habits. They show that habits, besides altering the level of long-term growth, can help to explain the transitional dynamics observed in terms of fertility choices (see the previous section).

Habits in a One-Sector Model of Endogenous Growth

Model and Equilibrium Conditions

In this sub-section, we integrate habit formation into an "AK" model of endogenous growth, i.e. one without any external effects in the form of learning-by-doing or investing, of the type discussed in Sect. "A Basic Growth Model with Two Status-Seeking Motives". In this context, we will be able to clearly identify the long-term effects of habit formation on consumer behaviour. To this end, we present the basic frameworks established by Carroll et al. (1997, 2000) and Gomez (2008) and summarise their main properties.

Specifically, the production technology of output, Y_t, is characterised by:

$$Y_t = AK_t, \tag{28}$$

where $A > 0$ is a productivity parameter and K_t is the amount of physical capital employed in the production process. As in Sect. "A Basic Growth Model with Two Status-Seeking Motives", the law of motion of physical capital, K_t, is given by:

$$Y_t = C_t + \dot{K}_t + \delta K_t, \tag{29}$$

where C_t is consumption and $\delta > 0$ is a given parameter measuring the rate of depreciation of physical capital. Finally, the preferences of individuals are represented by the utility function:

$$U = \int_0^\infty \frac{\{(C_t))^{1-\gamma}(C_t/Q_t))^{\gamma}\}^{1-\theta} - 1}{1-\theta} e^{-\rho t} dt, \tag{30}$$

where (as before) $\theta > 1$ is the inverse of the elasticity of substitution, $\rho > 0$ is the rate of time preference (discount rate) and $0 < \gamma < 1$ is a measure of the weight of current consumption relative to the comparison component of such variable to past habits denoted by the stock variable, Q_t. In line with Carroll et al. (1997, 2000) and Gomez (2008), we assume that the law of motion of habits is given by Eq. (27) in which we set: $X_t \equiv C_t$. In other words, individuals compare their current level of consumption to their habits in consumption.

Maximising (30) subject to (27–29), taking $\overline{C_t}$, K_0 and Q_0 as given, the first-order conditions for an interior equilibrium are:

$$(C_t)^{-\theta}(Q_t)^{\gamma(\theta-1)} + \mu_t \xi \nu = \lambda_t, \tag{31}$$

$$A - \delta + \frac{\dot{\lambda}_t}{\lambda_t} = \rho, \tag{32}$$

$$\frac{-\gamma(C_t)^{1-\theta}(Q_t)^{\gamma(\theta-1)-1}}{\mu_t} - \varrho + \frac{\dot{\mu}_t}{\mu_t} = \rho, \tag{33}$$

where λ_t and μ_t are the co-state variables associated with the law of motions of physical capital and habits, respectively, and where we use the property of symmetry at the equilibrium, i.e. $\overline{C_t} = C_t$. The transversality conditions are: $\lim_{t\to\infty} \lambda_t K_t e^{-\rho t} = 0$ and $\lim_{t\to\infty} \mu_t Q_t e^{-\rho t} = 0$.

Similarly to Sect. "A Basic Growth Model with Two Status-Seeking Motives", Eq. (31) is an efficiency condition which must be satisfied at each instant for every individual. It states that the marginal utility gain of an additional unit of consumption, $(C_t)^{-\theta}(Q_t)^{\gamma(\theta-1)}$, plus its marginal impact on habit formation measured by $\mu_t \xi \nu$, must be equal to the shadow price of physical capital. Equation (32) is a standard asset pricing equation stating that the net marginal productivity of physical capital, $A - \delta$, plus the change in the growth rate of its shadow price must be equal to the rate of time preference. Finally, Eq. (33) is another kind of asset pricing equation involving the habit stock. It establishes that the utility loss from a greater stock of habits in consumption plus the cost involved by the abandonment of some habits (depreciation rate), ϱ, and the change in the growth rate of the shadow price of habits must be equal to the rate of time preference.

Discussion

It is crucial to highlight that incorporating habit formation in consumption, as outlined by Eq. (27), carries at least two significant implications. Firstly, by allowing the economy-wide average consumption level to influence habit formation, we implicitly introduce an external effect. Secondly, the inclusion of such a reference stock, i.e. integrating an additional state variable into the utility function, profoundly impacts individuals' dynamic optimisation problems and, consequently, the dynamics of the economy itself. As a result, in contrast to a basic "AK" model without habits, authors such as Carroll et al. (1997) and Gomez (2008) demonstrate that such a framework now exhibits transitional dynamics, resulting in the existence of a unique asymptotic steady state that is saddle point stable.[15]

The primary result we might highlight from the analysis of the transitional dynamics is the inverse relationship between the speed of convergence of variables and the strength of internalisation of the external effect, as quantified by ν (refer to Gomez 2008; Proposition 3, p. 20). The rationale is the following: as ν increases, individuals tend to prioritise their own consumption relative to the economy-wide average in the formation of their habits in consumption. In other words, this is akin to diminishing the impact of the external factors. This results in individuals being more aware of the repercussions of their present actions on their future welfare through the adverse effects of their habits. In other words, this essentially translates into a greater reluctance towards consumption changes (or an increase in risk aversion, following the terminology of Carroll et al. 1997). Consequently, we obtain a slower speed of convergence towards the asymptotic steady state. This latter is characterised by common and constant levels of the growth rate for consumption, physical capital, and habits. Denoting them by$g$, simple computations lead to:

$$g = \frac{A - \delta - \rho}{\gamma + \theta(1 - \gamma)}. \tag{34}$$

Note that in the special case of no habits in utility ($\gamma = 0$), the growth rate in (34) boils down to the standard growth rate of the AK model. With this in mind, examination of Eq. (34) reveals that $\partial g / \partial \gamma > 0$ (under the maintained assumption of $\theta > 1$, as noted above). In essence, stronger preferences for comparing current actions to past habits in consumption positively impact the long-term growth rate. Therefore, the model posits that habit formation, through comparing current consumption to past actions, plays a role akin to social status comparisons in wealth. As highlighted by Carroll et al. (1997), this property arises because an increase in γ can be interpreted as a rise in the intertemporal elasticity of substitution

[15] Readers interested in the analysis of the (saddle point) stability of equilibrium can refer to Carroll et al. (1997, 2000) and Gomez (2008).

in consumption. Notably, as depicted in Eq. (34), the term $\gamma + \theta(1 - \gamma)$ serves a function analogous to the parameter representing the inverse of the elasticity of substitution,θ, in a standard model (with equality between the two when $\gamma = 0$). Consequently, as Carroll et al. (1997, p. 345) emphasise, it implies that "[individuals are] more willing to substitute intertemporally because the gain or loss in utility associated with a given increase or decrease in consumption will be diminished by the reference stock".[16]

Examination of Eq. (34) also reveals an intriguing parallel reminiscent of the findings discussed in Sect. "Steady State" concerning status comparisons in consumption. Specifically, the external effect stemming from the influence of the economy-wide average consumption level on habits is shown to have no enduring effects on the long-run level of growth. In the same way as before, such a result can easily be overturned by considering, for instance, a model with endogenous labour supply. Introducing of that, however, would complicate drastically the characterisation of the steady state without adding much to the analysis.

References

Abel, A. 1990. Asset Pricing under Habit Formation and Catching up with the Joneses. *American Economic Review* 80 (2): 38–42.

Aghion, P., and P. Howitt. 1992. A Model of Growth through Creative Destruction. *Econometrica* 60 (2): 323–351.

Alonso-Carrera, J. 2001. More on the Dynamics in the Endogenous Growth Model with Human Capital. *Investigaciones Economicas* 25 (3): 561–583.

Alonso-Carrera, J., J. Caballé, and X. Raurich. 2004. Consumption Externalities, Habit Formation and Equilibrium Efficiency. *Scandinavian Journal of Economics* 106 (2): 231–251.

Alvarez-Cuadrado, F., G. Monteiro, and S. Turnovsky. 2004. Habit Formation, Catching Up with the Joneses, and Economic Growth. *Journal of Economic Growth* 9 (1): 47–80.

Arrow, K.J. 1962. The Economic Implication of Learning by Doing. *Review of Economic Studies* 29 (3): 55–173.

Arrow, K.J. 1971. Political and Economic Evaluation of Social Effects and Externalities. In *Frontier of Quantitative Economics*. Edited by M. Intriligator. Amsterdam: North-Holland.

[16] See also Carroll et al. (2000) for a detailed discussion of this interpretation.

Alstadsaeter, A. 2011. Measuring the Consumption Value of Higher Education. *Cesifo Economic Studies* 57 (3): 458–479.

Barro, R.J. 1990. Government Spending in a Simple Model of Endogenous Growth. *Journal of Political Economy* 98 (5): S103–S125.

Barro, R.J. 1991. Economic Growth in a Cross Section of Countries. *Quarterly Journal of Economics* 106 (2): 407–443.

Becker, G.S. 1991. *A Treatise on the Family*. Cambridge, MA: Harvard University Press.

Becker, G.S., K.M. Murphy, and R. Tamura. 1990. Human Capital, Fertility, and Economic Growth. *Journal of Political Economy* 98 (5): S12–S37.

Bertola, G. 1993. Factor Shares and Savings in Endogenous Growth. *American Economic Review* 83 (5): 1184–1198.

Black, S.E., and C. Juhn. 2000. The Rise of Female Professionals: Are Women Responding to Skill Demand? *American Economic Review* 90 (2): 450–455.

Bloom, D.E., and J.D. Sachs. 1998. Geography. *Demography, and Economic Growth in Africa* 1998 (2): 207–295.

Boonprakaikawe, J., and F. Tournemaine. 2006. Production and Consumption of Education in a R&D-Based Growth Model. *Scottish Journal of Political Economy* 53 (5): 565–585.

Boserup, E. 1965. *The Conditions of Agricultural Growth: The Economics of Agrarian Change under Population Pressure*. London: George Allen and Unwin Ltd.

Carroll, C.D., J. Overland, and D. Weil. 1997. Comparison Utility in a Growth Model. *Journal of Economic Growth* 2 (4): 339–367.

Carroll, C.D., J. Overland, and D. Weil. 2000. Saving and Growth with Habit Formation. *American Economic Review* 90 (3): 341–355.

Corneo, G., and O. Jeanne. 1997. On Relative Wealth Effects and the Optimality of Growth. *Economics Letters* 54 (1): 87–92.

Corneo, G., and O. Jeanne. 1998. Social Organization, Status and Saving Behaviour. *Journal of Public Economics* 70 (1): 37–52.

Crenshaw, E., A. Ameen, and M. Christenson. 1997. Population Dynamics and Economic Development: Age Specific Population Growth and Economic Growth in Developing Countries, 1965 to 1990. *American Sociological Review* 62 (6): 974–984.

Croix (de la), D. and M. Doepke (2004) Public Versus Private Education when Differential Fertility Matters. *Journal of Development Economics* 73 (2): 607–629.

Dodge, D.A., and D.A.A. Stager. 1972. Economic Returns to Graduate Study in Science, Engineering and Business. *Canadian Journal of Economics* 5 (2): 182–198.

Doepke, M. 2004. Accounting for Fertility Decline During the Transition to Growth. *Journal of Economic Growth* 9 (3): 347–383.

Dolado, J., F. Felgueroso, and J.F. Jimeno. 2001. Female Employment and Occupational Changes in the 1990s: How is the EU Performing Relative to the US? *European Economic Review* 45 (4–6): 875–879.

Ehrlich, I., and F. Lui. 1997. The Problem of Population and Growth: A Review of the Literature from Malthus to Contemporary Models of Endogenous Population and Endogenous Growth. *Journal of Economic Dynamics and Control* 21 (1): 205–242.

Fershtman, C., K.M. Murphy, and Y. Weiss. 1996. Social Status, Education and Growth. *Journal of Political Economy* 104 (1): 108–132.

Fisher, W.H., and F.X. Hof. 2000. Relative Consumption, Economic Growth and Taxation. *Journal of Economics* 73 (3): 241–262.

Frankel, M. 1962. The Production Function in Allocation and Growth: A Synthesis. *American Economic Review* 52 (5): 995–1022.

Futagami, K., and A. Shibata. 1998. Keeping One Step Ahead of the Joneses: Status, the Distribution of Wealth and Long Run Growth. *Journal of Economic Behavior and Organization* 36 (1): 109–126.

Galor, O., and D.N. Weil. 1999. From Malthusian Stagnation to Modern Growth. *American Economic Review* 89 (2): 150–154.

Ghosh, S., and R. Wendner. 2017. Positional Preferences and Efficient Capital Accumulation when Households Exhibit a Preference for Wealth. *Oxford Economic Papers* 70 (1): 114–140.

Gomez, M.A. 2008. Convergence Speed in the AK Endogenous Growth Model with Habit Formation. *Economics Letters* 100 (1): 16–21.

Grossman, G.M., and E. Helpman. 1991. Quality Ladders in the Theory of Growth. *Review of Economic Studies* 58 (1): 557–586.

Gullason, E.T. 1989. The Consumption Value of Schooling. An Empirical Estimate of One Aspect. *Journal of Human Resources* 24 (2): 287–298.

Hall, R.E. 1988. Intertemporal Substitution in Consumption. *Journal of Political Economy* 96 (2): 339–357.

Haveman, R.H., and B.L. Wolfe. 1984. Schooling and Economic Well-Being: The Role of Nonmarket Effects. *The Journal of Human Resources* 9 (3): 377–407.

Hiraguchi, R. 2011. A Two-Sector Endogenous Growth Model with Habit Formation. *Journal of Economic Dynamics and Control* 35 (4): 430–441.

Jones, C.I. 1995a. Time Series Tests of Endogenous Growth Models. *Quarterly Journal of Economics* 110 (2): 495–525.

Jones, C.I. 2003. Population and Ideas: A Theory of Endogenous Growth. In *Knowledge, Information, and Expectations in Modern Macroeconomics, in Honor of Edmund S Phelps*. Edited by P. Aghion, R. Frydman, J. Stiglitz, and M. Woodford. Princeton: Princeton University Press.

Kelley, A.C. 1988. Economic Consequences of Population Change in the Third World. *Journal of Economic Literature* 26 (4): 1685–1728.

Kremer, M. 1993. Population Growth and Technological Change: One Million B.C. to 1990. *Quarterly Journal of Economics* 108 (3): 681–716.

Lee, R.D. 1988. Induced Population Growth and Induced Technological Progress: Their Interaction in the Accelerating Stage. *Mathematical Population Studies* 1 (3): 265–288.

Li, D. 2002. Is the AK model still alive? The long-run relation between growth and investment re-examined. *Canadian Journal of Economics* 35: 93–113.

Li, T., S. Wang, and J. Yang. 2021. Robust Consumption and Portfolio Choices with Habit Formation. Economic Modelling 98 (C): 227–246.

Ljungqvist, L., and H. Uhlig. 2000. Tax Policy and Aggregate Demand Management Under Catching Up with the Joneses. *American Economic Review* 90 (3): 356–366.

Lucas, R.E. 1988. On the Mechanics of Economic Development. *Journal of Monetary Economics* 22 (1): 3–42.

Maddison, A. 2001. *The World Economy: A Millennial Perspective OECD*. Paris.

Malthus, T.R. 1798. *An Essay on the Principle of Population*. London: W. Pickering.

Mankiw, N.G., D. Romer, and D.N. Weil. 1992. A Contribution to the Empirics of Economic Growth. *Quarterly Journal of Economics* 107 (2): 407–437.

McGrattan, E.R. 1998. A defense of AK growth models. *Federal Reserve Bank of Minneapolis Quarterly Review* 22: 13–27.

Oosterbeek, H., and H.V. Ophem. 2000. Schooling Choices: Preferences, Discount Rates, and Rates of Return. *Empirical Economics* 25 (1): 15–34.

Pham, T.K.C. 2005. Economic Growth and Status-Seeking Through Personal Wealth. *European Journal of Political Economy* 21 (2): 404–427.

Phelps, E.S. 1968. Population Increase. *Canadian Journal of Economics* 1 (3): 497–518.

Rauscher, M. 1997. Conspicuous consumption, economic growth and taxation. *Journal of Economics* 66: 35–42.

Romer, P. 1986. Increasing Returns and Long-Run Growth. *Journal of Political Economy* 94 (5): 1002–1037.

Romer, P. 1990. Endogenous Technological Change. *Journal of Political Economy* 98 (5): S71–S102.

Saint-Paul, G. 1993. Economic Reconstruction in France: 1945–58. In Postwar Economic Reconstruction and Lessons for the East Today. Edited by R. Dornbusch, W. Nolling, and R. Layard. Cambridge MA: MIT Press.

Schaafsma, J. 1976. The Consumption and Investment Aspects of the Demand for Education. *Journal of Human Resources* 11 (2): 233–242.

Schafer, A., and S. Valente. 2011. Habit Formation, Dynamic Altruism, and Population Dynamics. *Macroeconomics Dynamics* 15 (3): 365–397.

Schultz, T.W. 1963. *The Economic Value of Education*. New York: Columbia University Press.

Simon, J.L. 1977. *The Economics of Population Growth*. Princeton: Princeton University Press.

Simon, H.A. 1981. Information-Processing Models of Cognition. *Journal of the American Society of Information Science* 32 (5): 364–377.

Smith, A. 1759, 1982. *The theory of moral sentiments*. Liberty Fund: Indianapolis.

Smith, A. 1776. *The Wealth of Nations*. W. Strahan and T. Cadell: London.

Tamura, R. 1991. Income Convergence in an Endogenous Growth Model. *Journal of Political Economy* 99 (3): 522–540.

Tournemaine, F. 2007. Can Population Promote Income Per-Capita Growth? *A Balanced Perspective, Economics Bulletin* 15 (8): 1–7.

Tournemaine, F. 2008. Social Aspirations and Choice of Fertility: Why Can Status Motive Reduce Per-Capita Growth? *Journal of Population Economics* 21 (1): 49–66.

Tournemaine, F., and P. Luangaram. 2012. R&D, Human Capital, Fertility, and Growth. *Journal of Population Economics* 25 (3): 923–953.

Tournemaine, F., and C. Tsoukis. 2008. Relative Consumption, Relative Wealth and Growth. *Economics Letters* 100 (2): 314–316.

Tournemaine, F., and C. Tsoukis. 2009. Status Jobs, Human Capital and Growth: The Effects of Heterogeneity. *Oxford Economic Papers* 61 (3): 467–493.

Tournemaine, F., and C. Tsoukis. 2010b. Status, Fertility, Growth and the Great Transition. *The Singapore Economic Review* 55 (3): 553–574.

Tournemaine, F., and C. Tsoukis. 2018. The Great Transition: Implication from Environmental Policy for the Quality-Quantity Trade-Off in Children-Rearing. *The Singapore Economic Review* 63 (5): 1155–1174.

Tsoukis, C. 2007. Keeping up with the Joneses, Growth, and Distribution. *Scottish Journal of Political Economy* 54 (4): 575–600.

Tsoukis, C. 2020. *Theory of Macroeconomic Policy*. Oxford: Oxford University Press.

Uzawa, H. 1965. Optimal Technical Change in an Aggregative Model of Economic Growth. *International Economic Review* 6 (1): 18–31.

Weiss, Y., and C. Fershtman. 1998. Social Status and Economic Performance: A Survey. *European Economic Review* 42 (3–5): 801–820.

Wolf, H. 1993. The Lucky Miracle: Germany 1945–1951. In *Postwar Economic Reconstruction and Lessons for the East Today*. Edited by R. Dornbusch, W. Nolling, and R. Layard. Cambridge MA: MIT Press.

Yand, Z., and R. Zhang. 2018. On the Diversity of Growth Patterns with Habit Formation. *Economics Letters* 170 (C): 155–158.

CHAPTER 5

Hyperbolic Discounting, Labour Supply, and Growth

1 Introduction

The aim of this Chapter is to combine hyperbolic discounting (HD) with status-seeking and to analyse the implications in terms of growth and income and wealth distribution. Of the two key features, the status motive has been discussed at length in previous Chapters; here, it will take the form of relative consumption affecting utility. The main focus of the Chapter, however, is on HD (e.g. Laibson 1997, 2001; al-Nowaihi and Dhami 2008): This is gaining attention in capturing various insights of psychology and experimental/behavioural economics about attitudes to time. The Chapter focuses mainly on HD, as a new element, but combines it with status and demonstrates how behavioural elements (exemplified here by HD) interact with social elements (exemplified by status) and thereby reinforce each other's effects, in line with arguments made by Frederick et al. (2002, p. 377).

The key idea behind hyperbolic discounting is that the same intertemporal dilemma, involving identical trade-offs and dates, will receive different resolutions depending on its proximity to the planning period. Considerable experimental evidence from humans and animals or birds (Ainslie 1992; Loewenstein and Prelec 1992; Angeletos et al. 2001; Frederick et al. 2002; DellaVigna and Malmendier 2006; DellaVigna 2009; Startz and Tsang, 2012; Sprenger 2015) shows that intertemporal

C. Tsoukis et al., *Social and Behavioural Macroeconomics*,
https://doi.org/10.1007/978-3-031-77748-6_5

decision-making involves present-bias: Individuals exhibit more impatience as the dilemma gets closer. Equivalently, taking the planning time (T) as invariant, and the dilemma involving the same trade-off between times $T + t$ and $T + t + 1$, the discount rate involved is higher if t is small—i.e. the dilemma involves the near future—and lower if t is high—the more distant future (Angeletos et al. 2001; Frederick et al. 2002). This feature is not allowed in the standard geometric/exponential discounting routinely employed in dynamic macroeconomics. Hyperbolic discounting (HD) does incorporate this present-bias, however. As argued below, both the modelling technique and the results are quite different under HD than under the standard discounting and the Euler equation it produces. There is a small but growing macroeconomics literature that incorporates HD. This Chapter aims to convey the flavour of the procedures used and the results in relation to labour supply, growth and others. While the Chapter aims to review existing work, it also offers new results; because the framework is less familiar and because of the new results, the exposition is somewhat more technical than in other Chapters. It is backed up by an accompanying paper (Tsoukis and Tournemaine 2024) that substantiates the even more technical aspects of the model.

Consider an individual who considers buying an item of consumption either at time $T + t$ ($T \geq 0, t \geq 1$) or $T + t + 1$. Roughly speaking, if the earlier date is chosen, the gain involved is Marginal Utility × Discount Rate (the latter capturing the benefit of earlier consumption); the loss is the interest rate (either as an opportunity cost of -not-saving or as the cost of a loan to facilitate the purchase). The benefit from later consumption is simply Marginal Utility. Comparing the net benefits from purchasing at $T + t$ or at $T + t + 1$ is the basic dilemma underlying intertemporal choice; the optimal solution will be to choose an intertemporal profile of consumption such that equates the two in the margin—the key insight underpinning the Euler equation we have seen in Chapter 3 and in all dynamic macroeconomic models. Obviously, the very existence of a (non-zero) discount rate implies aversion towards postponing consumption (i.e. impatience). The baseline assumption in standard models is that the discount rate is constant, as embodied in exponential or geometric discounting in continuous or discrete-time models, respectively. The implication of such discounting is that the timing of planning (T) does not matter: The same intertemporal consumption profile will arise irrespective of when the planning takes place, and hence the planning time is not specified in Euler equations. Such planning is said to be time-consistent: Any plan will be validated as time comes to put it into effect.

The experimental evidence, as mentioned, shows quite emphatically that the discount rate, while always positive, is not constant over time; it is higher if t is small and the dilemma takes place nearer the planning time (T). Hence, in addition to the standard impatience, there is an added "present-bias" when the dilemma concerns the near future. E.g. Laibson et al. (2007) find considerable divergence between discount rates within lifetimes: In one of their estimates, the short-term discount rate is 15% and the long-term discount rate is 3.8%. See also Ainslie (1992), Frederick et al. (2002), Starz and Tsang (2012). The evolutionary origins of differentiated time preferences are investigated by Gowdy et al. (2013) and Galor and Özak (2016). The implications of hyperbolic discounting, on which there is no consensus about a functional form, are potentially far-reaching. The relevance of HD has been investigated in relation to the social valuation of very long-term issues such as climate change mitigation and biodiversity preservation (Gowdy et al. 2013), pollution (Six and Wirl 2015; Strulik 2021) and renewable-resource use with or without property rights (Strulik 2021).

Such behaviour can be captured by a discount factor that takes the form of a generalised hyperbola, leading to the label "hyperbolic discounting" (HD).[1] A geometric and an HD discount factors are shown in Fig. 1 (for discrete time). The slope of the (log) discount factor is the discount rate; it is constant in the geometric case, but in the HD case it is higher early on, while asymptotically the discount rate implicit in the HD case is assumed to fall to the discount rate of the geometric case. But beyond this basic fact, the various contributions do not agree on the exact form of the HD discount factor (see e.g. Frederick et al. 2002, footnote 13; O'Donoghue and Rabin 2015; Findley and Caliendo 2014; al-Nowaihi

[1] There is of course a literature that assumes declining impatience by letting the discount factor depend on consumption (see Frederick et al. 2002); this insight is outside our scope.

and Dhami 2008).[2,3] Much of the literature adds an HD portion to the geometric/exponential discount factor (as implicitly shown in Fig. 1); following Tsoukis et al. (2017), we follow this approach here.[4]

Unlike in exponential/geometric discounting, under HD, the same intertemporal dilemma will receive different resolutions as the planning period gets nearer to it in time. The various plans (about the same dilemma) will be time-inconsistent—they will change just because of the passage of time, without any extraneous change forcing the change (Strotz 1956; Phelps and Pollak 1968; see also Frederick et al. 2002; Sprenger 2015). We do not need to look hard to find evidence of this: I know (today) that it is good for my long-term well-being to start jogging, but when tomorrow comes (when jogging should occur, and the pain from exercise incurred), the plan changes. Psychologists may argue (see Chapter 2) that the root cause of such behaviour is the tension between conflicting goals, the long-term one (health, in the above example) and the short-term one (immediate gratification or avoidance of pain). Thus, HD has the potential to explain prevarication (postponing to implement hard decisions), regret (I will regret tomorrow the TV that I buy impulsively with a loan today), and similar features of real life, yet not allowed by geometric/exponential discounting (and full rationality).

Therefore, the time of the planning matters and the perturbation arguments that underlie the Euler equation are not valid. As a result, both the modelling technique and the results are quite different under HD. To proceed, one may assume full commitment to the initial plan: e.g. people enrol at the gym so as to force themselves to do exercise regularly; students ask professors to give them deadlines spread over the entire semester rather than allowing them flexibility as in that case they end up with a big load at the end of the term; employees commit to

[2] An early approach by Phelps and Pollak (1968) and others was to postulate a "beta-delta" discounting scheme, whereby the discount factor at times T, $T + 1$, $T + 2$, …, $T + \mathrm{t}$, … is 1, $\beta\delta$, $\beta\delta^2$, … $\beta\delta^{\mathrm{t}}$, …, for $0 < \beta, < \delta 1$. In other words, the present (with discount factor 1) is sharply differentiated from the "future" by the existence of the "beta" (β), but the future is treated as relatively homogeneous (note that the discount factor from the $T + 1$ standpoint is 1, δ, δ^2, δ^3, …, with no β).

[3] Rubinstein (2003) points out the observational equivalence of exponential and hyperbolic discounting, and argues that the deeper economic, psychological and decision-making micro-foundations need to be investigated further.

[4] Cabo et al. (2016) have shown that non-exponential discounting facilitates the appearance of non-standard, non-exponential patterns of growth.

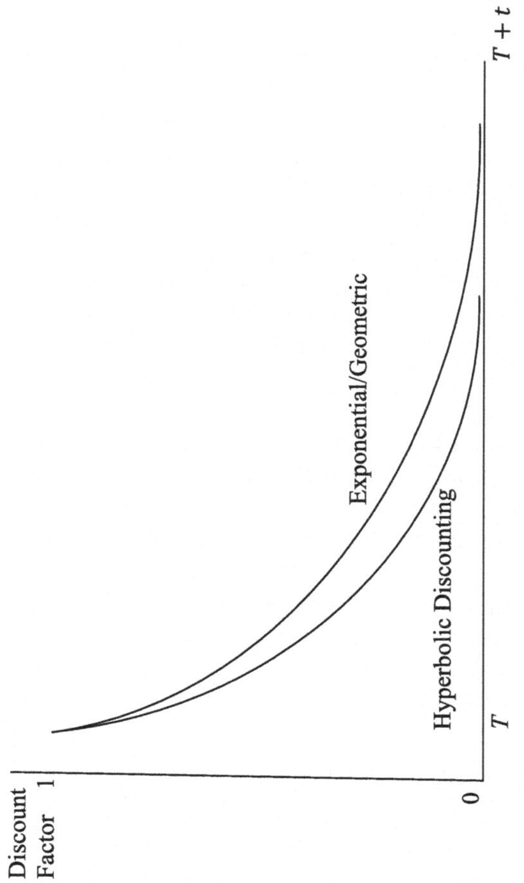

Fig. 1 The discount factor

pension schemes so as to retire with adequate means; or we commit against impulsive spending by tying our wealth to illiquid assets such as housing.[5] Evidence for commitment is ample, from enrolment at the gym to pensions and other saving products (see Attanasio and Weber 2010). In other words, individuals find it optimal to "tie their hands" in relation to saving decisions, so, as a result, they save more.[6] In the presence of full commitment, the modeller need only consider optimisation once (at the beginning of time); the plan will be adhered to, and the Euler equation is re-instated.

But commitment is not, cannot be, full. Additionally, commitment is often not sought even if there are grounds to believe that it may be beneficial (Laibson 2015; O'Donoghue and Rabin 2015). In its absence, there are various approaches to dealing with time inconsistency. Laibson (1997) and a follow-up literature (Harris and Laibson 2001; Krusell and Smith 2003) consider the discrete-time case. Their main approach, following the insights from psychology mentioned above, is to assume the "game" between two "selves" within each of us: the longer-thinking self thinks of the long-term benefit (e.g. knows that exercise is good), while the short-term self seeks immediate gratification (why bother with exercise, s/he asks lazily). The course of action we decide on is represented by the Nash equilibrium in this game. One advantage of this approach is that it introduces mechanisms of psychological self-control in real-world economic behaviour. However, analytically, this approach is quite involved; moreover, in continuous time, this modelling strategy is not available. For these reasons, this approach does not seem to have been integrated within mainstream macroeconomics; we therefore do not present it here.

[5] Ulysses and the Sirens offers a well-known example of time-inconsistent behaviour and commitment. Shall we repeat the story? Ulysses' long-term goal was to return home; but this would be jeopardised by listening to the alluring song of the Sirens, which would prompt him to visit them (immediate gratification) and thereby forget the return home (time inconsistency). Ulysses' solution was to let his comrades block their ears so as not to listen to the song and to tie him up on the mast (commitment) so that he could not visit the Sirens impulsively.

[6] The potential advantage of "tying one's hand" (i.e. denying oneself flexibility) underpins the logic behind the modern institutional architecture related to monetary policy, with Central Bank independence, inflation targeting, and the like (see e.g. Tsoukis 2020, Chapter 7). The avoidance of time inconsistency and the enhancement of the credibility of policy announcements was a key motivation for the introduction of such institutions.

One alternative is to assume a "naïve short-termist": Someone who will re-optimise tomorrow and alter the plan devised today but does not know that today. In this case (as in Strulik 2015; Caliendo and Aadland 2007; Farzin and Wendner 2014), the individual plans today (via an Euler equation), completely unaware that they will change the plan tomorrow. Yet another, more satisfactory, approach is to assume a "sophisticated short-termist": Someone who knows today that they will alter the plan tomorrow and they incorporate that in today's thinking.[7] Barro (1999) follows this approach and devises a time-consistent maximisation procedure, which is then incorporated into a continuous-time dynamic macro model; see Tsoukis, Tournemaine and Gillman (2017—henceforth TTG) for subsequent work.[8] It is clear from these and related analyses that HD plays an important role in issues related to growth theory, such as capital accumulation, saving and labour supply. This Chapter aims to showcase this importance in a setup that follows the original analysis of Barro (1999) and the subsequent development of TTG (2017) in a setup that is as general as possible, while allowing for a closed-form solution: endogenous labour supply, and constant-elasticity-of-intertemporal substitution utility and constant-elasticity of substitution (CES) production functions. As this generalises the earlier results (the discounting scheme is more general than any we are aware of; Barro 1999, considers mostly the log-utility case, and TTG, 2017, consider an AK model so labour is fixed), there is a considerable element of originality in the results, in addition to the survey element.

To preamble, we derive a rich set of results and we promise the reader that the long walk through the Chapter will be rewarding. We show that an exogenous measure of present-bias, embedded in the discounting scheme, has important implications for a whole range of key macroeconomic variables and issues of concern, such as growth, labour supply, factor shares, the fiscal spending multiplier and the difference between the real interest rate and the growth rate (the "$r - g$" question). As may

[7] Schematically, a naïve person will decide on Monday to go jogging on Tuesday but will not do it (will alter the plan); and will again decide on Tuesday to go on Wednesday and again will not go, but will yet again decide on Wednesday, and so on. A sophisticate will know that they will not carry out the plan and incorporate that into their thinking; for example, they may decide instead to do milder exercise that will be carried out.

[8] One may say that this approach treats the long run as a succession of short runs: The hapless Zeno of the caption goes from one "last" smoke to the next.

be expected of short-termism, a rise in present-bias raises the marginal propensity to consume out of intertemporal resources but decreases labour supply and growth. By increasing labour, assuming an elasticity of substitution between capital and labour in production less than unity, as the bulk of the evidence shows, then the labour share in national income falls. Furthermore, the "$r - g$" difference rises, which may increase the rate at which the capital share is rising in relation to the economy at large—according to the arguments of Piketty (2014) which we review briefly below. Thus, the rise in present-bias has important implications for both the size and growth of the overall "pie" but also its distribution and inequality.

The model also has implications for the government spending multiplier, which is positive but below unity; the latter being a point of contention in both theoretical and empirical literatures, as we review below. We show that a rise in present-bias reduces the size of the multiplier, which is somewhat surprising. Finally, we also derive the effects of the status-seeking motive on all these variables. Importantly, we show that the effects of status depend on the level of present-bias; an indication of the interplay between social and behavioural traits, as mentioned. Thus, in all hyperbolic discounting and the framework here relate to a number of issues and debates in macroeconomics. In a final Section, we discuss an extension that we have pursued in unpublished research, namely to combine status and HD more fundamentally; which can arguably strengthen the above results and relate to yet more debates in the literature.

2 The Model

The Discounting Scheme

We begin with a discussion of discounting schemes. A discounting scheme satisfies four properties:

P1. The discount factor is: $0 < \Psi(\tau, t) \leq 1$ for all $\tau \geq t$, where t is the planning time and $\tau \geq t$ the future time to which discounting applies.

P2. For the present ($\tau = t$), we have: $\Psi(t, t) = 1$

P3. The discount rate is defined as: $\frac{-\frac{d\Psi(\tau,t)}{d\tau}}{\Psi(\tau,t)} \equiv \psi_{\tau-t} \geq \frac{-\frac{d\Psi(\tau',t)}{d\tau'}}{\Psi(\tau',t)} \equiv \psi_{\tau'-t} \geq \rho$ for any $\tau' > \tau \geq t$.

P4. A positive asymptotic discount rate exists: $\lim_{\tau\to\infty} \frac{-\frac{d\Psi(\tau,t)}{d\tau}}{\Psi(\tau,t)} \equiv \rho > 0$

Geometric/exponential discounting satisfies Properties 1, 2, and 4; and 3 with equality. As mentioned, the form of HD used in the literature is not standard; any scheme that involves P3 with inequality will qualify as an HD scheme. Using the asymptotic discount rate (ρ) as the hallmark of rationality, we can define present-bias as the extra discounting that happens in the short run (i.e. the difference $\frac{-\frac{d\Psi(\tau,t)}{d\tau}}{\Psi(\tau,t)} - \rho$ for a finite τ).

For instance, in their formulation of HD, TTG (2017) uses:

$$\Psi(\tau, t) \equiv \exp\{-\rho(\tau - t)\}(1 + \delta(\tau - t))^{-\frac{\varphi}{\delta}}, \rho, \varphi, \delta \geq 0$$

which involves a mix of exponential and HD-based discounting: The former involves the standard discount rate, $\rho > 0$; the latter is parameterised by (a) the strength of HD discounting, $0 \leq \varphi < 1$, and (b) an index of present-bias, $\delta > 0$.[9] The associated discount rate is:

$$-\frac{\frac{d\Psi(\tau,t)}{d\tau}}{\Psi(\tau, t)} = \rho + \frac{\varphi}{1 + \delta(\tau - t)},$$

It is shown in the paper that this scheme satisfies all of P1–P4. In particular, this discount rate begins high and asymptotically drops to the exponential discount rate (ρ). As a result, the individual is more "presently-biased", exhibiting higher impatience in any intertemporal dilemma the nearer it appears in the future. It is easy to check that a rise in δ decreases the distant-future discount rate in relation to the near-future one, i.e. makes the present-bias more pronounced.

Using this scheme as an example, we can see the root of the time inconsistency problem. According to the above discount rate, discounting

[9] This discounting scheme adds a geometric discount rate ($\rho > 0$) to the pure HD portion used by al-Nowaihi and Dhami (2006). The reason is that in the absence of ρ, the discount rate will fall to 0 asymptotically; there is no reason to think that this should be the case. See TTG (2017) for more discussion.

between two future times $\tau' > \tau > t$ depends not only on the difference $\tau' - \tau$ (as in the exponential case) but also on the time of planning period (t) itself; to see this, write such discounting between these future dates evaluated now as:

$$\overline{\Psi}(\tau'\tau;t) \equiv \frac{\Psi(\tau',t)}{\Psi(\tau,t)} = \exp\{-\rho(\tau'-\tau)\}\frac{(1+\delta(\tau-t))^{-\varphi/\delta}}{(1+\delta(\tau'-t))^{-\varphi/\delta}}.$$

As emphasised, such a discount rate makes the optimal plan contingent on the planning time, with the resulting consequences we have described. Developing the analyses of Strotz (1956) and Phelps and Pollak (1968), Barro (1999) has presented a perturbation argument which is time-consistent as it depends on a "policy" rule (consumption rule) and the resulting consumption dynamics that are both time-consistent. We follow this procedure here.

In this Chapter, we use a more general discount factor, as follows:

$$\Psi(\tau,t) \equiv \exp\left\{-\int_t^\tau \psi_v dv\right\},\ \psi_v > \psi_s > 0\ or\ v < \mathrm{s},\ \lim_{s\to\infty}\psi_s \equiv \rho > 0 \quad (1)$$

where the $\psi_v > 0$ are the instantaneous discount rates. The property we are imposing here is that it declines monotonically over time to $\rho > 0$. We may think that, asymptotically, the discount rate is the same as the exponential one, but the HD nature of discounting adds extra discounting in the near term. It can be easily checked that all Properties above are satisfied, with 3 as inequality. Otherwise, we do not restrict the form of discounting. Let $\psi > 0$ be an "average" discount rate defined as:

$$\frac{1}{\psi} = \int_t^\infty \exp\{-\psi(\tau-t)\}d\tau := \int_t^\infty \Psi(\tau,t)d\tau \quad (2)$$

In intuitive terms, ψ is a (constant) discount rate that does the "same amount of discounting" under exponential discounting as scheme (3) will do. It is an important benchmark in what follows. Since HD imposes more discounting in the short run while asymptotically it declines to the exponential rate, we have: $\frac{\psi}{\rho} > 1$. The monotonically declining nature of ψ_v guarantees the existence of a unique positive ψ. The reason for its introduction is that going from exponential to HD involves potentially two changes, firstly in form and second in quantity. If the discount rate is high early on, as present-bias suggests, then obviously there is heavier discounting, as well as of a different form. Comparing the effects of the scheme defined in (3) with a hypothetical exponential scheme with a discount rate ψ involves a comparison of two schemes of different form that do "equally heavy" discounting. To provide more context here, there is a debate as to whether the form as well as the amount of discounting matters; TTG (2017) show that form matters, even among schemes that do an equal amount of discounting. We validate this result below.

Apart from the total extra discounting that an HD scheme imparts, encapsulated in ψ, there is also the question of the curvature of $\Psi(\tau, t)$—when the extra discounting occurs. To see that, consider Fig. 2, in which HD1 and HD2 are two profiles of hyperbolic discount rates that yield (by construction) the same ψ, but HD1 obviously imparts a higher present-bias than HD2.[10] To analyse that, we first take deviations of the discount rate around the benchmark ψ:

$$\Psi(\tau, t) \equiv \exp\left\{-\psi(\tau - t) - \int_t^\tau \tilde{\psi}_{v-t} dv\right\} \equiv \exp\left\{-\psi(\tau - t) - \tilde{\Psi}(\tau, t)\right\} \tag{1'}$$

$\tilde{\Psi}(\tau, t)$ is the corresponding discount factor in deviations form, more formally defined as:

$$\tilde{\Psi}(\tau, t) := \int_t^\tau \tilde{\psi}_v dv \tag{3}$$

Hence, the deviation discount rates $\tilde{\psi}_v \equiv \psi_v - \psi$ inherit the monotonicity property (declining) of the original discount rates but are no longer necessarily positive; they start as positive early on and become negative from a point onwards. But they do remain bounded below: $\tilde{\psi}_v > \lim_{s\to\infty} \psi_s - \psi > -\psi$.

[10] The two profiles of discount rates generate the same ψ when they produce profiles of discount factors whose integrals (areas under the curve) are equal.

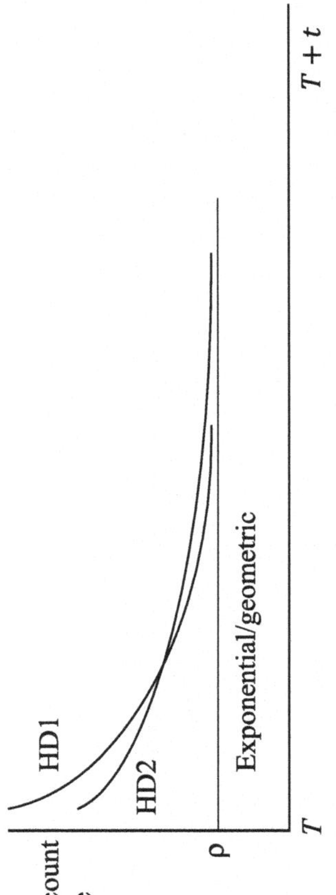

Fig. 2 Exponential/geometric and HD discount rates

To proceed, approximating $\exp\left\{-\tilde{\Psi}(\tau,t)\right\} \approx 1-\tilde{\Psi}(\tau,t)$, we have the approximate equality:

$$\Psi(\tau,t) = \exp\left\{-\psi(\tau-t)-\tilde{\Psi}(\tau,t)\right\} \approx \exp\{-\psi(\tau-t)\}\left[1-\tilde{\Psi}(\tau,t)\right] \quad (4)$$

The reason why the approximation is plausible is that, for τ − t small, $\tilde{\Psi}(\tau,t)$ will be small, while for larger τ, $\tilde{\Psi}(\tau,t)$ will again be small as an average of positive and negative values. Furthermore, using the information above, we have for $\tau \to \infty$:

$$\int_t^\infty \exp\{-\psi(\tau-t)\}d\tau := \int_t^\infty \Psi(\tau,t)d\tau = \int_t^\infty \exp\left\{-\psi(\tau-t)-\tilde{\Psi}(\tau,t)\right\}d\tau$$

Implying that:

$$\int_t^\infty \exp\{-\psi(\tau-t)\}\tilde{\Psi}(\tau,t)d\tau \approx 0 \quad (5)$$

The approximate equality (5) makes clear the sense in which $\tilde{\Psi}(\tau,t)$ is an average of discount rates (in deviations form). Now, keeping ψ constant, a greater present-bias implies that $\tilde{\Psi}(\tau,t)$ is higher early on and lower later on. Since the profile is such that (6) holds (approximately), if discounting takes place at a rate higher (lower) than a given ψ, e.g. $\overline{\psi} > (<)\psi$, then this would "penalise" the later values of $\tilde{\Psi}(\tau,t)$ more heavily (lightly). It follows that $\boldsymbol{\Psi} \equiv \int_t^\infty \exp\left\{-\overline{\psi}(\tau-t)\right\}\tilde{\Psi}(\tau,t)d\tau$ takes its sign and magnitude from the earlier (later) values, which are less penalised. Therefore, $\text{sgn}\{\boldsymbol{\Psi}\} = \text{sgn}\left\{\overline{\psi}-\psi\right\} > (<)0$. The value of Ψ depends on $\overline{\psi}$ and the curvature of $\tilde{\Psi}(\tau,t)$. For a given $\overline{\psi} > \psi$, a greater present-bias, i.e. higher early discount rates, implies a greater Ψ; in other words, the curvature of the discount factor, given the total "amount" of discounting (ψ), can be taken as an index of present-bias. We shall use this index of present-bias in what follows, cf. Sect. "The Discount Factor" (in which it turns out that $\overline{\psi} = \psi + (\sigma-1)(r-\lambda) > \psi$). Furthermore, it is obvious that the integral can be relabelled as $\Psi = \int_0^\infty \exp\{-\overline{\psi}\tau\} \tilde{\Psi}(\tau, 0)d\tau.$. The absence of time (t) makes it clear that, since $\overline{\psi}$ is constant, the integral converges to a constant independent of t.

Individuals

Except the hyperbolic discounting, the setup is standard; e.g. as in Turnovsky and Garcia-Penalosa (2006, 2007), but with hyperbolic discounting (and without agent heterogeneity). We comment on its various aspects briefly, and the interested reader should pursue more details by referring to any standard macro text (e.g. Tsoukis 2020). There is a unit mass of identical individuals. Lower cases refer to the variables of the representative individual while capitals refer to aggregate variables. Because of the unit mass and agent homogeneity, the two will be identical, except that aggregates are exogenous to the individual.[11]

The utility of the representative individual is a variant to that encountered in Chapter 4 (Eq. 4.3):

$$U_t \equiv \int_t^\infty \frac{(c_\tau - \theta C_\tau)^{(1-\sigma)}}{1-\sigma}(1 - l_\tau)^{(1-\sigma)\eta}\Psi(\tau, t)d\tau, \tag{6}$$
$$0 < l_\tau < 1; \sigma \geq 1, 0 < \theta < 1, \eta \geq 0$$

The elasticity of intertemporal substitution in consumption is $1/\sigma$; the bulk of the evidence shows it to be less than unity (Hall 1988; Turnovsky and Garcia-Penalosa 2006), so we assume $\sigma \geq 1$. The equality is allowed against the evidence, in order to incorporate log-utility, a very useful theoretical benchmark. $0 < \theta < 1$ parameterises the "status" or "keeping up with the Joneses" effect (see Chapters 3 and 4). C_τ is average consumption (given to the individual) and the reference standard for the social comparisons. $\eta \geq 0$ is the "Frisch" elasticity of labour supply, which is the elasticity of the substitution effect only—see King, Plosser and Rebelo (1988). The AK model is the special case of $\eta = 0$, therefore $l = L =$

[11] The homogeneity specification allows the determination of aggregate variables to be made independently of the distribution of individuals; this facilitates aggregation. On the other hand, distribution does depend on aggregate variables. In general, homogeneity (the structural parameters of all individuals are identical, and only initial endowments can vary), allows a limited discussion of distribution (the "representative-agent theory of distribution", see Caselli and Ventura 2000).

1, for all τ, see below. This special case facilitates the comparison of the results obtained here with those that consider the AK model (such as Tsoukis et al., 2017, and much of the HD literature).

Equation (6) above essentially re-parameterises Eq. (4.3) of Chapter 4. Aside from trivial parameter re-labelling, the more essential differences are: (i) the status effect is subtractive and not relative; (ii) there is no status effect related to capital or wealth (only to consumption); and (iii) discounting takes the hybrid HD-exponential form, rather than the pure exponential as in (4.3).

We next turn to the budget constraint of the representative individual. As commonly assumed, the individuals of this economy own all the capital stock (K), which they rent to the perfectly competitive firms and earn the real interest rate (r) per unit. Individuals also earn the real wage (w) for their labour services. There are no taxes. Both r and w are taken as given by both individuals and firms. Therefore, the individual's budget constraint is:

$$\frac{dk_t}{dt} = r_t k_t + w_t l_t - c_t, \tag{7}$$

The First-Order-Condition (FOC) for labour is (in obvious notation), $U_l/U_C = w$; therefore, we get:

$$\frac{\eta(c_t - \theta C_t)}{(1 - l_t)} = \mathrm{w}_t \tag{8}$$

The real wage acts as the opportunity cost of leisure and the marginal rate of transformation between labour and consumption). Imposing symmetry ($c_t = C_t$, $l_t = L_t$), we get:

$$\frac{\eta C_t(1 - \theta)}{(1 - L_t)} = w_t \tag{8$'$}$$

The real wage $\mathrm{w_t}$ is common across individuals. So, an alternative form of (8′) is:

$$0 < L_t = 1 - \frac{\eta(1 - \theta)C_t}{w_t} \leq 1 \tag{9}$$

The restriction is imposed as labour is positive and a fraction of the available time. And leisure $(1 - L)$ valued at the wage becomes:

$$w_t(1 - L_t) = \eta(1 - \theta)C_t \tag{10}$$

This is intuitive: the two goods (consumption and leisure) are in proportion to each other, determined by the Frisch elasticity and the status motive. Therefore, consumption gets a fraction of total possible income (i.e. that obtainable by working the full-time endowment of 1) and leisure (valued at the wage) gets the rest. The greater is $\eta(\theta)$, the more (less) is leisure and the less (more) labour and consumption. In other words, a greater status motive induces more labour (as we have already seen) and a greater labour elasticity more leisure. With $\eta = 0$, there is no leisure and $l_t = L_t = 1$ in all t. So, η can be taken as an index of labour flexibility.

We next turn to the intertemporal optimality condition, which is now more complicated in view of the time inconsistency. It will be recalled that the procedure based on the Euler equation is no longer valid. To proceed, we re-write utility (6) with (8) as:

$$U_t \equiv \int_t^\infty \frac{(c_\tau - \theta C_\tau)^{(1-\sigma)(1+\eta)}}{1-\sigma} \left(\frac{\eta(1-\theta)}{w_\tau}\right)^{(1-\sigma)\eta} \Psi(\tau, t)d\tau, \qquad (6')$$

$$0 < l_\tau < 1; \sigma \geq 1, 0 < \theta < 1, \eta \geq 0$$

In analogy to Barro (1999; see also TTG, 2017), we linearise this for a small time period $[t, t+\varepsilon]$, with $\varepsilon > 0$:

$$\frac{(1-\sigma)U_t}{H} = \varepsilon(c_t - \theta C_t)^{(1-\sigma)(1+\eta)} w_t^{-(1-\sigma)\eta} + \int_{t+\varepsilon}^\infty (c_\tau - \theta C_\tau)^{(1-\sigma)(1+\eta)} w_\tau^{-(1-\sigma)\eta} \Psi(\tau, t)d\tau \qquad (11)$$

where $H \equiv (1-\theta)^{(1-\sigma)\eta} \eta^{(1-\sigma)\eta}$.

We also linearise the individual's budget constraint (7) likewise:

$$k_{t+\varepsilon} = (1 + \varepsilon r_t)k_t + \varepsilon w_t l_t - \varepsilon c_t \qquad (7')$$

The latter equality uses (8). The FOC for maximisation of (11) with respect to c_t subject to the budget constraint (7′) is:

$$\frac{1}{H(1+\eta)}\frac{dU_t}{dc_t} = \varepsilon(c_t - \theta C_t)^{(1-\sigma)(1+\eta)-1} w_t^{-(1-\sigma)\eta}$$
$$+ \left\{ \int_{t+\varepsilon}^{\infty} (c_\tau - \theta C_\tau)^{(1-\sigma)(1+\eta)-1} w_\tau^{-(1-\sigma)\eta} \frac{dc_\tau}{dc_{t+\varepsilon}} \Psi(\tau, t) d\tau \right\} \frac{dc_{t+\varepsilon}}{dk_{t+\varepsilon}} \frac{dk_{t+\varepsilon}}{dc_t} = 0. \tag{12}$$

Equation (12) replaces the perturbation argument underlying the Euler equation with one with essentially the same logic but couched somewhat differently (in terms of a variable λ_t, as will be seen shortly). The first part on the right gives the marginal utility from a current rise in consumption now, while the second part gives the corresponding sacrifice in future consumption that just about satisfies the intertemporal budget constraint; when the intertemporal profile of consumption is optimal, the two parts will sum up to zero, and there will not be any scope of reallocating consumption across time.

Where we obtain from the linearised budget constraint (7′):

$$\frac{dk_{t+\varepsilon}}{dc_t} = -\varepsilon. \tag{13}$$

Furthermore, Barro (1999) and Tsoukis et al. (2017) hypothesise the existence of a $0 < \lambda_t < 1$ such that:

$$c_t = \lambda_t(k_t + \overline{w}_t), 0 < \lambda_t < 1 \tag{14}$$

Accordingly, λ_t is a postulated marginal propensity to consume out of lifetime resources. (Note that this is not a Lagrange multiplier). λ_t is assumed to be independent of position in any form of distribution of income or consumption, so it is common across individuals, but time-varying. In fact, it turns out to be a key variable in the model.

Life-time labour earnings, $\overline{w}_t$, is defined as[12]:

$$\overline{w}_t \equiv \int_t^{\infty} w_\tau l_\tau \exp\left\{-\int_t^{\tau} r_v dv\right\} d\tau, \tag{15}$$

so that:

$$\frac{d\overline{w}_t}{dt} = -w_t l_t + r_t \overline{w}_t \tag{15'}$$

Finally, time-differentiating (14), with the shorthand $\dot{x}_t \equiv \frac{dx_t}{dt}$, and using (7) and (15′), gives:

$$\dot{c}_t = (r_t - \lambda_t)c_t + \dot{\lambda}_t c_t / \lambda_t \tag{16}$$

Therefore, integrating (16), we obtain as in Tsoukis et al. (2017):

$$c_\tau = \exp\left\{\int_{t+\varepsilon}^{\tau} (r_v - \lambda_v + \dot{\lambda}_v/\lambda_v) dv\right\} C_{t+\varepsilon}, \tag{16'}$$

With $\dot{\lambda}_v \equiv d\lambda_v/dv$. Or, using the shorthand notation:

$$\Lambda_{\tau-t-\varepsilon} \equiv \int_{t+\varepsilon}^{\tau} (r_v - \lambda_v + \dot{\lambda}_v/\lambda_v) dv \tag{17}$$

$$c_\tau = \exp\{\Lambda_{\tau-t-\varepsilon}\} c_{t+\varepsilon}, \tag{18}$$

This further implies:

$$\frac{dc_\tau}{dc_{t+\varepsilon}} = \exp\{\Lambda_{\tau-t-\varepsilon}\}, \tag{18'}$$

[12] It will be noticed that the discounting of future labour earnings takes place in a "rational manner" at the economy-wide real interest rate (which is assumed known with certainty). However, an argument can be made that present-bias or myopia may extend to monetary sums as well as utility; the future is inherently uncertain and its treatment varies even among the best-informed agents. In that case, the discounting should obey a scheme like (1), with higher discount rates in the short run than in the long run. We know however of no analysis that deals with that case, which we leave to future research work. A conjecture may be made that this type of present-bias may reinforce that in utility; but this is no more than a conjecture.

and

$$c_\tau{}^{-\sigma} = \exp\{-\sigma\Lambda_{\tau-t-\varepsilon}\}c_{t+\varepsilon}{}^{-\sigma}. \tag{18''}$$

Now, we use all the information from (13), (14), (18), and (18′) into (12), to obtain:

$$\begin{aligned}&(c_t - \theta C_t)^{(1-\sigma)(1+\eta)-1} w_t^{-(1-\sigma)\eta}\\ &= \left\{\int_{t+\varepsilon}^{\infty} (c_\tau - C_\tau)^{(1-\sigma)(1+\eta)-1} w_\tau^{-(1-\sigma)\eta} \exp\{\Lambda_{\tau-t-\varepsilon}\}\Psi(\tau,t)d\tau\right\}\lambda_{t+\varepsilon}\end{aligned} \tag{19}$$

Now, Eqs. (14, 15, 18, 18′) can be readily aggregated using the symmetry property, as before. Therefore we have:

$$C_t = \lambda_t\left(K_t + \overline{W}_t\right), \quad 0 < \lambda_t < 1 \tag{20a}$$

$$\overline{W}_t \equiv \int_t^{\infty} w_\tau L_\tau \exp\left\{-\int_t^{\tau} r_v dv\right\}d\tau \tag{20b}$$

$$C_\tau = \exp\{\Lambda_{\tau-t-\varepsilon}\}C_{t+\varepsilon}, \tag{20c}$$

$$C_\tau{}^{-\sigma} = \exp\{-\sigma\Lambda_{\tau-t-\varepsilon}\}C_{t+\varepsilon}{}^{-\sigma} \tag{20d}$$

$$\frac{\dot{C}_t}{C_t} = (r_t - \lambda_t) + \frac{\dot{\lambda}_t}{\lambda_t} \tag{20e}$$

(20e) is written in the form of usual Euler equation which it replaces. We then use (20a–20d) into (19) to obtain:

$$\begin{aligned}&C_t^{(1-\sigma)(1+\eta)-1} w_t^{-(1-\sigma)\eta}\\ &= \left\{\int_{t+\varepsilon}^{\infty} C_\tau^{(1-\sigma)(1+\eta)-1} w_\tau^{-(1-\sigma)\eta} \exp\{\Lambda_{\tau-t-\varepsilon}\}\Psi(\tau,t)d\tau\right\}\lambda_{t+\varepsilon}.\end{aligned}$$

Letting $\Omega_t \equiv \frac{C_t}{w_t} > 0$ be a shorthand for the consumption-wage ratio, we can express the optimal consumption profile as:

$$C_t^{-\sigma}\Omega_t^{(1-\sigma)\eta} = \lambda_{t+\varepsilon} C_{t+\varepsilon}^{-\sigma}\left\{\int_{t+\varepsilon}^{\infty}\Omega_\tau^{(1-\sigma)\eta}\exp\{(1-\sigma)\Lambda_{\tau-t-\varepsilon}\}\Psi(\tau,t)d\tau\right\} \tag{19'}$$

Letting $\varepsilon \to 0$, and imposing $C_{t+\varepsilon} \to C_t$ so that there is no arbitrary jump in consumption as in Barro (1999) and Tsoukis et al. (2017). we get:

$$\lambda_t = \frac{\Omega_t^{(1-\sigma)\eta}}{\left\{\int_t^{\infty}\Omega_\tau^{(1-\sigma)\eta}exp\{(1-\sigma)\Lambda_{\tau-t}\}\Psi(\tau,t)d\tau\right\}}. \tag{21}$$

Equation (21) is one of the key equations of the model, giving the dynamics of λ_t. It replaces the Euler equation-based consumption dynamics of standard models. It relies on the perturbation argument underlying equation (12), which embodies optimisation. Although the discount rates decline over time, their inclusion in an integral implies that they, and thus λ_t, can be constant (in the steady state); something that could not happen in the conventional Euler equation. A further remark is that Ω_t is introduced because of endogenous labour. This term disappears in the standard AK model (as e.g. in Tsoukis et al., 2017).

The rest of the model is quite standard; we turn to it now.

Firms

We next turn to firms. There is a unit mass of identical, perfectly competitive firms. The hire labour and capital from the individuals in equal measure; so, each individual person rents an equal amount of labour to all firms, and similarly with capital. Firms employ them with a production function of the CES form[13]:

$$y_t = A\left(\phi(k_t)^{\frac{\varphi-1}{\varphi}} + (1-\phi)(K_t l_t)^{\frac{\varphi-1}{\varphi}}\right)^{\frac{\varphi}{\varphi-1}}, \quad 0 < \phi < 1, \quad 0 < \varphi \leq 1 \tag{22}$$

where y_t, k_t, and l_t (in lower cases) are the variables that pertain to the individual firm (and not, as in the earlier Section, to the individual person) and capital cases refer to aggregates (e.g. capital K_t). $A > 0$ is general-purpose technology (available equally to all firms without cost), which we keep constant but parametric. $\varphi > 0$ is the elasticity of substitution between capital and labour in production (note that $\phi \neq \varphi$). The balance of evidence suggests that $\varphi < 1$ (see Tsoukis 2020, Chapter 1). However, as an important benchmark, we shall also allow the case of $\varphi = 1$, the Cobb–Douglas production function with the unitary elasticity of substitution. $K_t l_t$ is labour in efficiency terms; the existence of aggregate capital captures externalities arising from "learning-by-investing" (Romer, 1986) or productive public services (Barro, 1990). As mentioned in Chapter 4, the constant returns to scale to broad capital (including the privately employed part and the effect from the externalities) guarantees perpetual growth. The diminishing marginal product to each factor employed in private production ensures interior solutions.

As is standard, the firm maximises profits: $y_t - r_t k_t - w_t l_t$, in obvious notation. Due to perfect competition, the first-order condition (FOC) with respect to labour equalises the market wage (given to the firm) with the marginal product of labour:

$$w_t = \frac{\partial y_t}{\partial l_t} = A\left(\phi(k_t)^{\frac{\varphi-1}{\varphi}} + (1-\phi)(K_t l_t)^{\frac{\varphi-1}{\varphi}}\right)^{\frac{1}{\varphi-1}}(1-\phi) l_t^{\frac{-1}{\varphi}} \tag{23}$$

Under symmetry, when $k_t = K_t$ and $l_t = L_t$, we may write:

$$y_t = AK_t f(l_t) \tag{22'}$$

[13] In fact, it is fairly straightforward to derive essentially the same results with a more general production function than even CES, providing they retain the key properties of diminishing marginal products of the privately employed factors and constant returns to scale to a broad definition of capital. See the companion research article for more information.

$$w_t = (1-\phi)Ak_t\left(\frac{f(l_t)}{l_t}\right)^{\frac{1}{\varphi}} = Ak_t f\prime(l_t) \tag{23'}$$

Using the shorthand notation:

$$f(L_t) = f(l_t) \equiv \left(\phi + (1-\phi)l_t^{\frac{\varphi-1}{\varphi}}\right)^{\frac{\varphi}{\varphi-1}} \tag{24}$$

Note that because of symmetry, the aggregate and individual version of $f(.)$ coincide (except the change in notation). For future reference, we also note that:

$$\frac{f(L_t)}{L_t} = \left(\frac{\phi + (1-\phi)L_t^{\frac{\varphi-1}{\varphi}}}{L_t^{\frac{\varphi-1}{\varphi}}}\right)^{\frac{\varphi}{\varphi-1}} = \left(\phi L_t^{\frac{1-\varphi}{\varphi}} + (1-\phi)\right)^{\frac{\varphi}{\varphi-1}} \geq 1 \tag{25}$$

The sign follows from $0 < l_t \leq 1$ and $0 < \phi < 1, 0 < \varphi \leq 1$. When $l_t = 1$ (under $\eta = 0$), the relation above becomes an equality. Furthermore, we have:

$$f\prime(L_t)L_t = (1-\phi)\left(\frac{f(L_t)}{L_t}\right)^{\frac{1}{\varphi}} L_t$$

and

$$\begin{aligned}\frac{d\{f'(L_t)L_t\}}{dL_t} &= \frac{1}{\varphi}(1-\phi)\left(\frac{f(L_t)}{L_t}\right)^{\frac{1-\varphi}{\varphi}}\left\{f'(L_t) - \frac{f(L_t)}{L_t}\right\} \\ &\quad + (1-\phi)\left(\frac{f(L_t)}{L_t}\right)^{\frac{1}{\varphi}} = \\ &= \frac{1}{\varphi}(1-\phi)\left(\frac{f(L_t)}{L_t}\right)^{\frac{1}{\varphi}}\left\{\varphi - 1 + \left(\frac{f(L_t)}{L_t}\right)^{\frac{1-\varphi}{\varphi}}\right\} > 0\end{aligned} \tag{25'}$$

As $\frac{f(L_t)}{L_t} \geq 1$. This information will be used below.

From (10), we get the consumption-wage ratio as[14]:

$$\Omega_t \equiv \frac{C_t}{w_t} = \frac{1 - L_t}{\eta(1-\theta)} \tag{26}$$

In the steady state, L_t and therefore Ω_t will be constant.
The FOC with respect to the interest rate is:

$$r_t = \phi A(f(L))^{\frac{1}{\varphi}} = A\frac{\phi}{\left(\phi + (1-\phi)L_t^{\frac{\varphi-1}{\varphi}}\right)^{\frac{1}{1-\varphi}}} = Af(L_t) - Af\prime(L_t)L_t \tag{27}$$

Symmetry is used; the second equality uses NIA (see below) and, apart from tax, it is often expressed in a similar way.

National Income Accounting (NIA)

There is a government sector that collects no tax, yet it engages in deficit-financed spending in proportion $0 < \gamma < 1$ of GDP.[15] This buys output symmetrically from all firms and distributes it as public goods and services free at the point of use. (Those public services/goods do not enter individual utility.) All output, inclusive of what is destined to be public services, is remunerated as either labour or rental income (there are no profits due to perfect competition). There is no capital depreciation and no external sector. Hence, the three sides of NIA (value-added, expenditure and income) read as:

$$Y_t = C_t + \gamma Y_t + \dot{K}_t = w_t L_t + r_t K_t \tag{28}$$

[14] It should be recalled that the lower-case notation in this sub-Section pertains to the firm, not the individual. Hence, because of symmetry, the representative firm uses (10), not (8).

[15] This is obviously not realistic but it is simplest, both analytically and also notionally: It disentangles the pure spending effect of government (included) from the disincentive(s) due to tax (excluded).

Equilibrium

Equilibrium satisfies individual behaviour, namely the first-order conditions of the individual (8) and (12), the budget constraint (7) and their aggregate equivalents under symmetry; the definition of the propensity to spend (λ_t) (14) and intertemporal labour earnings (15); the representative firm's production function (22) and FOC (23′), (27); and NIA (28). Thus, all markets clear: The output market clears by (28), consumption expenditure (20a, b, e) and supply (the production function 22); the labour market clears by demand (given inversely from the aggregate version of 23′) and supply (10); the capital market clears by demand (inversely from 27) and supply that can be read off the income side of GDP (28). Because of symmetry, individual and aggregate markets clear simultaneously.

The Full System

The final equations of the model are the dynamics of λ_t (21) with definition (26), consumption dynamics (20e), labour (10) and investment derived as a residual from the income Eq. (28). The system is usually consolidated into two final dynamic equations as follows. Using the shorthand $z_t \equiv \frac{C_t}{K_t}$ as the consumption-capital ratio, we combine the consumption and investment Eqs. (20e and 28) with the aggregate version of production (22), to get:

$$\frac{\dot{z}_t}{z_t} = \frac{\dot{C}_t}{C_t} - \frac{\dot{K}_t}{K_t} = r_t - \lambda_t + \frac{\dot{\lambda}_t}{\lambda_t} - Af(L_t)(1-\gamma) + z_t \tag{29}$$

Note the existence of labour in both the production function and implicitly the interest rate (cf. the interest rate 27); we want to substitute labour out. Combining the labour Eq. (10) with the firm FOC (23′), we have:

$$(1-\phi)AK_t\overline{L}(L_t) = \eta(1-\theta)C_t$$

Where $\overline{L}(L_t) \equiv (1-L_t)\left(\frac{f(L_t)}{L_t}\right)^{\frac{1}{\varphi}}$, with $\overline{L}\prime(.) = -\left(\frac{f(L_t)}{L_t}\right)^{\frac{1}{\varphi}} + \frac{1}{\varphi}\frac{(1-L_t)}{L_t}\left(\frac{f(L_t)}{L_t}\right)^{\frac{1}{\varphi}}\left[\frac{df(L_t)}{dL_t}\frac{L_t}{f(L_t)} - 1\right] < 0$. The negative sign is guaranteed by: $\frac{df(L_t)}{f(L_t)} - \frac{dL_t}{L_t} = \frac{(1-\phi)L_t^{\frac{\varphi-1}{\varphi}}}{\phi+(1-\phi)L_t^{\frac{\varphi-1}{\varphi}}}\frac{dL_t}{L_t} - \frac{dL_t}{L_t} < 0$, hence $\frac{df(L_t)}{dL_t}\frac{L_t}{f(L_t)} \leq 1$. Solving for the consumption-capital ratio, we obtain:

$$z_t = \frac{C_t}{K_t} = \frac{A(1-\phi)}{\eta(1-\theta)}\overline{L}(L_t) \tag{30}$$

Finally, solving for labour:

$$L_t = L\left(\frac{\eta(1-\theta)}{A(1-\phi)}z_t\right), \tag{30'}$$

where $L(.) \equiv \overline{L}^{-1}(.)$ and therefore $L\prime(.) = \left(\overline{L}^{-1}\right)\prime(.) < 0$.

Finally, (27—the right-hand part) and (30′) into (29) deliver:

$$\frac{\dot{z}_t}{z_t} = \gamma Af(L_t) - Af\prime\left(L\left(\frac{\eta(1-\theta)}{A(1-\phi)}z_t\right)\right)L\left(\frac{\eta(1-\theta)}{A(1-\phi)}z_t\right) - \lambda_t + \frac{\dot{\lambda}_t}{\lambda_t} + z_t \tag{29'}$$

Since $-\frac{d\{f\prime(L)L\}}{dL} + \gamma\frac{d\{f(L_t)\}}{dL_t} < 0$ (see 25′ above) and $L'(.) < 0$, , it follows that the right-hand side of (29′) depends positively on z_t.

The other dynamic equation is Eq. (21), with Ω_t substituted out as follows: Using definition (26), the aggregate version of the wage-FOC Eq. (23′) and the solution for labour (30′), we have:

$$\Omega_t \equiv \frac{C_t}{w_t} = z_t\frac{K_t}{w_t} = \frac{z_t}{Af\prime\left(L\left(\frac{\eta(1-\theta)}{A(1-\phi)}z_t\right)\right)} \equiv \Omega(z_t) \tag{26'}$$

With $\Omega\prime(z_t) = \frac{\Omega_t}{z_t} - \Omega_t\frac{f\prime\prime(L(.))}{f\prime(L(.))}L\prime(.)\frac{\eta(1-\theta)}{A(1-\phi)}$ and approximating from (30′): $L_t \approx 1 + L\prime(.)\frac{\eta(1-\theta)}{A(1-\phi)}z_t$ (note from 10 that $L_t = 1$ when $z_t = 0$), we have:

$$\Omega\prime(z_t) = \frac{\Omega_t}{z_t}\left[1 - \frac{f''(L(.))L(.)}{f\prime(L(.))} + \frac{f''(L(.))}{f\prime(L(.))}z_t\right] > 0 \tag{31}$$

The sign follows from $\frac{f''(L(.))L(.)}{f\prime(L(.))} = \frac{\varphi-1}{\varphi}(1-\phi) < 0$ (cf. 25′). With (26′), we may finally write:

$$\lambda_t = \frac{(\Omega(z_t))^{(1-\sigma)\eta}}{(1+\eta)\left\{\int\limits_t^{\infty} (\Omega(z_\tau))^{(1-\sigma)\eta} exp\{(1-\sigma)\Lambda_{\tau-t}\}\Psi(\tau,t)d\tau\right\}} \tag{21′}$$

We are finally there. Equations (21′) and (29′) form a 2 × 2 dynamic system in λ_t and z_t. The discussion of the dynamics is beyond our scope here and therefore omitted. The interested reader can consult an unpublished companion piece for more information.[16] Instead, we proceed directly to the analysis of the steady state, after a brief digression on factor shares.

Factor Shares

Straightforward derivations from the FOC (23′) and (27) yield the following labour and capital shares in GDP:

$$\frac{w_t L_t}{Y_t} = \frac{f\prime(L_t)L_t}{f(L_t)} = \frac{(1-\phi)}{\phi L_t^{\frac{1-\varphi}{\varphi}} + (1-\phi)} \tag{32a}$$

and

$$\frac{r_t K_t}{Y_t} = \frac{f(L_t) - f\prime(L_t)L_t}{f(L_t)} = \frac{\phi L_t^{\frac{1-\varphi}{\varphi}}}{\phi L_t^{\frac{1-\varphi}{\varphi}} + (1-\phi)} \tag{32b}$$

The two shares add up to one, i.e. they exhaust output (as there are not taxes).

3 Steady State

As discussed below, there exists a unique steady state, in which the labour supply (L), the marginal propensity to consume out of intertemporal resources (λ), the real interest rate (r), the real wage (w), the

[16] The system is saddle point stable, with two eigenvalues of positive sign and one negative, corresponding to one predetermined variable ($c_t = C_t/A_t K_t$) and two "jump" ones related to the marginal propensity to consume out of lifetime resources, λ_t.

consumption-capital ratio (C_t/K_t) and the consumption-wage ratio ($\Omega = C_t/w_t$), all remain constant. As ratios remain constant, a balanced-growth occurs: The growing variables grow at the same rate (g), which is recovered from (20e) as: $g = r - \lambda$.

The Discount Factor

With a constant Ω, the version of (21′) that applies in the steady state is:

$$\lambda = \frac{1}{\left\{\int_t^\infty \exp\{(1-\sigma)\Lambda_{\tau-t}\}\Psi(\tau,t)d\tau\right\}} = \frac{1}{\int_t^\infty \exp\left\{[-\psi-(\sigma-1)(r-\lambda)](\tau-t)-\tilde{\Psi}(\tau,t)\right\}d\tau} \qquad (33)$$

The second equation uses the definition (17) for the steady state (when $r_v = r$, $\lambda_v = \lambda$ and $\dot{\lambda}_v = 0$) and the decomposition (1′). This equation and its implications for the marginal propensity to spend out of intertemporal resources (λ) is worth discussing in some detail. First, do let us note that the integral in the denominator converges to a positive constant. This is guaranteed because in steady-state growth, $r > \lambda$, and $\sigma > 1$, therefore in terms of the discussion surrounding Eq. (5), $\overline{\psi} \equiv \psi + (\sigma-1)(r-\lambda) > \psi$. Hence, following on from that discussion, $\boldsymbol{\Psi} \equiv \int_t^\infty \exp\left\{-\overline{\psi}(\tau-t)-\tilde{\Psi}(\tau,t)\right\}d\tau > 0$ and the integral converges to a positive constant. For future reference, and following from the discussion of Sect. "The Discounting Scheme", with $\overline{\psi} > \psi$ therefore $\boldsymbol{\Psi} > 0$, a rise in present-bias will raise Ψ; this will be used shortly.

A second remark concerns some special cases:

- Consider the purely exponential case, whereby $\psi = \rho$ and $\tilde{\Psi}(\tau,t) = 0$, therefore:
  $$\lambda^{EXP} = \frac{1}{\int_t^\infty \exp\{[-\rho-(\sigma-1)(r-\lambda^{EXP})](\tau-t)\}d\tau} = \rho + (\sigma-1)(r-\lambda^{EXP}),$$
  in which case
  $\lambda^{EXP} = \frac{\rho+(\sigma-1)r}{\sigma}$ and the growth rate is $g = r - \lambda^{EXP} = \frac{r-\rho}{\sigma}$ as in the standard model.
- The purely exponential case with unitary elasticity of intertemporal substitution ($\sigma = 1$): In that case : $\lambda = \rho, g = r - \rho$.

- The existence of present-bias implies that $\lambda \geq \lambda^{\mathrm{EXP}}$. To see that, use the decomposition in (4), the definition of Ψ and $\overline{\psi} \equiv \psi + (\sigma - 1)(r - \lambda)$, to write λ as:

$$\lambda = \frac{1}{\int_t^\infty \exp\{-\overline{\psi}(\tau - t)\}\left[1 - \tilde{\Psi}(\tau, t)\right]d\tau}$$
$$= \frac{1}{\int_t^\infty \exp\{-\overline{\psi}(\tau - t)\}d\tau - \Psi} > \overline{\psi} = \psi + (\sigma - 1)(r - \lambda) \geq \lambda^{EXP},$$

with equality when $\psi = \rho$.

The Full System

From (9), labour supply is:

$$0 < L = 1 - \eta(1 - \theta)\Omega < 1 \tag{9'}$$

where Ω is taken from (26). As the wage grows at rate g, the intertemporal labour earnings (20b) becomes:

$$\overline{W}_t = \frac{w_t}{r - g}L \tag{20b'}$$

From (20e) growth is:

$$g = r - \lambda \tag{20e'}$$

Therefore, with (26), consumption (20a) becomes:

$$C_t = \lambda(K_t + w_t L/(r - g)) = \lambda K_t + w_t L \tag{20a'}$$

The intuition behind consumption (20a′) is straightforward as well as illuminating: Individuals consume a fraction of their wealth plus (all of) their wage bill. This equation generalises the solution for consumption obtained under exponential discounting, which is $C_t = \rho K_t + w_t L$ (see e.g. Alesina and Rodrik, 1994) and which becomes a special case in our framework when there is no present-bias. As a greater present-bias increases λ, as will be shown shortly, the present-bias increases the fraction of lifetime resources consumed currently.

From the aggregate version of (23′) and (25), the wage-capital ratio is:

$$\frac{w_t}{K_t} = Af'(L) \tag{23''}$$

where it should be recalled that $f''(.) < 0$. And from (27):

$$r = Af(L) - Af\prime(L)L \tag{27'}$$

We have that $r\prime(L) = Af\prime(L) - Af\prime(L) - Af''(L)L = -Af''(L)L > 0$.
Further, from (9′) and (20a′), we get: $C_t = \lambda_t K_t + w_t - \eta(1-\theta)C_t$, so consumption becomes:

$$C_t = \frac{1}{1+\eta(1-\theta)}(\lambda K_t + w_t) \tag{34a}$$

It is intuitive to digress momentarily to derive leisure from (10) with (34a): valued at the wage:

$$\mathrm{w}_t(1 - \mathrm{L}_t) = \frac{\eta(1-\theta)}{1+\eta(1-\theta)}(\lambda K_t + w_t) \tag{34b}$$

This is intuitive: consumption gets a fraction of total (flow) income (evaluated at the total time endowment of 1) and leisure (valued at the wage) gets the rest. Given λ, the greater is η, the more is leisure and the less labour and consumption.

The aggregate budget constraint (28), with consumption (34a), the wage (23″), growth (20e′) and the interest rate (27′) gives:

$$Af(L)(1-\gamma) = \frac{\lambda + Af\prime(L)}{1+\eta(1-\theta)} + Af(L) - Af\prime(L)L - \lambda$$

Or after simplifications:

$$\eta(1-\theta)\lambda = Af\prime(L)[1-(1+\eta(1-\theta))L] + \gamma Af(L)(1+\eta(1-\theta)) \tag{35}$$

Note that this places a natural restriction on labour supply:

$$0 \leq L \leq \frac{1}{(1+\eta(1-\theta))} < 1 \tag{36}$$

This restriction is due to the instantaneous preferences and not to the discounting scheme.

Equation (35) implies a negative relation between λ and L because:

$$\eta(1-\theta)\frac{d\lambda}{dL} = Af''(L)[1 - L(1+\eta(1-\theta))]$$

$$- Af'(L)(1-\gamma)(1+\eta(1-\theta)) < 0 \tag{37}$$

The sign follows from $f''(L) < 0$ due to diminishing marginal product, from (36), and $\gamma < 1$.

Equations (33) and (35) are a two-dimensional static system in (λ, L) that completely characterises the steady state. Once determined, this yields the rest of the variables from the preceding equations. The system is depicted in Fig. 3. Because $r'(L) > 0$, and $\sigma > 1$, equation implies (33) a positive relation between the two variables:

$$\frac{d\lambda}{dL} = \frac{\frac{d}{dr}\frac{1}{\int_t^{\infty}\exp\{[-\psi-(\sigma-1)(r(L)-\lambda)](\tau-t)-\tilde{\Psi}(\tau,t)\}d\tau}}{1-\frac{d}{d\lambda}\frac{1}{\int_t^{\infty}\exp\{[-\psi-(\sigma-1)(r(L)-\lambda)](\tau-t)-\tilde{\Psi}(\tau,t)\}d\tau}} r'(L)$$

$$= \frac{(\sigma-1)\lambda^2 r'(L)}{1+(\sigma-1)\lambda^2} > 0$$

The sign follows since $r\prime(L) = -Af''(L) > 0$. Furthermore, given any level of L, $\frac{d\lambda}{dL}$ is higher the higher is the (exogenous) present-bias (evident in λ). This information will be used shortly.

Therefore, in terms of Fig. 3, Eq. (33), shown as Eq. 1, has a positive slope. On the other hand, because of (37), Eq. (35), shown as Eq. 2, has a negative slope. A simple geometric argument shows that there exists a unique steady state; see the accompanying paper for more details.

Proposition 1a: Existence and uniqueness of a steady state:

There exists a unique, steady-state, balanced-growth path, in which the growth rate of output, consumption and capital is common and constant,

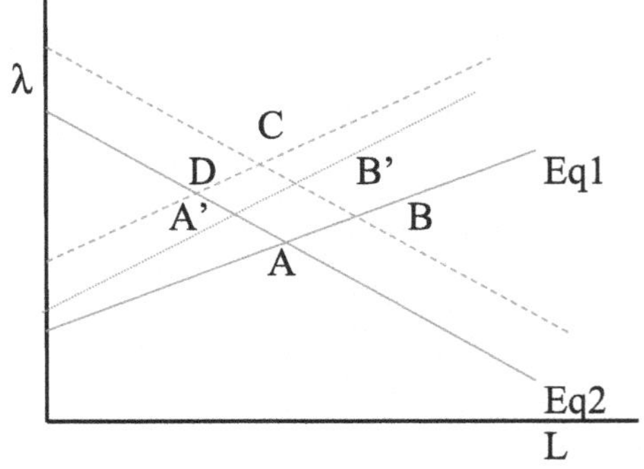

Fig. 3 The steady-state system

and where the "marginal propensity to consume out of intertemporal resources" (λ), labour supply (L), all the "grand ratios" (e.g. C/K) and the real interest are all constant.

Proposition 1b: The properties of the system are as follows:

- A fall in η but rise in θ: At first sight, the effect is ambiguous. Rewriting (35), we have:

$$\lambda = \frac{A\left[f\prime(L)(1 - L(1 + \eta(1 - \theta))) + \gamma f(L)(1 + \eta(1 - \theta))\right]}{\eta(1 - \theta)} \qquad (35')$$

  The effect on all terms on the RHS is a rise, therefore λ rises: The Eq2 curve shifts up (broken line). Hence, with an upward-sloping Eq1, both L and λ rise: Equilibrium moves from A to. This is intuitive: greater status motivation produces more work effort and consumption per unit of resources, while less value to leisure does the same.
- Interactions between different socio-behavioural traits: Moreover, the effects of the changes above depend on the level of present-bias in existence. As mentioned, both the position and slope of Eq. 1 are higher when present-bias is higher (dotted line); in that case, we move from A′ to B′, with a greater effect on λ and less on labour supply. This is an instance of an interaction between the behavioural and social factors that concern us in this book. Specifically, two deviations from the standard setup of exponentially discounted intertemporal optimisation: hyperbolic discounting and status (and the elasticity of labour supply) interact with each other and can offer richer results and predictions. As Frederick et al. (2002, p. 377) argue, this increases the model's normative and predictive appeal.
- A rise in government spending (γ) raises λ in Eq. 2, therefore shifts the curve up (A to B). The result is an increase in both λ and L: Government spending is expansionary, a result that bears on the issue of the fiscal multiplier, to which we return below. As before, this effect too interacts with the level of present-bias; e.g. more of the latter leads to B′ instead of B.
- A rise in productivity (A), raises λ via the interest rate in Eq. (35) and also obviously raises λ in (37). In Fig. 3, both Eqs. 1 and 2 will

shift up to the broken lines—moving from A to C. The result is a higher propensity to consume (λ), but the effect on L is ambiguous.

- An exogenous rise in present-bias. From the discussion of sub-Sects. "The Discounting Scheme" and "The Discount Factor", this raises Ψ; writing $\lambda = \frac{1}{\int_t^\infty exp\{-\overline{\psi}(\tau-t)\}d\tau-\Psi}$ as in sub-Section "The Discount Factor", we see that the result is a rise in λ given $r(L)$. Again, Eq1 increases in slope as well as shifts up (to the broken line)—A to D, delivering a rise in λ and a fall in L.

4 Further Results

Growth

The model has important implications for growth and thereby contributes to the relevant extensive literature. To see the implications, it is convenient and intuitive to convert the steady-state system into 2 × 2 in λ and g. The first equation is readily obtained from (33) with growth (20e′):

$$\lambda(g) = \frac{1}{\int_t^\infty \exp\left\{[-\psi - (\sigma - 1)g](\tau - t) - \widetilde{\Psi}(\tau, t)\right\}d\tau} \tag{38a}$$

The second equation arises by combining (35) and growth (20e′) with the interest rate (27), to obtain:

$$g = Af(L)\left[1 - \gamma\frac{1 + \eta(1 - \theta)}{\eta(1 - \theta)}\right] - \frac{Af\prime(L)}{\eta(1 - \theta)}(1 - L) \tag{39}$$

With $dg/dL > 0$. Combining the interim relationship (39) again with (35), which implies $L = L(\lambda)$, $L'(.) < 0$ (from 35′ and concomitant discussion), we finally get:

$$g = g(\lambda) \tag{38b}$$

with $g\prime(\lambda) < 0$.

Equations (38a, b) make up the transformed system. In (λ, g) space, the first one is upward-sloping, the second down-sloping. In view of the centrality of growth as an issue in macroeconomics and as a topic in our book, it is worth graphing the transformed system in Fig. 4.

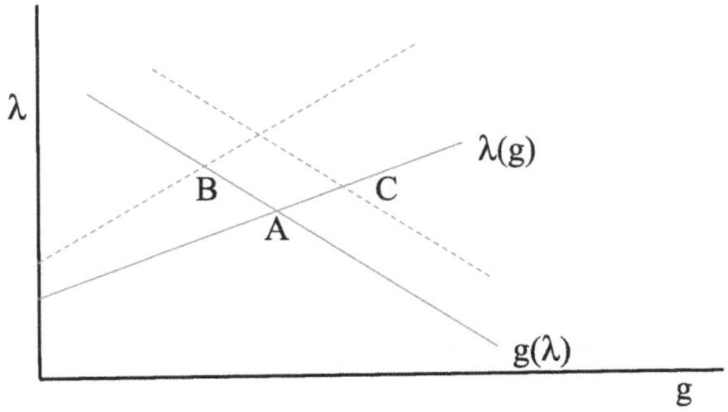

Fig. 4 The transformed steady-state system

Of most interest are the effects of a rise in present-bias on λ (already discussed) and g. Following the same line of reasoning as with (33), we see that a rise in present-bias raises λ for any given g, and thereby shifts the $\lambda(g)$ line (with an increase in slope as well) up to the broken line in Fig. 4. We move from A to B, thereby increasing λ, as discussed, and reducing g. The potential relevance of this result is dual: On the one hand, it may be part of the explanation as to why differences in growth rates persist across countries and "club convergence" appears. The other potential contribution is towards an explanation of the emergence of "secular stagnation", whereby growth is expected to be lower in the foreseeable future than it has been over recent decades. The reasons for this are being debated, as is the very existence or not of "secular stagnation". Our results show that societies (or generations) with a higher present-bias are likely to experience less growth than others; if present-bias has increased presently, the result may well be lower growth. This analysis then pushes the argument one step further, namely to understand why present-bias may have increased now compared to the past; but this is in the domain of sociologists more than economists.

As discussed around Eq. (35′), a fall in η but a rise in θ lead to a rise in λ given any level of L. In view of the inverse relationship between λ and L (the downward-sloping Eq. 2 in Fig. 3), the same exogenous changes also raise L given λ. Furthermore, from (39) above, we see that the same also raises g given λ. Therefore, the $g(\lambda)$ schedule in Fig. 4 shifts up—A to C: Both λ and g increase.

Finally, a rise in government spending (γ) has both a direct and an indirect—via L—effect on $g(\lambda)$. From (35′), λ rises given L and also L rises given λ (the shift up in Eq. 2 shown in Fig. 3); hence the indirect effect is positive. However, the indirect effect is obviously negative, so things are unclear at first sight. But here we can be guided by the results derived above: If the total effect of γ on $g(\lambda)$ is expansionary (contractionary), the line shifts up (down) in Fig. 4, producing a rise (fall) in λ. Since the effect on λ is expansionary, as derived above, it must be the case that the total effect on g is expansionary, the $g(\lambda)$ line shifts up (A to C) and both λ and g rise. As before, in other words, the effect of government spending is expansionary, and this result extends to growth as well (due to the rise in labour supply).

Labour Supply

The labour supply has received some attention in recent years. Two issues appear as focal points: Firstly, the difference between the US and Europe; the former has a higher labour hour per person than the latter (taken as a whole, while of course there are important differences between individual countries); see e.g. Blundell et al. (2013) and Prescott (2004). Various suggestions in the literature include the possible effect of higher taxation in Europe, which disincentivises work effort, or the greater value Europeans possibly place on leisure. A second focal point is the falling tendency of the hours in the labour market (particularly among white men, and particularly in continental Europe, see Blundell et al. 2013) and the rise of inactivity (due to demographics, early retirement, and the like). Our analysis of socio-economic factors adds a couple of suggestions to this candidate list: We see that a greater status motive (θ) and lower present-bias lead towards a greater labour supply. Again, if these results are to contribute to an explanation of differences in labour supply between the US and Europe, it must be explained why the US may feature a greater status motivation and less present-bias. While notions such as the "American dream" may argue towards the former, it is left to others to provide a conclusive account.

The Government Spending Multiplier

The government spending multiplier continues to be an area of active research interest, motivated by its profound policy relevance and by the fact that our understanding of its empirical magnitude continues to be rather vague and therefore debated. While practically everyone agrees that the multiplier is positive, a focal point of debate among Keynesians and others is whether the pure (unfunded) spending multiplier exceeds unity or not. Our framework has implications for this issue, too, which we proceed to show.

We begin from Eq. (35), repeated here for ease, with the introduction of government spending in levels, $G = \gamma A f(L)$:

$$\eta(1-\theta)\lambda = Af\prime(L)[1-(1+\eta(1-\theta))L] + G(1+\eta(1-\theta)) \qquad (35')$$

Given the capital stock, the government spending multiplier is given by:

$$\frac{\partial A f(L)}{\partial G} = A f\prime(L)\frac{\partial L}{\partial G}$$

Equation (35′) implies through a series of tedious substitutions:

$$\eta(1-\theta)\lambda = Af\prime(L)[1-(1+\eta(1-\theta))L] + G(1+\eta(1-\theta))$$

Or

$$[1+\eta(1-\theta)] = (1+\eta(1-\theta))Af'(L)\frac{dL}{dG} - Af''(L)[1-(1+\eta(1-\theta))L]\frac{dL}{dG} + \eta(1-\theta)\frac{d\lambda}{dG}$$

and

$$[1+\eta(1-\theta)] = (1+\eta(1-\theta))Af'(L)\frac{dL}{dG} - \frac{f''(L)}{f'(L)}[1-(1+\eta(1-\theta))L]Af'(L)\frac{dL}{dG} + \eta(1-\theta)\frac{d\lambda}{dr}\frac{dr}{dL}\frac{dL}{dG}$$

Using $f\prime(L) = (1-\phi)\left(\frac{f(L)}{L}\right)^{\frac{1}{\varphi}}$, $\frac{f\prime(L)L}{f(L)} = (1-\phi)\left(\frac{f(L)}{L}\right)^{\frac{1-\varphi}{\varphi}}$, and $\frac{f\prime\prime(L)}{f\prime(L)} = \frac{1}{\varphi}\left[\frac{f\prime(L)}{f(L)} - \frac{1}{L}\right] = \frac{1}{\varphi L}\left[(1-\phi)\left(\frac{f(L)}{L}\right)^{\frac{1-\varphi}{\varphi}} - 1\right]$, also $\frac{dr}{dL} = -Af''(L)L$ and $\frac{d\lambda}{dr} = (\sigma-1)\lambda^2 > 0$, we have:

$$[1+\eta(1-\theta)] = (1+\eta(1-\theta))Af\prime(L)\frac{dL}{dG}$$
$$+\frac{1}{\varphi L}\left[1-(1-\phi)\left(\frac{f(L)}{L}\right)^{\frac{1-\varphi}{\varphi}}\right][1-(1+\eta(1-\theta))L]Af\prime(L)\frac{dL}{dG}$$
$$+\eta(1-\theta)(\sigma-1)\lambda^2\frac{1}{\varphi L}\left[1-(1-\phi)\left(\frac{f(L)}{L}\right)^{\frac{1-\varphi}{\varphi}}\right]Af\prime(L)\frac{dL}{dG}$$

Collecting terms, we finally get the multiplier as:

$$\frac{d\left(\frac{Y}{K}\right)}{dG} = Af\prime(L)\frac{dL}{dG} = M < 1 \tag{40}$$

Where
$0 < M \equiv \frac{1+\eta(1-\theta)}{1+\eta(1-\theta)+\frac{1}{\varphi L}\left[1-(1-\phi)\left(\frac{f(L)}{L}\right)^{\frac{1-\varphi}{\varphi}}\right][1+\eta(1-\theta)(\sigma-1)\lambda^2-(1+\eta(1-\theta))L]} <$
1

The inequality follows from $(1-\phi)\left(\frac{f(L)}{L}\right)^{\frac{1-\varphi}{\varphi}} = \frac{(1-\phi)}{\phi L^{\frac{1-\varphi}{\varphi}}+(1-\phi)} < 1$ and $L \leq \frac{1}{(1+\eta(1-\theta))}$ and the baseline assumption of $(\sigma-1) > 0$ as discussed.

The positive effect of γ is not driven by spending but by the rise in labour supply. In other words, the multiplier derived here belongs to the class of "neoclassical" multipliers (Hall 2009; Mulligan 2011; Woodford 2011) that motivate the expansion from the supply and not the demand side. As discussed in more detail in Tsoukis (2020, Ch. 8), unlike the more familiar, demand-side "Keynesian" multiplier, the neoclassical multiplier is based on the crowding out of (private) consumption by government spending; this then raises the marginal utility of both consumption and leisure, implying less leisure and more work effort. While there is an expansion, therefore, there must be a crowding out of consumption, hence a less than unity multiplier, otherwise there would be no expansion in the first place. The fact that the multiplier is less than unity implies that the multiplier is a "neoclassical" and not a "Keynesian" one.

Furthermore, a rise in present-bias, hence a higher λ given all else, reduces M and therefore the multiplier. This is at first sight counterintuitive: one would have expected that a rise in the propensity to consume would raise the multiplier. Yet, the effect of present-bias arises via investment, which depends on the growth rate: $g = r - \lambda$. As government spending rises, labour rises, leading to a rise in r and thereby in λ; the total effect of G on growth and investment is: $\frac{dg}{dG} = \frac{dr}{dG}\left[1 - \frac{d\lambda}{dr}\right] = \frac{dr}{dG}\left[1 - (\sigma - 1)\lambda^2\right]$; thus, an exogenous rise in present-bias renders the expansionary effect less effective, because essentially investment responds by less. This is a novel effect in the discussion of the multiplier that seems not to have been highlighted in extant literature. Note that the effect would disappear under log-utility ($\sigma = 1$).

The Labour Share

Factor (capital-labour) shares have been under intensive interest lately, for the dual reason that they are related to inequality, and because inequality has been increasing in recent decades in developed economies. The labour share (labour income as a share of net national income) was traditionally considered to be one of the constants of macroeconomics, typically thought to be 2/3; but, in recent years it has shown a tendency to decrease (see Karabarbounis and Neiman 2014; Ronglie 2015; Autor et al. 2017; and Tsoukis 2020, Ch. 10 for a review). The capital (profits and rents) share is the mirror image of the labour share, as they add up to 1 (they exhaust national income net of income taxes). Factor shares are related to inequality: As capital income is more unequally distributed than wage/labour income, because of the inequality in asset ownership (higher than overall income inequality), the higher (lower) is the capital (labour) income, the greater is inequality. The reasons for the current decline in labour income are not well understood and continue to be debated. Our framework can contribute to this discussion.

The labour share was derived above (Eq. 32a) and repeated here for convenience (steady-state version):

$$\frac{w_t L}{Y_t} = \frac{(1-\phi)}{\phi L^{\frac{1-\varphi}{\varphi}} + (1-\phi)} \tag{32a'}$$

The labour share falls with labour (with the empirically plausible elasticity $\varphi < 1$) as the latter reduces the wage (due to a diminishing marginal product) but because of limited substitutability, the reduction is proportionately bigger than the increase in labour. Hence, the effects of various exogenous changes on the labour share will be the opposite of the ones on labour itself. Such effects disappear under a Cobb–Douglas technology ($\varphi = 1$), when the labour share boils down to an exogenous technical parameter ($1 - \phi$). Our framework offers an avenue of enquiry on rising inequality based on socio-behavioural factors, via the decline in the labour share.

"$r - g$"

The issue of whether the real interest rate exceeds the growth rate or not has achieved prominence since at least Piketty's (2014) demonstration that the formal reflects the growth rate of capital and therefore capital income (in the long run), whereas the latter is the growth of the economy at large. If $r - g > 0$, the capital income grows faster than the (rest of the) economy, therefore as a share over GDP, the capital share will tend to rise. This has important (adverse) implications for inequality, as pointed out above. The issue is far from settled or agreed upon (see the contributions to the Spring 2015 issue of the *Journal of Economic Perspectives* for more insights and Tsoukis 2020, Ch. 10 for a review). One set of issues concerns the question of "dynamic inefficiency" or not. If $r - g < 0$, at a very basic level, the present value of growing sums, that are routinely found in growth economics, is infinite. Furthermore, the economy is "dynamically inconsistent". A further set of issues concerns the fact that, empirically, the riskless real rate of return is almost invariably less than the growth rate, offering a challenge to Piketty's claim (as well as dynamic efficiency). However, it has been shown that the risky real interest rate, which is the relevant rate of return on wealth, has historically been higher than the growth rate (see Jorda et al. 2019), and hence dynamic efficiency can thereby be salvaged. It is unclear, however, what that implies for Piketty's (2014) argument that capital income may be growing as a share of the economy. Nor is it clear what various extensions, such as e.g. the existence of overlapping generations, may imply for Piketty's claim.

We do not aim to resolve these ambiguities here. We only wish to point out that our framework may offer some perspectives on these issues. As our framework is deterministic, the distinction between riskless and risky interest rate cannot be addressed; we just consider the rate here as a proxy for the more empirically relevant risky rate, which is greater than the growth rate. From the growth Eq. (20e′), we readily have:

$$r - g = \lambda \tag{41}$$

Everything that raises the marginal propensity to consume out of intertemporal resources, λ, including present-bias, the status motive and government spending, as discussed, raises the "$r - g$" difference. Therefore, the socio-behavioural traits discussed here are likely to have implications for the capital share and inequality at large, as well as dynamic (in)efficiency. In other words, such traits do not only have implications for the size of the aggregate "pie" but for its distribution and inequality, as well.

Finally, we note that the implications of status and hyperbolic discounting for inequality are discussed in Chapter 7. We summarise in the following Proposition:

Proposition 2: Effects of the present-bias. An exogenous rise in present-bias:

- Increases the propensity to consume out of intertemporal resources (λ);
- Decreases growth;
- Decreases labour supply;
- Reduces the government spending multiplier (as that is of the "neoclassical" type);
- Increases the labour share, thus indirectly affecting (negatively) inequality;
- Increases "$r - g$", which is said to increase wealth as a share of national income and thereby to exacerbate inequality.

References

Ainslie, G.W. 1992. *Picoeconomics*. Cambridge, UK: Cambridge UP.

Alesina, A. and D. Rodrik. 1994. Distributive Politics and Economic Growth, *Quarterly Journal of Economics*. 109 (2): 465–490.

Al-Nowaihi, A., and S. Dhami. 2006. A Note on the Loewenstein-Prelec Theory of Intertemporal Choice. *Mathematical Social Sciences* 52 (1): 99–108.

Al-Nowaihi, A., and S. Dhami. 2006. A Note on the Loewenstein-Prelec Theory of Intertemporal Choice. *Mathematical Social Sciences* 52 (1): 99–108.

Angeletos, G.-M., D. Laibson, A. Repetto, J. Tobacman, and S. Weinberg. 2001. The Hyperbolic Consumption Model: Calibration, Simulation, and Empirical Evaluation. *The Journal of Economic Perspectives* 15 (3): 47–68.

Attanasio, O.P., and G. Weber. 2010. Consumption and Saving: Models of Intertemporal Allocation and Their Implications for Public Policy. *Journal of Economic Literature* 48 (3): 693–751.

Autor, D., D. Dorn, L.F. Katz, C. Patterson and J. Van Reenen. 2017. Concentrating on the Fall of the Labor Share. *American Economic Review*. 107 (5): 180–85.

Barro, R.J. 1990. Government Spending in a Simple Model of Endogenous Growth. *Journal of Political Economy* 98 (5): S103–S125.

Barro, R.J. 1999. Ramsey Meets Laibson in the Neoclassical Growth Model. *Quarterly Journal of Economics* 114 (4): 1125–1152.

Blundell, R., A. Bozio and G. Laroque. 2013. Extensive and Intensive Margins of Labour Supply: Work and Working Hours in the US, the UK and France. *Fiscal Studies*. 34: 1–29.

Cabo, F., G. Martín-Herrán, and M.P. Martínez-García. 2016. Unbounded Growth in the Neoclassical Growth Model with Non-constant Discounting. *Mathematical Social Sciences* 84 (C): 93–104.

Caliendo, F.N., and D. Aadland. 2007. Short-Term Planning and the Life-Cycle Consumption Puzzle. *Journal of Economic Dynamics and Control* 31 (4): 1392–1415.

Caselli, F., and J. Ventura. 2000. A Representative Consumer Theory of Distribution. *American Economic Review* 90 (4): 909–926.

DellaVigna, S. 2009. Psychology and Economics: Evidence from the Field. *Journal of Economic Literature* 47 (2): 315–372.

DellaVigna, S., and U. Malmendier. 2006. Paying not to Go to the Gym. *American Economic Review* 96 (3): 694–719.

Farzin, Y.H., and R. Wendner. 2014. The Time Path of the Saving Rate: Hyperbolic Discounting and Short-Term Planning, FEEM WP No. 063.2014.

Findley, T.S., and F.N. Caliendo. 2014. Interacting Mechanisms of Time Inconsistency. *Journal of Economic Psychology* 41 (C): 68–76.

Frederick, S., G. Loewenstein, and T. O'Donoghue. 2002. Time Discounting and Time Preference: A Critical Review. *Journal of Economic Literature* 40 (2): 351–401.

Galor, O., and Ö. Özak. 2016. The Agricultural Origins of Time Preference. *American Economic Review* 106 (10): 3064–3103.

García-Peñalosa, C. and S.J. Turnovsky. 2006. Growth and income inequality: a canonical model. *Economic Theory*. 28: 25–49.

García-Peñalosa, C. and S.J. Turnovsky. 2007. Growth, Income Inequality, and Fiscal Policy: What Are the Relevant Trade-offs?. *Journal of Money, Credit and Banking*. 39: 369–394.

Gowdy, J., J.B. Rosser, and L. Roy. 2013. The Evolution of Hyperbolic Discounting: Implications for Truly Social Valuation of the Future. *Journal of Economic Behavior and Organization* 90 (Supplement): S94–S104.

Hall, R.E. 1988. Intertemporal Substitution in Consumption. *Journal of Political Economy* 96 (2): 339–357.

Hall, R.E. 2009. By How Much Does GDP Rise If the Government Buys More Output?, *Brookings Papers on Economic Activity*. 2009 (2): 183–249.

Harris, C., and D. Laibson. 2001. Dynamic Choices of Hyperbolic Consumers. *Econometrica* 69 (4): 935–957.

Jordà, O., K. Knoll, D. Kuvshinov, M. Schularick and A.M. Taylor. 2019. The Rate of Return on Everything, 1870–2015, *Quarterly Journal of Economics*, 134 (3): 1225–1298.

Karabarbounis, L. and B. Neiman. 2014. The Global Decline of the Labor Share, *Quarterly Journal of Economics*, 129 (1): 61–103.

King, R.G., C.I. Plosser, and S.T. Rebelo. 1988. Production, Growth and Business Cycles I. The Basic Neoclassical Model. *Journal of Monetary Economics* 21 (2–3): 195–232.

Krusell, P.B., and A.A. Smith Jr. 2003. Consumption-Savings Decisions with Quasi-Geometric Discounting. *Econometrica* 71 (1): 365–375.

Laibson, D. 1997. Golden Eggs and Hyperbolic Discounting. *Quarterly Journal of Economics* 112 (2): 443–477.

Laibson, D. 2001. A Cue-Theory of Consumption. *Quarterly Journal of Economics* 116 (1): 81–119.

Laibson, D. 2015. Why Don't Present-Biased Agents Make Commitments? *American Economic Review: Papers & Proceedings* 105 (5): 267–272.

Laibson, D., A. Repetto, and J. Tobacman, 2007. Estimating Discount Functions with Consumption Choices over the Lifecycle, NBER Working Paper No. 13314.

Loewenstein, G., and D. Prelec. 1992. Anomalies in Intertemporal Choice: Evidence and an Interpretation. *Quarterly Journal of Economics* 107 (2): 573–598.

Mulligan, C.B. 2011. Simple Analytics and Empirics of the Government Spending Multiplier and Other 'Keynesian' Paradoxes, *The B.E. Journal of Macroeconomics*, 11 (1): Article 19.

O'Donoghue, T., and M. Rabin. 2015. Present Bias: Lessons Learned and to Be Learned. *American Economic Review: Papers and Proceedings* 105 (5): 273–279.

Phelps, E.S. and R.A. Pollak. 1968. On Second-Best National Saving and Game-Equilibrium Growth, *The Review of Economic Studies*. 35 (2): 185–199.

Picketty, T. 2014. *Capital in the Twenty-First Century*. Boston, MA: Belknap (Harvard) Press.

Prescott, E.C. 2004. Why Do Americans Work So Much More than Europeans? Federal Reserve Bank of Minneapolis Quarterly Review. 28 (1): 2–14.

Rognlie, M. 2015. Deciphering the fall and rise in the net Capital share: Accumulation or scarcity? *Brookings Papers in Economic Activity*. 2015 (1): 1–54.

Romer, P. 1986. Increasing returns and long-run growth, *Journal of Political Economy*. 94 (5): 1002–1037.

Rubinstein, A. 2003. Economics and Psychology? *The Case of Hyperbolic Discounting, International Economic Review* 44 (4): 1207–1216.

Six, M., and F. Wirl. 2015. Optimal Pollution Management When Discount Rates Are Endogenous. *Resource and Energy Economics* 42: 53–70.

Sprenger, C. 2015. Judging Experimental Evidence on Dynamic Inconsistency. *American Economic Review: Papers and Proceedings* 105 (5): 280–285.

Startz, R., and K.-P. Tsang. 2012. Nonexponential Discounting: A Direct Test and Perhaps A New Puzzle. *The B.E. Journal of Macroeconomics* 12 (1): 1–35.

Strotz, R.H. 1956. Myopia and Inconsistency in Dynamic Utility Maximization. *Review of Economic Studies* 23 (3): 165–180.

Strulik, H. 2021. Hyperbolic Discounting and the Time-Consistent Solution of Three Canonical Environmental Problems. *Journal of Public Economic Theory* 23: 462–486.

Strulik, H. 2015. Hyperbolic Discounting and Endogenous Growth. *Economics Letters* 126 (C), 131–134.

Tsoukis, C., F. Tournemaine and M. Gillman. 2017. Hybrid exponential-hyperbolic discounting and growth without commitment, *The Manchester School*, 85 (S2): e45–e74.

Tsoukis, C. 2020. *Theory of Macroeconomic Policy*. Oxford: Oxford University Press.

Tsoukis, C., and F. Tournemaine. 2024. *Hyperbolic Discounting, Labour Supply and Growth*. Mimeo.

CHAPTER 6

Hyperbolic Discounting and Macroeconomic Policy

1 Introduction

This chapter analyses the implications of hyperbolic discounting (HD) for macroeconomic policy. We shall take monetary policy, in the form of a "Taylor rule" for interest rates, as a concrete example of macroeconomic policy and its stabilisation potential, but the chapter has relevance for other types of policy, namely fiscal policy. While that was discussed also in the last chapter, here we derive fresh insights because the setup is more "Keynesian" than in the last chapter, as it allows for a demand-determined output in the form of an output gap, whereas the setup of the last chapter was "neoclassical" in the sense that output is entirely supply-side based. For this reason, the insights we offer on fiscal policy (see Result 3) differ from those of last chapter.

HD was introduced in the last chapter; it was argued that there exists sizeable experimental evidence that suggests that behaviour does not conform to the implications of the traditionally used discounting scheme, the exponential (in continuous time) or equivalently, the geometric (in discrete time). In particular, there is evidence of time inconsistency, which is incompatible with exponential/geometric (EG) discounting. To rectify this, some contributions have started using HD, which implies that the discount rate decreases as we contemplate further into the future—in sharp contrast to EG, which involves a constant discount rate. As discussed, the structure of HD invalidates the perturbation arguments

C. Tsoukis et al., *Social and Behavioural Macroeconomics*,
https://doi.org/10.1007/978-3-031-77748-6_6

underlying the Euler equation. Various approaches for an alternative have been tried in the literature; as in Chapter 5, we shall follow the approach introduced by Barro (1999), which uses a time-consistent procedure, in the face of HD.

The chapter then analyses the implications of HD for the optimal design of monetary policy. As mentioned, the latter is used here as the most obvious form of short-run stabilisation policy, so some of the wider results we derive are more broadly applicable to stabilisation policy at large. HD seems not to have been pursued in connection with monetary or stabilisation policy in the literature, so the nature of the analysis here is more exploratory rather than a review of established results. As HD was introduced and discussed in Chapter 5, the exposition in this chapter will be brief, yet full enough to be readable on its own. We first begin (Sect. 2) with a brief review of the discounting scheme; it is very similar to that of Chapter 5, except slightly more specific in order to allow tractability in the dynamics. One inconsequential difference with Chapter 5 is the use of discrete time here, necessitated by the presence of shocks, which motivate the monetary/stabilisation policy.

A further difference is that we restrict attention to an AK production process with fixed labour, in the place of the CES production function of the last chapter. The reason is that short-run fluctuations are mostly due to movements of labour along the "extensive margin", i.e. movements in and out of employment, rather than along the "intensive margin" (changes in the amount of labour offered), which may be more relevant in the long run and for comparisons across countries; see Tsoukis (2020, Ch. 1) for a review; as noted there, Erosa et al. (2016) present an estimate that seems to be average of the literature, namely that the extensive margin accounts for 62% of the total labour response across the business cycle. The incorporation of the intensive–extensive distinction would get us too far and therefore is outside our scope. The presence of flexible labour, therefore, with its minority contribution to business analysis, would offer little insight about stabilisation policy while it would greatly complicate the analysis. Thus, for the purposes of this chapter, it is best to abstract from labour via the AK model. We let output fluctuations captured by an output gap that responds to both demand and supply shocks. The AK setup has been used previously by Tsoukis, Tournemaine and Gillman (2017) which extended Barro's (1999) analysis. Thus, the analysis here may be seen as an application of Tsoukis et al. (2017) to issues of stabilisation and monetary policy.

The model will broadly follow the logic of the "three-equation" New Keynesian (NK) model. This comprises an IS-type equation, an inflation equation (also known as the NK Phillips Curve) and a "Taylor rule" that summarises monetary policy. The IS equation will be derived from the behaviour of the representative agent, analysed in Sect. 3, which incorporates HD. The inflation equation and monetary policy/Taylor rule are discussed in Sect. 3. Section 4 then analyses a simple model of optimal monetary policy design and discusses the implications of HD. To preamble, we derive a few quite strong results. Result 4 concerns the effect of present bias on the fiscal multiplier; it is shown that present bias increases the multiplier. This contrasts with the result shown in the previous chapter; the difference arises because model of the previous chapter was "neoclassical", based on optimisation, endogenous labour supply, and supply-determined output. The setup here is more "Keynesian" as it allows for a demand-determined output gap. This difference lies at the heart of the difference in the multipliers of the two chapters. Importantly, a higher present bias brings us a step closer to the textbook Keynesian model, where future resources matter less for current output determination (Result 1). Arguably, the notion of a "Keynesian consumption function" is associated with more reliance on current output and resources and less on notions of opportunity cost of consumption or of future resources (what may be called a "neoclassical consumption function"); see, e.g. D'Orlando and Sanfilippo (2010). Furthermore, regarding the optimal design of monetary policy, we find that the relative response of the interest rate to the output gap and inflation is not affected by present-bias; but the overall responsiveness of the interest rate ratio should increase when present bias increases (Result 5). This is a stark result, which we believe should be more closely studied in the context of optimal monetary policy design.

Furthermore, in his analysis of the effects of myopia on monetary policy design, Gabaix (2020) highlights a paradox, namely that in standard New Keynesian (NK) models, future monetary policy seems to matter now too much, in a counter-factual way. Our framework can help resolve the puzzle as present value reduces the relevance of future interest rates and future monetary policy for the determination of current output (Result 2), and therefore the result helps resolve the puzzle. In fact, the hyperbolic structure of discounting postulated here may provide an additional rationalisation to myopia postulated and analysed by Gabaix (2020), on top of the cognitive reasons and "rational inattention" discussed there.[1] In any case, Gabaix' (2020) important analysis serves as one of the key motivations for the present chapter. The analysis here is more suggestive about what is at play when there is hyperbolic discounting; it leaves various important issues for a more thorough treatment in the future.

A series of Appendices conclude the chapter. Appendices T1-7 elaborate on straightforward but tedious analytical material. Before those, in Appendix A, the chapter pursues a further theme that seems not to have been taken up in the literature. As in Chapter 5, the model postulates and analyses a propensity to consume out-of-lifetime resources (λ). Those resources include (physical) capital and the present value of labour earnings (which are a postulated fraction of output). Now, the present value of that sums future earnings discounted by a geometric discounting. Even though this is a sum of monetary values and not utility, one could argue that the present-bias, or myopia, embedded in HD, may be present in the discounting of monetary values as well. This myopia may be motivated by impatience and an aversion to the "future" as a whole, with less differentiation between near and distant future. Appendix A analyses how the present value of labour earnings may look like in the presence of such myopia. As mentioned, this chapter is exploratory in nature and Appendix A is in that spirit; both highlight possibilities and offer roadmaps for promising future research.

2 The Representative Agent

A Model of Hyperbolic Discounting (HD)

As in Barro (1999) and others, the framework assumes a unit mass of identical, infinitely lived agents. Intertemporal preferences are characterised by HD and there is no commitment mechanism. Period utility is assumed iso-elastic. Time is discrete. The setup is deterministic. At the

[1] More specifically, Gabaix (2020) postulates that the individual perceives dimly or "sparsely" the evolution of their own individual wealth and develop similarly limited expectations of the state vector—cf. Eqs. (6) and (8). These mechanisms of myopia parallel the discounting mechanism analysed here; in the spirit of cognitive myopia is the brief analysis of Appendix A on hyperbolic discounting of wealth.

time of planning (t), the representative individual maximises[2]:

$$U_t = \sum_{\tau=0}^{\infty} \frac{C_{t+\tau}^{1-\sigma}}{1-\sigma} \phi(t+\tau, t) \tag{1}$$

σ is the inverse of the elasticity of substitution. Empirical evidence suggests that the intertemporal elasticity of substitution is less than unity, see the previous chapter, i.e. $\sigma > 1$; we maintain this assumption in the sequel, but we shall also consider the common benchmark case of log-utility ($\sigma = 1$).

Assumption 1 $\sigma \geq 1$.

The discount factor, $\phi(t+\tau, t)$, is a discrete-time version of that used in Chapter 5.[3] It discounts sums that occur (with certainty) at time $t + \tau$ to time t equivalents. It is characterised by:

$$\phi(t, t) = 1 \tag{2a}$$

$$\phi(t+\tau, t) \equiv \frac{1}{(1+\rho)^{\tau} \prod_{s=1}^{\tau} (1+\varphi^{s})}, \tau,\ s \geq 1, \rho > 0, \varphi \geq 0 \tag{2b}$$

This discount factor is a hybrid of standard geometric discounting (EG), exemplified by the discount rate $\rho>0$, and of "hyperbolic discounting" (HD), introduced by $\varphi \geq 0$, on which more below. This discount factor obeys the standard requirements of any discounting scheme:

$$\phi(t, t) = 1, lim_{\tau \to \infty} \phi(\tau, t) = 0 \tag{3}$$

Furthermore, to gain more intuition, we list the elements for $t + 1$ and $t + 2$:

$$\phi(t+1, t) = \frac{1}{(1+\rho)(1+\varphi)}, \phi(t+2, t) = \frac{1}{(1+\rho)^2(1+\varphi)\left(1+\varphi^2\right)} \tag{4}$$

[2] Because of the unit mass, the individual and aggregate variables coincide, hence agent-specific subscripts are suppressed. See Chapter 5 for more details.

[3] For tractability, this discount factor assumes a more specific functional form than the equivalent of Chapter 5. There are also inconsequential notational differences between the two.

This discount factor shares with exponential discounting the properties that $\phi(t, t) = 1$ and $lim_{\tau\to\infty}\phi(\tau, t) = 0$ for any φ. For $t < \tau < \infty$, however, a higher φ essentially "front-loads" the discounting more heavily, thereby deviating from EG.

The associated discount rate is:

$$-\frac{\phi(t+\tau+1,t)-\phi(t+\tau,t)}{\phi(t+\tau,t)}=\frac{\rho+(1+\rho)\varphi^{\tau}}{1+\rho+(1+\rho)\varphi^{\tau}} \tag{5}$$

This is greater than the geometric discount rate of $\frac{\rho}{1+\rho}$ (except in the special case of $\varphi = 0$), and it increases with φ. As discussed in Chapter 5, the hallmark of HD is that the discount rate (5) decreases with τ, in sharp contrast to the (purely) geometric discount rate, which is constant. Asymptotically, this discount rate declines to the geometric rate. This feature of a higher discount rate in the nearer future and lower later is called present bias.[4] It implies that the near future is discounted more heavily, so we are more impatient in intertemporal dilemmas in that frame, whereas we are less impatient regarding intertemporal dilemmas in the long term.

Thus, $\varphi > 0$ captures hyperbolic discounting in this chapter. It is our key parameter of interest; we shall analyse how it affects steady-state values, the speed of adjustment in dynamics, and the optimal design and effectiveness of monetary policy. This formulation of HD is by no means unique, and other formulations have been proposed.[5] The specification in (2) is less general than that used in Chapter 5, but it is tractable, thus allowing the derivation of analytical results. Though our formulation is a

[4] See Chapter 5 for more discussion.

[5] Again as discussed previously, the question of the appropriate form of the discount factor in (2) is not settled; see, e.g. Frederick et al. (2002, footnote 13), O'Donoghue and Rabin (2015). Barro (1999) uses an exponential discount *rate*, while al-Nowaihi and Dhami (2008) use (and refine) the generalised hyperbola first proposed by Loewenstein and Prelec (1992): $\phi(\tau, t) = (1 + \varphi(\tau - t))^{-b/\varphi}$. This however implies that the discount rate in the distant future is arbitrarily low, implying arbitrarily high patience by the "coolly rational" "future self"; there is no particular reason to think that this is the case. Furthermore, there is a sense in which more present-bias (a higher ϕ), in fact, implies a lower volume of total discounting over time (as the future discount rate becomes arbitrarily small). This may have counter-intuitive consequences; e.g. Strulik (2015) finds that current consumption falls and the growth rate rises with the degree of short-termism. This motivates our use of the hybrid HD-geometric discount factor in (2b). See also Farzin and Wendner (2014) for further discussion on HD factors.

hybrid, we shall call it "hyperbolic discounting" (HD) to distinguish it from the pure EG scheme.

As is well known, discounting in another form except purely geometric (or equivalently, in a continuous-time setup, exponential) introduces time inconsistency. The essence of this is that the same intertemporal dilemma (that involves two fixed future dates, say τ' and τ) will receive different resolutions as the planning period gets nearer to it in time (t in what follows, where t < τ < τ'). The root of this problem is that, according to the scheme in (2), discounting between two future times τ' > τ (>t), standing at time t, depends not only on the difference τ'- τ (as in the exponential/geometric case) but also on the time of planning period (t) itself. As a result, the perturbation argument underlying the standard Euler equation is not valid as the results depend on the horizon which we are considering. This is unlike the EG discounting, in which the same intertemporal dilemma will receive the same resolution, irrespective of the planning time. Hence, unlike in the EG case, under HD discounting, the choice of the planning time is not trivial.

To see this dependence on the planning horizon, consider for simplicity two consecutive time periods relevant to the dilemma (or trade-off): τ' = τ + 1. Note that τ is effectively the distance from the planning period. In this case (planning at t), consider the discount factor between these two future dates:

$$\overline{\phi}(\tau+1,\tau/t) \equiv \frac{\phi(\tau+1,t)}{\phi(\tau,t)} = \frac{(1+\rho)^{\tau}\prod_{s=1}^{\tau}(1+\varphi^{s})}{(1+\rho)^{\tau+1}\prod_{s=1}^{\tau+1}(1+\varphi^{s})} = \frac{(1+\rho)^{-1}}{\left(1+\varphi^{\tau+1}\right)}.$$

The distance from the planning period is now obvious. If, instead, planning took place at t + 1, the intertemporal dilemma at the same fixed future dates would now be only τ-1 periods away. Following the same reasoning, we see that the relevant discount factor is:

$$\overline{\phi}(\tau,\tau-1/t) = \frac{\phi(\tau,t)}{\phi(\tau-1,t)} = \frac{(1+\rho)^{-1}}{(1+\varphi^{\tau})}.$$

In this case, the discount factor is smaller ($\varphi^{\tau} > \varphi^{\tau+1}$)—discounting between two fixed time periods is "heavier" as the planning period comes closer. Standing at the planning period t + 1, we have a stronger preference for a unit of consumption to occur at the earlier date (we are more impatient) than if we stood at t. As a result, we are prepared to pay a higher price (e.g. incur a loan at a higher interest rate to bring the given unit of consumption one period earlier) if the dilemma takes place in the nearer rather than the more distant future.

Since the planning time matters, the question arises as to when planning should take place; to which there is no obvious answer, hence the standard intertemporal optimisation analysis is not applicable in this case. Developing the analyses of Strotz (1956) and Pollak (1976), using mainly log-utility, Barro (1999) has proposed a time-consistent procedure. Tsoukis, Tournemaine, and Gillman (2017) generalises this setup to a more general utility function and considers richer dynamics. We essentially follow this procedure here.

A Time-Consistent Procedure

As mentioned, the procedure below follows Barro (1999) and Tsoukis et al. (2017), but proceeds in discrete time.[6] Except for the discrete time, it parallels closely that of Chapter 5. The strategy is to consider a possible perturbation whereby the consumer changes consumption for one period (at t), and then uses the proceeds of that change to reset their consumption at t + 1 and beyond; this information is given by the consumer's budget constraint and some postulated but time-consistent consumption dynamics. Thus, the procedure is time-consistent as it depends on a "policy" rule (consumption rule) and the resulting consumption dynamics that are both time-consistent.

Formally, the perturbation should leave utility at time t unaltered, if the consumer is on an optimal path. Accordingly, the change in lifetime utility from a change in C_t is[7]:

$$\frac{dU_t}{dC_t} = C_t^{-\sigma} + \sum_{\tau=1}^{\infty} \left\{ C_{t+\tau}^{-\sigma} \phi(t+\tau, t) \frac{dC_{t+\tau}}{dC_{t+1}} \frac{dC_{t+1}}{dK_{t+1}} \frac{dK_{t+1}}{dC_t} \right\} = 0. \tag{6}$$

[6] Our procedure pre-supposes a "sophisticated present-biased" individual, i.e. someone who is aware of their present-bias. This contrasts with the "naïve short-termist" who is not (see Chapter 5).

[7] Expressing (1') as $(1-\sigma)U_t = C_t^{1-\sigma} + (t, t+1)(1-\sigma)U_{t+1}$ brings out the formal analogy between our approach and that of "selves-based" discrete-time models such as that of Krusell and Smith (2003, cf. Eqs. 1 and 2) and Harris and Laibson (2001, cf. Eqs. 2 and 3). The policy rule determining consumption (see 6 below) is analogous to the time-invariant policy rule arising from such analyses (that both the current and future selves are using, therefore: time-consistent in the sub-game perfect equilibrium).

This approach allows the entire stream of consumption, and not only consumption at a specific point in time as in the perturbation underlying the Euler equation, to be potentially affected after the initial change; this is key to delivering time consistency. The total effect on utility from a change in current consumption is made up of the sum of the direct effect on utility at time t, plus the effect on discounted utility from the change in consumption at $\tau \geq t + 1$. Furthermore, to gauge the change in future consumption, one needs an evolution formula for consumption from t + 1 onwards (the first ratio inside the curly brackets), the effect of altered assets at t + 1 on consumption at t + 1 (a kind of propensity to consume out of assets, the second ratio), times the effect on assets at t + 1 from changed consumption at t (the third ratio). We consider these effects in turn.

In the beginning-of-period formulation, the individual's budget constraint is:

$$K_{t+1} = (1 + r_t)[K_t + W_t - C_t], \tag{7}$$

where K_t is assets, r_t is the rate of interest (assumed to accrue overnight between t and t + 1), and W_t is the labour income of the individual (all in real terms). The real interest rate need not be time-invariant; in fact, as it reflects the marginal productivity of capital, we shall take it as an exogenous driver of growth in what follows. Labour income (W_t) will be linked to the production function, to be specified below. The main point here is, it is exogenous to the individual.

Therefore,

$$\frac{dK_{t+1}}{dC_t} = -(1 + r_t). \tag{8}$$

Evaluating the effect of higher assets at t + 1 on consumption at that time and beyond (dC_{t+1}/dK_{t+1}) is trickier. Following Barro (1999), we conjecture that there is a "propensity to consume" out of current assets and lifetime labour income, defined by[8]:

$$\lambda_t \equiv \frac{C_t}{K_t + \overline{W}_t} > 0. \tag{9}$$

This "propensity to consume", λ_t, is the individual's hypothesised policy rule determining consumption out of lifetime wealth. We restrict this to be positive but not time-invariant; even so, the resulting outcome is time-consistent, as we explain below.

It also falls with the interest rate due to the unmodelled cost of credit.

This implies a consumption path equal to:

$$C_t = \lambda_t \left(K_t + \overline{W}_t \right), \tag{10}$$

This may be considered a "policy" rule for the individual. Lifetime labour earnings, $\overline{W}_t$, are defined as:

$$\overline{W}_t \equiv \sum_{\tau=0}^{\infty} \left\{ W_{t+\tau} R_{t+\tau,t} \right\}, \tag{11}$$

The discount factor is defined as:

$$R_{t+\tau,t} = 1 \text{ for } \tau = 0;\ R_{t+\tau,t} = \prod_{s=0}^{\tau-1} (1 + r_{t+s})^{-1} \quad \text{for } \tau \geq 1 \tag{12}$$

This discount factor is characterised by the two iterative formulas $R_{t+\tau,t} = (1 + r_t)^{-1} R_{t+\tau,t+1}$ and $R_{t+\tau+1,t} = (1 + r_{t+\tau})^{-1} R_{t+\tau,t}$. With this, (11) becomes:

$$\overline{W}_t = W_t + \sum_{\tau=1}^{\infty} \left\{ W_{t+\tau} R_{t+\tau,t} \right\} = W_t + (1 + r_t)^{-1} \sum_{\tau=1}^{\infty} \left\{ W_{t+\tau} R_{t+\tau,t+1} \right\} \tag{11'}$$

The interpretation of Eq. (11) (applied to the steady state for clearer intuition) is that an annuity equal to $r\overline{W}_t = W_t$ would be equal to the real

[8] Thus, consumption is postulated to be a fraction of total lifetime resources. But this assumption is not unduly restrictive; the same is true in the standard model (where λ_t itself turns out to be a non-linear function of the interest rate and the exponential rate of time preference).

wage, and if it were consumed every period, the lifetime labour earnings would just be exhausted.

From (11′), we obtain:

$$\overline{W}_t = W_t + (1 + r_t)^{-1}\overline{W}_{t+1} \tag{13}$$

Using (13) and the resource constraint (7) into (10), we also obtain:

$$C_t = \lambda_t\left(K_t + \overline{W}_t\right) = \lambda_t\Big((1 + r_t)^{-1}\left(K_{t+1} + \overline{W}_{t+1}\right) + C_t\Big)$$

Therefore, shifting (10) one period forward and substituting the above, we get:

$$C_t = \lambda_t\left(\frac{C_{t+1}}{(1 + r_t)\lambda_{t+1}} + C_t\right), \tag{14}$$

This is re-written as:

$$C_{t+1} = \Lambda(t + 1, t)C_t, \tag{15}$$

With:

$$\Lambda(t + 1, t) \equiv (1 + r_t)\lambda_{t+1}\left[\frac{1 - \lambda_t}{\lambda_t}\right] \tag{16}$$

Equation (15) replaces the Euler equation of consumption dynamics. The novelty of this setup in relation to standard theory is the existence of the propensity to consume, λ_t. Generalising, for any distance from the planning period:

$$C_{t+\tau} = C_t \prod_{s=0}^{\tau-1} \Lambda(t + 1 + s, t + s), \tau \geq 1 \tag{15′}$$

From this, we have, in a straightforward way:

$$\frac{dC_{t+\tau}}{dC_t} = \prod_{s=0}^{\tau-1} \Lambda(t + 1 + s, t + s), \tau \geq 1$$

Also:

$$\frac{C_{t+\tau}^{-\sigma}}{C_t^{-\sigma}} = \prod_{s=0}^{\tau-1}[\Lambda(t+1+s,t+s)]^{-\sigma}, \tau \geq 1$$

And therefore:

$$\frac{C_{t+\tau}^{-\sigma}}{C_t^{-\sigma}}\frac{dC_{t+\tau}}{dC_t} = \left(\frac{C_{t+\tau}}{C_t}\right)^{1-\sigma} = \prod_{s=0}^{\tau-1}[\Lambda(t+1+s,t+s)]^{1-\sigma}, \tau \geq 1.$$

With this information, alongside the effect of consumption on capital (8), the policy rule (10) and consumption dynamics (15), we are able to express the perturbation in (6) after division across by $C_t^{-\sigma}$ and re-arrangement as:

$$0 = 1-(1+r_t)\frac{dC_t}{dC_{t+1}}\frac{dC_{t+1}}{dK_{t+1}}\sum_{\tau=1}^{\infty}\left\{\left(\frac{C_{t+\tau}}{C_t}\right)^{1-\sigma}\phi(t+\tau,t)\right\}, \tag{17}$$

Or:

$$1 = \frac{(1+r_t)\lambda_{t+1}}{\Lambda(t+1,t)}\sum_{\tau=1}^{\infty}\left\{\phi(t+\tau,t)\prod_{s=0}^{\tau-1}[\Lambda(t+1+s,t+s)]^{1-\sigma}\right\}$$

where the first ratio simplifies to:

$$\frac{(1+r_t)\lambda_{t+1}}{\Lambda(t+1,t)} = \frac{(1+r_t)\lambda_{t+1}}{(1+r_t)\lambda_{t+1}\left[\frac{1-\lambda_t}{\lambda_t}\right]} = \frac{\lambda_t}{1-\lambda_t}$$

With this information, we get a value for the propensity to consume:

$$\frac{\lambda_t}{1-\lambda_t} = \frac{1}{\sum_{\tau=1}^{\infty}\left\{\phi(t+\tau,t)\prod_{s=0}^{\tau-1}[\Lambda(t+1+s,t+s)]^{1-\sigma}\right\}} \tag{18}$$

We now see how time consistency has been achieved: The propensity to consume λ_t does not depend on τ (after integration); therefore, it imposes the same rule on consumption at any given time (that depends on the "fundamentals" of lifetime resources and the propensity itself) irrespective of how long before the event the planning took place. In other words, the propensity to consume is time-varying yet time-consistent: Its dynamics depends entirely on extraneous developments and not on the timing of planning.

It is now instructive to pause and take a look at the implications of (18) for the steady state. In the balanced-growth-path steady state, all levels of variables grow at the same, constant growth rate, and all growth rates and "grand ratios" are constant. The real interest rate (r) and the marginal propensity to consume (λ) are also constant. From the definition of $\Lambda(t+1,t)$ in (16), we have:

$$\Lambda(t+1+s,t+s) = (1+r)(1-\lambda) \approx 1+r-\lambda \tag{16'}$$

for all t and s. Consumption growth in the steady state equals the economy-wide growth rate (g), therefore from Eq. (15), we have:

$$g = r - \lambda \tag{19}$$

Regarding discounting, it is instructive to consider first the purely geometric case, where $\varphi = 0$ and the discount factor is: $\phi(t+\tau,t) = (1+\rho)^{-\tau}$. To this end, we approximate:

$$[\Lambda(t+1+s,t+s)]^{1-\sigma} \approx 1+(1-\sigma)(r-\lambda) \tag{16''}$$

Therefore, the quantity on the right of (18) becomes:

$$\sum_{\tau=1}^{\infty}\left\{\phi(t+\tau,t)\prod_{s=0}^{\tau-1}[\Lambda(t+1+s,t+s)]^{1-\sigma}\right\} \approx \sum_{\tau=1}^{\infty}\frac{[1+(1-\sigma)(r-\lambda)]^{\tau}}{(1+\rho)^{\tau}}$$
$$= \frac{1+(1-\sigma)(r-\lambda)}{\rho-(1-\sigma)(r-\lambda)}$$

Hence, (18) implies:

$$\frac{\lambda^{GEO}}{1-\lambda^{GEO}} = \frac{\rho-(1-\sigma)\left(r-\lambda^{GEO}\right)}{1+(1-\sigma)\left(r-\lambda^{GEO}\right)} \tag{20}$$

Some tedious re-writing gives:

$$0 < \lambda^{GEO} = \frac{\rho+(\sigma-1)r}{\sigma+\rho} < 1 \tag{21a}$$

From (19), the steady-state growth rate (of consumption and all other variables) is:

$$g^{GEO} = r - \lambda^{GEO} = \frac{r(1+\rho) - \rho}{\sigma + \rho} \approx \frac{r - \rho}{\sigma} \tag{21b}$$

The last approximate equality gives the EG growth rate in continuous time (see Chapter 5; and Tsoukis et al., 2017, Eqs. 25–26); so, except for the second-order terms, the discrete-time and continuous-time cases coincide.

We next proceed to get the steady-state results under the general case that incorporates HD. In that case, the denominator on the right of (18) becomes:

$$\sum_{\tau=1}^{\infty}\left\{\phi(t+\tau,t)\prod_{s=0}^{\tau-1}[\Lambda(t+1+s,t+s)]^{1-\sigma}\right\} = \frac{1+(1-\sigma)(r-\lambda)}{(1+\rho)(1+\varphi)} + \\ + \frac{[1+(1-\sigma)(r-\lambda)]^2}{(1+\rho)^2(1+\varphi)\left(1+\varphi^2\right)} \cdots =$$

Intuitively, we see that the present of HD (φ) decreases this sum. In other words, a "greater amount" of total intertemporal discounting takes place than under purely geometric discounting, and this is not surprising as the discount factor that applies to the near future is higher, while that of the distant future asymptotically approaches the geometric discount rate. Therefore, the MPC (λ) increases: More consumption results out of a given amount of intertemporal resources. Therefore, less resources are available for investment, and the growth rate drops given the real interest rate, as can be checked from the equality $g = r\text{-}\lambda$. It is also clear that the higher the φ (given ρ), the higher the λ and the lower the growth rate.

Straightforward but rather tedious calculations, outlined in Technical Appendix T1, yield:

$$\frac{\lambda}{1-\lambda} = \frac{\rho - (1-\sigma)(r-\lambda)}{1+(1-\sigma)(r-\lambda)} \frac{1+\rho-\varphi G}{(1-\varphi)(1+\rho)-\varphi G}, \tag{22}$$

where:

$$G \equiv 1 + (1-\sigma)(r-\lambda) \tag{23}$$

Comparison of (20) with (22) and (23) establishes that $\lambda \geq \lambda^{GEO}$, with equality when $\varphi = 0$. Appendix T1 presents a simple geometric argument that makes this clear. In fact, λ rises with φ. As the growth rate then depends negatively on λ from (19), given the real interest rate, the growth rate declines with φ and present bias. The result that more present-bias increases the propensity to consume and thereby reduces growth is also familiar from the last chapter.

We next linearise Eq. (18), in order to obtain a difference equation for the propensity to consume (λ). Much of what follows involves a long series of tedious manipulations, detailed in Technical Appendix T2, so here we go straight to the result, Eq. (24) or (26):

$$\frac{\tilde{\lambda}_t}{\lambda}\frac{G}{(1-\lambda)(\sigma-1)} = \frac{(1-\lambda)\tilde{r}_t + \frac{1+r}{\lambda}\left[(1-\lambda)\tilde{\lambda}_{t+1} - \tilde{\lambda}_t\right]}{1 - \frac{G}{1+\rho}L^{-1}} \tag{24}$$

Equation (24) offers an intuitive interpretation of λ. The right side of (24) is the (linearised) growth rate of consumption, cf. (15) and (16). Therefore, the current λ is the present value of all these future growth rates, discounted at rate $G/(1 + \rho)$. Note that although φ does not feature explicitly, present-bias is indirectly present via the steady-state value of λ (which is higher, it will be recalled, with more present-bias).

Furthermore, using the approximation in (T1.3): $\frac{1}{1+\lambda} \approx 1 - \lambda \approx \frac{G}{1+\rho}$, we can simplify to:

$$\left[\frac{G}{(1-\lambda)(\sigma-1)} + 1 + r\right]\frac{\tilde{\lambda}_t}{\lambda} = \frac{(1-\lambda)\tilde{r}_t}{1 - \frac{G}{1+\rho}L^{-1}} \tag{25}$$

The main property of (25) is that it involves a forward-looking structure and that the propensity to consume ($\tilde{\lambda}_t$) depends on all current and future (deviations of) interest rates.

Using (24) once again, we are able to relate the growth rate of consumption to the interest rate—again, Appendix T2 has the details:

$$(1-\lambda)\tilde{r}_t + \frac{1+r}{\lambda}\left[(1-\lambda)\tilde{\lambda}_{t+1} - \tilde{\lambda}_t\right] = M\tilde{r}_t \tag{26}$$

$$0 < M \equiv \frac{(1-\lambda)G}{G + (1-\lambda)(\sigma-1)(1+r)} \approx \frac{(1-\lambda)G}{\sigma} < 1$$

Equation (26) is a linearised version of the key Eq. (18) and is one of the key dynamic equations of the model. It will play a prominent role in what follows. With this, we are able to express the growth rate of consumption (cf. Eq. 16) as a positive function of the interest rate. With $\sigma > 1$ (our default assumption), we get the restriction $0 < M < 1$. The positive relation between the growth rate of consumption and the interest rate is reminiscent of the Euler equation: There, the interest rate stimulates saving and hence consumption growth. As Tsoukis et al. (2017) points out, this equation degenerates and hence λ is a constant, when there are no time-varying changes in the real interest rate.

The rest of the chapter proceeds now to integrate this setup in a complete, yet simple, macroeconomic model.

Production and National Income Accounting

The production function is of the "AK" form. This allows for analytic balanced-growth-path equilibrium; but while in the standard AK model, there is no dynamics, here there will be dynamics due to the hyperbolic discount factor. Thus, when shocks occur (introduced below), the dynamics allow for a gradual return to equilibrium, and this gives scope for a stabilisation policy. Potential output (with overbar) is proportional to the capital stock:

$$\overline{Y}_t = AK_t \tag{27}$$

where K_t is capital defined in a broad sense, inclusive of productivity supported by "learning-by-doing" externalities (Arrow 1962; Frankel 1962; and Romer 1986) and public services (Barro 1990). As discussed in Chapter 4, both these types of effect are assumed to be proportional to the capital stock (equivalently: output) and ensure that the marginal return to a broad definition of capital is constant and therefore growth is perpetual. Implicitly, the AK model assumes that labour is inelastically supplied and equal to the time endowment of one.

In order to introduce a potential for stabilisation policy, we introduce a distinction between potential and actual output (the latter is simply Y_t—without overbar). The difference between the two is (the negative of) the output gap, defined formally as[9]:

$$y_t \equiv \frac{Y_t - \overline{Y}_t}{\overline{Y}_t} \tag{28a}$$

Intuitively, the output gap is due to either part of the (unmodelled) labour or part of capital falling idle due to lack of demand. It is also due to productivity deviating temporarily from A. Therefore, output becomes:

$$Y_t = \overline{Y}_t(1 + y_t) = AK_t(1 + y_t) \tag{28b}$$

We assume that the output deviations, y_t, are characterised by persistence:

$$y_{t+1} = (1 - \psi)y_t \tag{29}$$

where $0 \leq 1\text{-}\psi \leq 1$ is the persistence parameter. This persistence will hold even if the shock is instantaneous (as below) and is implicitly assumed to exist because of such factors as labour market (search) frictions, time-to-build considerations in investment, or persistence in productivity. For consistency, we shall assume below that this parameter is such that the persistence of output is the same as the persistence of the consumption-capital ratio (deviations from the steady-state value).

In this model, there is generally no government (except a monetary authority or Central Bank). But we shall allow for a demand shock that will initiate a business cycle (and hence create the potential for stabilisation). One shock is a spending shock, assumed for simplicity to be a government spending shock of size $\gamma_t Y_t$ ($0 < \gamma_t < 1$). This spending is assumed to be debt-financed, so there is no taxation (and no other debt). This, admittedly simplistic, setup allows us to focus entirely on the demand-side implications of government spending. It also lets the government spending shock be observationally equivalent to any other spending shock, and hence broaden its relevance.

Furthermore, we assume that net exports are proportional to the value of the currency, and this in turn is inversely proportional to the real interest rate:

$$NetEx_t = -\mu(r_t - r)Y_t \tag{30}$$

[9] In empirical business cycles research, y_t is also referred to as detrended output (assuming that $\overline{Y}_t$ captures trend).

This is a simple way by which we allow monetary policy to exert an effect on output; the effect of the interest rate on net exports is captured by $\mu > 0$. Otherwise, the external sector remains unmodelled.[10] Both the shocks and the monetary policy effect are proportional to output.

The national resource constraint is standard[11]:

$$Y_t = C_t + K_{t+1} - K_t + \gamma_t Y_t + NetEx_t \tag{31}$$

Using the production function (27), the output gap (28a), and net exports (30) and collecting terms, we can re-write (31) as:

$$[1 + y_t - \gamma_t + \mu(r_t - r)]A = \frac{C_t}{K_t} + \frac{K_{t+1} - K_t}{K_t} \tag{32}$$

The intuition here is standard but it may help: Given the level of consumption and capital accumulation, a higher spending shock will imply a higher output. Alternatively, given the output level, higher government spending crowds out consumption and/or capital accumulation. A similar interpretation, with the opposite sign, holds for the effect of monetary policy on net exports and demand.

At this point, an appropriate transversality condition should be added that would rule out runaway capital accumulation; appropriately discounted capital at the end of time should approach zero. We leave it to future research to specify the precise form of this transversality condition in the presence of present-bias; note that normally, future capital is discounted at the constant, exponential/geometric discount rate.

It is useful at this point to compare our setup with the standard model; the latter would have:

- A consumption Euler equation—replaced here by (18) or linearised form (24), giving rise eventually to (26);

[10] Alternatively, monetary policy can affect output through the workings of the financial system, with an effect of the type emphasised by the voluminous literature on the "credit channel", but that would be more difficult to model. The exchange-rate and credit channels are not mutually exclusive, in fact, they can reinforce each other.

[11] Formally, the national resource constraint should be the sum of the representative individual's budget constraint (7) and the (unmodelled) firm's budget constraint. But, if we allowed for net exports/trade balance, that would also require modelling foreign assets and their accumulation dynamics; which would take us too far afield. So, Eq. (32) is correct, but it should be derived and not postulated.

- Production function—here (28b) with absent labour, so essentially an "AK" production function with an added output gap caused by shocks;
- National Income Accounting and capital accumulation, here (32).

As is well known, because of its "AK" nature, the standard model would feature a constant growth rate and would always be on a balanced-growth-path (equal growth rates across all variables and agents)—see, e.g. García-Peñalosa and Turnovsky (2006). If, instead, the production function was "neoclassical", with constant returns to capital and (elastic) labour but diminishing returns to aggregate capital, then the model would be of the "Ramsey" type, with asymptotic growth equal to the population growth rate (so that per-capita values are constant)—see, e.g. Turnovsky and García-Peñalosa (2007).

Therefore, we have developed two dynamic equations: Eq. (26) characterises the path of the marginal propensity to consume and replaces the traditional Euler equation of the standard framework built on geometric discounting; Eq. (32) with output from (28b) is essentially the resource constraint. A third equation will be derived from monetary policy and inflation below. We next proceed to characterise the steady state of the system more fully. Let us add that the tricky issue of dynamics in this setup is bypassed by letting shocks occur only once and imposing an exogenous decay (inverse persistence) on the output gap. With this, we can obtain an analytical solution and get results for macroeconomic (mainly monetary) policy in the face of present bias. A full treatment of dynamics is left for future research.

Steady State

As mentioned above, in the steady-state, balanced-growth-path, all K, C, and Y (all real) grow at the same, constant growth rate (g), and "grand ratios" (such as the consumption-capital ratio, C/K), interest rates and the propensity to consume are all constant; there is no output gap. Therefore, the steady-state version of the resource constraint Eq. (31) is:

$$\frac{C_t}{K_t} = A - g \tag{33a}$$

The growth rate (to repeat, common across variables) is obtained from the consumption Eq. (19), repeated here:

$$g = r - \lambda \tag{33b}$$

The propensity to consume is given by Eq. (23′), repeated here with minor re-writing from the definition of G in (21a):

$$\frac{\frac{1-\lambda}{\lambda}}{\frac{1-(\sigma-1)(r-\lambda)}{\rho+(\sigma-1)(r-\lambda)}} = \frac{1+\rho-\varphi+\varphi(\sigma-1)(r-\lambda)}{(1-\varphi)(1+\rho)-\varphi+\varphi(\sigma-1)(r-\lambda)} \tag{33c}$$

The steady-state interest rate (r) is exogenously given, reflecting the marginal product of privately owned capital (refer to Chapter 5 for more details). Implicitly, the capital in the production function is a Cobb–Douglas composite of privately owned capital to an extent $0 < \kappa < 1$, and the positive externalities (such as learning-by-doing, or from public services) engendered by aggregate capital to an extent $1\text{-}\kappa$. With the labour fixed at unity, the real interest rate is κA. From (33a) and the consumption function (10) with $C_t = \lambda_t\left(K_t + \frac{W_t}{r-g}\right)$ and the growth rate (19 or 33b), we have:

$$\frac{C_t}{K_t} = \lambda\left(1 + \frac{\overline{W}_t}{K_t}\right) = \lambda + \frac{W_t}{Y_t}A(1+\lambda) = A - g = A - r + \lambda$$

Simplifying:

$$\frac{W_t}{Y_t}A(1+\lambda) + r = A$$

The interpretation is familiar from national income accounting and the theory of income distribution. The left is labour plus interest income and this, on the right, equals gross output (-capital ratio). Therefore, with r = κA, the wage-gross output ratio is:

$$\frac{W_t}{Y_t} = \frac{1-\kappa}{1+\lambda} \tag{33d}$$

The present value of labour earnings then becomes:

$$\frac{\overline{W}_t}{K_t} = \frac{W_t}{Y_t}\frac{A(1+\lambda)}{\lambda} = \frac{(1-\kappa)A}{\lambda} \tag{33e}$$

Thus, the division of gross output is as follows: A fraction $0 < \kappa < 1$ goes to capital income (interest), out of which λ/A finances investment; the rest is consumed. Net income (i.e. net of investment) represents a fraction $1/(1 + \lambda)$ of gross income; of that, a fraction $1\text{-}\kappa$ goes to labour, all of which is consumed. We now get an important intermediate result, namely that the wage share in gross output is determined not only by the technical parameter κ but also by the propensity to consume (λ) which is affected by present-bias. Thus, present-bias has also important implications for factor shares and income inequality (see also the last chapter).

All variables have now been determined. The effects of parameters of interest, such as productivity (A) and the geometric discount rate (ρ) are essentially the same is in standard models, so we shall not dwell upon them. The exception is the effect of hyperbolic discounting, introduced by φ, which merits a comment. Do let us recall the assumption that $\sigma \geq 1$. With this, the ratio on the right-hand side of (33c) increases with φ and decreases with λ; the left-hand side also decreases with λ. Therefore, given productivity and the real interest rate, a rise in φ will elicit a fall in the propensity to consume (λ). From (33a), the consumption-capital ratio will rise. Thus, consumption rises out of given capital but the latter will be growing at a lower rate.

A "Keynesian Consumption Function" and a Modified IS Equation (MIS)

In this brief section, we develop a new dynamic equation, consolidating the consumption dynamics, (15), with (16), and the national income accounting equation, (32). Using the linearisation of the growth rate of consumption (16) as in the numerator of the right side of Eq. (24—cf. also T2.1a, b), the former is re-expressed as:

$$\frac{C_{t+1} - C_t}{C_t} = (1 - \lambda)\tilde{r}_t + \frac{1 + r}{\lambda}\left[(1 - \lambda)\tilde{\lambda}_{t+1} - \lambda_t\right] \qquad (34)$$

Subtracting (32) by parts from the above, we get:

$$\frac{C_{t+1} - C_t}{C_t} - \frac{K_{t+1} - K_t}{K_t} = -(1 + y_t - \gamma_t + \mu(r_t - r))A + \frac{C_t}{K_t}$$
$$+ (1 - \lambda)\tilde{r}_t + \frac{1 + r}{\lambda}\left[(1 - \lambda)\tilde{\lambda}_{t+1} - \lambda_t\right]$$

If we let $c_t \equiv \log\left(\frac{C_t}{K_t}\right)$ be the log C-K ratio, then we may write: $\frac{C_t}{K_t} \approx \frac{C}{K}(1 + c_t)$, and with $\frac{K_{t+1}-K_t}{K_t} - \frac{C_{t+1}-C_t}{C_t} = -c_{t+1} + c_t$, and using (26), the above may be re-expressed as:

$$c_{t+1} - c_t = -(1 + y_t - \gamma_t + \mu(r_t - r))A + \frac{C}{K}(1 + c_t) + M\tilde{r}_t \qquad (35)$$

As mentioned, Eq. (35) consolidates and replaces Eqs. (15) and (33); it is a key equation in our dynamic system. There are two noteworthy features. Firstly, notice the greater than unity coefficient of c_t on the right. This implies a dual possibility: If there are no time-varying external drivers (e.g. if any exogenous change takes place once-and-for-all), then the equation is unstable: the constant on the right (C/K) implies that c_{t+s} will become ever higher at higher s, eventually approaching infinity. (Note that C/K will also jump to its new value instantaneously and permanently—hence, it is constant). Thus, the endogenous variables (including the growth rate, g) all jump to their new permanent values immediately when a (permanent) change occurs. (See, e.g. Turnovsky 1995; Garcia-Penalosa and Turnovsky 2007; Tsoukis 2020). Things change in our setup, however, because shocks are assumed to occur once only.

If we get deviations from the steady state (reminder: to be denoted by tildes, so that $\tilde{c}_t \equiv c_t - c$, and similarly for all other variables), Eq. (35) becomes:

$$\left(1 + \frac{C}{K}\right)\left[1 - \frac{1}{1 + \frac{C}{K}}L^{-1}\right]\tilde{c}_t = A(y_t - \gamma_t + \mu\tilde{r}_t) - M\tilde{r}_t \qquad (36a)$$

{L}^{-1} is the lead operator, explained below. This key dynamic equation is essentially a resource constraint. To gain intuition, these are the elements of this equation:

- $\frac{C}{K}\tilde{c}_t$ is private consumption;
- the capital growth rate (investment) is made up of two components: The effect of the interest rate on consumption dynamics (essentially saving), $M\tilde{r}_t$, plus, the dynamics of the consumption-capital ratio, $(1 - L^{-1})\tilde{c}_t$;
- on the right, we have output (capacity), net of government spending and net exports (itself negatively dependent on the interest rate).

Note the structure of (36a): The less than unity coefficient of the lead of $\tilde{c}_t$, implies that the equation must be solved "forward"; this is standard. Solving forward presents the present value of the terms on the right side:

$$\left(1+\frac{C}{K}\right)\tilde{c}_t = A(£_1(\tilde{y}_t) - £_1(\gamma_t)) + (A\mu - M)£_1(\tilde{r}_t) \tag{36b}$$

where $£_1(x_t) \equiv \frac{x_t}{1-\frac{1}{1+\frac{C}{K}}L^{-1}}$. It is clear from (36a) and (36b) that the cumulative effect of the interest rate is C/K; but a higher C/K spreads the future sum further into the future as the discounting is lighter. Thus, as C/K rises with λ and present-bias, one intermediate result is that the sum of shocks and other drivers of the consumption-capital ratio both rise and become more forward-looking. This might appear counterintuitive (present-bias making future shocks more relevant) but it makes more sense if we remember from (18) that the λ cumulates future discount factors. This is how time consistency is achieved. So, the higher the early discount rate (present bias), the more forward-looking the sum ought to be.

There are two alternative ways of presenting (36b) that help intuition. Firstly, re-arrange it to get:

$$A\tilde{y}_t = \left(1+\frac{C}{K}\right)\tilde{c}_t + A£_1(\gamma_t) - (A\mu - M)£_1(\tilde{r}_t) + \frac{A\tilde{y}_{t+1}}{1+\frac{C}{K}} \tag{37a}$$

According to (37a), output is made up of two components: the elements of current aggregate demand (the first three items on the right), plus the expected future resources (future output). The first element is emphasised by the textbook Keynesian analysis, the latter is a feature of "neoclassical" intertemporal optimisation. One contribution of our framework is to show that present bias (λ) increases C/K and therefore reduces the relevance of future resources. In other words, a higher present bias brings us a step closer to the textbook Keynesian model. This gives rise to Result 1:

Result 1 A rise in present bias reduces the relevance of future resources in determining current output.

It is also instructive to show (36b) with the persistence rule (29) for output, in which case the present value of output is: $£_1(y_t) =$

$\frac{y_t}{1-\frac{1}{1+\frac{C}{K}}(1-\psi)} \approx y_t \frac{1+\frac{C}{K}}{\frac{C}{K}+\psi}$; hence, by re-arrangement, we get:

$$\frac{A}{\frac{C}{K}+\psi} y_t = \tilde{c}_t + \frac{\pounds_1(\gamma_t)}{1+\frac{C}{K}} - (A\mu - M)\frac{\pounds_1(\tilde{r}_t)}{1+\frac{C}{K}} \tag{37b}$$

This is another form of the resource constraint; in the standard way, output is affected by demand (consumption; the spending shock; and net exports via the interest rate), but it is also affected positively by the interest rate as that creates incentives to save and invest. In what follows, we assume that the net effect of the interest rate is negative, i.e. $A\mu - M > 0$, hence the interest rate affects output negatively, which gives it a stabilisation role in the first instance.

A number of further remarks are noteworthy, in relation to our focus on present bias. Firstly, both the shock and the interest rate appear as present values, i.e. both current and future values matter. This gives monetary policy a "forward guidance" role, in that it can affect current decision simply by announcing the future course of policy (i.e. without any current actions). This has given rise to paradox, namely that future monetary policy seems to matter now too much, in a counter-factual way (see Gabaix, 2020). Our framework can help resolve the puzzle as λ increases C/K and therefore reduces the discount factor in $\pounds_1(\tilde{r}_t)$; hence, the relevance of future monetary policy is moderated by the presence of present value. We summarise thus:

Result 2 A rise in present bias decreases the relevance of future interest rates for the determination of current output and therefore reduces the relevance of future monetary policy.

Secondly, the total effect of the spending shock and/or the interest rate (given consumption) increases with λ. Assuming for a moment that both the shock and the interest rate stayed constant at γ and $\tilde{r}$, then the equation becomes:

$$\frac{A}{\frac{C}{K}+\psi} y_t = \tilde{c}_t + \frac{\gamma}{\frac{C}{K}} - (A\mu - M)\frac{\tilde{r}}{\frac{C}{K}}$$

With the assumed structure of the shocks, the present value of the spending shock is: {\pounds }_{1}\left({\{gamma }}_{t}\right)={\{gamma}}_{t}. To close the system, we solve for c_t as follows: We take log-deviations from the fundamental Eq. (10), to obtain:

$$\tilde{c}_t = \frac{\tilde{\lambda}_t}{\lambda} + dlog\left(1 + \frac{\overline{W}_t}{K_t}\right) = \frac{\tilde{\lambda}_t}{\lambda} + \frac{d\left(\frac{\overline{W}_t}{K_t}\right)}{1 + \frac{\overline{W}_t}{K_t}} \tag{38}$$

where d() is the change of the variable from its initial steady-state value. From (11) and (33d):

$$\begin{aligned}\overline{W}_t &= \sum_{\tau=0}^{\infty}\{W_{t+\tau}R_{t+\tau,t}\} = \frac{W_t}{Y_t}A\sum_{\tau=0}^{\infty}\{K_{t+\tau}R_{t+\tau,t}\} \\ &= \frac{1-\kappa}{1+\lambda}AK_t\sum_{\tau=0}^{\infty}\left\{\prod_{s=0}^{\tau}(1+g_s^K)R_{t+\tau,t}\right\}\end{aligned} \tag{39a}$$

In taking deviations,$d\left(\frac{\overline{W}_t}{K_t}\right)$, we must allow for the output gap,$y_{t+\tau}$. The quantity in (38) involves the growth rate of capital,g_s^K, with the convention that$g_0^K = 1$. As discussed above in going from (34) to (35), this equals:

$$g_s^K \equiv \frac{K_{t+1} - K_t}{K_t} = \frac{C_{t+1} - C_t}{C_t} - (c_{t+1} - c_t) \tag{39b}$$

where a reminder is that $c_t \equiv \log\left(\frac{C_t}{K_t}\right)$, the log C-K ratio. We shall use (39a) in deviations form and will also make free use of (19). The result is derived in detail in Technical Appendix T3, and presented below in Eq. (40a):

$$(1+\overline{\omega})\tilde{c}_t\left[1 - \frac{1+(1+\lambda)\overline{\omega}}{(1+\lambda)(1+\overline{\omega})}L^{-1}\right] = \omega\tilde{r}_t + \overline{\omega}y_t, 0 < \overline{\omega}, \omega < 1 \tag{40}$$

$$\tilde{c}_t = \frac{\overline{\omega}y_t + \omega\tilde{r}_t}{1+\overline{\omega}} + \frac{1+(1+\lambda)\overline{\omega}}{(1+\lambda)(1+\overline{\omega})}\tilde{c}_{t+1}, 0 < \overline{\omega}, \omega < 1 \tag{40a}$$

The precise expressions for $\overline{\omega}, \omega$ are given in Appendix T3. Equation (40a) writes current consumption as a weighted average of current resources (output) adjusted by the interest rate as the opportunity cost of consumption and of future consumption as an indicator of future resources. With $\frac{\partial\overline{\omega}}{\partial\lambda} > 0$, $\frac{\partial\omega}{\partial\lambda} < 0$ (see Appendix T3), the coefficient of current output $(\frac{\overline{\omega}}{1+\overline{\omega}})$ rises, while that of the interest rate $(\frac{\omega}{1+\overline{\omega}})$ and of future consumption $(\frac{1+(1+\lambda)\overline{\omega}}{(1+\lambda)(1+\overline{\omega})})$ decline with λ. Therefore, a rise in present bias increases the relevance of current resources (associated more with a "Keynesian consumption function", e.g. D'Orlando & Sanfilippo, 2010) while it reduces the relevance of the opportunity cost and future resources, as emphasised by the "neoclassical, intertemporal optimisation-based approach". We have Result 3:

Result 3 A rise in present bias takes us closer to a "Keynesian" and away from the (spirit of a) "neoclassical" consumption function.

Re-writing Eq. (40a) to bring out the future sums, as we did with (36b), we have:

$$(1+\overline{\omega})\tilde{c}_t = \omega £_2(\tilde{r}_t) + \overline{\omega} £_2(\tilde{y}_t) \tag{40b}$$

where $£_2(x_t) \equiv \frac{x_t}{1-\frac{1+(1+\lambda)\overline{\omega}}{(1+\lambda)(1+\overline{\omega})}L^{-1}}$. The cumulative effect of the interest rate is $\frac{1+\lambda}{\lambda}$. Again, we can apply the persistence rule of output, in analogy to (36b), with $\frac{1+(1+\lambda)\overline{\omega}}{(1+\lambda)(1+\overline{\omega})}(1-\psi) \approx \frac{1+(1+\lambda)\overline{\omega}-\psi}{(1+\lambda)(1+\overline{\omega})}$. In this case, we get:

$$(1+\overline{\omega})\tilde{c}_t = \omega £_2(\tilde{r}_t) + (1+\overline{\omega})\overline{\omega}\frac{1+\lambda}{\lambda+\psi}y_t, 0 < \overline{\omega}, \omega < 1 \tag{40c}$$

It is instructive to compare (36b) and (40b) under the assumption that there is no labour income ($\kappa = 1$ in Appendix T3), hence all consumption is $C_t = \lambda K_t$. In this case, it turns out that $\frac{1}{1+\frac{C}{K}} = \frac{1}{1+\lambda} = \frac{1+(1+\lambda)\overline{\omega}}{(1+\lambda)(1+\overline{\omega})}$ (cf. T3.2), therefore $\overline{\omega} = 0$, and the two equations combine to:

$$\omega\tilde{r}_t = \frac{A(y_t - \gamma_t + \mu\tilde{r}_t) - M\tilde{r}_t}{1+\frac{C}{K}} \tag{41}$$

In this case, the forward sums are such that they essentially cancel out,[12] leaving only a static equation.

In the general case of a positive labour share ($0 < \kappa < 1$), then:

$$\frac{1}{1+\frac{C}{K}} < \frac{1}{1+\lambda} < \frac{1+(1+\lambda)\overline{\omega}}{(1+\lambda)(1+\overline{\omega})} \tag{42}$$

[12] This can be seen by quasi-differencing.

In this case, Eq. (40c) becomes (after straightforward re-arrangement):

$$\frac{Ay_t}{\frac{C}{K}+\psi}-\overline{\omega}\frac{1+\lambda}{\lambda+\psi}y_t=\frac{A\gamma_t}{1+\frac{C}{K}}-\frac{(A\mu-M)\pounds_1(\tilde{r}_t)}{1+\frac{C}{K}}+\frac{\omega\pounds_2(\tilde{r}_t)}{1+\overline{\omega}} \tag{43}$$

On the left, we have the cumulative coefficient of output—production, minus the effect of output on consumption, applying the persistence rule (29). On the right, we have the spending shock (which occurs only once, so there is no present value). Further, on the right, we have the cumulative effects of the interest rate that occur because of the effect on the trade balance (the $-\mu < 0$ term) and the two positive terms that reflect the total effect of the interest rate on saving and consumption growth.

It is worth elaborating on the coefficient of output, which can be re-written as (with T3.2):

$$A\Omega_1 \equiv \left[\frac{A}{\frac{C}{K}+\psi}-\frac{(1-\kappa)A}{1+C/K}\frac{1+\lambda}{\lambda+\psi}\right](>0) \tag{44a}$$

As it is not easy to ascertain the sign in the square brackets, we take a Taylor expansion around $\psi = 1$ (no persistence), to get:

$$A\Omega_1 \approx \frac{\kappa A}{1+\frac{C}{K}}+\frac{1-\psi}{1+\frac{C}{K}}\left[\frac{A}{1+\frac{C}{K}}-\frac{(1-\kappa)A}{1+\lambda}\right] \tag{44b}$$

With plausible assumptions,[13] the expression in square brackets is positive, hence the inequality in parentheses in (44a). As we shall show below, this coefficient declines with λ.

In terms of the 3-equation NK model, Eq. (43) is a Modified IS curve (MIS), linking output to current and future interest rates and the fiscal shock. In the final section, we proceed to consider inflation and monetary

[13] This is a sufficient (not necessary) condition. It is also a plausible one, as would be obvious if we put back-of-the-envelope numbers on these variables. Plausible figures would be, C/K = 2/9 (C/Y = 2/3, Y/K = 1/3), and the intertemporal labour income (to which a tax rate of 1/3 should realistically apply) would be 2/3 (labour share in income) × 2/3 (net of tax) × 1/3 (Y/K) = 4/27. With C/K = λ + labour income/K, we have $\lambda = 2/27 \approx 7\%$. In our setup, there is no taxation, but that means that C/K should be greater than the number above. So, these figures are plausible. Thus, $(1-\kappa)A\frac{2}{9} < 1$ and $(1+\lambda) > (1+\frac{C}{K})(1-\kappa)A$ as this can be written $(1+\lambda)\frac{29}{27} > \frac{(1-\kappa)^2A^2}{1-(1-)A} = \frac{4}{81}\cdot\frac{9}{7} = \frac{4}{63}$. Hence, the square brackets is positive.

policy. This will result in an inflation equation or New Keynesian Phillips Curve and a monetary policy rule (Taylor rule). Together with the MIS Eq. (43), this will be a 3×3 system in inflation, y_t and$\tilde{r}_t$; in other words, we will have developed a version of the "three-equation New Keynesian model". The emphasis will be to see how present bias affects that system and the design of monetary policy.

The Fiscal (Government Spending) Multiplier

Before moving on to inflation and monetary policy, it is worth digressing briefly on the fiscal multiplier; a topic which is not our main focus, but on which our framework has insights to offer. Considering Eqs. (41) and (43a), the government expenditure multiplier is[14]:

$$\frac{\partial y_t}{\partial \gamma_t} = \frac{1}{(1+\frac{C}{K})\Omega_1} = \frac{1}{\left(1+\frac{C}{K}\right)\left[\frac{1}{\frac{C}{K}+\psi} - \frac{(1-\kappa)A}{1+\frac{C}{K}}\frac{1+\lambda}{\lambda+\psi}\right]} \tag{45a}$$

It should be emphasised that this multiplier takes the current and future interest rates as given; as we shall see below, things change when the response of interest rates to the output gap is factored in. To gain more perspectives, consider the impact multiplier which is derived by "shutting down" all future output because of no persistence at all ($\psi = 1$), so that we get[15]:

Impact multiplier:

$$\left.\frac{\partial y_t}{\partial \gamma_t}\right|_{\psi=1} = \frac{1}{[1-(1-\kappa)A]} > 1 \tag{45b}$$

as $\overline{\omega} = \frac{(1-\kappa)\lambda A}{1+\frac{C}{K}}$ (cf. T3.2). This multiplier is discussed in Technical Appendix T4 (cf. T4.1). Equation (45b) offers some quite strong results. As discussed in Chapter 5, there is a voluminous literature on the fiscal (spending) multiplier. (For a survey, the reader can consult—what else—Tsoukis (2020, Ch. 8), or practically any other text). A focal point is whether the multiplier is above or below unity, which is practically the

[14] Obviously, this involves government spending funded implicitly by government borrowing, as there is no taxation.

[15] Recall that the shock only occurs once.

dividing line between the "Keynesian" (demand) and the "neoclassical" multipliers. The multiplier here is a hybrid, with some Keynesian elements (notably, the output gap) grafted onto an intertemporally optimising setup but with exogenous labour. The fact that the multiplier is above unity makes this a Keynesian multiplier, in contrast to the one derived in the last chapter. Here, the expansionary effect comes from the fact that a rise in output expands consumption because of the wage element (captured by $(1 - \kappa)A$ in the denominator) and hence output demand, which is of course the textbook Keynesian mechanism.

With full persistence ($\psi = 0$), we get the cumulative multiplier shown in equation (T4.2). The general case uses the approximation in (44b) and is shown below (cf. also T4.3):

$$\left.\frac{\partial y_t}{\partial \gamma_t}\right|_{0\leq\psi<1} = \frac{1}{1-(1-\kappa)A+(1-\psi)\left[\frac{1}{1+\frac{C}{K}}-\frac{(1-\kappa)A}{1+\lambda}\right]} \tag{45c}$$

With $\psi < 1$, it is unclear whether this is above or below unity. But, as shown in (T4.4), a rise in present bias and λ raises this multiplier. Again, this is in sharp contrast to the neoclassical multiplier of the last chapter, and in the spirit of the Keynesian multiplier. More present bias implies more consumption now, raising the impact multiplier.

Result 4 In the general case (where $0 \leq \psi < 1$, i.e. excluding the case of no persistence at all), the government spending multiplier increases with present bias and λ.

3 Inflation and Monetary Policy

We now turn to inflation and monetary policy. The treatment here will be brief as we are on more standard ground. The change in inflation is linked to future inflation and the output gap:

$$\Delta\pi_t = \Theta\Delta\pi_{t+1} + \Xi_1 y_t - \Xi_2\alpha_t + v_t \tag{46}$$

where π_t is the inflation rate, Δ the difference operator (i.e. for any variable x,$\Delta x_t \equiv x_t - x_{t-1}$) and y_t is the (inverse) output gap, v_t is an exogenous pricing shock that fuels inflation, and α_t is a positive supply shock that reduces inflation as it decreases the marginal cost. A common interpretation of (37) is the New Keynesian Phillips Curve (NKPC), where the change in inflation is positively related to (the negative of) the output gap.

Unravelling the forward structure in (46), we get that the change in inflation is fuelled by the present and all future output gaps and pricing shocks minus the productivity shocks, all discounted by $0 < \Theta < 1$. This is intuitive: A buoyant output market accelerates inflation; a productivity shock checks inflation, while a pricing shock accelerates it. The interpretation of Θ will be discussed below; the key point is that Θ rises with all the forward-looking elements in the inflation process, in which case future developments matter more for current inflation acceleration.

Equation (46) is derived from a more general New Keynesian inflation equation of the following form (see Tsoukis, Kapetanios and Pearlman, 2011; and Tsoukis, 2020, Chapters 3 and 6):

$$\pi_t = \vartheta_1 \pi_{t-1} + \vartheta_2 \pi_{t+1} + \xi_1 y_t - \xi_2 \alpha_t \tag{46'}$$

This equation has Calvo (1983)-type pricing, and the many variants and elaborations since the original Calvo paper (see Tsoukis et al., 2011), at its core. As in the original Calvo (1983) paper, $\psi_1 > 0$ incorporates price flexibility, therefore inversely also price stickiness: it tells us that as price stickiness rises (ψ falls), the output gap will have a lower effect on inflation, as the latter is more sluggish (prices change more infrequently). $\psi_2 > 0$ adds the direct (adverse) effect of a supply shock on the marginal cost and inflation, as the subsequent literature has pointed out.

Equation (46′) relies on numerous very stylised and hence rather implausible assumptions, and has therefore been extended in various directions (see again Tsoukis et al., 2011, for a review). But engaging with such extensions would take us too far; hence, the simple (46′) equation serves to integrate inflation into an HD-based model of business cycles and monetary policy, while preserving tractability.

A Calvo (1983)-type pricing structure motivates the existence of a lead in Eq. (46′).[16] The existence of the lag is a more moot point; only a couple of variants imply it, namely models that assume wage as well as price stickiness and/or models that assume infrequent fully optimal revision of prices but inflation-indexed adjustment of prices between fully

[16] Note that our setup is deterministic, so future variables are known; there is no need to take expectations.

calculated revisions. In fact, there exist good analytical reasons as well as empirical evidence that argue towards two features: (i) a homogeneity restriction $\vartheta_1 + \vartheta_2 = 1$, and (ii) the lag being more important than the lead, i.e. $0.5 < \vartheta_1 < 1$ (see Tsoukis et al., 2011). Hence, we make these two assumptions here. Factoring the leads and lags under these two assumptions leads to Eq. (37) that we use here, where $\Xi_1 \equiv \frac{\xi_1}{\vartheta_1}$, $\Xi_2 \equiv \frac{\xi_2}{\vartheta_1}$ and $\Theta \equiv \frac{\vartheta_2}{\vartheta_1} = \frac{1-\vartheta_1}{\vartheta_1} < 1$. It follows that Ψ_1 is an inverse index of price stickiness, inflation indexation, and wage stickiness. Θ is an index of the relative importance of price stickiness (which argues in favour of forward-looking elements in the inflation equation, therefore$\vartheta_2 = 1 - \vartheta_1$) versus wage stickiness (which argues in favour of lags, therefore ϑ_1). Adding a pricing shock (due, e.g. to rising energy prices) is a straightforward extension to this framework.

The model is completed with monetary policy that takes the form of the standard Taylor rule (Taylor 1993; for an introduction to the subsequent voluminous literature, see, e.g. Tsoukis 2020, Chapter 7):

$$i_t = r + \pi_t + \eta_\pi \Delta\pi_t + \eta_y[y_t - \alpha_t] \tag{47}$$

Apart from inflation, monetary policy responds to output minus the productivity shock as this part of output will not elicit inflationary pressures.

Where i_t is the nominal interest rate (we assume it is the unique interest rate of this simple economy). We also assume $\eta_\pi > 1$, as is customary. Note a couple of simplifications that are made in the interests of tractability. Firstly, we assume no lags of the interest rate and hence no persistence in interest rate setting. Secondly, the above equation is slightly different from the usual formulation which has $\overline{\pi} + \eta_\pi(\pi_t - \overline{\pi})$ instead of the $\pi_t + \eta_\pi \Delta\pi_t$ term assumed here; the change is made for tractability. The implications of the two formulations are largely equivalent: when inflation is rising, the real interest rate ($r_t \equiv i_t - \pi_t$) is above its long-run level of the steady-state real interest rate I. There may be a loss of information as we do not specify a target inflation rate; the implication of this is that the level of inflation (as opposed to its change) is not determinate in this model. However, as before, this simplification is necessary if we wish to keep things manageable. We note that in the steady state: $\Delta\pi_t = 0$. Therefore, (47) is readily transformed to deviations form:

$$\tilde{r}_t = \eta_\pi \Delta\pi_t + \eta_y[y_t - \alpha_t] \tag{47'}$$

We have now developed three equations, IS Eq. (43), inflation equation/NKPC (46), and monetary policy—Taylor Rule for the interest rate (47′). The endogenous variables are,y_t, $\tilde{r}_t$ and$\Delta\pi_t$. Conditional on the solution of the model, the dynamics of the propensity to consume,$\tilde{\lambda}_t$, can be read off Eq. (26). This system of three equations corresponds to the well-known three-equation New Keynesian model. In the steady state, inflation will be constant, but our model is silent on the level at which it will settle (technically, the long-run inflation rate is "indeterminate"). This is a consequence of the fact that we do not specify a target inflation rate in the Taylor rule; it is the price to pay for tractability, as noted. As our emphasis here is on the business cycle and therefore on dynamics, not on the long run and the steady state, this is a price worth paying.

To proceed to an analytical solution, we consolidate (46) and (47′). In a straightforward manner, we get:

$$\tilde{r}_t = \Theta\tilde{r}_{t+1} + \left[\eta_y + \eta_\pi \Xi_1\right]y_t - \Theta\eta_y y_{t+1} - \eta_y\alpha_t - \eta_\pi[\Xi_2\alpha_t - v_t] \quad (48)$$

Or

$$\tilde{r}_t = \eta_y y_t + \eta_\pi \Xi_1 \frac{y_t}{1 - \Theta L^{-1}} - \frac{\eta_y\alpha_t + \eta_\pi[\Xi_2\alpha_t - v_t]}{1 - \Theta L^{-1}} \quad (48')$$

Applying the output persistence formula and considering that shocks take place only at t, we have:

$$\tilde{r}_t = Hy_t - \eta_y\alpha_t - \eta_\pi[\Xi_2\alpha_t - v_t] \quad (49a)$$

$$H \equiv \left[\eta_y + \eta_\pi \frac{\Xi_1}{1 - (1 - \psi)\Theta}\right]$$

Now, if -t- is the time when shocks occur (only once), then with the output persistence rule (29), future interest rates will be:

$$\tilde{r}_{t+1} = Hy_{t+1} = H(1 - \psi)y_t, \tilde{r}_{t+2} = H(1 - \psi)^2 y_t, \quad (49b)$$

Therefore, at the time when shocks occur, the interest rate rises with the output gap (as it fuels inflation), falls with the productivity shock (α_t) and rises with the pricing shock (v_t)—for quite similar reasons. In subsequent times, the interest rate only responds to the output gap which is getting eliminated at its own exogenous rate of decay (ψ, inverse of persistence). We call Eqs. (49a, b) the Modified LM equation (MLM). Note that without wage stickiness ($\Theta = 0$) or any persistence ($\psi = 1$), there would be no forward structure of the interest rate in (48). Hence, both wage stickiness (Θ) and output persistence ($1\text{-}\psi$) increase the bearing that the output gap has on the interest rate.

To proceed, we combine the MLM Eqs. (49a, b) with the IS Eq. (43). The result is (with details to be found in Appendix T5):

$$[A\Omega_1 + \Omega_3 H]y_t = \frac{A\gamma_t}{1+\frac{C}{K}} + \Omega_2\left[\eta_y\alpha_t + \eta_\pi(\Xi_2\alpha_t - v_t)\right] \tag{50}$$

$$A\Omega_1 \equiv \left[\frac{A}{\frac{C}{K}+\psi} - \varpi\frac{1+\lambda}{\lambda+\psi}\right] = \left[\frac{A}{\frac{C}{K}+\psi} - \frac{(1-\kappa)A}{1+\frac{C}{K}}\frac{1+\lambda}{\lambda+\psi}\right] > 0 \tag{51a}$$

$$\Omega_2 \equiv \frac{(A\mu - M)}{1+\frac{C}{K}} - \frac{\omega}{1+\varpi} = \frac{(A\mu - M)}{1+\frac{C}{K}} - \omega\frac{1+\frac{C}{K}}{1+\frac{C}{K}+(1-\kappa)A}(>)0 \tag{51b}$$

$$\Omega_3 \equiv \frac{(A\mu - M)}{\frac{C}{K}+\psi} - \omega\frac{1+\lambda}{\lambda+\psi}(>0) \tag{51c}$$

A number of remarks are in order: Firstly, a comparison with (45a) shows that Ω_1 is essentially the fiscal multiplier, which was shown to be positive; hence the sign in (51a). Secondly, Ω_2 gives the impact effect of the shocks: Productivity and pricing shocks will surely have beneficial and harmful effects, respectively, on output. Therefore, on grounds of realism, we impose the positive sign (in parenthesis) in (51b). In other words, we assume that μ is high enough for this to happen. The motivation here is that the interest rate must have a negative cumulative effect on output for monetary policy to take a stabilisation role; as is common thinking and practice.

Next, consider Ω_3. We see that the fiscal multiplier is:

$$\frac{\partial y_t}{\partial \gamma_t} = \frac{A}{(1+\frac{C}{K})[A\Omega_1 + \Omega_3 H]}\left(< \frac{1}{(1+\frac{C}{K})\Omega_1}\right) \tag{45a'}$$

This is the fiscal multiplier with the interest rate now allowed to respond to the output gap. It will be remembered that, in (45a), the interest rate was taken as given. In other words, the $\Omega_3 H$ element represents the well-known crowding out effect from the endogenous interest rate. This allows us to sign this element; it must be positive (hence the positive sign in parenthesis in 51c) as this decreases the multiplier; but the multiplier is still positive, as crowding out partially offsets the change in output but cannot reverse its sign. Hence, the new multiplier must be smaller than the one with the given interest rate in (45a) (cf. the inequality in parenthesis in 51c).

We shall also need an inflation equation, which is (46) with minor re-writing:

$$\Delta\pi_t = \frac{\Xi_1 y_t - \Xi_2\alpha_t + v_t}{1 - \Theta L^{-1}} = \frac{\Xi_1 y_t}{1 - (1 - \psi)\Theta} - \Xi_2\alpha_t + v_t \qquad (46'')$$

With these analytics, we can now proceed to the optimal design of monetary policy.

4 Present Bias and Optimal Monetary Policy Design

The policy objective of the monetary authority is primarily to stabilise inflation, captured by minimising the variance of its change; secondarily, to stabilise output (i.e. to minimise its variance). The first two objectives are captured by a weighted sum of $\mathrm{Var}(\Delta\pi_t)$ and $\mathrm{Var}(y_t)$, in standard notation. Therefore, the aim is to:

$$\min_{\eta_\pi,\eta_y} Var(\Delta\pi_t) + \varepsilon Var(y_t), 0 < \varepsilon < 1 \qquad (52)$$

It will be recalled that the policy parameters, η_π, η_y, are the responses of the interest rate to inflation and the output gap in the Taylor rule (47′). Let the frequency of the various shocks be p_γ, p_α, $p_\upsilon > 0$, in obvious notation. All shocks are white noise: with unitary variance (as well as mean zero) and are uncorrelated. Therefore, the variance of inflation from (4.6″) is:

$$Var(\Delta\pi_t) = \left(\frac{\Xi_1}{1 - (1 - \psi)\Theta}\right)^2 Var(y_t) + p_\alpha^2(\Xi_2)^2 + p_\upsilon^2 \qquad (53)$$

Ignoring the constant $p_{\alpha}^2(\Xi_2)^2 + p_v^2$ which cannot be affected by policy, (52) implies:

$$\min_{\eta_\pi,\eta_y}\left[\left(\frac{\Xi_1}{1-(1-\psi)\Theta}\right)^2 + \varepsilon\right] Var(y_t), \qquad (52')$$

In other words, the monetary authority ends up minimising the variance of output; in this setup, it does not matter how much the monetary authority cares about inflation or output stabilisation: Stabilising the latter accounts for both. From (50), the variance of output becomes:

$$Var(y_t) = p_{\gamma}^2 A^2 \Gamma^2 + p_{\alpha}^2 \varsigma^2 (\eta_y + \eta_\pi \Xi_2)^2 + p_v^2 \varsigma^2 (\eta_\pi \Xi_2)^2 \qquad (54)$$

$$\Gamma \equiv \frac{1}{(1+\frac{C}{K})[A\Omega_1 + \Omega_3 H]}, \; \varsigma \equiv \frac{\Omega_2}{[A\Omega_1 + \Omega_3 H]}$$

After straightforward manipulations, detailed in Appendix T6, the first-order conditions deliver the following conditions. Firstly, the optimal response of the interest rate in the Taylor rule (47') to output versus inflation is:

$$\frac{\eta_y}{\eta_\pi} = \frac{p_{\alpha}^2(\Xi_2)^2 + p_v^2(\Xi_2)^2 - p_{\alpha}^2 \frac{\Xi_2\Xi_1}{1-(1-\psi)\Theta}}{p_{\alpha}^2\left[\frac{\Xi_1}{1-(1-\psi)\Theta} - \Xi_2\right]} \qquad (55a)$$

Implicitly, the denominator is assumed positive. A detailed interpretation of this rule is not so interesting here; what is striking, and somewhat counterintuitive, is that this optimal ratio does not depend on any terms that are affected by λ. Thus, it does not depend on present-bias (or any other element of optimisation); just the elements of the inflation equation/Phillips Curve (46) matter here—forward-lookingness, price stickiness, output persistence, and the relative frequencies of the various shocks.

Furthermore, we get an equation that determines the optimal responsiveness of the interest rate to inflation and the output gap, η_π, given the ratio from (55a). In other words, this gives us the joint responsiveness of the interest rate in the Taylor rule, not only the responsiveness to inflation:

$$\eta_\pi = \frac{p_\gamma^2(\eta + \Xi_2)}{p_\alpha^2(\eta + \Xi_2)^2 + p_v^2(\Xi_2)^2} \frac{1}{\left(1 + \frac{C}{K}\right)^2 (\Omega_1)^2} \frac{A\Omega_1}{\Omega_2} \frac{\Omega_3}{\Omega_2} \tag{55b}$$

This formula is neater than it looks. Apart from the first ratio, which involves the various parameters that appear in condition (55a), we now have two additional elements: the middle ratio, which will be recognised as the fiscal multiplier with a given interest rate (45a); this rises with λ and present bias (cf. Result 1 and Eq. T4.4 of Appendix 4). We also have two ratios, $\frac{A\Omega_1}{\Omega_2} \frac{\Omega_3}{\Omega_2}$, which are affected by λ in the way discussed in Appendix 7. $\frac{\Omega_3}{\Omega_2}$ unambiguously rises with λ. Furthermore, if the pure demand effect of the interest rate is sufficiently stronger than its (positive) effect on investment via saving and on the effect on the present value of wage income overall, then the ratio $\frac{A\Omega_1}{\Omega_2}$ also rises with λ.

Result 5 Under a mild condition, namely that the pure demand effect of the interest rate is sufficiently stronger than its effect on investment and the present value of wage income, a rise in present bias and λ implies that the interest rate in the Taylor rule of monetary policy should become more responsive to the output gap and the inflationary shock.

Appendix A: A Model of Financial Myopia

In this Appendix, we introduce financial myopia, in addition to the utility-related myopia, which we have termed "present-bias". To distinguish the two, we shall call simply "myopia" the myopia related to financial or monetary sums. A good example is provided by the calculation of the present value of labour earnings, Eq. (11) of the text. In this Appendix, we outline how this would change if labour earnings were discounted by a more myopic discount rate than simply the interest rate. Financial or monetary myopia could arise because of a number of inter-related reasons, either sheer lack of foresightedness, or as farther future is more uncertain (not modelled explicitly due to the deterministic setup) so that we implicitly discount more heavily, or finally because of mortality and the associated uncertainty of the future earnings. If there is such myopia, then both the definitional Eq. (11) and the subsequent dynamics will change. This is a theme that, to our knowledge, has not been pursued in the literature, so this Appendix offers some original results.

We begin with the analogue of Eq. (11), the present value of labour earnings, but with now a discount factor $\phi'(t+\tau, t)$ that embodies discounting by the interest rate (constant, for simplicity) with added (financial) myopia:

$$\phi'(t,t) = 1, \phi'(t+1,t) = \frac{1}{(1+r)(1+\varphi')}, \phi'(t+2,t) = \frac{1}{(1+r)^2(1+\varphi')\left(1+\varphi'^2\right)} \tag{TA.1}$$

The myopia factor $\varphi' \geq$ may or may not be the same as the present bias (φ) assumed in (4) in relation to utility. This discount factor replaces $R_{t+\tau,t}$ in (12) and is the analogue of (4) for discounting utility.

Now, the present value of labour earnings, replacing (11), is:

$$\widehat{W}_t \equiv \sum_{\tau=0}^{\infty}\left\{W_{t+\tau}\phi'(t+\tau,t)\right\} \tag{TA.2}$$

With this, the consumption Eq. (10) must be re-written as:

$$C_t = \lambda_t\left(K_t + \widehat{W}_t\right) \tag{TA.3}$$

Straightforward development follows (using the lead operator as appropriate):

$$\widehat{W}_t = W_t + \frac{W_{t+1}}{(1+r)(1+\varphi')} + \frac{W_{t+2}}{(1+r)^2(1+\varphi')\left(1+\varphi'^2\right)} + \ldots \approx$$

$$\approx W_t + \frac{W_{t+1}\left(1-\varphi'\right)}{1+r} + \frac{W_{t+2}\left(1-\varphi'-\varphi'^2\right)}{(1+r)^2}$$

$$+ \frac{W_{t+3}\left(1-\varphi'-\varphi'^2-\varphi'^3\right)}{(1+r)^3} + \ldots =$$

$$= \overline{W}_t - \frac{\varphi'\overline{W}_{t+1}}{1+r} - \frac{\varphi'^2\overline{W}_{t+2}}{(1+r)^2} - \ldots = 2\overline{W}_t - \frac{\overline{W}_t}{1-\frac{\varphi'}{1+r}L^{-1}}$$

where $\overline{W}_t$ is as in (11). Now, in the steady state, both W_t and $\overline{W}_t$ will be growing at the constant rate g = r-λ. This allows us to write the discount factor as: $\frac{\varphi}{1+r}L^{-1} = \frac{\varphi'}{1+r}(1+g) \approx \frac{\varphi'}{1+\lambda}$. Hence:

$$\widehat{W}_t = 2\overline{W}_t - \frac{\overline{W}_t}{1 - \frac{\varphi'}{1+\lambda}} = \overline{W}_t \frac{1+\lambda-2\varphi'}{1+\lambda-\varphi'} \leq \overline{W}_t$$

with equality when $\varphi' = 0$. Therefore the same rule of motion as (13) applies. Multiplying across (13) by $\frac{1+\lambda-2\varphi'}{1+\lambda-\varphi'}$, we have:

$$\widehat{W}_t = \frac{1+\lambda-2\varphi'}{1+\lambda-\varphi'} W_t + (1+r_t)^{-1}\overline{W}_{t+1} \tag{TA.4}$$

Equation (TA.3) replaces Eq. (13) of the text. It practically means that, for the scheme to work, the wage as a share over output must decline. This means that the $0 < 1\text{-}\kappa < 1$ factor (the labour share) must decline. This has no implications for the rest of Sects. "A Time-Consistent Procedure", "Production and National Income Accounting", and the steady-state analysis of Sect. "Steady state"; in particular, steady-state λ in Eq. (18) remains unaltered. Thus, so does the growth rate (g), conditional on the steady-state interest rate, and the consumption-capital ratio (33a).

But things are different with respect to wage income. Note that the national income Eq. (33a) with consumption (TA.3) becomes in the steady state:

$$\frac{C_t}{K_t} = \lambda\left(1 + \frac{\widehat{W}_t}{K_t}\right) = A - g \tag{TA.5}$$

We now have:

$$\frac{\widehat{W}_t}{K_t} = \frac{1+\lambda-2\varphi'}{1+\lambda-\varphi'}\frac{W_t}{K_t}\frac{1+\lambda}{\lambda} \tag{TA.6}$$

This is the same formula as before, with the addition of the factor $\frac{1+\lambda-2\varphi'}{1+\lambda-\varphi'} \leq 1$. (TA.5) and (TA.6) with the growth rate (19), following the same steps that took us from (33a) to (33d), we get:

$$\frac{W_t}{Y_t} = \frac{1-\kappa}{1+\lambda}\frac{1+\lambda-\varphi'}{1+\lambda-2\varphi'} \tag{TA.7}$$

Comparison with (33d) immediately reveals that the wage share in gross output increases by the financial myopia factor. This has important implications for income inequality.

The model considers an exogenous steady-state real interest rate due to the AK production function. A more fruitful analysis of the above setup of financial myopia would require an endogenous interest rate, which would arise in a CES production function with explicit modelling of labour (as in last chapter). This is on the agenda for future research.

Technical Appendix T1: On the geometric (GEO) and HD solutions

Firstly, note that (20a) is derived from re-writing (20) as:

$$\lambda^{GEO} = \frac{\rho - (1-\sigma)\left(r - \lambda^{GEO}\right)}{1+\rho}$$

Then, (20a) is a small step away.

To derive (21), i.e. λ in the general case, we first repeat the definition of G in (22):

$$G \equiv 1 + (1-\sigma)(r-\lambda) \tag{T1.1a}$$

Therefore, from (18) and the above expression, we have:

$$\frac{1-\lambda}{\lambda} = \frac{G}{(1+\rho)(1+\varphi)} + \frac{G^2}{(1+\rho)^2(1+\varphi)\left(1+\varphi^2\right)} + \frac{G^3}{(1+\rho)^3(1+\varphi)\left(1+\varphi^2\right)\left(1+\varphi^3\right)} + \ldots \tag{T1.1b}$$

In order to get sharper results, we may approximate: $\frac{1}{(1+\varphi)} \approx 1-\varphi$, $\frac{1}{(1+\varphi)\left(1+\varphi^2\right)} \approx 1-\varphi-\varphi^2$, etc. We therefore have:

$$\frac{1-\lambda}{\lambda} \approx \frac{G(1-\varphi)}{(1+\rho)} + \frac{G^2\left(1-\varphi-\varphi^2\right)}{(1+\rho)^2} + \frac{G^3\left(1-\varphi-\varphi^2-\varphi^3\right)}{(1+\rho)^3} + \ldots =$$

$$= \frac{\frac{G}{1+\rho}}{1-\frac{G}{1+\rho}} - \frac{\varphi\frac{G}{1+\rho}}{1-\frac{G}{1+\rho}}\frac{1}{1-\varphi\frac{G}{1+\rho}} = \frac{1+(1-\sigma)(r-\lambda)}{\rho-(1-\sigma)(r-\lambda)}\frac{(1-\varphi)(1+\rho)-\varphi G}{1+\rho-\varphi G} \tag{T1.2}$$

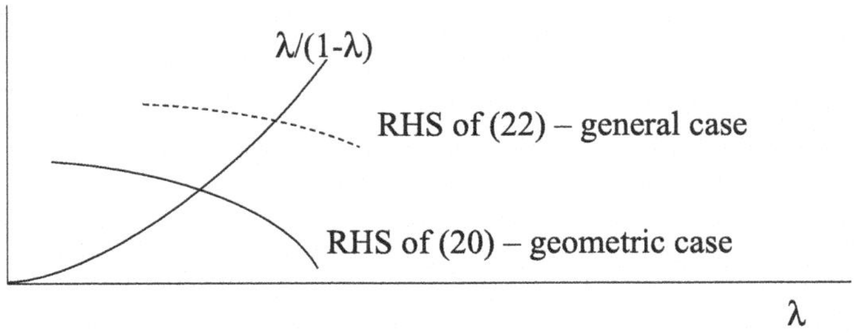

Fig. 1 Comparison of λ in (20) and (22)

Recall that the λ under purely geometric discounting is given by (19). The inequality $\lambda \geq \lambda^{GEO}$ is established by reference to the following Fig. 1:

The upward-sloping line gives the left-hand side (LHS) of (20) and (22), essentially the same function. The downward-sloping lines are the right side (RHS) of (20) (solid line) and that of (21) (broken line). The latter line is to the right and above the former because $\frac{1+\rho-\varphi G}{(1-\varphi)(1+\rho)-\varphi G} > 1$.[17] Clearly, λ is higher than in the geometric case; in fact, it rises with φ, as the factor given above that differentiates the two lines rises with φ.

Next, we shall derive an expression that is useful in the text in the discussion of present values. The discount factor of growing variables is effectively $\frac{1}{1+r-g} = \frac{1}{1+\lambda}$ (from 19); we therefore derive a tractable approximation to that. To this end, re-write (22) as:

$$\frac{\lambda}{1-\lambda} = \frac{1+\rho-G}{G}\frac{1+\rho-\varphi G}{(1-\varphi)(1+\rho)-\varphi G} = \frac{1-\overline{G}}{\overline{G}}\frac{1-\varphi\overline{G}}{1-\varphi-\varphi\overline{G}}$$

where $\overline{G} \equiv \frac{G}{1+\rho}$. Therefore:

$$\lambda = \frac{\frac{1-\overline{G}}{\overline{G}}\frac{1-\varphi\overline{G}}{(1-\varphi)-\varphi\overline{G}}}{1+\frac{1-\overline{G}}{\overline{G}}\frac{1-\varphi\overline{G}}{(1-\varphi)-\varphi\overline{G}}}$$

[17] The RHS of (21) continues to be downward sloping if  is not too large. But its slope is less than that of the RHS of (19)—an inessential detail.

and

$$1+\lambda=\frac{1+2\frac{1-\overline{G}}{\overline{G}}\frac{1-\varphi\overline{G}}{(1-\varphi)-\varphi\overline{G}}}{1+\frac{1-\overline{G}}{\overline{G}}\frac{1-\varphi\overline{G}}{(1-\varphi)-\varphi\overline{G}}}=\frac{2(1-\varphi\overline{G})-\overline{G}\left[1+\varphi-\varphi\overline{G}\right]}{\left(1-2\varphi\overline{G}\right)}$$

Or

$$\frac{1}{1+\lambda}\approx 1-\lambda=\frac{1}{1+\frac{1-\overline{G}}{\overline{G}}\frac{1-\varphi\overline{G}}{(1-\varphi)-\varphi\overline{G}}}=\frac{\overline{G}\left[1-\varphi-\varphi\overline{G}\right]}{(1-2\varphi G)}$$
$$\approx\overline{G}\left[1-\varphi(1-\overline{G})\overline{G}\right]\approx\overline{G}$$

where the second approximation is around $\varphi = 0$ and the third around $\overline{G} = 1$. Hence, we shall use:

$$0<\frac{1}{1+\lambda}\approx 1-\lambda\approx\overline{G}\equiv\frac{G}{1+\rho}<1 \tag{T1.3}$$

Technical Appendix T2

In this Appendix, we describe the derivation of Eq. (24) of the text, i.e. the linearised version of (18), giving the dynamics of λ. We start from a linearisation of (16) in the same spirit as (16''), but now allow for deviations from the steady state:

$$[\Lambda(t+1+s,t+s)]^{1-\sigma}\approx 1+(1-\sigma)(r-\lambda+X_{t+1}) \tag{T2.1a}$$

where X_t is the deviation of $\Lambda(t+1,t)$ from its steady state, $r-\lambda$. Using tildes to indicate deviations from steady-state values, i.e. $\tilde{r}_t\equiv r_t-r$ and $\tilde{\lambda}_t\equiv\lambda_t-\lambda$, we have:

$$X_t\equiv(1-\lambda)\tilde{r}_t+\frac{1+r}{\lambda}\left[(1-\lambda)\tilde{\lambda}_{t+1}-\tilde{\lambda}_t\right]= \tag{T2.1b}$$
$$=(1-\lambda)\tilde{r}_t-(1+r)\tilde{\lambda}_t+(1+r)\frac{1-\lambda}{\lambda}\left(\tilde{\lambda}_{t+1}-\tilde{\lambda}_t\right)$$

Furthermore, the product terms involved in $\prod_{s=0}^{\tau-1}[\Lambda(t+1+s,t+s)]^{1-\sigma}$ will be linearised as follows (using the definition of G in 21):

$$[1 + (1-\sigma)(r - \lambda + X_t)]\big[1 + (1-\sigma)(r - \lambda + X_{t+1})\big]$$
$$\approx G^2 + G(1-\sigma)(X_t + X_{t+1})$$

To aid intuition, note that the X_{t+s} terms involve short-run deviations, whereas the stand-alone G terms are the steady-state values. So, the sum in the denominator on the right side of Eq. (18) becomes:

$$\frac{1-\lambda_t}{\lambda_t} = \frac{G + (1-\sigma)X_t}{(1+\rho)(1+\varphi)} + \frac{G^2 + G(1-\sigma)(X_t + X_{t+1})}{(1+\rho)^2(1+\varphi)\big(1+\varphi^2\big)}$$
$$+ \frac{G^3 + G^2(1-\sigma)(X_t + X_{t+1} + X_{t+2})}{(1+\rho)^2(1+\varphi)\big(1+\varphi^2\big)} \cdots$$

Using (22) to separate the steady-state terms, this equals:

$$\frac{1-\lambda_t}{\lambda_t} = \frac{1-\lambda}{\lambda} + \frac{(1-\sigma)X_t}{(1+\rho)(1+\varphi)} + \frac{G(1-\sigma)(X_t + X_{t+1})}{(1+\rho)^2(1+\varphi)\big(1+\varphi^2\big)}$$
$$+ \frac{G^2(1-\sigma)(X_t + X_{t+1} + X_{t+2})}{(1+\rho)^3(1+\varphi)\big(1+\varphi^2\big)\big(1+\varphi^3\big)} + \ldots =$$

With the approximations described in Appendix T1, this becomes:

$$\frac{1-\lambda_t}{\lambda_t} = \frac{1-\lambda}{\lambda} + \frac{(1-\varphi)}{1+\rho}(1-\sigma)X_t + \frac{G\big[1-\varphi-\varphi^2\big]}{(1+\rho)^2}(1-\sigma)(X_t + X_{t+1})$$
$$+ \frac{G^2\big[1-\varphi-\varphi^2-\varphi^3\big]}{(1+\rho)^3}(1-\sigma)(X_t + X_{t+1} + X_{t+2}) + \ldots$$

In order to add up, we find it useful to define a new quantity:

$$Z_t \equiv X_t + \frac{G}{1+\rho}X_{t+1} + \left(\frac{G}{1+\rho}\right)^2 X_{t+2} +$$

Then, we first add up all the "1" elements ...

$$+\frac{1-\sigma}{1+\rho}Z_t\left\{1 + \frac{G}{1+\rho} + \left(\frac{G}{1+\rho}\right)^2 + \ldots\right\} = \frac{1}{1+\rho}\frac{1-\sigma}{1-\frac{G}{1+\rho}}Z_t$$

… subtracting all the "φ " elements, so to speak …

$$-(1-\sigma)\frac{\varphi}{1+\rho}Z_t\left\{1+\frac{G}{1+\rho}+\left(\frac{G}{1+\rho}\right)^2+\ldots\right\}=-\frac{\varphi}{1+\rho}\frac{1-\sigma}{1-\frac{G}{1+\rho}}Z_t$$

… and then all the "φ^2" elements…

$$-G(1-\sigma)\left(\frac{\varphi}{1+\rho}\right)^2Z_t\left\{1+\frac{G}{1+\rho}+\left(\frac{G}{1+\rho}\right)^2+\ldots\right\}$$
$$=-G\left(\frac{\varphi}{1+\rho}\right)^2\frac{1-\sigma}{1-\frac{G}{1+\rho}}Z_t$$

… and so on, to finally obtain the following version of Eq. (18):

$$\frac{1-\lambda_t}{\lambda_t}=\frac{1-\lambda}{\lambda}+\frac{1}{1+\rho}\frac{1-\sigma}{1-\frac{G}{1+\rho}}Z_t-\frac{\varphi}{1+\rho}\frac{1-\sigma}{1-\frac{G}{1+\rho}}\frac{1}{1-\frac{\varphi G}{1+\rho}}Z_t=\frac{1-\lambda}{\lambda}+\frac{1-\lambda}{\lambda}\frac{1-\sigma}{G}Z_t \tag{T2.2}$$

Note that we have used (T1.2) to re-write the coefficient of Z_t as $\frac{1-\lambda}{\lambda}\frac{1-\sigma}{G}$. The coefficient of Z_t decreases with φ: λ increases, as shown above, and G increases as well (note that σ > 1, and given the real interest rate).

A digression on the lead operator and geometric sums is now is in order. In the above, we have used the lead operator, L: For any variable, e.g. x_t, we have $Lx_t \equiv x_{t-1}$ and therefore the inverse is the lead operator: $L^{-1}x_t \equiv x_{t+1}$ (without expectations, due to the deterministic setup). With these definitions, we can then use L and L^{-1} as any standard constant parameter. The lead operator, in particular, is very in handling present-value sums, as shown below.

From the definition of geometric sums (using Z_t as an example), we can write:

$$Z_{t+1}\equiv L^{-1}Z_t=X_{t+1}+\frac{G}{1+\rho}X_{t+2}+\left(\frac{G}{1+\rho}\right)^2X_{t+3}+\ldots$$

Therefore, multiplying by $\frac{G}{1+\rho}$ and subtracting from Z_t in an elementary way, we have:

$$Z_t-\frac{G}{1+\rho}L^{-1}Z_t=Z_t\left(1-\frac{G}{1+\rho}L^{-1}\right)=X_t$$

Re-arranging, using the fact that these operators can be handled as constants, we have:

$$Z_t = \frac{X_t}{1 - \frac{G}{1+\rho}L^{-1}} \tag{T2.3}$$

As (T2.3) makes clear, the discounted sum $X_t + \frac{G}{1+\rho}X_{t+1} + \left(\frac{G}{1+\rho}\right)^2 X_{t+2} + \ldots$ and the ratio $\frac{X_t}{1-\frac{G}{1+\rho}L^{-1}}$ are equivalent; the latter is equivalent to the present value of (all current and future) X_t discounted at the coefficient of L^{-1}, i.e. in this case $\frac{G}{1+\rho}$.

We can now re-write equation (T2.2), as:

$$\frac{1-\lambda_t}{\lambda_t} = \frac{1-\lambda}{\lambda} + \frac{1-\lambda}{\lambda}\frac{1-\sigma}{G}\frac{(1-\lambda)\tilde{r}_t + \frac{1+r}{\lambda}\left[(1-\lambda)\tilde{\lambda}_{t+1} - \lambda_t\right]}{1 - \frac{G}{1+\rho}L^{-1}} \tag{T2.4}$$

Using deviations, since $\frac{1-\lambda_t}{\lambda_t} \approx \frac{1-\lambda}{\lambda} - \frac{\tilde{\lambda}_t}{\lambda^2}$, we get an intermediate expression:

$$\frac{\tilde{\lambda}_t}{\lambda}\left[1 - \frac{G}{1+\rho}L^{-1}\right]\frac{G}{(1-\lambda)(\sigma-1)} = (1-\lambda)\tilde{r}_t + \frac{1+r}{\lambda}\left[(1-\lambda)\tilde{\lambda}_{t+1} - \lambda_t\right] \tag{T2.5}$$

From here, Eq. (24) of the text follows by simple division by $\left[1 - \frac{G}{1+\rho}L^{-1}\right]$.

Finally, we turn to the derivation of Eq. (25) of the text. Firstly, rewrite (24′) as:

$$\frac{\tilde{\lambda}_t}{\lambda}\left[1 - \frac{G}{1+\rho}L^{-1}\right] = \frac{(1-\lambda)\tilde{r}_t}{\frac{G}{(1-\lambda)(\sigma-1)} + 1 + r} = \frac{(1-\lambda)(\sigma-1)(1-\lambda)\tilde{r}_t}{G + (1-\lambda)(\sigma-1)(1+r)}$$
$$\approx \frac{(\sigma-1)}{\sigma}(1-\lambda)^2\tilde{r}_t \tag{T2.6}$$

The approximation uses the definition of G in (T1.1a). From (25), the right side of (24) is:

$$(1-\lambda)\tilde{r}_t + \frac{1+r}{\lambda}\left[(1-\lambda)\widetilde{\lambda_{t+1}} - \lambda_t\right] = M\tilde{r}_t \tag{T2.7}$$

$$M \equiv (1-\lambda)\left[1 - \frac{1+r}{\frac{G}{(1-\lambda)(\sigma-1)} + 1 + r}\right] = \frac{(1-\lambda)G}{G + (1-\lambda)(\sigma-1)(1+r)}$$
$$\approx \frac{(1-\lambda)G}{\sigma} \tag{T2.8}$$

This is Eq. (26) of the main text.

Technical Appendix T3

The purpose of this Appendix is to present the derivations that take us from Eqs. (37)–(40a). We start from the product in (39a):

$$\prod_{s=0}^{\tau}(1+g_s^C)R_{t+\tau,t} = (1+r-g)^{-\tau}\left[1 - \sum_{s=0}^{\tau}\frac{\tilde{r}_s - \tilde{g}_s^K}{1+r-g}\right]$$

From (15), (16) and (26), the difference on the right is (see also 32 for $\tilde{g}_s^C$):

$$\tilde{r}_s - \tilde{g}_s^K = \tilde{r}_t - (1-\lambda)\tilde{r}_t - \frac{1+r}{\lambda}\left[(1-\lambda)\widetilde{\lambda_{t+1}} - \lambda_t\right] - \Delta c_{t+1}$$
$$= (1-M)\tilde{r}_t - \Delta c_{t+1}$$

where we also use the shorthand notation: $\Delta c_{t+1} \equiv c_{t+1} - c_t$. Therefore:

$$\prod_{s=0}^{\tau}(1+g_s^K)R_{t+\tau,t} = (1+\lambda)^{-\tau}\left[1 - \sum_{s=0}^{\tau}\frac{(1-M)\tilde{r}_{t+s} - \Delta c_{t+1}}{1+\lambda}\right]$$

Hence, we have, using also the wage from (33d):

$$d\frac{\overline{W}_t}{K_t} = \frac{W_t}{Y_t}A\sum_{\tau=0}^{\infty}\left[\left\{\frac{1+g}{1+r}\right\}^{\tau} y_t - (1+\lambda)^{-\tau}\sum_{s=0}^{\tau}\frac{(1-M)\tilde{r}_{t+s}}{1+\lambda}\right]$$
$$= \frac{(1-\kappa)A}{1+\lambda}\sum_{\tau=0}^{\infty}(1+\lambda)^{-\tau}\left[y_t - \frac{(1-M)\tilde{r}_{t+s} - \Delta\tilde{c}_{t+1}}{\lambda}\right]$$

where $0 < \kappa < 1$ is the implicit share of capital in the product (assumed constant and not modelled here—see the previous chapter). The derivations use the approximation $\frac{1+g}{1+r} \approx \frac{1}{1+r-g} = \frac{1}{1+\lambda}$. Therefore, with $\overline{\omega} \equiv \frac{(1-\kappa)A/(1+\lambda)}{1+(1-\kappa)A/(1+\lambda)} = \frac{(1-\kappa)A}{1+\lambda+(1-\kappa)A}$, Eq. (37) becomes:

$$\tilde{c}_t = \frac{\tilde{\lambda}_t}{\lambda} + \overline{\omega}\frac{y_t - (1-M)\tilde{r}_t + \Delta\tilde{c}_{t+1}}{1 - \frac{1}{1+\lambda}L^{-1}} = \frac{\tilde{\lambda}_t}{\lambda} + \overline{\omega}\frac{y_t - (1-M)\tilde{r}_t + \Delta\tilde{c}_{t+1}}{1 - \frac{1}{1+\lambda}L^{-1}}$$

$$\overline{\omega} \equiv \frac{(1-\kappa)A/(1+\lambda)}{1+(1-\kappa)A/(1+\lambda)}$$

And M from (T2.8). Or:

$$\tilde{c}_t\left[1 - \frac{1}{1+\lambda}L^{-1}\right] = \frac{\tilde{\lambda}_t}{\lambda}\left[1 - \frac{1}{1+\lambda}L^{-1}\right] + \overline{\omega}\left[y_t - (1-M)\tilde{r}_t + \Delta\tilde{c}_{t+1}\right]$$

And using again (25):

$$\tilde{c}_t\left[1 - \frac{1}{1+\lambda}L^{-1}\right] = \frac{(\sigma-1)}{\sigma}(1-\lambda)^2\tilde{r}_t + \overline{\omega}\left[y_t - (1-M)\tilde{r}_t + \Delta\tilde{c}_{t+1}\right]$$

And using the definition of M in (T2.8), from which: $0 < 1 - M = 1 - \frac{(1-\lambda)G}{\sigma} < 1$. From (T1.1a), $G \equiv 1 + (1-\sigma)(r-\lambda) \approx \sigma - (\sigma-1)(1-r)(1+\lambda)$, hence

$$\frac{(\sigma-1)}{\sigma}(1-\lambda)^2 - \overline{\omega}(1-M) = \frac{(\sigma-1)}{\sigma}(1-\lambda)^2 - \overline{\omega}\left[\lambda + \frac{(\sigma-1)(1-r)(1-\lambda^2)}{\sigma}.\right]$$

$$\approx \frac{(\sigma-1)}{\sigma}\left[(1-\lambda)^2 - \overline{\omega}\left(1-\lambda^2\right)\right] - \overline{\omega}\left[\lambda - \frac{(\sigma-1)r}{\sigma}.\right]$$

And with $\overline{\omega} = \frac{(1-\kappa)A}{1+\lambda+(1-\kappa)A}$, we get: So, $(0 <)\omega < 1$.
Therefore, we finally have:

$$(1+\overline{\omega})\tilde{c}_t\left[1 - \frac{1+(1+\lambda)\overline{\omega}}{(1+\lambda)(1+\overline{\omega})}L^{-1}\right] = \omega\tilde{r}_t + \overline{\omega}y_t \qquad \text{(T3.1)}$$

$$(0 <)\omega \equiv \frac{(\sigma-1)}{\sigma}(1-\lambda)^2 - \overline{\omega}(1-M)(< 1)$$

With a slight re-arrangement, we get Eq. (40a) of the text. Again, likely signs appear in parentheses. With $\frac{\partial \overline{\omega}}{\partial \lambda} < 0, \frac{\partial \omega}{\partial \lambda} < 0$.

For the purposes of the text around Eq. (41), note that:

$$0 < \overline{\omega} = \frac{(1-\kappa)A}{1+\lambda+(1-\kappa)A} = \frac{\left(\frac{C}{K}-\lambda\right)}{1+C/K} < 1 \tag{T3.2}$$

Appendix T4: On the Fiscal Multiplier

This Appendix discusses the properties of the impact and cumulative government expenditure multipliers, Eqs. (45b, c), respectively. From (44a), the impact multiplier (45b) is re-written as:

$$\left.\frac{\partial y_t}{\partial \gamma_t}\right|_{\psi=1} = \frac{1}{[1-(1-\kappa)A]} > 1 \tag{T4.1}$$

The ratio is greater than unity as realistically $(1-\kappa)A \ll 1$ (cf. Footnote 12 and the discussion around the output coefficient 43a). Neither persistence (assumed zero in this case) nor present bias, and λ play any role here.

Turning attention now to the case of full persistence ($\psi = 0$), we get:

$$\left.\frac{\partial y_t}{\partial \gamma_t}\right|_{\psi=0} = \frac{\lambda\frac{C}{K}}{\left[\lambda\left(1+\frac{C}{K}\right)-\frac{C}{K}(1-\kappa)A(1+\lambda)\right]} \tag{T4.2}$$

As it is unclear whether this is above or below unity, we may use the expansion in (44b) to get from (45a):

$$\left.\frac{\partial y_t}{\partial \gamma_t}\right|_{0\leq\psi<1} = \frac{1}{1-(1-\kappa)A+(1-\psi)\left[\frac{1}{1+\frac{C}{K}}-\frac{(1-\kappa)A}{1+\lambda}\right]} \tag{T4.3}$$

As the square brackets is positive (see again Footnote 12), this multiplier, in fact, declines as output becomes more persistent (i.e. as ψ declines). This counterintuitive result arises because the output effect lasts longer but it is also more heavily discounted (as taking place in the farther future). This intermediate result speaks to literature that analyses whether the fiscal multiplier is larger in static or intertemporally optimising models (see Tsoukis, 2020, Ch. 8).

Of more importance is the effect of present bias and λ. We have:

$$\frac{\partial\left[\frac{1}{1+\frac{C}{K}}-\frac{(1-\kappa)A}{1+\lambda}\right]}{\partial\lambda}=-\frac{1}{\left(1+\frac{C}{K}\right)^{2}}+\frac{(1-\kappa)A}{(1+\lambda)^{2}}<0$$

This follows from $(1+\lambda)^2 > \left(1+\frac{C}{K}\right)^2(1-\kappa)A$ or $(1+\lambda) > (1+\frac{C}{K})\sqrt{(1-\kappa)A}$ or $(1+\lambda) > \frac{(1-\kappa)A}{1-\sqrt{(1-\kappa)A}}$. For an illustration with plausible numbers, see again Footnote 12. The end result is:

$$\frac{\partial\left\{\frac{1}{\left(1+\frac{C}{K}\right)\Omega_1}\right\}}{\partial\lambda}=\frac{\partial\left\{\left.\frac{\partial y_t}{\partial\gamma_t}\right|_{0\leq\psi<1}\right\}}{\partial\lambda}>0 \quad \text{(T4.4)}$$

Appendix T5: The Total Effect of the Interest Rate on Output

This brief Appendix outlines the development of Eq. (50) of the text and discusses it. Firstly, we develop some intermediate expressions about the present value of the interest rate in (49a, b):

$$\pounds_1(\tilde{r}_t)=\frac{Hy_t-\eta_y\alpha_t-\eta_\pi[\Xi_2\alpha_t-v_t]}{1+\frac{C}{K}}$$
$$+\frac{1}{1+\frac{C}{K}}\left\{\frac{(1-\psi)}{\left(1+\frac{C}{K}\right)}+\frac{(1-\psi)^2}{\left(1+\frac{C}{K}\right)^2}+\ldots\right\}y_t=$$
$$=\frac{Hy_t}{\frac{C}{K}+\psi}-\frac{\eta_y\alpha_t+\eta_\pi[\Xi_2\alpha_t-v_t]}{1+\frac{C}{K}} \quad \text{(T5.1a)}$$

And similarly, using the definition of $\overline{\omega}$ in (T3.2):

$$\frac{\omega\pounds_2(\tilde{r}_t)}{1+\overline{\omega}}=-\frac{\omega\left[\eta_y\alpha_t+\eta_\pi(\Xi_2\alpha_t-v_t)\right]}{1+\overline{\omega}}+\frac{\omega(1+\lambda)H}{\lambda+\psi}y_t \quad \text{(T5.1b)}$$

Inserting (T5.1a, b) into (43) and collecting terms gives:

$$\frac{A+(A\mu-M)H}{\frac{C}{K}+\psi}y_t-\frac{1+\lambda}{\lambda+\psi}[\overline{\omega}+\omega H]y_t$$

$$= \frac{A\gamma_t}{1+\frac{C}{K}} + \left[\frac{(A\mu - M)}{1+\frac{C}{K}} - \frac{\omega}{1+\overline{\omega}}\right]\left[\eta_y\alpha_t + \eta_\pi(\Xi_2\alpha_t - v_t)\right] \qquad \text{(T5.2)}$$

This is essentially Eq. (50) of the text.

Technical Appendix T6

Equation (50) of the text is re-written as:

$$y_t = \frac{A\gamma_t + \left(1+\frac{C}{K}\right)\Omega_2\left[\eta_y\alpha_t + \eta_\pi(\Xi_2\alpha_t - v_t)\right]}{\left(1+\frac{C}{K}\right)[A\Omega_1 + \Omega_3 H]} \qquad \text{(T6.1)}$$

Or

$$y_t = A\Gamma\gamma_t + \varsigma\left[\eta_y\alpha_t + \eta_\pi(\Xi_2\alpha_t - v_t)\right] \qquad \text{(T6.1')}$$

From here, obtaining the variance of output (Eq. 54 of the text) is a small step away. The first-order conditions (FOC) with respect to the policy parameters η_π, η_y are:

$$Var(y_t)\frac{\Omega_3}{[A\Omega_1 + \Omega_3 H]}\frac{\partial H}{\partial \eta_\pi} = p_\alpha^2\varsigma^2\Xi_2(\eta_y + \eta_\pi\Xi_2) + p_v^2\varsigma^2\eta_\pi(\Xi_2)^2 \qquad \text{(T6.2a)}$$

$$Var(y_t)\frac{\Omega_3}{[A\Omega_1 + \Omega_3 H]}\frac{\partial H}{\partial \eta_y} = p_\alpha^2\varsigma^2(\eta_y + \eta_\pi\Xi_2) \qquad \text{(T6.2b)}$$

H is given below Eq. (49a). Division by parts yields:

$$p_\alpha^2\varsigma^2(\eta_y + \eta_\pi\Xi_2)\frac{\Xi_1}{1-(1-\psi)\Theta} = p_\alpha^2\varsigma^2\Xi_2(\eta_y + \eta_\pi\Xi_2) + p_v^2\varsigma^2\eta_\pi(\Xi_2)^2$$

In relative terms: $\eta \equiv \eta_y/\eta_\pi$. Hence, we get:

$$p_\alpha^2\eta\left[\frac{\Xi_1}{1-(1-\psi)\Theta} - \Xi_2\right] = p_\alpha^2(\Xi_2)^2 + p_v^2(\Xi_2)^2 - p_\alpha^2\frac{\Xi_2\Xi_1}{1-(1-\psi)\Theta} \qquad \text{(T6.3)}$$

As mentioned in the text, an implicit assumption is that the square brackets is positive. Also, the optimal ratio of policy parameters does not depend on present bias and λ.

Then, given η, we have from FOC (T6.2a, b):

$$Var(y_t)\frac{\Omega_3}{[A\Omega_1+\Omega_3 H]}\frac{\eta_\pi \Xi_1}{1-(1-\psi)\Theta} = p_\alpha^2 \varsigma^2 \eta_\pi \Xi_2(\eta_y+\eta_\pi \Xi_2) + p_\upsilon^2 \varsigma^2(\eta_\pi \Xi_2)^2$$

$$Var(y_t)\frac{\Omega_3}{[A\Omega_1+\Omega_3 H]}\eta_y = p_\alpha^2 \varsigma^2 \eta_y(\eta_y+\eta_\pi \Xi_2)$$

Combining the two, we have:

$$Var(y_t)\frac{\Omega_3 H}{[A\Omega_1+\Omega_3 H]} = p_\alpha^2 \varsigma^2(\eta_y+\eta_\pi \Xi_2)^2 + p_\upsilon^2 \varsigma^2(\eta_\pi \Xi_2)^2 \tag{T6.4}$$

Using (54) and re-arranging, we have:

$$p_\gamma^2 = \frac{\varsigma^2}{A^2\Gamma^2}\frac{1-\overline{\overline{\Omega}}}{\overline{\overline{\Omega}}}(\eta_\pi)^2\left[p_\alpha^2(\eta+\Xi_2)^2 + p_\upsilon^2(\Xi_2)^2\right], \overline{\overline{\Omega}} \equiv \frac{\Omega_3 H}{[A\Omega_1+\Omega_3 H]}$$

Therefore, using the definition of H:

$$p_\gamma^2 = \frac{(\Omega_2)^2}{A^2}\frac{A\Omega_1}{\Omega_3(\eta+\Xi_2)}\eta_\pi\left[p_\alpha^2(\eta+\Xi_2)^2 + p_\upsilon^2(\Xi_2)^2\right]$$

or

$$\eta_\pi = \frac{p_\gamma^2(\eta+\Xi_2)}{p_\alpha^2(\eta+\Xi_2)^2 + p_\upsilon^2(\Xi_2)^2}\frac{1}{\left(1+\frac{C}{K}\right)^2}\frac{A}{(\Omega_2)^2}\frac{\Omega_3}{\Omega_1} \tag{T6.5b}$$

This is essentially Eq. (55b) of the main text. Apart from the parameters of the inflation equation and the frequencies, and in contrast to condition (55a), we now have elements that depend on λ. The effect of that on $\frac{\Omega_3}{\Omega_1}$ and Ω_2 is worked out in the next Appendix T7.

Technical Appendix T7

Our purpose here is to show the effect of λ on $\frac{A\Omega_1}{\Omega_2}\frac{\Omega_3}{\Omega_2}$. The discussion here is more suggestive than fully rigorous. To facilitate comparison, we write the ratios as:

$$\frac{A\Omega_1}{\Omega_2} = \frac{\frac{A}{\frac{C}{K}+\psi} - \overline{\omega}\frac{1+\lambda}{\lambda+\psi}}{\frac{(A\mu-M)}{1+\frac{C}{K}} - \frac{\omega}{1+\overline{\omega}}} = \frac{C.B}{D.\begin{bmatrix}\alpha & 0\\ 0 & \beta\end{bmatrix}.B}$$

And:

$$\frac{\Omega_3}{\Omega_2} \equiv \frac{\frac{(A\mu - M)}{\frac{C}{K}+\psi} - \omega\frac{1+\lambda}{\lambda+\psi}}{\frac{(A\mu - M)}{1+\frac{C}{K}} - \frac{\omega}{1+\overline{\omega}}} = \frac{D.B}{D.\begin{bmatrix} \alpha & 0 \\ 0 & \beta \end{bmatrix}.B}$$

$$C \equiv \left[A \; \overline{\omega} \right], B \equiv \left[\frac{1}{\frac{C}{K}+\psi} \; -\frac{1+\lambda}{\lambda+\psi} \right], D \equiv \left[A\mu - M \; \omega \right],$$

$$\alpha \equiv \frac{\frac{C}{K}+\psi}{1+\frac{C}{K}}, \beta \equiv \frac{\lambda+\psi}{(1+\lambda)(1+\overline{\omega})}$$

Consider the ratios $0 < \beta = \frac{\lambda+\psi}{(1+\lambda)} \frac{1+\frac{C}{K}}{1+\frac{C}{K}+(1-\kappa)A} < \alpha = \frac{\frac{C}{K}+\psi}{1+\frac{C}{K}} < 1$ (using T3.2). The inequalities can easily be verified. Furthermore, as can easily be checked, $0 < \frac{\partial \alpha}{\partial \lambda} < \frac{\partial \beta}{\partial \lambda}$. This fact, together with $\Omega_2 > 0$ strongly suggests that the ratio Ω_3/Ω_2 increases with λ.

Furthermore:

$$\frac{\partial \Omega_2}{\partial \lambda} = \frac{\partial (A\mu - M)/\partial \lambda}{1+\frac{C}{K}} - \frac{(A\mu - M)}{\left(1+\frac{C}{K}\right)^2} - \frac{\frac{\partial \omega}{\partial \lambda}}{1+\overline{\omega}} - \omega \frac{(1-\kappa)A}{\left[1+\frac{C}{K}+(1-\kappa)A\right]^2}$$

The sign of this expression is ambiguous, essentially because both $\frac{\partial M}{\partial \lambda}, \frac{\partial \omega}{\partial \lambda} < 0$. To make progress, we invoke intuitive arguments. It will be recalled that Aμ is the pure demand effect of the interest rate (here: through net exports), the effect that gives the interest rate its stabilisation scope; M captures the effect on investment (via the encouragement to saving); and ω is the net effect on the present value of wage income (allowing for the effect of the interest rate on λ). If the effects of λ on M and ω are sufficiently weak such that $\frac{\partial \Omega_2}{\partial \lambda}/\Omega_2 < \frac{\partial \Omega_1}{\partial \lambda}/\Omega_1$, then the ratio Ω_1/Ω_2 will increase with λ and Eq. (55b) will imply that the responsiveness of the interest rate to the output gap and inflationary shocks should increase with the present bias. The economic interpretation of this condition is that the effects of the interest rate on investment and the present value of wages is weak relative to the effect on demand (μ); as the latter is not affected by present bias and λ, the effect on Ω_2 will be weak enough so that Ω_1/Ω_2 rises. The argument here is more suggestive than full proof, however, the condition is fairly weak and Result 4 stated in the text therefore appears justified.

References

Al-Nowaihi, A., and S. Dhami. 2008. A Note on the Loewenstein-Prelec Theory of Intertemporal Choice. *Mathematical Social Sciences* 52 (1): 99–108.

Arrow, K.J. 1962. The Economic Implication of Learning by Doing. *Review of Economic Studies* 29 (3): 55–173.

Barro, R.J. 1990. Government Spending in a Simple Model of Endogenous Growth. *Journal of Political Economy* 98 (5): S103–S125.

Barro, R.J. 1999. Ramsey Meets Laibson in the Neoclassical Growth Model. *Quarterly Journal of Economics* 114 (4): 1125–1152.

Calvo, G.A. 1983. Staggered prices in a utility-maximizing framework.*Journal of Monetary Economics*. 12 (3): 383–398.

D'Orlando, F., and E. Sanfilippo. 2010. Behavioral foundations for the Keynesian Consumption Function. *Journal of Economic Psychology* 31 (6): 1035–1046.

Farzin, Y.H., and R. Wendner. 2014. The Time Path of the Saving Rate: Hyperbolic Discounting and Short-Term Planning, FEEM WP No. 063.2014.

Frankel, M. 1962. The Production Function in Allocation and Growth: A Synthesis. *American Economic Review* 52 (5): 995–1022.

Frederick, S., G. Loewenstein, and T. O'Donoghue. 2002. Time Discounting and Time Preference: A Critical Review. *Journal of Economic Literature* 40 (2): 351–401.

Gabaix, X. 2020. A Behavioral New Keynesian Model. *American Economic Review* 110 (8): 2271–2327.

García-Peñalosa, C., and S.J. Turnovsky. 2006. Growth and Income Inequality: A Canonical Model. *Economic Theory* 28 (1): 25–49.

García-Peñalosa, C., and S.J. Turnovsky. 2007. Growth, Income Inequality, and Fiscal Policy: What Are the Relevant Trade-offs?. *Journal of Money, Credit and Banking*. 39: 369–394.

Harris, C., and D. Laibson. 2001. Dynamic Choices of Hyperbolic Consumers. *Econometrica* 69 (4): 935–957.

Krusell, P.B., and A.A. Smith Jr. 2003. Consumption-Savings Decisions with Quasi-Geometric Discounting. *Econometrica* 71 (1): 365–375.

Loewenstein, G., and D. Prelec. 1992. Anomalies in Intertemporal Choice: Evidence and an Interpretation. *Quarterly Journal of Economics* 107 (2): 573–598.

O'Donoghue, T., and M. Rabin. 2015. Present Bias: Lessons Learned and to Be Learned. *American Economic Review: Papers and Proceedings* 105 (5): 273–279.

Pollak, R.A. 1976. Interdependent Preferences. *American Economic Review*. 66 (3): 309–320.

Romer, P. 1986. Increasing Returns and Long-Run Growth. *Journal of Political Economy* 94 (5): 1002–1037.

Strotz, R.H. 1956. Myopia and Inconsistency in dynamic Utility Maximization. *Review of Economic Studies* 23 (3): 165–180.

Strulik, H. 2015. Hyperbolic Discounting and Endogenous Growth. *Economics Letters* 126 (C), 131–134.

Taylor, J.B. 1993. Discretion Versus Policy Rules in Practice. *Carnegie-Rochester Conference Series on Public Policy* 39 (1): 195–214.

Tsoukis, C. 2020. *Theory of Macroeconomic Policy*. Oxford: Oxford University Press.

Tsoukis, C., F. Tournemaine and M. Gillman. 2017. Hybrid exponential-hyperbolic discounting and growth without commitment, *The Manchester School*, 85 (S2): e45–e74.

Tsoukis, C., G. Kapetanios and J. Pearlman. 2011. Elusive Persistence: Wage And Price Rigidities, The New Keynesian Phillips Curve And Inflation Dynamics. *Journal of Economic Surveys*. 25 (4): 737–768.

Turnovsky, S.J. 1995. *Methods of Macroeconomic Dynamics*. Boston, MA: MIT Press.

Turnovsky, S.J. and C. Cecilia García-Peñalosa. 2008. Distributional dynamics in a neoclassical growth model: The role of elastic labor supply. *Journal of Economic Dynamics and Control*. 32 (5): 1399–1431.

CHAPTER 7

Socio-Behavioural Traits and Inequality

Inequality is not traditionally considered a part of macroeconomics, yet it richly deserves a place in it for a number of inter-related reasons: Firstly, because of the importance of inequality[1]; secondly, because inequality has been rising in many developed economies in the last 40 years[2]; lastly, because macroeconomic models can shed light on this development. This chapter will review the implications of socio-behavioural macroeconomic models for inequality.[3] This should be taken as an implicit call for intensifying the efforts in that direction, in view of our belief that socio-behavioural traits have lots of insights to offer in this respect.

The chapter is organised as follows. The first section deals with some key facts on the inequality of income and wealth, particularly, and outlines the long-running challenges they present for macroeconomic theory.

[1] If anyone needs to be convinced of this, a look at Wilkinson and Pickett (2009a, 2009b) will suffice.

[2] See, e.g. The World Bank: World Social Report 2020: Inequality in a Rapidly Changing World, Tables 1.1 and 1.2; https://www.un.org/development/desa/dspd/wp-content/uploads/sites/22/2020/02/World-Social-Report2020-FullReport.pdf.

[3] We shall not engage with the macroeconomics of inequality outside the socio-behavioural domain. For a review of that literature, see Tsoukis (2020), which devotes a chapter (no. 10) on inequality. Unfortunately, including analyses on inequality is not standard practice in macroeconomics textbooks. Picketty (2014, 2015) puts inequality centre stage in macroeconomics.

C. Tsoukis et al., *Social and Behavioural Macroeconomics*,
https://doi.org/10.1007/978-3-031-77748-6_7

Secondly, we review the main conclusions of the literature on the growth-inequality connection. Furthermore, we review the literature discussing the impact of status motives on this relationship. We show that there are diverse mechanisms that have a bearing on the growth-inequality trade-off. Finally, we show how we can tackle these issues in a theoretical endogenous growth model.

1 Wealth and Income Inequality

Key Facts and Challenges

Socio-behavioural models may shed useful light on key aspects of wealth and income inequality that standard analyses seem to struggle to explain. So, in this section, we discuss some avenues of research that appear promising. Key facts about the distribution of wealth have been pointed out by, among others, Cagetti and De Nardi (2008), Kennickell (2009), Wolff (2010), and Allegretto (2012). Firstly, wealth is very concentrated; e.g. currently, in the US, the richest 1% of the population owns about one-third of wealth; in the UK and similar economies, it is only slightly less. Secondly, wealth inequality is considerably higher than income or earnings inequality. This finding is a challenge to more conventional models of intertemporal choice as in those models, wealth distribution is closely linked to that of income or earnings (De Nardi 2004; Francis 2009). Finally, as mentioned, there is a positive correlation between lifetime income and saving rates (see, e.g. Dynan et al. 2004; De Nardi and Fella, 2017).

Another relevant issue is the question of whether income and wealth heterogeneity are due to unequal endowments of physical or human capital or due to heterogeneous preferences or shocks within the lifetime. In this respect, Chatterjee (1994) explores the dynamics of wealth inequality in a model with common preferences but with initial wealth dispersion. Caselli and Ventura (2000) add heterogeneity in initial tastes and skills and characterise the joint evolution of distributions and averages for consumption, income, and wealth. De Nardi and Fella (2017) add human capital, bequests across generations, entrepreneurship, and medical expenses to a standard overlapping generations model and find some role for all these factors in explaining the facts related to wealth inequality. In an influential paper, Keane and Wolpin (1997) have argued that 90% of lifetime earnings dispersion is accounted for by factors that are predetermined at the time individuals enter the labour market. Additionally, Guvenen (2016) argues that the pure permanent-transitory model is statistically hard to distinguish, in a typical panel dataset, from a model where income profiles are ex ante heterogeneous, and shocks are much less persistent (e.g. with autocorrelation around 0.8). Under this approach, most of life-cycle inequality is the result of initial heterogeneity (in the slope of earnings profiles). Various theoretical approaches have built on these empirical findings, and we review them below.

The "Capitalist Spirit" and Wealth and Income Inequality

A first promising line of research emphasises the "capitalist spirit", as discussed in Chapter 3. This involves the assumption that accumulation of capital and wealth are objectives in their own right (alongside consumption), and not only means to an end. Practically, capital (as a proxy for wealth) is an argument in the utility function. Introducing this feature into the analysis of Sect. 1 of Chapter 4, and adopting a specification in the spirit of Francis (2009), the intertemporal utility becomes:

$$U = \int_0^\infty \frac{\{(C_t)^\alpha + (K_t)^\beta\}^{1-\theta} - 1}{1-\theta} e^{-\rho t} dt, \quad \beta, \alpha > 0, \theta > 1,$$

where all variables and parameters are as before. The novelty is physical capital that enters (as a level, and not in a relative form) in the utility function. Following the standard procedure, the first-order conditions yield:

$$\frac{(K_t)^{\beta-1}}{(C_t)^{\alpha-1}} + R_t - \delta + \frac{\dot{\lambda}_t}{\lambda_t} = \rho.$$

This replaces Eq. (4.9) of Chapter 4. To appreciate the possibilities here, note that $\frac{\dot{\lambda}_t}{\lambda_t}$ is inversely related to the growth rate of consumption; in turn, that is essentially proportional to the saving rate.[4] Therefore, the extra term $\frac{(K_t)^{\beta-1}}{(C_t)^{\alpha-1}}$ implies that saving is higher, as has been highlighted in the relevant literature on the "capitalist spirit" (see Chapter 3). This is also implied by relative capital in the utility function, as Eq. (9)

[4] A higher consumption growth arises because of more saving early on.

of Chapter 4 shows. The new element here is the possibility that, if the "capitalist spirit" is strong, i.e. $\beta > \alpha > 1$ (as is the case e.g. in Francis, 2009), then the higher the capital, the more the saving rate. Therefore, there is a positive correlation between capital/wealth and saving, which standard models find difficult to predict. Such a fact has obvious implications for inequality, as it implies that the richer an individual is, the faster their wealth grows.

Status, Hyperbolic Discounting, and Inequality

A second possible avenue for research is to combine some of the social and behavioural elements we have explored in previous chapters. Specifically, we may allow a direct interaction between status, in the sense of relative consumption in utility, and hyperbolic discounting (HD). This extension has been pursued in unpublished work by Tsoukis (2014) and arguably leads to important results linked to inequality. All else equal, the present-bias is assumed to be higher (lower) among the poorer (richer) individuals. Following findings about the importance of heterogeneity in initial endowments, mentioned above, the assumption is made that heterogeneity in initial conditions is key. The model shows that the initial heterogeneity can be perpetuated and amplified through the interaction of status and discounting, giving rise to predictions such as poverty traps.

There are good reasons why status may interact with our attitudes to time: As discussed in Chapters 5 and 6, such attitudes involve the conflict between two aims, immediate self-gratification (which weighs the present more and discounts heavily the future) and longer-term goals (which take the future into account). For longer-term goals to prevail, one needs to exercise discipline over the tendency, or instinct, of immediate self-gratification, something that may be more difficult in a less favourable context such as lack of status. Banerjee and Duflo (2012) provide evidence of short-termism among the poor, as the poor have less inner incentive to fight the instinct of self-gratification. This is partly due to neurological reasons (the disproportionately high levels of cortisol—the hormone produced by stress) and partly due to psychological reasons (the will to discipline oneself weakens when the chances of success in the task for which discipline is required are minimal). As discussed in Chapter 2, there is also evidence that all effort is sustained ultimately from the same pool of mental resources (see Kahneman, 2011). For individuals preoccupied more with the effort of day-to-day living, the resources available for exercising discipline to further longer-term goals may thus be more limited. As a result, poor people are likely to exercise less self-control and may be more present-biased.

Further evidence on how socio-economic status may affect reasoning and choices, including intertemporal ones, is provided by Wilkinson and Pickett (2009a); they survey studies that relate a wide range of social problems and dysfunctions, including obesity, drug abuse, and drug abuse-related deaths, to income inequality within each country or US state; in other words, income inequality is positively correlated with symptoms of lack of ability to pursue long-term goals, even vital ones like maintenance of a healthy lifestyle. They also review studies of experiments with non-human primates which show that cortisol is related to lack of status. From these arguments and findings, the following logical chain emerges: low status produces cortisol, resulting in low self-control, therefore less ability to sacrifice current gratification for longer-term goals. Furthermore, they argue, "[e]xposure to chronic stress shifts physiological priorities: Processes that are not essential when responding to immediate threat or danger—such as tissue maintenance and repair, digestion, growth, and reproductive functions—are all downregulated in favour of processes that improve reaction times and provide energy for muscular activity" (Wilkinson and Pickett, 2009a, p. 505). The authors argue that these physiological implications of stress are an important intermediary mechanism by which the social environment has serious consequences for health. For our line of reasoning, this argument is important because those deprived of status are less capable of functions that contribute to longer-term well-being. An additional plausible chain link is, from socio-economic status to health (as per the evidence in Wilkinson and Pickett, 2009a, 2009b), to higher future discounting due to a lower probability of survival (Chakraborty, 2004).[5] The bottom line is that there are a variety of channels and good empirical support for the premise that status-seeking interacts with discounting and that lack of status increases the discount rate, making an individual more present-biased. Thus, we have here implications for inequality arising from the combination of two deviations from the standard setup of intertemporal optimisation: hyperbolic discounting and status. As Frederick et al. (2002, p. 377) argue, combining insights

[5] Naturally, the causal direction may be two-way, as has been pointed out in the health economics literature (e.g. Ikeda, Kang, and Ohtake, 2010, show that temporal decision biases result in obesity and lower health).

from more than one behavioural model may improve the intertemporally optimising model's normative and predictive appeal.

The assumption in Tsoukis (2014) that poorer individuals, who are under more pressure from the status motive, are more prone to impatience and short-termism has important implications. With attitudes to time linked to income distribution, with the richer individuals having lower discount rates and therefore exercising more patience and saving, the rich save proportionately more, a fact not easily explained along more traditional lines of reasoning, as mentioned. Additionally, models with hyperbolic discounting may be better placed to account for the gap in wealth and income inequality. In this respect, the analysis reinforces the findings of Hendricks (2007) on the importance of discount factor heterogeneity for wealth inequality. Furthermore, there is evidence of co-movement between consumption and predictable income evolution that standard optimisation models find difficult to explain (Attanasio and Weber 2010; Frederick et al. 2002). The introduction of status as a determinant of HD may better account for the excess co-movement of income and consumption or for under-saving (see O'Donoghue and Rabin 2001a, b). Thus, this extension is arguably able to account for several key puzzles in economics in a more satisfactory way than either the standard model with exponential discounting or with non-exponential discounting but without status.

2 Status, Growth, and Distribution

In this section, we discuss the effect of status on growth and distribution/inequality. We begin with a brief review of the growth-inequality relationship. We then discuss the role of status on this relationship in a variety of setups. We begin with one-sector models. Moving on to two-sector models, we discuss the notion of "status jobs", i.e. the idea that social status comparisons can be made in relation to the job of individuals, as an example of a two-sector model. In the next and final sub-section, we discuss the choice of public versus privately funded education and the effect of the status motive on this choice. We furthermore discuss the possibility that social status comparisons can impact government policies in terms of education (and healthcare).

The Relation Between Inequality and Growth

The relation between growth and distribution is both a subject of intensive research and a focus of debate. Some economists argue that inequality can have a negative impact on economic growth, while others suggest that inequality can be a natural by-product of economic development. Such a debate is interesting per se, but it also has important policy implications. Economic policies designed towards favouring economic growth are usually seen to be desirable because growth can lift people out of poverty (see, e.g. Becker et al. 1990). Besides, it leads to higher incomes, improved living standards, and a better quality of life for individuals as it enables them to access better education, healthcare, housing, and other essential goods and services. Economic policies aiming at reducing inequality stem from ethical considerations and involve questions of fairness, social justice, and the well-being of individuals and communities. The crux of the debate is that, potentially, there is a trade-off between growth and inequality. Therefore, understanding the mechanisms at work with respect to this relationship is crucial, notably to policymakers who intend to design effective policies to improve societal outcomes.

On one side of the debate on the growth-inequality relationship, authors such as Stiglitz (2012), Piketty (2014, 2015), Acemoglu and Robinson (2013), and Rodrik (2014) among others, defend the view of a negative correlation between growth and inequality. For instance, Stiglitz (2012) notes that inequality can be harmful for growth because it can induce a reduction of investments in human capital and innovation, which are important drivers of long-term growth. Piketty (2014, 2015) explains that where the returns on capital are greater than the rate of economic growth, income inequality between individuals can lead to a decrease in economic growth. Acemoglu and Robinson (2013) argues that greater inequality between individuals can lead to political instability, which can in turn have negative effects on economic growth. In a similar vein, Rodrik (2014) explains that high levels of inequality can create political polarisation and undermine social cohesion. On the other side of the debate, we find authors such as Conard (2016). They defend the notion that income inequality can drive economic growth because it provides an incentive for individuals to take more risks and invest in innovations and new technologies which are beneficial behaviours for growth. In this vein, Cowen (2017) asserts that, in an equal world, individuals tend to become less motivated to strive for success. Inequality, instead, can be a driving force to motivate them to work harder and invest in growth-enhancing activities such as Research and Development (R&D).

The empirical evidence supporting these ideas seems more limited. Some empirical studies find a negative relationship between economic growth and income inequality (Barro, 1991; Birdsall et al. 1995). Knowles (2010) finds a negative correlation between income inequality and economic growth, but he also shows that the relationship is non-linear. Notably, he finds that, in some cases, higher levels of income inequality can be associated with greater rates of economic growth, particularly in middle-income countries. More recently, Cerra et al. (2021) reviewed many studies examining the relationship between growth, inequality, and poverty. They conclude that, if growth is important with respect to poverty reduction, its relationship with inequality is not clear-cut. The outcome ultimately depends on the channel of transmission of the various effects. While high levels of inequality can lead to reduced access to education or healthcare, which can limit long-term growth, inequality might be a source of motivation for those at the bottom of the status ladder. In the context of this book's topic, we may then argue that it may, in turn, lead to greater investments in growth-enhancing activities (such as, among other things, human capital accumulation) in a sort of catching-up spirit.

Regarding the impact of economic policies, the idea of the existence of a trade-off between growth and distribution is potent. It can be argued that those aiming at promoting economic growth via encouragement of entrepreneurship and investment in innovative activities may provide greater incentives and rewards for those who are already wealthy and have more resources. This can lead to an increase in income and wealth disparities, as those with more capital and skills can benefit from greater growth opportunities than those with limited resources. In sectors driven by innovation and technological progress, such policies may lead to an increase in the demand for skilled workers which translates into a greater variation of wages between individuals and contributes to income inequality (see, e.g. Aghion et al. 2015; Levine and Rubinstein 2017). On the other hand, it can be claimed that policies aimed at reducing inequality often involve public investments in education, healthcare, social welfare programmes, and progressive taxation. While these policies can enhance social equity, they may divert resources from other areas of economic activity, potentially harming overall growth (see, e.g. Alesina and Rodrick, 1994; Garcia-Penalosa et al. 1999).

Social Status Comparisons, Inequality, and Growth

In this section, we discuss the growth-inequality trade-off issue in a model in which individuals are driven by social status comparisons. We argue that the interactions between sociological considerations and economic policies impact the relationship. The literature analysing the impact of social status comparisons on the growth-inequality relationship is fairly open-ended in terms of approaches and results. In terms of methodology, we can count three possible approaches to introduce the notion of inequality/heterogeneity. First, it can be assumed that individuals have different preferences. For instance, Futagami and Shibata (1998) assume a different rate of time preference between individuals, which influences their willingness to save and accumulate wealth. Tournemaine and Tsoukis (2015a, 2015b) adopt a more direct strategy in considering that some individuals are more motivated or status-driven. Thereby, they introduce heterogeneity between individuals via the weight they attribute to social status considerations. Second, it can be assumed that firms have access to different technologies. For instance, depending on the level of infrastructures in different regions, firms may benefit from various external effects in the form of knowledge spillover effects resulting in various levels of productivity for the workers and so heterogeneous wage incomes across regions (see. E.g., Aloi et al. 2022).

Third, individuals may have different initial endowments (see, e.g. Alesina and Rodrick 1994; Pahm 2005). This relates to the discussion in the first section above. For instance, some individuals might be born with a greater level of wealth than others. This could translate into greater access to resources and opportunities and lead to disparities in education, healthcare, and other important aspects of life and impact the macroeconomic outcome. Note that we could also cite differentiated innate skills as a source of disparities between individuals. They can take various forms such as the ability to learn new materials at school, practice a physical activity, or play a musical instrument (see, e.g. Tsoukis, 2007; Tournemaine and Tsoukis, 2008; 2010a, b). Thus, there is a variety of effects at work and the choice of setup is not trivial.

One-Sector Growth Models with Status

Long and Shimomura (2004) use an exogenous growth model "à la Ramsey-Cass-Koopmans" to show that, even if individuals are born with heterogeneous endowments in physical capital (see Sect. "Wealth and Income Inequality"), as long as they are motivated to improve their social rank, they all end up sharing the same levels of income, consumption and wealth in the long run. Therefore, social status comparisons appear as a force driving the economy towards a more egalitarian society. Although the analysis seems appealing from a theoretical perspective, we must admit that it is limited by an important drawback. As long-term growth is exogenous by construction, its interaction with inequality cannot be studied.

Using an "AK" model, Corneo and Jeanne (1999) introduce the idea that individuals have imperfect information with respect to the perception of social status by others. In such a setting, where inequality is introduced exogenously, they show that individuals' initial distribution of wealth is essential for long-term growth. Specifically, extreme cases of great initial equality and inequality are detrimental to long-term growth. In a similar setting, Corneo and Jeanne (2001) show that, if individuals care about their rank in the distribution of wealth (and not their relative standing), long-term growth is positively correlated with the strength of preferences for social status and equality.

Futagami and Shibata (1998) introduce heterogeneity in individuals' rates of time preference in a model where social comparisons are based on wealth. As explained in Chapter 4, they implicitly introduce the idea that some individuals are more patient than others, i.e. some are more willing to save and others less so. Their main result is twofold. First, there is a result on the cross-sectional distribution. Less patient individuals, who seek to maintain their position (keeping up with the Joneses), are pushed to pursue their wealth accumulation at a faster pace than what they would choose otherwise. Hence, the interaction of preference heterogeneity with the status motive has implications for distribution.[6] Second, greater preferences for social status comparisons can have a negative long-term effect on growth. The reason is that a stronger preference for social status for an individual is both synonymous with a greater willingness to save for him/herself and a decrease in the social ranking for others. For the latter, this

[6] This is reminiscent of the analysis in Tsoukis (2014) discussed above; the difference being that in Futagami and Shibata (1998), the heterogeneity stems from differences in the rate of time preference, whereas in Tsoukis (2014), it is due to capital endowments.

implies a reduction of their incentive to accumulate wealth; at the aggregate level, it is therefore possible to observe both a decrease in the rate of accumulation of wealth and a negative effect on long-term growth.

Using a model with government expenditures "à la Barro (1990)", Pham (2005) assumes that individuals have heterogeneous preferences regarding their valuation of social status comparisons based on wealth. Not surprisingly, individuals who put a greater weight on social status comparisons in their preferences end up with larger shares of the total wealth in the economy. The induced impact on the relationship between inequality and growth is, however, unclear. The outcome ultimately depends on the relative proportion of "rich" and "poor" in the economy.

Tournemaine and Tsoukis (2010a) use a model in which individuals are differentiated according to some innate skills that render them more productive. Moreover, two important features are added to this formulation. First, labour supply is endogenous. Second, the authors use a "social status function" that separates the notion of "average" status effect (that we encounter in the standard literature cited above) and "differential" status effect (see Chapter 3, Sect. 3). They show that social status comparisons induce individuals to work harder, which positively impacts inequality and growth.

Two-Sector Growth Models with Status: "Status Jobs"

Referring to our arguments developed earlier in Chapter 4, the advantage of using a two-sector model of endogenous growth is its richness and flexibility. A model with human capital accumulation lends itself nicely to a discussion of the interplay between social status comparisons, inequality, and growth. Key considerations in this regard are: (i) the crucial empirical observation stating that human capital is a strong factor favouring economic development; (ii) the interpretation that education and health of individuals can be taken as proxies for human capital (see Chapter 4); (iii) the notion that education can be a source of social status comparisons; finally, (iv) the idea that the government can directly influence the provision of funds to education and healthcare through economic policies. In other words, the channel of human capital is a natural framework for the discussion of policy.

As mentioned in Chapter 3, the factors that can be used to account for status considerations are various. Besides consumption, wealth or education, the quality of jobs can be an instrument of comparisons as valid as the others. The quality of a job can effectively signal the potential successes of an individual. For instance, positions such as engineers, surgeons, judges, lawyers, professors, and diplomats, among others, are highly regarded in any society. Fershtman et al. (1996) and Tournemaine and Tsoukis (2009) take this approach and identify the quality of jobs by the amount of human capital accumulated by individuals. The argument is that education is a means for individuals to obtain the job they seek and, in turn, reach a social position in society. This is an important issue as job comparisons may have repercussions on several grounds such as the allocation of time between leisure, work, and education, which in turn may affect inequality and growth. Moreover, as discussed in Chapter 4, exercising a well-regarded job can for instance induce some "non-pecuniary" benefits in the form of status and induce individuals to allocate more resources to human capital accumulation than they would do otherwise. In this vein, Fershtman et al. (1996) argue that this effect may lead to a misallocation of talents in the sense that individuals with low innate skills, but high wealth may end up with a better job than individuals with high innate skills but low wealth. In turn, this could even negatively impact long-term economic growth. Extending on this work by allowing for endogenous labour supply, Tournemaine and Tsoukis (2009) show that the status effect captured by the fear of being left behind induces individuals to work harder. As the effect is more pronounced for those lower down the status ladder, they show that growth and equality are positively related. In other words, there is no trade-off between growth and inequality.

Choice of Regime of Education (Public–Private) and Educational Policy

It is usually argued that one of the main goals of education and healthcare policies is primarily to reduce inequality (see, e.g. Schultz 1961, 1963, 1964). Intuitively, through the provision of unrestricted access to publicly funded education and healthcare via schools and hospitals, the government facilitates the acquisition and maintenance of knowledge and skills by individuals who may lack the necessary resources to do so. Extensive research conducted by Glomm and Ravikumar (1992), Saint-Paul and Verdier (1993), Zhang (1996), and Sylwester (2002), among others, has thoroughly examined the correlation between inequality and education, affirming the validity of this assertion from both theoretical and empirical perspectives. In essence, the uniform provision of education acts as a means of mitigating disparities and promoting egalitarianism.

These articles compare the outcomes of a pure publicly funded education system to a pure private one to assess their impact on long-term growth and distribution. However, a unique system prevails in equilibrium, i.e. the possibility of a simultaneous co-existence of the two systems is not formalised and/or cannot occur. Such an issue, though, has been tackled by Tournemaine and Tsoukis (2015a, 2015b), who analyse the effects of heterogeneous preferences for social status comparisons on differences in motivation among individuals. They notably point out a distributive conflict between beneficiaries and non-beneficiaries from the publicly funded system and demonstrate that such conflict impacts the growth-inequality relationship. Their model echoes arguments in sociology whereby it is argued that individuals, who are ranked higher up on the social status ladder, usually favour privately funded schools over publicly funded ones for their children.[7] In this spirit, Ball (1993, 1997) and Ball et al. (1995) assert that the decision regarding the type of education system in the US or UK is a way of boosting or maintaining a position in the society. In his empirical work, Anderson (1988) even suggests the existence of links between status, religious beliefs, and choice of education regime.

Let us finally mention that the spectrum of motives behind the decision to invest in education is rather large and may even affect the shape of the educational system itself. Specifying a democratic (median voter) system, Tournemaine and Tsoukis (2015a, 2015b) demonstrate that social status considerations can shape the educational system in terms of the mix between privately and publicly funded systems. They show that lower inequality and higher long-term economic growth are compatible policy goals, i.e. there is not necessarily a trade-off between the two.

In economic sociology, some authors have developed the idea that the fear of being left behind (as mentioned earlier) and the need to catch up in terms of education, could also help explain the importance of tutoring or extra schooling activity besides the formal educational system. These activities are sometimes referred to as "shadow education". For example,

[7] Bernal (2005) argues that individuals in the middle and upper social classes choose to send their children to private education, while poorer populations including ethnic minorities and immigrants attend state education for free.

Davies (2004), Glewwe and Kremer (2006), and Kim and Lee (2010) claim that tutoring activities exist because individuals seek to compensate for the poor quality of publicly funded schools. Other reasons, such as clarifying the content of lessons learned in class (see, e.g. Banerjee et al., 2007), training for an entrance examination (see, e.g. Tansel and Bircan, 2006) or acquiring additional skills to improve abilities (see, e.g. Dang, 2007) are also reasons discussed in the literature.

This is an important issue and we elaborate on it more formally in the next section. To preamble, authors like Russell (1997) and Dang and Rogers (2008) explain that the tutoring activity, which we can define as the supplementary education that individuals obtain on top of the compulsory (or formal) one, is a standard practice both in developing and developed countries, though we may observe great disparities between countries regarding the choice of individuals to invest or not in extra schooling activities. For instance, Dang and Rogers (2008) argue that 83 per cent of children in South Korea receive extra schooling and households spend on aggregate an amount of funds in private tutoring which is almost equivalent to the total amount of government expenditures in education. On the other side of the picture, a report of the European Commission (2011) establishes that this activity is almost absent in the Scandinavian countries.[8]

3 The "Shadow Education Sector": A Formal Analysis

Introduction

In this sub-section, we show more formally the arguments developed previously. In other words, we propose examining the issue of the relationship between long-term growth and inequality in a formal model of endogenous growth in which individuals are driven by social status aspirations and decide on the amount of extra schooling activities they pursue. There are at least two reasons to justify this choice of approach. First, to

[8] Countries may also differ in terms of timing for investments in extra schooling activities. For instance, countries like France and Greece mainly invest during several years of high school in preparation for higher education entry exams via additional schooling for languages and music. Others such as the UK and Thailand, mainly invest during the last stages of primary school, in preparation for high school entry through more intensive extra schooling in (extracurricular) activities such as music and drama.

our knowledge, there has not been any attempt so far at integrating the notion of extra schooling activities in a growth or other macroeconomic economic model and examine its implications for growth or inequality or other macroeconomic outcomes. This sub-section, therefore, shall contribute to the growth and human capital literatures by bringing all these issues into an integrated framework. This, we believe, is important because there can be two-way interactions between macroeconomic outcomes and the choice by individuals of how much extra education to pursue. Second, our approach can be apprehended as a complement to the existing literature on education cited earlier. Indeed, this latter mainly focuses on the growth-inequality nexus in models where individuals must choose between private and publicly funded regimes (see, e.g. Glomm and Ravikumar, 1992; Saint-Paul and Verdier, 1993; Zhang, 1996; Sylwester, 2002; Tournemaine and Tsoukis, 2009; 2015a, b). Therefore, considering the interplay between public spending on education and the choice of individuals to invest or not in extra schooling departs from this literature, we seek to contribute to a better understanding of the mechanisms at work.

This is important as the issue of the potential impact of extra schooling activities on growth and inequality has already been a topic of discussion among scholars (see, e.g. Dang, 2007; Dang and Rogers, 2008). Regarding distribution, it could be argued that extra schooling activities should foster inequality because only richer and more educated individuals can allocate the necessary resources to these activities. On the other hand, if individuals indirectly benefit from the knowledge accumulated by others through spillover effects, this conclusion might not be as obvious. On growth, it could be argued that extra schooling activities are likely to participate in and even foster economic development as it can be interpreted as a complement of compulsory education. In this context, it seems important to formally assess the consequences of public spending in education on the growth-inequality nexus in a framework where extra schooling activities are formalised in an endogenous manner.

To proceed, as stated previously, we propose to bring forward the social status motive as a key factor to explain the choice of individuals to invest (or not) in extra schooling activities.[9] Our motivation is dual. First, the

[9] Advancing the status motive as a possible explanation to explain the differences we observe between countries with respect to additional spending in education also concurs, to some extent, with Blanchard (2004). The author explains for instance that shifting

notion that individuals are driven by status motives and that their utility depends, among other things, on their position in the distribution (see, e.g. Clark and Oswald 1996; McBride 2001; Choudhary et al. 2007; Maurer and Meier 2008), is shown to have important effects related to both growth and distribution (see, e.g. Futagami and Shibata 1998; Corneo and Jeanne 1999; Pham 2005; Tournemaine and Tsoukis 2009; 2010a, b; 2015a, 2015b). Second, we can argue that, for the most part, the reasons for which individuals are willing to invest in extra schooling activities derive from their status motive which pushes them into a quest for success and recognition.[10]

To conduct the analysis, we develop a simple model with human capital accumulation where heterogeneous individuals are differentiated via an idiosyncratic parameter measuring their status motivation. The key element of the model, fitting with the arguments given above, is that individuals, who receive a kind of compulsory education depending on the amount of funds allocated to public education and on a minimum amount of time to spend at school, are free to choose whether or not to invest additional resources in extra schooling activities.

Although simple, the model is rich enough to allow the examination of a number of important and various issues. Notably, we discuss the impact of government spending in education on growth and inequality. While we show that government spending in education has a positive effect on growth, we obtain that their impact on inequality is ambiguous. The positive impact on growth is the outcome of an increase in individuals' productivity in their human capital accumulation process. The reduction or increase in inequality, on the other hand, depends on the combination of several factors such as the amount of public funds allocated to education, the amount of compulsory time spent at school, the cultural encouragement that extra schooling receives from society, and the overall level of status motive of individuals. What we show, though, is that the critical element to check to infer the impact of the policy change

attitudes and more broadly social norms play an important role in respect to the difference in the number of hours of work per week per person in the US and Europe.

[10] The European commission report (2011) states, p. 3: "[P]rivate tutoring is much less about pupils who are in real need of help that they cannot find at school, and much more about maintaining the competitive advantages of the already successful and privileged". Interested readers can also refer to Fershtman, Murphy and Weiss (1996) and Tournemaine and Tsoukis (2009) for the connections between social aspirations and education achievement.

on distribution is the initial share of individuals content with compulsory education. In the case where this share is large enough, we show that greater public funds allocated to education can yield a reduction in economy-wide inequality. This outcome arises even if more individuals decide to invest in extra schooling activities.

Despite the idea that government spending in education can increase inequality seems a striking result at first glance, it echoes the empirical finding of Antoninis and Tsakloglou (2001). Indeed, the authors argue that if government spending is allocated to primary and secondary education, this should reduce inequality. If, however, funds are allocated to tertiary education the opposite should occur. On the theoretical side, some authors also provide various explanations for this feature. For instance, Benabou (1996) argues that, in countries like the US, where public schools are funded by local taxes, the quality of education may vary across cities and states. More recently, Zhang (2008) argues that lobbying from the richest and more powerful communities can induce a bias in the allocation of public spending in education.

In this sub-section, we provide a complementary explanation. We argue that the desire to acquire more education is related to the motivation of individuals who seek to achieve a social position in society. That is, the interaction between status motive and education implies that a more educated population can come along with more inequality.

Another interesting contribution of the theoretical model we propose concerns its implication with respect to political-economy issues. In the same spirit as Alesina and Rodrik (1994), we discuss the distributive conflict between individuals and the resulting relationship between growth and distribution. In our framework, conflict arises between those who are content with the formal system of education and those who prefer to invest additional resources in education. We show that the former group of individuals prefers a smaller public education sector (i.e. less tax) than the latter because their productivity gain from a greater size of the government is lower. Thereby, and as a consequence of this result, we conclude that, in a democratic system, the actual size of the government is either above or below the welfare-maximising one.

The Model

We consider a closed economy in continuous time populated by a mass [0 1] of infinitely lived individuals indexed by: $i : i \in [0\ 1]$. Time, denoted by

t, goes from zero to infinity. Every individual is initially endowed with a given amount T of labour-time and $h_{i,0} \equiv h_0 > 0$ units of human capital. Individuals allocate their time between: (i) the production of an output, $y_{i,t}$; (ii) education which takes the form of a human capital accumulation process $h_{i,t}$; and (iii) leisure.

As we will see, out of the unit mass of individuals, an endogenous mass at one end will choose a compulsory (or formal) regime of education, i.e. they will choose not to spend any additional resources on extra schooling; the rest, $1-p$, on the other hand, will choose to allocate extra units of time to education to acquire extra units of human capital. For notational clarity, we will use the upper-script, j, with "$j = A$" if individuals are content with compulsory schooling and the upper-script "$j = B$" if they prefer to invest additional units of time in extra schooling.

Following Saint-Paul and Verdier (1992), we assume that output is produced with a linear technology of the form:

$$y_{i,t}^{j} = \Omega l_{i,t}^{j} h_{i,t}^{j}, \; i \in [0, 1], \; j = A, B, \tag{1}$$

where $\Omega > 0$ is a constant productivity parameter, and $l_{i,t}^{j}$ and $h_{i,t}^{j}$ represent the labour supply and human capital level of individual i choosing educational system j.[11]

In the same spirit as Kempf and Moizeau (2009), the law of motion of individual human capital depends on the level of public investments and on the amount of time that each individual allocates to human capital accumulation.[12] Public investments in human capital accumulation are funded by an income flat tax rate, $\tau > 0$, levied on each individual income. The budget constraint of the individual is thus given by:

$$c_{i,t}^{j} = (1 - \tau)\Omega l_{i,t}^{j} h_{i,t}^{j}, i \in [0, 1], \; j = A, B. \tag{2}$$

For simplicity, we assume that the budget constraint of the government is balanced at each moment. That is, the government spending in education matches exactly the amount of funds collected at each moment.

[11] For simplicity, like Saint-Paul and Verdier (1992), we do not incorporate physical capital in the production function. Adding physical capital would complicate, but not "wash away", the effects we are discussing here.

[12] Blankenau and Simpson (2004) assume that the law of motion of individual human capital depends on the level of public investments and on the (private) investment of each individual that can be interpreted as private material resources.

We depart from Kempf and Moizeau's (2009) human capital specification as we assume that the time allocated to education depends on two elements: (i) a compulsory and common to every individual amount of time spent in education, denoted by e and (ii) a free to choose amount of time, denoted by $\varepsilon_{i,t} > 0$ representing the additional units of time individuals spend in education. The law of motion of human capital capturing these features is set to:

$$\dot{h}_{i,t}^{j} = \varphi(\tau\overline{y}_t)^{\phi}\left[(e + \eta\varepsilon_{i,t})h_{i,t}^{j}\right]^{1-\phi}, \; i \in [0, 1], \; j = A, B, \tag{3}$$

where $0 < \varphi < 1$, $\phi > 0$ is a constant productivity parameter, $\eta \geq 0$ is a measure of the efficiency of extra schooling investments or more broadly a measure of the cultural encouragement that extra schooling receives from society, $\overline{y}_t$ is the average level of output in the economy, whereby $\tau\,\overline{y}_t$ represents the per-capita amount of public spending in the form of material resources in education. For technical simplicity, we follow Abel (2005) and assume a geometric aggregation rule for individual variables. We define: $\overline{y}_t = (\overline{y}_t^A)^p(\overline{y}_t^B)^{1-p}$ and $\overline{h}_t = \left(\overline{h}_t^A\right)^p\left(\overline{h}_t^B\right)^{1-p}$, where $\overline{y}_t^A = \exp\left[\int_0^p \log y_{i,t}^A di/p\right]$, $\overline{y}_t^B = \exp\left[\int_p^1 \log y_{i,t}^B di/1 - p\right]$, $\overline{h}_t^A = \exp\left[\int_0^p \log h_{i,t}^A di/p\right]$ and $\overline{h}_t^B = \exp\left[\int_p^1 \log h_{i,t}^B di/(1-p)\right]$.

Individuals derive utility from their level of consumption, their social status in society and leisure. As it is standard in the literature, the social status of individuals is defined by the ratio of their level of consumption, $c_{i,t}$ to the average of the others, $\overline{c}_t$, where $\overline{c}_t = (\overline{c}_t^A)^p(\overline{c}_t^B)^{1-p}$, with $\overline{c}_t^A = \exp\left[\int_0^p \log c_{i,t}^A di/p\right]$ and $\overline{c}_t^B = \exp\left[\int_p^1 \log c_{i,t}^B di/(1-p)\right]$.[13]

[13] There exist other ways to account for social status. For instance, status could be defined as: (i) the relative level of human capital of an individual to that of others (see, e.g. Fershtman, Murphy and Weiss, 1996; Tsoukis and Tournemaine, 2009) or (ii) the relative amount of wealth (physical capital) of an individual to that of others (see, e.g. Corneo and Jeanne, 1997; Pham, 2005). It is important to mention that none of the results we derive hinge on our particular specification.

Preferences are represented by:

$$U_{i,t}^{j} = \int_{0}^{\infty} \begin{bmatrix} \log\left(c_{i,t}^{j}\right) + \Delta_i \log\left(c_{i,t}^{j}/\overline{c}_t\right) \\ +\beta\left(T - l_{i,t}^{j} - e - \varepsilon_{i,t}\right) \end{bmatrix} e^{-\rho t} dt,\ i \in [0, 1],\ j = A, B, \tag{4}$$

where $\rho > 0$ is the rate of time preference, $\beta > 0$ represents the marginal utility of leisure, this latter being given by $T - l_{\mathrm{i,t}}^{j} - e - \varepsilon_{\mathrm{i,t}}$, and $\Delta_i \log\left(c_{\mathrm{i,t}}^{j}/\overline{c_t}\right)$ represents the preference of an individual for social status. Parameter Δ_i is the strength of the taste for status in consumption, that is, it captures the idea that some individuals are more motivated for status, antagonistic, or rivalrous, others less so. For technical simplicity, we assume that $\delta_i \equiv \log(1 + \Delta_i)$ is uniformly distributed on the support $[\delta^{\min}, \delta^{\max}]$ with mean $\overline{\delta} = \left(\delta^{\max} + \delta^{\min}\right)/2$ and variance $\sigma_{\delta}^2 = \left(\delta^{\max} - \delta^{\min}\right)^2/12$.

We will see shortly that it is important to distinguish between economy-wide, sector A-wide, and sector B-wide variables. In what follows, we denote $\left(\overline{\delta}^{A}, \sigma_{\delta A}^2\right)$ and $\left(\overline{\delta}^{B}, \sigma_{\delta B}^2\right)$ as the average and variance of individuals' motivation opting for no extra schooling and those investing extra time in education, respectively. An important feature here is that the values of these variables depend on the parametric p, although $\left(\overline{\delta}, \sigma_{\delta}^2\right)$ do not. Moreover, as δ_i is uniformly distributed on the support $[\delta \min, \delta \max]$, we have $\overline{\delta}^{A} = \left(\delta^{\min} + \delta_p\right)/2 < \overline{\delta} < \overline{\delta}^{B} = \left(\delta^{\max} + \delta_p\right)/2$, $\sigma_{\delta A}^2 = \left(\delta_p - \delta^{\min}\right)^2/12 < \sigma_{\delta}^2$ and $\sigma_{\delta B}^2 = \left(\delta^{\max} - \delta_p\right)^2/12 < \sigma_{\delta}^2$, where $\delta_p = p(\delta_{\max} - \delta_{\min}) + \delta_{\min}$ denotes the motivation of the marginal individual, i.e. the one who is indifferent between the compulsory regime (j = A) and investing extra units of time in education (j = B). An important step for the analysis will be the determination of the share of individual content with compulsory education, p, to analyse its behaviour and relation with growth, inequality, and welfare when a policy change occurs.

Equilibrium

In this sub-section, we proceed as follows. First, we solve two optimisation problems: One for the typical individual choosing compulsory education only, and one for the individual choosing to allocate extra time to schooling activities. Second, we determine which type of education regime an individual chooses in the first place. Third, we characterise the steady-state equilibrium. Fourth, we analyse the main properties of the equilibrium, more particularly, the effects of a policy change on the growth-inequality relation and welfare. For simplicity, we restrict the analysis to the steady-state outcome and relegate the transitional dynamics, which shows that the equilibrium is saddle point stable around the steady state, to the Appendix at the end of this Chapter.

It is assumed that agents build status-seeking in consumption, as analysed, into their optimality conditions, taking the averages as given. In doing so, they are also assumed to be able to accurately forecast the relevant aggregate statistics (mean consumption) one instant ahead.[14] The outcome of this process is a Nash equilibrium, whereby agents respond optimally to aggregate outcomes and, in so doing, reproduce them (or the distributions from which aggregate statistics are drawn). The assumption of an (infinitesimal) lag between the time on which information is based and the realisation of outcomes allows us to avoid explicit game-theoretic considerations (that is, following Pollack 1976, p. 310; and the "catching up" model of Abel 1990).

Individual Problem with the Compulsory Regime Only

If an individual is content with compulsory education, the optimisation problem reduces to the choice of consumption, $c_{i,t}^A$, and labour-time devoted to output production, $l_{i,t}$, that maximises (4) subject to (1) and the budget constraint given by (2). After some manipulations, we obtain:

$$l_i^A = \frac{1 + \Delta_i}{\beta} = \frac{\exp(\delta_i)}{\beta}, \ for\, all, \ i \in [0, p], \tag{5}$$

where we have used the usual convention of dropping the index of time for constant variables in a steady state.

[14] This is the assumption of "rational myopic foresight", which is a standard hypothesis in macroeconomics, see, e.g. Turnovsky, (1996, Chapter 3) for more discussion.

Equation (5) says that the marginal benefit of an additional unit of labour allocated to the production of goods equals its marginal cost in utility terms. The marginal benefit comprises two components: the direct benefit from an additional unit of consumption plus the indirect gain due to the improvement in social status, Δ_i.

For future reference, from (3), we compute the growth rate of individual human capital for those who choose $\varepsilon_{i,t} = 0$:

$$g_i^A = \varphi\left(\frac{\tau\overline{y_t}}{h_{i,t}^A}\right)^{\phi}(e)^{1-\phi},\ for\ all,\ i \in [0, p]. \tag{6}$$

Individual Problem with Extra Schooling

Individuals who spend extra time in education choose consumption, $c_{i,t}^B$, labour-time spent in output production, $l_{i,t}^B$, and the extra time, $\varepsilon_{i,t}$. After manipulations, the current-value Hamiltonian of this problem is: $CVH_{i,t}^B = \log\left[\left(c_{i,t}^B\right)\left(c_{i,t}^B/\overline{c_t}\right)^{\Delta_i}\right] + \beta\left(T - l_{i,t}^B - \varepsilon_{i,t}\right) + \mu_{i,t}^B\varphi(\tau\overline{y}_t)^{\phi}\left[\left(e + \eta\varepsilon_{i,t}\right)h_{i,t}^B\right]^{1-\phi}$ where $\mu_{i,t}^B$ is the co-state variable associated to the law of motion of human capital (see 3) and $c_{i,t}^B = (1-\tau)\Omega\ l_{i,t}^B h_{i,t}^B$ (see 2). The first-order conditions are: $\partial CVH_{i,t}^B/\partial l_{i,t}^B = (1+\Delta_i)l_{i,t}^B - \beta = 0$, $\partial CVH_{i,t}^B/\partial\varepsilon_{i,t} = -\beta + \mu_{i,t}^B\eta(1-\phi)\dot{h}_{i,t}^B/(e+\eta\varepsilon_{i,t}) = 0$,, $\partial CVH_{i,t}^B/\partial h_{i,t}^B = (1+\Delta_i)/h_{i,t}^B + \mu_{i,t}^B(1-\phi)\dot{h}_{i,t}^B/h_{i,t}^B + = -\dot{\mu}_{i,t}^B + \rho\mu_{i,t}^B$. The transversality condition is: $\lim_{t\to\infty}\mu_{i,t}^B h_{i,t}^B e^{-\rho t} = 0$.

Under the assumption that the economy is in steady state, we have $l_{i,t}^B = l_i^B$, $\varepsilon_{i,t} = \varepsilon_i$ and $\dot{\mu}_{i,t}^B/\mu_{i,t}^B + \dot{h}_{i,t}^B/h_{i,t}^B = 0$ at each instant. Using this information, simple manipulations of the first-order conditions yield:

$$l_i^B = \frac{1+\Delta_i}{\beta} = \frac{\exp(\delta_i)}{\beta},\ for\ all\ i \in [p, 1], \tag{7}$$

$$\begin{aligned} e + \eta\varepsilon_i &= \frac{\eta(1+\Delta_i)}{\beta}\left[\frac{(1-\phi)g_i^B}{\phi g_i^B + \rho}\right] \\ &= \frac{\eta\exp(\delta_i)}{\beta}\left[\frac{(1-\phi)g_i^B}{\phi g_i^B + \rho}\right],\ for\ all\ i \in [p, 1], \end{aligned} \tag{8}$$

and, from Eq. (3), the growth rate of human capital of individual i, $p<i<1$, choosing to invest in extra schooling is given by:

$$g_i^B = \varphi\left(\frac{\tau \overline{y_t}}{h_{i,t}^B}\right)^{\phi} (e + \eta\varepsilon_i)^{1-\phi}, \ for\ all\ i \in [p, 1]. \tag{9}$$

Choice of the Education Regime

Having set out the optimisation of each type of individual conditional on the choice of education (i.e. compulsory or extra schooling), we determine what type of education the individual chooses in the first place. To proceed, we compare the level of utility attained under the two regimes for the marginal individual p, i.e. the one who is indifferent between the two regimes. To avoid complexity, we assume that the choice between education regimes happens only once: at date zero and that the system is in a steady state. This presupposes perfect foresight, an assumption in line with the deterministic nature of our model.

An important property of the steady state is that the growth rates attainable in both regimes must be equal. This outcome results from the presence of the average output, $\overline{y_t}$, in the technology of production of human capital (3): This implies that, as the level of individual human capital forges ahead of $\overline{y_t}$, it acts to slow down its growth rate. This is likely to bring a convergence of human capital to common growth rates, as found in the literature (see, e.g. Tamura 1991; de la Croix and Doepke 2004; Alonso-Carrera 2001). We thus have: $g_i^A = g_i^B = g, \forall i \in [0,1]$, where a "$g$" without any upper-script will henceforth indicate the growth rate common across sectors and individuals.

The marginal individual, with ambition δ_p, is such that:

$$\int_0^{\infty} \left[\exp(\delta_p)\log\left(\frac{c_{p,t}^B}{c_{p,t}^A}\right) - \beta\varepsilon_{p,t}\right] e^{-\rho t} dt = 0. \tag{10}$$

Equation (10) is derived from the utility function (4) applied to the case of the individual choosing compulsory education or investing extra time in human capital accumulation. Had Eq. (10) been greater (lower) than zero, the utility of investing extra time in human capital accumulation would be greater (lower) than from the compulsory regime. In other words, Eq. (10) is used to define the threshold status-seeking, or rivalry, level δ_p of the agent who is exactly indifferent between the two regimes. Any $i < p$ would indicate those who prefer the compulsory regime, and those $i > p$ who prefer to invest extra time in education.

Using (2), (5), (7) and (8), we can simplify the critical condition (10) to obtain:

$$\log\left(\frac{h_{p,t}^B}{h_{p,t}^A}\right) = \frac{(1-\phi)g}{\phi g + \rho} - \frac{\beta e}{\exp(\delta_p)}. \tag{11}$$

Equation (11) captures the two key effects of the long run for the marginal individual with motivation δ_p: in equilibrium, consumption considerations captured by the log-human capital gap between regimes (left-hand side) equalises leisure considerations (right-hand side).

We can derive another equation in relative human capital by using (3). After straightforward manipulations, we obtain:

$$\log\left(\frac{\overline{h}_t^B}{h_{i,t}^B}\right) = (1-\phi)\left(\delta^{-B} - \delta_i\right),\ i \in [p,\ 1]. \tag{12}$$

From Eq. (12), the steady-state human capital of an individual choosing to invest extra time in education differs from the average in that sector by the difference between the motivation of that person from sector-wide average. The dependence of sector-wide motivation on the fraction, p, of the population in each sector is implicit here. We have indeed $d\overline{\delta}^B/\mathrm{dp} > 0$.

Using the property that the human capital of individuals in the regime is the same as the average, i.e. $h_{i,t}^A = \overline{h}_t^A$ for all $i < p$ (see (6) given that $g_i^A = g$ at the steady state), we can combine (11) and (12) in which we set $i = p$, to obtain:

$$\log\left(\frac{\overline{h}_t^B}{\overline{h}_t^A}\right) = \frac{(1-\phi)g}{\phi g + \rho} - \frac{\beta e}{\exp(\delta_p)} + (1-\phi)\left(\overline{\delta}^B - \delta_p\right) \tag{13}$$

Equation (13) is decomposed into an intra-group component coming from (11) and a between-groups component coming from (12). In other words, the log-difference between the average human capital of those investing in extra schooling and the human capital attainable with compulsory education combines the difference in the human capital of the *p-th* individual across the two educational regimes and the difference between average human capital when individuals invest extra units of time in education and the human capital of the *p-th* individual (also investing).

Characterisation of the Steady State

In this section, we characterise the steady state. For convenience, results are gathered in the next Proposition.

Proposition 1 There exists a unique steady-state equilibrium characterised by a constant individual amount of labour allocated to output production given by.

$$l_i = \frac{\exp(\delta_i)}{\beta} \; for\, all\, i \in [0,\ 1]. \tag{14}$$

The amount of time spent in extra schooling by an individual i, $0 < p < i < 1$, *is given by*

$$\varepsilon_i = \frac{\exp(\delta_i)}{\beta}\left[\frac{(1-\phi)g}{\phi g+\rho}\right] - \frac{e}{\eta}, i \in \left[\mathrm{p,1}\right], j = \mathrm{B}. \tag{15}$$

The share of individuals content with compulsory education, p (so the remaining share of those choosing to have extra schooling, 1 − p) and long-run growth are implicitly solutions of the following two equations:

$$(g)^{\phi}(\phi g+\rho)^{1-\phi} = \frac{\varphi}{\beta}(1-\phi)^{(1-\phi)}\left[\tau\Omega\exp\left(\overline{\delta}\right)\right]^{\phi}\left[\eta\exp\left(\overline{\delta}^{B}\right)\right]^{1-\phi}\left(\frac{\overline{h}_t^{A}}{\overline{h}_t^{B}}\right)^{p\phi}, \tag{16}$$

and

$$g = \varphi\left[\frac{\tau\Omega\exp\left(\overline{\delta}\right)}{\beta}\right]^{\phi}\left(\frac{\overline{h}_t^{A}}{\overline{h}_t^{B}}\right)^{(p-1)\phi}(e)^{1-\phi}. \tag{17}$$

where

$$\delta_p = p(\delta^{\max} - \delta^{\min}) + \delta^{\min},$$

and the relative average human capital and consumption between sectors are given by

$$\frac{\overline{h}_t^B}{\overline{h}_t^A} = \frac{\overline{c}_t^B}{\overline{c}_t^A} = \exp\left[\frac{(1-\phi)g}{\phi g+\rho} - \frac{\beta e}{\exp(\delta_p)} + \frac{1-\phi}{\phi}\left(\frac{\delta^{\max}-\delta_p}{2}\right)\right]. \tag{18}$$

Finally, the economy-wide level of inequality, defined as the relative log-consumption to the log-average, $\sigma_y^2 = E_i\left[\log(c_{i,t}) - \log(\overline{c}_t)\right]^2$, *is given by*

$$\sigma_y^2 = \sigma_{\delta A}^2 + \frac{\sigma_{\delta B}^2}{\phi^2} + p(1-p)\left[\log\left(\frac{\overline{c}_t^B}{\overline{c}_t^A}\right)\right]^2 \tag{19}$$

Proof. See the Appendix.

Examination of Eq. (14) shows that the constant quantity of labour-time spent in the production of output positively depends on the degree of status-seeking, δ_i. In other words, as social aspirations induce greater work efforts, they are synonymous with motivation. This is a crucial element of the model as it differentiates individuals in terms of income and consumption even if they do not spend extra time on education, i.e. $\varepsilon_i = 0$ and $\mathrm{h}_{i,t} = \overline{\mathrm{h}}_t^{A}$ for all $i < p$. In the same vein, Eq. (15) shows that status motivation has also a positive effect on individuals' extra investments in education: $\partial\varepsilon_i/\partial\delta_i > 0$. In other words, not only do individuals work harder but they also allocate more time to education. Therefore, in this case, the status motive acts via two channels which may have important consequences on inequality (see Sect. "Status, Growth, and Distribution").

The analysis of the set of Eqs. (16)–(19) is more complex. Starting with the relationship between the long-run level of growth, *g*, and the share of population content with compulsory education, *p*, we can simplify (16)–(18) to obtain the following 2 × 2 system in *(g, p)*:

$$g = \left\{\begin{array}{c}\varphi\left[\frac{\tau\Omega\exp(\overline{\delta})}{\beta}\right]^{\phi}(e)^{1-\phi} \\ \times\left\{\exp\left[\begin{array}{c}\frac{(1-\phi)g}{\phi g+\rho} + \frac{\beta e}{\exp\left[p\left(\delta^{\max}-\delta^{\min}\right)+\delta^{\min}\right]} \\ +\frac{1-\phi}{\phi}\frac{(1-p)\left(\delta^{\max}-\delta^{\min}\right)}{2}\end{array}\right]\right\}^{(1-p)\phi}\end{array}\right\}, \tag{20}$$

And

$$(g)^{\phi}(\phi g+\rho)^{1-\phi} = \left\{ \begin{array}{c} \frac{\varphi}{\beta}(1-\phi)^{(1-\phi)}\left[\tau\Omega\exp(\bar{\delta})\right]^{\phi}\left[\eta\exp(\bar{\delta}^{B})\right]^{1-\phi} \\ \times\left\{\exp\left[\frac{(1-\phi)g}{\phi g+\rho}+\frac{\beta e}{\exp\left[p\left(\delta^{\max}-\delta^{\min}\right)+\delta^{\min}\right] + \frac{1-\phi}{\phi}\frac{(1-p)\left(\delta^{\max}-\delta^{\min}\right)}{2}}\right]\right\}^{-p\phi} \end{array} \right\}. \quad (21)$$

Equation (20) is a reduced form of the growth equation for those who are content with public education. It shows an unambiguous negative relation between g and p. Intuitively, as more individuals are willing to invest extra time in education (i.e. p decreases), only the less motivated remain content with compulsory education which has a negative impact on growth. Similarly, Eq. (21) is a reduced form of the growth equation for those who invest extra units of their time in education. The sign of the relation between and cannot be determined a priori as two effects going in opposite directions are at work: A lower number of individuals investing extra time in education leads to a drop in overall investments in human capital which has a negative impact on growth; but also, it leads to an increase of average motivation of those who prefer to invest in extra schooling which is beneficial to growth.

To complete the analysis, we make a graphical representation of the 2 × 2 system (20)–(21) and show the existence and uniqueness of a solution for g and p (see Fig. 1). To get there, we calibrate the model by choosing benchmark parameter values shown in Table 1, chosen so as to obtain a credible growth rate of around 2 per cent, but close to the standard values used in the literature (see, e.g. Barro and Sala-i-Martin, 2004). Moreover, we set $\tau = 0.05$ which roughly corresponds to the share of GDP an OECD country would spend on education[15]

[15] With the parameter values given in Table 1, we find: $p = 0.280322$, $g = 0201895$, $\overline{h}_t^A/\overline{h}_t^B = 0.857086$, $\sigma_y^2 = 0.0994307$.

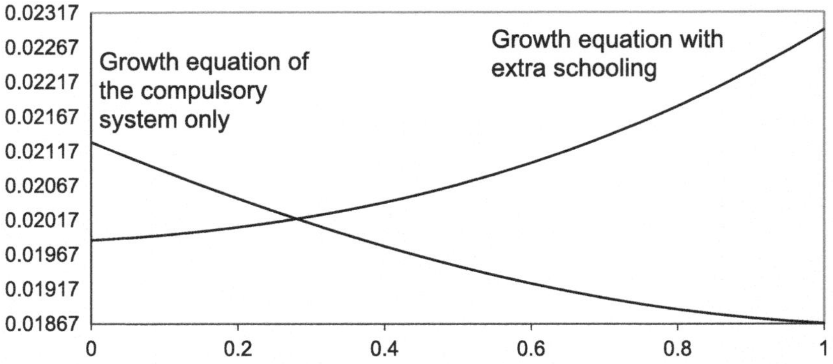

Fig. 1 Graphical representation of Eqs. (20)–(21)

Table 1 Benchmark parameter values

Description	*Parameter*	*Parameter value*
Income tax	τ	0.05
Productivity in output production	Ω	1
Share of private/public resources in human capital	φ	0.7
Productivity parameter in human capital	ϕ	0.1
Effciency in extra schooling investments	η	1
Disutility of labour	β	0.5
Discount rate	ρ	0.05
Compulsory time in education	e	0.25
Status parameter	$\delta_i \in [\delta^{min}, \delta^{max}]$	$\delta^{min} = 0$ $\delta^{max} = 1$

To close this sub-section, we note from (19) that the economy-wide level of inequality, σ_y^2, is given as a within- and between-groups decomposition of income heterogeneity. Its value is the sum of the variances between individuals choosing the same education system $\left(\sigma_{\delta A}^2, \sigma_{\delta B}^2\right)$, plus a measure of the income gap between the two separate cohorts of individuals. Interestingly, σ_y^2 depends on p, which is itself endogenously determined. Thus, we can raise the issue of the impact of an increase in public education spending on the share of individuals choosing compulsory schooling or investing extra units of time in education, the long-run level of growth and inequality. This task is carried out next.

Policy Implications

Basic Properties

We study the effects of a change in τ on the share of individuals in each educational system, p (and $1 - p$), long-run growth, g, relative average human capital across sectors, $\overline{h}_t^A/\overline{h}_t^B$, extra time spent in education, ε_i, and economy-wide variance, σ_y^2. For that purpose, we suppose that the economy is initially in a steady state, and the government decides to implement an unanticipated and permanent increase in τ. As in the previous section, we can use numerical simulations across a wide range of values, or simply use Fig. 1 noting that an increase in τ leads to an upward shift of (20). In both cases, we obtain Table 2 that depicts the signs of the derivatives of $p, g, \overline{h}_t^A/\overline{h}_t^B, \varepsilon_i, \sigma_y^2$ with respect to the policy instrument τ.

Table 2 shows that a larger share of individuals starts investing in extra schooling as the size of the government increases (i.e. $dp/d\tau < 0$ and $d(1-p)/d\tau > 0$). Such a result concurs with the arguments of Dang and Rogers (2008) who explain that a better public education system can increase the willingness of less motivated individuals to acquire more education. In our model, the mechanism leading to this outcome is intuitive: it is the result of an increase in individuals' productivity in their human capital accumulation process (see 3). The consequence is obviously an increase in growth ($dg/d\tau > 0$), but also an increase in the human capital gap across those who are content with compulsory education and those who prefer to spend extra time in education $\left(d\left(\overline{h}_t^A/\overline{h}_t^B\right)/d\tau < 0\right)$. This latter effect comes from the fact that the more motivated individuals

Table 2 Effects of educational policy change

$\frac{dp}{d\tau} < 0$	$\frac{dg}{d\tau} > 0$	$\frac{d\left(\overline{h}_t^A/\overline{h}_t^B\right)}{d\tau} < 0$	$\frac{d\varepsilon_i}{d\tau} > 0$	$\frac{d\sigma_y^2}{d\tau} \lesseqgtr 0$

spend more time in education, as $d\varepsilon_i/d\tau > 0$ (see 15) which also fosters the pace of their human capital accumulation process.

An immediate consequence of the above results is that the effect of an increase in τ on economy-wide inequality, σ_y^2, is not clear-cut. Using the uniform distribution property for δ_i and Eq. (19), we have:

$$\frac{d\sigma_y^2}{d\tau} = \left\{ \begin{array}{c} \frac{(\delta_p - \delta^{\min})}{6}\frac{d\delta_p}{d\tau} - \frac{1}{\phi^2}\frac{(\delta^{\max} - \delta_p)}{6}\frac{d\delta_p}{d\tau} \\ +2p(1-p)\frac{\overline{c}_t^A}{\overline{c}_t^B}\log\left(\frac{\overline{c}_t^B}{\overline{c}_t^A}\right)\frac{d(\overline{c}_t^B/\overline{c}_t^A)}{d\tau} \\ +(1-2p)\left[\log\left(\frac{\overline{c}_t^B}{\overline{c}_t^A}\right)\right]^2\frac{dp}{d\tau} \end{array} \right\}.$$

This expression shows that the effect of a rise in the tax rate induces a number of conflicting effects: It raises the variance of those choosing compulsory education only (first term), while reducing the variance of those investing extra time in human capital accumulation (second term). Although the sum of these two effects can be of either sign, we can infer that it is likely to be negative at least if δp is high initially ($p > 1/2$), i.e. a majority of individuals are content with the compulsory regime of education. If a majority of individuals choose to invest in extra schooling ($p < 1/2$), however, the reverse is more likely to apply. Similarly, we can analyse the impact of the average income gap between the two cohorts of individuals (third and fourth term). We can see that the third term is unambiguously positive as $\overline{c}_t^B/\overline{c}_t^A > 1$ and a greater size of the public sector induces an increase in human capital gap across individuals (see, e.g. Table 2, $\left(d\overline{h}_t^A/\overline{h}_t^B\right)/d\tau < 0$). The fourth term, finally, is positive if p >1/2 and negative if p < 1/2.

Due to the difficulty of drawing an unambiguous conclusion with respect to the sign of $d\sigma_y^2/d\tau$, we use numerical methods. Using the benchmark parameter values given in Table 1, the simulation exercise allows us to obtain Fig. 2 which shows that, in general, there is a U-shaped relation between σ_y^2 and τ.

The intuition behind the shape of the relation between σ_y^2 and τ is straightforward. When the tax rate is low, we are likely to observe a majority of individuals content with compulsory education because individual productivity in the human capital sector is low. In this case, the reduction in $\sigma_{\delta A}^2$ is sufficient to dominate the other effects. As the tax rate increases, however, more people start investing in extra schooling,

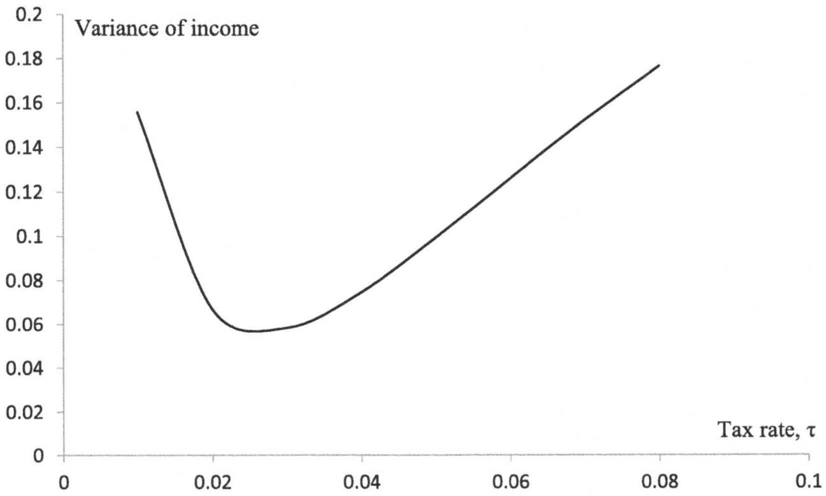

Fig. 2 Variance of income

thereby implying a reduction in the weight of $\sigma^2_{\delta A}$ in the overall determination of the variance, σ^2_y. When τ is sufficiently high, synonymous with a low p, economy-wide inequality increases, i.e. $\sigma^2_{\delta B}$ dominates. We recall that when individuals invest in extra schooling two forces act in the same direction to produce greater inequalities: not only do individuals work harder but they also spend more time in education (see 14 and 15).

The Growth-Inequality Relation Revisited

The role of public spending in education and its implication on the growth-inequality relation cannot be analysed in isolation. Besides being intuitive, we can easily check that a greater amount of compulsory time in education and lower overall status motives (i.e. lower $\delta^{\min}$ and/or $\delta^{\max}$) would reduce the incentives of individuals to spend extra resources in education (i.e. $dp/de > 0$ and $dp/d\delta^{\min} < 0$, $dp/d\delta^{\max} < 0$). On the other hand, a greater productivity in extra schooling activities would induce more individuals to spend additional resources in education: $dp/d\eta < 0$. Therefore, depending on the country specificity, i.e. both from a political and cultural perspective (notably via the status motivation, δ_I, and the cultural encouragement that extra schooling receives from society, η), there exist various reasons that can explain why a majority of individuals are content (or not) with compulsory education, thereby why we observe great disparities between countries with respect to investments in extra schooling.

Interestingly, what comes out from the discussion of the previous sub-section, is that more extra schooling does not necessarily go along with more inequality. Formally, we have shown that countries in which a majority of the population is initially content with compulsory education, like in Scandinavian countries, should experience higher growth and lower inequality if they increase the amount of funds allocated to public education. For others, such as South Korea, however, higher growth should come with a higher level of inequality. The amount of compulsory education, the status motive of individuals, and the cultural encouragement that extra schooling receives from society clearly play a role in the determination of these outcomes. Importantly though, it also naturally begs the question of the size of the government, i.e. the amount of tax, τ, which is the key variable that the policy-maker can easily modify to affect the economy's outcome. To complete our analysis, we discuss this issue in the following sub-section.

Government Size in a Democratic System

The aim of this sub-section is to determine the choice of tax rate, τ, that is the size of the public education sector and analyse its implications for welfare. To tackle this issue, we assume the existence of a majority voting system, whereby the tax rate level, τ, is chosen by the median voter who is referenced by $i = 0.5$. To conduct the analysis, as previously, we assume that the economy has reached a steady state. In this context, the long-run level of utility of the median voter, $i = 0.5$, is given by $U_{0.5}^j = \exp(\delta_{0.5}) \log\left[(1-\tau)\Omega 1^{j} h_{0.5,0}^j\right]/\rho - \Delta_{0.5} \log(\overline{c}_0)/\rho + \beta\left(T - l_{0.5}^j - e - \varepsilon_{0.5}\right)/\rho + g/\rho^2$, where $i_{0.5} = \exp(\delta_{0.5})/\beta$ (see 14) and $\varepsilon_{0.5} = 0$ if $j = A$ and $\varepsilon_{0.5} = \exp(\delta_{0.5})[(1-\varphi)g/(\varphi g+\rho)]/\beta - e$ if $j = B$ (see 15). Using this information, we can derive the lifetime utility of the median individual, $U_{0.5}^j$, with respect to τ, where $\overline{c}_0$ and $h_{0.5,0}^j$ are taken as given. We obtain:

$$\rho \frac{dU_{0.5}}{d\tau} = -\frac{\exp(\delta_{0.5})}{(1-\tau)} + \frac{1}{\rho}\frac{dg}{d\tau} + \frac{d\varepsilon_{0.5}}{d\tau}. \tag{22}$$

As shown by the first two terms on the right-hand side of expression (22), a change in τ has two effects that are common to every individual. They correspond to the consumption loss induced by a higher income tax rate (first term) and the growth effect of such policy change (second term). The third term, which by use of (15) is strictly positive, corresponds to the change in the time allocated to extra schooling when the amount of funds allocated to education increases.

Denoting by τ^{med-A} and τ^{med-B} the tax rate level chosen by a median voter attending public and private education, respectively, we can use (22) to establish:

Proposition 2: In the steady state, the democratic system sets a tax rate verifying.

$$0 < \tau^{\text{med}-A} < \tau^{\text{med}-B} < 1, \tag{23}$$

where

$$\frac{1}{\rho}\frac{dg}{d\tau^{med-A}} = \frac{\exp(\delta_{0.5})}{\left(1 - \tau^{med-A}\right)}, \tag{24}$$

and

$$\frac{1}{\rho}\frac{dg}{d\tau^{med-B}} = \frac{\exp(\delta_{0.5})}{\left(1 - \tau^{med-B}\right)} + \frac{d\varepsilon_{0.5}}{d\tau^{med-B}}. \tag{25}$$

Proof. The result follows directly from (22).

Proposition 2 highlights the conflict between those who choose to allocate resources to extra schooling who are more motivated and likely to wish to have a higher tax rate, and those who are less motivated and not willing to invest extra resources in human capital accumulation and who are likely to prefer less rather than more tax (see 23). From the comparison between (24) and (25), this result is the outcome of the additional effect in (25) not present in (24) and captured by $d\varepsilon_{0.5}/d\tau^{med-B} > 0$. This term measures the positive welfare impact of additional spending in public education on the amount of extra time spent at school. That is, the more motivated (richer) individuals prefer a higher tax level because they integrate the notion that public spending in education allows them to accumulate human capital at a faster rate.

From Proposition 2, we can also infer the implications of our analysis for societal welfare. Clearly, if the tax rate is below (above) the preferred rates of both groups, i.e.$\tau < \tau^{\text{med}-A}(\tau^{\text{med}-B} < \tau < 1)$, more public education increases (decreases) the welfare of all individuals. In either of these cases, the policy prescription is clear: while the tax rate should be increased if$\tau < \tau^{\text{med}-A}$, it should be reduced if$\tau^{\text{med}-B} < \tau < 1$. If, however,$\tau^{\text{med}-A} < \tau < \tau^{\text{med}-B}$, i.e. the tax rate is between the preferred rates of the two groups, a rise in the tax rate will only benefit the more motivated, while the welfare of the less motivated will decline. Viewed from an opposite angle, this implies that no group has an incentive to set a tax rate that maximises societal welfare given by, at date zero,$W_0 = \mathrm{p}U_0^A + (1-p)U_0^B$. Since, $\tau^{\text{med}-j} = \text{argmax } U_{0.5}^j, j = \text{A,B}$, it follows that$0 < \tau^{\text{med}-A} < \tau^{\omega} < \tau^{\text{med}-B} < 1$, where τ^{ω}=argmaxW_0. Thus, the preferences of the two groups differ, on either side of the maximum welfare, but none has an incentive to vote for it. Nonetheless, if we assume that the less motivated group is more numerous ($0.5 < p < 1$) to capture the stylised fact of a right-skewed motivation (and therefore income distribution), we conclude that the chosen tax rate is given by τ^{med-A} and verifies $\tau^{med-A} < \tau^{\omega}$. The actual tax rate is lower than the one maximising societal welfare. Therefore, in this situation, greater societal welfare would necessarily go along with a reduction of inequality and an increase in the long-run growth rate.

Further Discussion and Extensions

As mentioned earlier, extra schooling (or shadow education) is an important phenomenon both in developed and developing countries raising several important issues. In fact, one of the main concerns of governments regarding this activity is probably its impact on inequality. The argument is often that extra schooling increases inequalities because only wealthier individuals can and are willing to invest in such activity.

Our results have been stated above, so we refrain from repeating them comprehensively. Let us mention, however, that we believe that the model we presented has given a different perspective to the debate. It has been done so by showing the key role of government expenditures in education on the choice of individuals driven by social aspirations to invest in extra schooling and the resulting impact on growth, inequality, and welfare.

It is important to mention that, to keep the analysis simple and focus on the key feature of the problem, we have presented a simple framework that abstracts from several issues that may play an important role in the real world. Thereby, several extensions are possible. An interesting one could be to analyse a model where compulsory schooling and extra schooling are treated separately, each one of them being characterised by its own technology. This would help to refine the analysis of the interaction between public spending and the decision to invest in extra schooling activities. In the same spirit, one could try to add a privately funded formal sector of education. Thereby, we could analyse not only the choice of individuals between a public or private regime of education (see, e.g. Tournemaine and Tsoukis, 2009; 2015a, b) but also their decision to take additional lessons.

Appendix

Proof of Proposition 1

Equation (14) follows directly from (5) and (7). To obtain (16), we combine (7), (9), (13) and use the fact that $\overline{h}_t = \left(\overline{h}_t^A\right)^p\left(\overline{h}_t^B\right)^{1-p}$. Similarly, (17) is the outcome of the manipulation of (6) with (5), (7), (13) and $\overline{h}_t = \left(\overline{h}_t^A\right)^p\left(\overline{h}_t^B\right)^{1-p}$.

To characterise the variance of log-consumption, we must solve the following equation: $\sigma_c^2 = E_{i|i<p}\left(\log c_{\mathrm{i,t}}^A/\overline{c}_t\right)^2 + E_{i|i>p}\left(\log c_{\mathrm{i,t}}^B/\overline{c}_t\right)^2$. Trivial decomposition yields: $\sigma_c^2 = E_{i|i<p}\left[\log\left(c_{\mathrm{i,t}}^A/\overline{c}_t^A\right) - \log\left(\overline{c}_t/\overline{c}_t^A\right)\right]^2 + E_{i|i>p}\left[\log\left(\overline{c}_{\mathrm{i,t}}^B/\overline{c}_t^B\right) - \log\left(\overline{c}_t/\overline{c}_t^B\right)\right]^2$. Since each parenthesis is a constant for each individual cohort separately, and using the fact that $\log\overline{c}_t = p\log\overline{c}_c^A + (1-p)\log\overline{c}_t^B$, we can simplify this expression to obtain:

$$\sigma_c^2 = \sigma_{cA}^2 + \sigma_{cB}^2 + p(1-p)\left(\log\overline{c}_t^B/\overline{c}_t^A\right)^2,$$

where σ_{cA}^2 and σ_{cB}^2 denote the variances between individuals choosing the same education system.

To compute σ_{cA}^2 and σ_{cB}^2, we note that $\log c_{i,t}^j/\overline{c}_t = \log l_{i,t}^j - E[\log l] + \log h_{i,t}^j/\overline{h}_t$. If i $<$ p, we have $h_{i,t}^j = \overline{h}_t^A$. Therefore, the variance of income of those who opt for the compulsory regime of education is given by: $\mathrm{Var}\left(\log c_{\mathrm{i,t}}^{A}/\overline{c_t}\right)_{i<p} = \mathrm{Var}\left(\log l_{\mathrm{i,t}}^{A}\right)_{i<p} = \sigma_{\delta A}^{2}$. If $i > p$, we have $Var\left(\log c_{i,t}^{B}/\overline{c}_t\right)i > p = Var\left(\log l_{i,t}^{B}\right)_{i>p} + Var\left(\log h_{i,t}^{B}/\overline{h}_t\right)_{t>p} + 2\mathrm{cov}\left(\log l_{i,t}^{B}, \log h_{i,t}^{B}/\overline{h}_t\right)_{i>p}$. Using (9) and taking logarithm, we obtain:

$$\log g = \log\left\{\frac{\eta^{1-\phi}}{\beta^{1-\phi}}\varphi\tau\phi\left[\frac{1-\phi g}{\phi g+\rho}\right]^{1-\phi}\right\} + \phi\log\left(\frac{\overline{y}_t}{h_{i,t}^{B}}\right) + (1-\phi)\delta_i,$$

which implies that:

$$Var\left[\log\left(h_{i,t}^{B}/\overline{h}_t\right)\right]_{i>p} = \frac{(1-\rho)^2}{\phi^2}\sigma_{\delta B}^{2}.$$

As $\mathrm{Var}\left(\log l_{\mathrm{i,t}}^{B}\right)_{i>p} = \sigma_{\delta B}^{2}$, we finally obtain: $\mathrm{Var}\left(\log c_{\mathrm{i,t}}^{B}/\overline{c_t}\right)_{i>p} = \frac{\sigma_{\delta B}^{2}}{\phi^2}$. To complete the computation, we note that $\overline{c}_t^{B}/\overline{c}_t^{A} = \log\overline{h}_t^{B}/\overline{h}_t^{A}$. Gathering the above results, we find (19).

Transitional Dynamics

In this sub-section, we characterise the transitional dynamics. To simplify the analysis, as mentioned in the main text, we recall that the choice between education regimes happens only once. Therefore, the share of individuals content with compulsory education, p, jumps immediately to its steady-state value. Moreover, to facilitate the analysis, we describe the dynamics corresponding to an average individual choosing compulsory schooling only and that which corresponds to the average individual investing in extra schooling. That is, to proceed, we take any $\mathrm{i} < \mathrm{p}$ as $h_{\mathrm{i,t}}^{A} = \overline{h}_t^{A}$ and assume that $h_{\mathrm{i,t}}^{B} = \overline{h}_t^{B}$ for $p < i < 1$, i.e. $\delta_i^{B} = \overline{\delta}^{B}$.

For more clarity, we proceed in three steps. First, we derive the key equations which are used to characterise the transitional dynamics. Second, due to the complexity of the model, we use numerical methods to show the saddle point stability property around the steady state. Third, we provide some intuitions of the results.

Preliminaries

We denote by $\hat{h}_t = \overline{h}_t^A / \overline{h}_t^B$ the ratio of average human capital in the two cohorts. Our aim is to characterise a 2 × 2 dynamic system in $\varepsilon_{i,t}$ and $\hat{h}_t$ and show that it is saddle point stable. For convenience, the first-order conditions for individuals who invest in extra education, are repeated below:

$$\beta = \frac{\mu_{i,t}^B \eta (1-\phi) \dot{h}_{i,t}^B}{(e + \eta \varepsilon_{i,t})}, \; p < i < 1, \tag{26}$$

$$\frac{(1+\Delta_i)}{\mu_{i,t}^B h_{i,t}^B} + \frac{(1-\phi)\dot{h}_{i,t}^B}{h_{i,t}^B} = -\frac{\dot{\mu}_{i,t}^B}{\mu_{i,t}^B} + \rho, \; p < i < 1. \tag{27}$$

Moreover, from (3), we have:

$$\frac{\dot{h}_{i,t}^j}{h_{i,t}^j} = \varphi \left[\tau \Omega \frac{\exp(\overline{\delta})}{\beta} \right]^{\phi} \left[\frac{\overline{h}_t}{h_{i,t}^j} \right]^{\phi} (e + \eta \varepsilon_{i,t})^{1-\phi}, \; j = 1,\, 2, \tag{28}$$

where we used $\overline{y}_t = \Omega \exp(\overline{\delta}) \overline{h}_t / \beta$. Using (28), we obtain:

$$\frac{\dot{\hat{h}}_t}{\hat{h}_t} = \varphi \left[\tau \Omega \frac{\exp(\overline{\delta})}{\beta} \right]^{\phi} \left\{ (\hat{h}_t)^{\phi(p-i)} (e)^{1-\phi} - (\hat{h})^{p\phi} (e + \eta \varepsilon_{i,t})^{1-\phi} \right\},$$

which is the first dynamic equation of the dynamic system.

We can manipulate the first-order conditions with the law of motion of human capital to obtain:

$$\frac{1}{\mu_{i,t}^B} = \frac{(1-\phi)}{\beta} \eta \varphi \left[\tau \Omega \frac{\exp(\overline{\delta})}{\beta} \right]^{\phi} \left(\frac{\overline{h}_t}{h_{i,t}^B} \right)^{\phi} h_{i,t}^B (e + \eta \varepsilon_{i,t})^{-\phi},$$

and

$$\left[\frac{\eta (1+\Delta_i)}{\beta (e + \eta \varepsilon_{i,t})} + 1 \right] \frac{(1-\phi) \dot{h}_{i,t}^B}{h_{i,t}^B} = -\frac{\dot{\mu}_{i,t}^B}{\mu_{i,t}^B} + \rho.$$

Deriving the first equation with respect to time and plugging the result in the second one, we obtain:

$$\frac{\phi\eta\varepsilon_{i,t}}{(e+\eta\varepsilon_{i,t})}\frac{\dot{\varepsilon}_{i,t}}{\varepsilon_{i,t}}=\phi p\frac{\dot{\hat{h}}_t}{\hat{h}_t}$$
$$-\left[\frac{\eta(1+\Delta_i)(1-\phi)}{\beta(e+\eta\varepsilon_{i,t})}\right]\varphi\left[\tau\Omega\frac{\exp(\bar{\delta})}{\beta}\right]^{\phi}(\hat{h}_t)^{p\phi}(e+\eta\varepsilon_{i,t})^{1-\phi}+\rho,$$

which is the second equation of the 2 × 2 system. The stability of the model is checked next.

Stability

We check the stability property of the model around the steady state. Taking a first-order Taylor approximation of the 2 × 2 system around the steady state, we obtain:

$$\begin{pmatrix}\dot{\varepsilon}_{i,t}/\varepsilon_{i,t}\\ \dot{\hat{h}}_t/\hat{h}_t\end{pmatrix}=M\times\begin{pmatrix}\varepsilon_{i,t}-\varepsilon^*\\ \hat{h}_t-\hat{h}^*\end{pmatrix},\tag{29}$$

where variables without subscript t indicate their steady-state value.

The $M-$matrix is given by:

$$M=\begin{pmatrix}m_{11}\ m_{12}\\ m_{21}\ m_{22}\end{pmatrix},$$

where we recall that $\delta_i^B=\overline{\delta}^B$ and $h_{i,t}^B=\overline{h}_t^B$ so that the elements of the M $-$Matrix are given by.

$$m_{12}=\frac{\partial\dot{\varepsilon}_{i,t}/\varepsilon_{i,t}}{\partial\hat{h}_t}=\begin{bmatrix}\phi p\frac{\partial\dot{\hat{h}}_t/\hat{h}}{\partial\hat{h}_t}\\ +\frac{\eta^2\exp\left(\overline{\delta}^B\right)(1-\phi)}{\beta}\left[\tau\Omega\frac{\exp(\bar{\delta})}{\beta}\right]^{\phi}(\hat{h}*)^{p\phi}(e+\eta\varepsilon*)^{-1-\phi}\\ -(1-\phi)\eta\left[\frac{\exp\left(\overline{\delta}^B\right)(1-\phi)}{\beta(e+\eta\varepsilon*)}-\phi\right]\\ \times\varphi\left[\tau\Omega\frac{\exp(\bar{\delta})}{\beta}\right]^{\phi}(\hat{h}*)^{p\phi}(e+\eta\varepsilon*)^{\phi}\end{bmatrix},$$

$$m_{12} = \frac{\partial \dot{\varepsilon}_{i,t}/\varepsilon_{i,t}}{\partial \hat{h}_t} = \begin{bmatrix} \phi p \frac{\partial \dot{\hat{h}}_t/\hat{h}}{\partial \hat{h}_t} \\ -p\phi\left[\frac{\eta \exp(\bar{\delta}^B)(1-\phi)}{\beta(e+\eta\varepsilon*)} - \phi\right] \\ \times\varphi\left[\tau\Omega\frac{\exp(\bar{\delta})}{\beta}\right]^{\phi}\left(\hat{h}*\right)^{p\phi-1}(e+\eta\varepsilon*)^{1-\phi} \end{bmatrix},$$

$$m_{21} = \frac{\partial \dot{\hat{h}}_t/\hat{h}_t}{\partial \varepsilon_{i,t}} = -(1-\phi)\eta\varphi\left[\tau\Omega\frac{\exp(\bar{\delta})}{\beta}\right]^{\phi}\left(\hat{h}*\right)^{p\phi}(e+\eta\varepsilon*)^{-\phi},$$

$$m_{22} = \frac{\partial \dot{\hat{h}}_t/\hat{h}_t}{\partial \hat{h}_t} = \varphi\left[\tau\Omega\frac{\exp(\bar{\delta})}{\beta}\right]^{\phi}\begin{Bmatrix} \phi(p-1)\left(\hat{h}*\right)^{\phi(p-1)-1}(e)^{1-\phi} \\ -p\phi\left(\hat{h}*\right)^{(p\phi-1)}(e+\eta\varepsilon*)^{1-\phi} \end{Bmatrix}.$$

Using numerical methods whose benchmark parameter values are summarised in Table 1, we find that the $M-$matrix evaluated at the asymptotic steady state has one positive and one negative eigenvalue.[16] Hence, since relative human capital,$\hat{h}_t$, is predetermined, while the amount of resources allocated to education,ε^*, is a jump variable, the unique steady state is saddle point stable. With this information in mind, we can analyse the impact of a change in income tax rate, τ, on $\varepsilon_{i,t}$ and $\hat{h}_t$ both on impact and along the transition. This task is carried out next.

Discussion

The aim of this sub-section is to discuss the properties of the model along the steady state. For this purpose, we assume that the government decides to increase marginally and permanently the tax rate level, τ. We restrict our attention to the case $\tau < \tau^{med-A}$ initially (see Proposition 2). Using the results derived previously, we can infer that, on impact, ε jumps up on the new saddle path and, afterwards, sluggishly decreases to its new steady state of higher value, i.e. approaches it from below.

Regarding the human capital ratio (state variable), there is no change in impact. Following the marginal increase of the tax rate, we can nevertheless deduce that it decreases after impact. That is, along the transition, $\hat{h}_t$ decreases progressively to its new steady state and attains it from above.

[16] With the benchmark parameter values given in Table 1, the eigenvalues of the $M-$Matrix are given by $q_1 = 0.180828 > 0$ and $q_2 = -0.0202657 < 0$.

More precisely, following an increase in the tax rate level, both types of individuals experience an increase in their human capital growth. The difference is that the boost for the more motivated individuals surpasses the boost for the less motivated individuals. It thus results in an increase in the average human capital gap across individuals along the transition to the new steady state.

From the results above, it is straightforward to identify the effects of a change in τ on consumption, $c_{i,t}$, on impact for both types of individuals. From the resource constraint (2) and Eqs. (5), (7), it emerges that, on impact, consumption drops down for both types of individuals. Moreover, as labour supply remains unchanged, we conclude that, although a marginal increase in the amount of resources devoted to public education induces welfare gains in the long run, its immediate effect (i.e. on impact) is always welfare-reducing.

References

Abel, A. 1990. Asset Pricing under Habit Formation and Catching up with the Joneses. *American Economic Review* 80 (2): 38–42.

Abel, A.B. 2005. Optimal Taxation when Consumers Have Endogenous Benchmark Levels of Consumption. *Review of Economic Studies* 72 (1): 21–42.

Acemoglu, D. and J.A. Robinson. 2013. *Why Nations Fail: The Origins of Power, Prosperity and Poverty*. New York: Profile Books.

Aghion, P., U. Akcigit, A. Bergeaud, R. Blundell and D. Hémous (2015): Innovation and Top Income Inequality, NBER working paper No. 21247

Alesina, A., and D. Rodrik. 1994. Distributive Politics and Economic Growth. *Quarterly Journal of Economics* 109 (2): 465–490.

Allegretto S.A. 2012. The State of Working America's Wealth, 2012: Through Volatility and Turmoil, the Gap Widens, Economic Policy Institute Briefing Paper #292. http://epi.3cdn.net/2a7ccb3e9e618f0bbc_3nm6idnax.pdf

Aloi, M., J. Poyago-Theotoki, and F. Tournemaine. 2022. The Geography of Knowledge and R&D-led Growth. *Journal of Economic Geography* 22 (6): 1149–1190.

Alonso-Carrera, J. 2001. More on the Dynamics in the Endogenous Growth Model with Human Capital. *Investigaciones Economicas* 25 (3): 561–583.

Anderson, D.S. 1988. Values, Religion, Social Class and the Choice of Private School in Australia. *International Journal of Educational Research* 12 (4): 351–373.

Antoninis, M., and P. Tsakloglou. 2001. Who Benefits from Public Education in Greece? *Evidence and Policy Implications, Education Economics* 9 (2): 197–222.

Attanasio, O.P., and G. Weber. 2010. Consumption and Saving: Models of Intertemporal Allocation and Their Implications for Public Policy. *Journal of Economic Literature* 48 (3): 693–751.

Ball, S.J. 1993. Education Markets, Choice and Social Class: The Market as a Class Strategy in the UK and the USA. *British Journal of Sociology of Education* 14 (1): 3–19.

Ball, S.J. 1997. On the Cusp: Parents Choosing Between State and Private Schools in the UK: Action within an Economy of Symbolic Goods. *International Journal of Inclusive Education* 1 (1): 1–17.

Ball, S.J., R. Bower, and S. Gewirtz. 1995. Circuits of Schooling: A Sociological Exploration of Parental Choice of School in Social Class Contexts. *Sociological Review* 43 (1): 52–78.

Banerjee, A.V., and E. Duflo. 2012. *Poor Economics*. London: Penguin Books.

Banerjee, A.V., S. Cole, E. Duflo, and L. Linden. 2007. Remedying Education: Evidence from Two Randomized Experiments in India. *Quarterly Journal of Economics* 122 (3): 1235–1264.

Barro, R.J. 1990. Government Spending in a Simple Model of Endogenous Growth. *Journal of Political Economy* 98 (5): S103–S125.

Barro, R.J. 1991. Economic Growth in a Cross Section of Countries. *Quarterly Journal of Economics* 106 (2): 407–443.

Barro, R.J., and X. Sala-i-Martin. 2004. *Economic Growth*. The MIT Press: Cambridge.

Becker, G.S., K.M. Murphy, and R. Tamura. 1990. Human Capital, Fertility, and Economic Growth. *Journal of Political Economy* 98 (5): S12–S37.

Benabou, R. 1996. Heterogeneity, Stratification, and Growth: Macroeconomic Implications of Community Structure and School Finance. *American Economic Review* 86 (3): 584–609.

Birdsall, N., D. Ross, and R. Sabot. 1995. Inequality and Growth Reconsidered: Lessons from East Asia. *The World Bank Economic Review* 9 (3): 477–508.

Blankenau, W.F., and N.B. Simpson. 2004. Public Education Expenditures and Growth. *Journal of Development Economics* 73 (2): 583–605.

Cagetti, M., and M. De Nardi. 2008. Wealth Inequality: Data and Models. *Macroeconomic Dynamics* 12 (52): 285–313.

Caselli, F., and J. Ventura. 2000. A Representative Consumer Theory of Distribution. *American Economic Review* 90 (4): 909–926.

Cerra, V., R. Lama, and N. Loayza. 2021. Links Between Growth, Inequality, and Poverty: A Survey, International Monetary Fund, Working Paper No. 2021/068.

Chakraborty, S. 2004. Endogenous Lifetime and Economic Growth. *Journal of Economic Theory* 116 (1): 119–137.

Chatterjee, S. 1994. Transitional Dynamics and the Distribution of Wealth in a Neoclassical Growth Model. *Journal of Public Economics* 54 (1): 97–119.

Choudhary, A., P. Levine, P. McAdam, and P. Welz. 2007. *Relative Preferences, Happiness and Corrective Taxation*. Mimeo: University of Surrey.

Clark, A.E., and A.J. Oswald. 1996. Satisfaction and Comparison Income. *Journal of Public Economics* 3 (61): 359–381.

Corneo, G., and O. Jeanne. 1999. Pecuniary Emulation, Inequality and Growth. *European Economic Review* 43 (9): 1665–1678.

Corneo, G., and O. Jeanne. 2001. Status, the Distribution of Wealth, and Growth. *Scandinavian Journal of Economics* 103 (2): 283–293.

Cowen, T. 2017. *The Complacent Class: The Self-Defeating Quest for the American Dream*. New York City: St Martin's Press.

Croix (de la), D., Doepke, M. (2004) Public versus private education when differential fertility matters. *Journal of Development Economics* 73(2): 607–629

Dang, H.A. 2007. The Determinants and Impact of Private Tutoring Classes in Vietnam. *Economics of Education Review* 26 (6): 683–698.

Dang, H.A., and F.H. Rogers. 2008. The Growing Phenomenon of Private Tutoring: Does It Deepen Human Capital, Widen Inequalities, or Waste Resources? *The World Bank Research Observer* 23 (2): 161–200.

De Nardi, M. 2004. Wealth Inequality and Intergenerational Links. *Review of Economic Studies* 71 (3): 743–768.

Dynan, K.E., J. Skinner, and S.P. Zeldes. 2004. Do the Rich Save More? *Journal of Political Economy* 112 (2): 397–444.

European Commission. 2011. The Challenge of Shadow Education: Private Tutoring and Its Implications for Policy Makers in the European Union, ISBN: 978-92-79-19986-8.

Fershtman, C., K.M. Murphy, and Y. Weiss. 1996. Social Status, Education and Growth. *Journal of Political Economy* 104 (1): 108–132.

Francis, J.L. 2009. Wealth and the Capitalist Spirit. *Journal of Macroeconomics* 31 (3): 394–408.

Frederick, S., G. Loewenstein, and T. O'Donoghue. 2002. Time Discounting and Time Preference: A Critical Review. *Journal of Economic Literature* 40 (2): 351–401.

Futagami, K., and A. Shibata. 1998. Keeping One Step Ahead of the Joneses: Status, the Distribution of Wealth and Long Run Growth. *Journal of Economic Behavior and Organization* 36 (1): 109–126.

Garcia-Penalosa, C., E. Caroli, and P. Aghion. 1999. Inequality and Economic Growth: The Perspective of the New Growth Theories. *Journal of Economic Literature* 37 (4): 1615–1660.

Glewwe, P., and M. Kremer. 2006. School, Teachers, and Education Outcomes in Developing Countries. In *Handbook of the Economics of Education*. Edited by Eric A. Hanushek, and Finis Welch. Amsterdam: North-Holland.

Glomm, G., and B. Ravikumar. 1992. Public Versus Private Investment in Human Capital: Endogenous Growth and Income Inequality. *Journal of Political Economy* 100 (4): 818–834.

Guvenen, F. 2016. *Quantitative Economics With Heterogeneity: An A-to-Z Guidebook*. Princeton: Princeton University Press.

Hendricks, L. 2007. How Important is Discount Rate Heterogeneity for Wealth Inequality? *Journal of Economic Dynamics and Control* 3 (9): 3042–3068.

Ikeda, S., M.-I. Kang, and F. Ohtake. 2010. Hyperbolic Discounting, the Sign Effect, and the Body Mass Index. *Journal of Health Economics* 29 (2): 268–284.

Keane, M.P., and K.I. Wolpin. 1997. The Career Decisions of Young Men. *Journal of Political Economy* 105 (3): 473–522.

Kempf, H., and F. Moizeau. 2009. Inequality, Growth, and the Dynamics of Social Segmentation. *Journal of Public Economic Theory* 11 (4): 529–564.

Kennickell, A.B. 2009. Ponds and Streams: Wealth and Income in the U.S., 1989 to 2007, Finance and Economics D.P. 2009–13, Board of Governors of the Federal Reserve System.

Kim, S., and J.H. Lee. 2010. Private Tutoring and Demand for Education in South Korea. *Journal Economic Development and Cultural Change* 58 (2): 259–296.

Knowles, S. 2010. Inequality and Economic Growth: The Empirical Relationship Reconsidered in the Light of Comparable Data. *Journal of Development Studies* 41 (1): 135–159.

Levine, R., and Y. Rubinstein. 2017. Smart and Illicit: Who Becomes an Entrepreneur and Do They Earn More? *The Quarterly Journal of Economics* 132 (2): 963–1018.

Maurer, J., and A. Meier. 2008. Smooth it Like the 'Joneses'? *Estimating Peer-Group Effects in Intertemporal Consumption Choice, Economic Journal* 118 (527): 454–476.

McBride, M. 2001. Relative Income Effects on Subjective Well-Being in the Cross-Section. *Journal of Economic Behavior and Organization* 45 (3): 251–278.

O'Donoghue, T., and M. Rabin. 2001b. Self Awareness and Self Control. In *Chapter in Now or Later: Economic and Psychological Perspectives on Intertemporal Choice*. Edited by R. Baumeister, G. Loewenstein, and D. Read. Russell Sage.

O'Donoghue, T., and M. Rabin. 2001a. Choice and Procrastination. *Quarterly Journal of Economics* 116 (1): 121–160.

Pham, T.K.C. 2005. Economic Growth and Status-Seeking Through Personal Wealth. *European Journal of Political Economy* 21 (2): 404–427.

Picketty, T. 2015. Putting Distribution Back at the Center of Economics: Reflections on Capital in the Twenty-First Century. *Journal of Economic Perspectives* 29 (1): 67–88.

Picketty, T. 2014. *Capital in the Twenty-First Century*. Boston, MA: Belknap (Harvard) Press.

Rodrik, D. 2014. *The Globalization Paradox: Democracy and the Future of the World Economy*. New York: W.W. Norton & Company.

Saint-Paul, G., and T. Verdier. 1993. Education, Democracy and Growth. *Journal of Development Economics* 42 (2): 399–407.

Schultz, T.W. 1963. *The Economic Value of Education*. New York: Columbia University Press.

Stiglitz, J.E. 2012. *The Price of Inequality*. London: Penguin.

Sylwester, K. 2002. Can Education Expenditures Reduce Income Inequality? *Economic Education Review* 21 (1): 43–52.

Tamura, R. 1991. Income Convergence in an Endogenous Growth Model. *Journal of Political Economy* 99 (3): 522–540.

Tansel, A., and F. Bircan. 2006. Demand for Education in Turkey: A Tobit Analysis of Private Tutoring Expenditures. *Economics of Education Review* 25 (3): 303–313.

Tournemaine, F., and C. Tsoukis. 2008. Relative Consumption, Relative Wealth and Growth. *Economics Letters* 100 (2): 314–316.

Tournemaine, F., and C. Tsoukis. 2009. Status Jobs, Human Capital and Growth: The Effects of Heterogeneity. *Oxford Economic Papers* 61 (3): 467–493.

Tournemaine, F., and C. Tsoukis. 2010a. Gain Versus Pain From Status and Ambition: Effects on Growth and Inequality. *The Journal of Socio-Economics* 39 (2): 286–294.

Tournemaine, F., and C. Tsoukis. 2010b. Status, Fertility, Growth and the Great Transition. *The Singapore Economic Review* 55 (3): 553–574.

Tournemaine, F., and C. Tsoukis. 2015a. Public Expenditures, Growth and Distribution in a Mixed Regime of Education with a Status Motive. *Journal of Public Economic Theory* 17 (5): 673–701.

Tournemaine, F., and C. Tsoukis. 2015b. The Growth-Distribution Nexus in a Mixed Regime of Education with a Status Motive: On the Macroeconomic of the Welfare State. *Economic Modelling* 47 (C), 235–243.

Tsoukis, C. 2007. Keeping up with the Joneses, Growth, and Distribution. *Scottish Journal of Political Economy* 54 (4): 575–600.

Tsoukis, C. 2014. Hyperbolic discounting, labour and growth, mimeo: (99+) Status, hyperbolic discounting, growth, and distribution.

Tsoukis, C. 2020. *Theory of Macroeconomic Policy*. Oxford: Oxford University Press.

Turnovsky, S.J. 1996. *Methods of Macroeconomic Dynamics*. Boston, MA: MIT Press.

Wilkinson, R.G., and K.E. Pickett. 2009a. Income Inequality and Social Dysfunction. *Annual Review of Sociology* 35 (1): 493–511.

Wilkinson, R.G., and K.E. Pickett. 2009b. *The Level Spirit*. London: Allen Lane.

Wolff, E.N. 2010. Recent Trends in Household Wealth in the United States: Rising Debt and the Middle-Class Squeeze—an Update to 2007, WP No. 589, March 2010, Levy Institute. http://www.levyinstitute.org/publications/?docid=1235

Zhang, J. 1996. Optimal Public Investments in Education and Endogenous Growth. *Scandinavian Journal of Economics* 98 (3): 387–404.

Zhang, L. 2008. Political Economy of Income Distribution Dynamics. *Journal of Development Economics* 87 (1): 119–139.

CHAPTER 8

Socio-Economics, Macroeconomics, and Finance

1 Introduction

Social and Non-Market Interactions

A standard criticism that is levelled against the methodological individualism of neoclassical theory is that it neglects all social influences on the atomistic agent who is at the core of the paradigm. An area called social economics or economic sociology, situated between economics and sociology, has by now developed to provide the analysis of the "socialised individual". As Backhouse and Fontaine (2018) have pointed out, the relation between economics and other social sciences has oscillated between synergy and isolation since about 1900s. At core, what divides economics from other social sciences are the main methodological assumptions underpinning (or seen as underpinning) the "home economicus": Rationality, optimisation, stable and exogenous preferences, selfishness, individual "sovereignty" in the sense that decisions are taken at the individual level; there is no decision-making power at the level of community, class or society, or any other group.

It may be useful to outline briefly the method of economics, reviewed in more detail in earlier Chapters: Mainstream ("neoclassical") economics proceeds based on a few basic building blocks (Manski 2000): Individuals maximise utility that encapsulates their preferences about everything material, typically consumption and leisure. Firms maximise profits. Both

C. Tsoukis et al., *Social and Behavioural Macroeconomics*,
https://doi.org/10.1007/978-3-031-77748-6_8

individuals and firms face constraints that summarise the resources available to them, such as income (or time, to be allocated between competing uses), or technology, or the prices that they take as given from their environment (e.g. prices of goods, wages, price of energy and raw materials). Both individuals and firms optimise, i.e. maximise their utility or profits subject to all relevant constraints (including the behaviour of others). Rationality is assumed in that individuals and firms can both think clearly and act accordingly. The market allows the exchange between willing parties (buyers-sellers). Equilibrium is reached when all parties optimise simultaneously and all markets clear, without unsold surpluses or excess demand; such "disequilibria" will be eliminated via the appropriate adjustment of various prices. The analysis of equilibrium allows (macro)economics to offer powerful predictions about the impact of the "fundamentals" (such as exogenously available resources, the nature preferences or utility, technology, market structure, economic policies) on outcomes (prices and quantities).

As mentioned, this approach of "choice under constraints" implies that decision-making power exists only at the level of an individual, person or firm. Furthermore, individuals and firms interact with one another only through their economic exchanges. In the pedagogically dominant perfect competition paradigm, the exchange is even entirely impersonal, with individuals and firms caring only about anonymously set market prices and wages, to the point that it can be said that there is no interaction at all.

However, as we all know and experience, to some extent individual behaviour is shaped by social interactions in various ways. Preferences are to some extent socially determined, via norms, conventions, fads or fashion. Individuals have preferences and emotions (envy or altruism, or status-seeking motives) towards one another, and they (may) exhibit behaviour of cooperation, trust or reciprocity. People (chose to) belong to groups and adopt their standards of behaviour, as the new "economics of identity" emphasises. Culture, morality and social capital are yet other manifestations of social processes that affect economic behaviour. Institutions and social structures also shape preferences and behaviour. As with relative position and status, many concepts are interconnected, e.g. norms, trust, and cooperation are associated with social capital, and group formation, culture or fashion are associated with identity. In Granovetter's (1985) terms, individual behaviour is "embedded" within social relations and structures.

Social sciences other than economics have emphasised social interactions and influences a lot more than individual optimality; indeed, this may be a salient difference between economics and other social sciences. For instance, in the analysis of crime or the decision to receive education, a social scientist may emphasise aspirations, tradition, and societal influences; whereas an economist will emphasise the structure of rewards and risk, and individual enjoyment (see e.g. Steuer 2003). This has given rise to the criticism by Granovetter (1985) that against the atomised, under-socialised actor of neoclassical economics, there is the "over-socialised" actor of much sociological analysis who is over-determined by social influences and has no personal agency. Instead, the appropriate mode of analysis, Granovetter argues, is to account for the social influences while allowing for a degree of agency of the individual.

In recent years, there has been an increasing awareness of, and effort to account for social (or non-market) interactions and combine or reconcile them with individual decision-making. Such a research agenda has also started to permeate macroeconomics; succinct reviews are contained in Manski (2000) and Scheinkman (2008). Indeed, Chapters 3 and 4 discussed one class of such interactions, namely the account of relative as well as individual consumption in utility (that goes under different guises and names but shares the same core idea). This Chapter outlines other approaches and perspectives. We begin first with a very brief account of the relationship between economics and other social disciplines, and the fields, old and new, that may be said to be in-between.

Economics and Other Social Sciences

From the late nineteenth century onwards, the gradual professionalisation of the US social sciences, specialisation, and the quest for greater disciplinary identity led to the increasing separation of economics from other social sciences. Some dialogue always existed, but by the late 1920s, this process had led to what may be described as disciplinary isolation. On the economics side, this is the time of the growing mathematical formulation and consolidation of neoclassical economics. The quest was for a discipline that was rigorous, dispassionate and "non-ideological", i.e. apolitical. The aim was to have a theoretical core, reference to which would enable all debates to be resolved. In these aims, most economists felt that they could derive little benefit from other social sciences.

The WWII saw US economists assisting the war effort by contributing to military intelligence and solving practical problems related to the conduct of the war (Backhouse and Fontaine 2018, p. 25n). This experience, together with the rise of macroeconomics under the influence of Keynes, the development of national income statistics and the increasing use of statistical-econometric methods carved a niche for post-war economists, particularly macroeconomists, as associated with quantitative and practical policy problems. However, the dialogue with sociology, history, psychology and politics was never extinguished and even picked up. The various disciplines were seen as complementary. This is the backdrop to Herbert Simon's multi- and interdisciplinary efforts in the 1950s and later.

From 1960 on, there is yet another turn towards specialisation and disciplinary purity. This is the era of growing rigour and mathematisation; much of standard microeconomic theory, in particular, dates from this period. The growing self-confidence of economists, resulting from making great theoretical advances, made them unwilling to learn from other social disciplines. The opposite happened in a way: Economists began applying their "rational choice" methodology to problems traditionally viewed as belonging to the domain of other disciplines: The economics of crime, family, electoral dynamics, law, and elsewhere. This was seen by some as economics trespassing on other sciences and was criticised as "economics imperialism" (Backhouse and Fontaine 2018, p. 30). We may add that forays of practitioners of one discipline into the traditional domains of others may actually be fruitful, not harmful; they should also be complemented, however, by a dialogue in the sense of learning from one another and from adapting key assumptions in the light of findings by others. It was these aspects of the multi-disciplinarity that seemed to be lacking; from the 1960s on, that made the various social disciplines look more competitive than synergistic.

In recent decades, this mindset has been challenged with the emergence of behavioural economics, drawing from areas such as economics, psychology and decision theory. As mentioned in Chapter 1, one reason for looking at the relationship between economics and sociology is that behavioural "imperfections" such as those reviewed in Chapter 2 may be coordinated and have an aggregate impact via social structures. For this reason, institutional contexts and social norms must be integrated into economics. Backhouse and Fontaine (2018) quote two prominent behavioural theorists:

"'What is imperfectly understood', he wrote, 'is the precise manner in which institutions serve as social tools that reinforce, even induce, individual rationality' (Smith 1991, p. 881). [...] Shira Lewin (1996) argued that to draw the lessons about the relationship between economics and psychology it is necessary for economists to pay more attention to sociological analyses [...]". Backhouse and Fontaine (2018, p. 33).

Economic Sociology and "Socio-Economics"

A digression on the field of economic sociology will be useful here. Although socio-economics is a relatively recent creation, economic sociology has a long history; see Swedberg (1991), whom we follow here. Both economists and sociologists have contributed to its creation. The distant roots of the field can be traced back to the late-nineteenth—early twentieth-century German Historical School of Economics and the Economic Sociology School, with Max Weber being the most familiar name (usually regarded as a sociologist, yet he was a professor of economics in Germany). A roughly contemporary French school is associated with the name of Emile Durkheim and others. A notable economist that has contributed to economic sociology was the inter-war Austrian economist Joseph Schumpeter. Around 1870–1914, the institutional economists (Thorstein Veblen and others) also contributed to the field. The modern economic institutionalist school (e.g. Ronald Coase, Oliver Williamson) contributes via the "transactions costs" approach to the building of institutions such as firms; in this, they augment the neoclassical theory with added assumptions (such as the aim of institutions to minimise transactions costs). A small minority of post-war economists also contributed to the field by departing from neoclassical theory in a more thorough way, to the point of being regarded as heterodox (John Kenneth Galbraith, Gunnar Myrdal). As American tradition of "Economy and Society" has always been present, to which Talcott Parsons, a leading light in post-WWII American sociology, contributed in the 1950s. Economic sociology also benefited from the forays of economics into social issues, as discussed, and has benefited from the encounter with the "rational choice" method of economics. It is outside our scope to engage more closely with all these contributions; the interested reader can consult Swedberg (1991) and Granovetter (2005), and also Backhouse and Fontaine (2018) and Zafirovski (2016). It is fair to say that much of this rich tradition, or traditions as there was not much unity, remained at the sociology-side of the fence. Yet, it has generated an awareness that the predictive power of economics remains limited if the economic actor is not placed in its social setting. In raising this awareness, these contributions have prepared the ground for the emergence of a new field, social economics, in the last few decades.

Socio-economics, as Zafirovski (2016) reminds us, goes beyond the application of rational choice, methodological individualism to other social sciences. This recognition is a common theme that unites economic sociology and socio-economics. In a nutshell, individual behaviour is socially conditioned: We live socially and this affects crucially our preferences and all types of behaviour, including economic behaviour. The *homo economicus* stands is sometimes contrasted to the *homo sociologicus* (e.g. Elster 1989), or Aristotle's *zoon politicon* (Bowles and Gintis 2006); the point of socio-economics is that all these species must be replaced by yet another, namely the *homo economico-sociologicus.* In this way, by combining individual agency (through optimisation) with external influences, we can meet Granovetter's (1985) criticism mentioned above—neither under-socialisation, nor over-socialisation of the economic actor. The real challenge, we argue, is to allow such setups to endogenise the social structures that individuals are subject to.

Macroeconomics saw the rise of the New Classicals from the 1970s onwards, placing paramount emphasis on "micro-foundations" (see Chapter 1) that, in the eyes of many, blurred the distinction between micro and macroeconomics. Prominent in their methodology is also the absence of any assumption that might characterise the "economic" man as more "social". But, under the influence of behavioural economics, and not only, dissenting voices have emerged. George Akerlof has been the prime advocate for the closer integration of economics, particularly macroeconomics, with psychology, sociology and even anthropology (see the references in Chapter 1). The spirit of his writing is that economics must learn from, as much as teach, other social sciences. In this way, the explanatory power of macroeconomic theories and models will arguably increase.

This Chapter will be devoted to the field of socio-economics, with applications to macroeconomics and finance. We dwelt on behavioural economics in Chapters 2 (mainly) and 1, so we shall not have much to add to it here. Instead, we shall focus more on the concept of socially determined preferences (via social norms, status-seeking and identity), cooperation and social capital; further ideas such as the "social contract", fairness and morality, though still relevant for social interactions, are more remotely related and therefore will be more lightly touched on.[1] The approach will be again to consider "portable extensions" to standard theory, as per Chapter 2. The approach will be more informal and open-ended, as opposed to analytically formal as in previous Chapters. Before we turn towards a closer examination of some key concepts, we review briefly some of the insights offered by the new and exciting field of "socio-biology".

2 Socio-Biology: Evolution and Human Sociality

The Origins of Human Sociality

"Socio-biology" is a new field, drawing on biology, anthropology and sociology, that tries to understand human behaviour by placing humans in their biological settings. A recent book that gives a good flavour of this field is Christakis (2019), and we shall draw on it in what follows. Synthesising a bewildering and fascinating array of scholarship, from anthropology to evolutionary biology to genetics to zoology to palaeontology, with additions from psychology, history, sociology, philosophy and literature, he in fact makes a much stronger point: Humans are evolutionarily programmed to behave according to a blueprint that he calls "the social suite". This comprises the following eight elements (Christakis 2019, p. 15):

- The capacity to have and recognise individual identity;
- Love for partners and offspring;
- Friendship;
- Social networks;
- Cooperation;
- Preference for one's own group ("in-group bias");
- Mild hierarchy (that is, relative egalitarianism);
- Social learning and teaching.

[1] Another area that has received a lot of attention is social networks; see e.g. Bramoullé, Galeotti, and Rogers (2016). Engaging with this vast and disparate area here will take us too far afield. It is also not clear how networks can be "summarised" at the aggregate (macroeconomic) level.

Naturally, there is variation both within and between societies; thankfully, there is no total uniformity. But, similarity is much greater than diversity. On the basis of the wide evidence that he presents, Christakis formalises this point in the following way: If we were to agree on the main dimensions (say, n) that characterise human behaviour (and there is no agreement on what those dimensions might be or indeed how many they are), and we actually measured the characteristics of all actual human societies, and then put the n-tuple that characterises each society in the n-dimensional space of characteristics, we would observe that the actual area of the n-dimensional space actually occupied is quite small: Only a small amount of variation from what may be conceivably possible has been realised—this is what a vast array of evidence shows, from anthropological to experimental studies to history of new communities or shipwrecks.[2]

But Christakis (2019) also makes two further important points. The common characteristics that are largely shared are the ones of the "social suite", which may characterise human nature as "good". As mentioned, there is no uniformity; as he writes (p. 203), we are "pre-wired rather than hardwired". But example after example of societies that have succeeded or failed and all the other evidence show that the societies that share the features of the social suite are more likely to survive and be successful. Furthermore, individual behaviour is socially conditioned, as mentioned. In a paragraph worth quoting in full, he writes:

> People often think that personality traits such as kindness are fixed. But our research with groups suggests something different; the tendency to be altruistic or exploitative may depend on how the world is organised. So, if we took the *same* [italics in the original] population of people and assigned them to one social world, we could make them really generous to one another, and if we put them in another sort of world, we could make them really mean or indifferent to one another. Crucially, this indicates that the tendency to cooperate is a property not only of individuals but

[2] This thought experiment follows an actual discovery made by the palaeontologist David Raup in 1966 (quoted in Christakis, 2019, Chapter 4). Raup showed that the shapes of all extant shells can be fully described in terms of three key characteristics. Taking the measurements of actual shells in these three respects and putting them in the three-dimensional space of characteristics, the morphology space or "morphospace", Raup showed that this morphospace is mostly empty. The actual shells shapes have quite a limited variation compared to what is conceivably possible. The analogy with the human "morphospace", which is n-dimensional, should be obvious.

> also of groups. Cooperation depends on the rules governing the formation of friendship ties. Good people can do good things (and vice versa) simply as a result of the structure of the network in which they are embedded, regardless of the convictions they hold or that the group espouses. It is not just a matter of being connected to 'bad people'; the number and pattern of social connections is also crucial. Aspects of the social suite such as cooperation and social networks work together.

(Christakis 2019, p. 120–21).

The coevolution of genes and culture is one of the most fascinating, but also intriguing, themes with which socio-biology is preoccupied; Christakis (2019, Chapters 6 and 8) discusses this area. Evolution has led human societies (mostly) down the path to monogamy and "pair-bonding", whereby the mating partners develop, apart from exclusivity, emotional attachment. This has fostered equality between the sexes but also co-existence within larger groups with enhanced cooperation (as cooperation leads to advantages, see below). This has further led to larger groups in which the degree of kinship gradually became smaller but, crucially, the level of cooperation was maintained. This has given rise to friendship with strangers (non-relatives). Hence, human groups have proceeded from the formation of the pair, to family, to extended family, to clan and to larger society, while maintaining a degree of positive sentiment and attachment to the expanding concentric circles. The evolutionary blueprint for modern human societies was thus set, with the emergence of culture, institutions and morality, all weaved around the "social suite".

Gene-culture coevolution, further explored at length in Chapter 11 of the book, requires three elements: (i) that genes affect culture, (ii) that culture itself evolves and spreads because of societal mechanisms and (iii) that culture alters genes via reverse feedback mechanisms. Channels (i) and (ii) are uncontroversial and the book provides ample examples and evidence.[3] The new and more debatable idea, one could argue, is (iii). It is debatable firstly because the time frames by which genes and culture

[3] But we should be aware of simplistic interpretations of effect (i), from genes to culture. As Gintis (2012, p. 178) says, "[n]o 'gene for cooperation' has been discovered", nor, we may add, any gene for culture. Also, genes do not prescribe certain behaviours or cultural traits; rather, they equip us for capabilities, and in particular, the ability to respond flexibly to the variations in our natural or social environment. As Christakis (2019) puts it (p. 411), "… when it comes to culture, our genes equip us to *flexibly* produce things".

operate are different by whole orders of magnitude—human genes are thought to require tens of thousands of years to change, while culture changes over just a few hundreds of years. Therefore, if culture has fed back into the genome, it must have been in its very early manifestations: E.g. the ability to engineer and control fire, something that humanoids learnt a million and more years ago, surely must count as culture in the sense that it required collective effort, learning and spreading by imitation. It surely then had effects (e.g. greater nutritional value of food enabling humans to live healthier and longer lives and to develop bigger brains, requiring less effort for chewing, therefore, also requiring less strong gum muscles and jaws), which then became encoded in genes via natural selection. The agricultural revolution, maybe ten to twenty thousand years ago, may have had similar effects by the production of more plentiful sources of food. Fast forward to more recent times (a few thousand years ago), the clustering of humans in the first cities fostered more social behaviour and greater immune systems. It is debatable to what extent these latter cultural features of sociality (and all that it entails) or indeed greater immune systems have had time to affect the human genome.[4] Concluding, it seems reasonable to assume that the gene-culture coevolution operates at the level of very broad characteristics of human sociality.

Evolution, Reciprocity and Cooperation, and Social Institutions

Explaining cooperation is a puzzle in evolutionary biology as Darwin himself knew (e.g. Apicella and Silk 2019). Both non-humans and, in particular, humans engage in activities that are individually costly but confer benefits at the social level—the essence of cooperation. The key element that needs explanation is how such formations show evolutionary success despite the fact that the recipient benefits at the expense of the donor. How can such a behaviour prevail although free-riding is tempting and fitness-enhancing for any individual? Christakis (2019, Chapter 8)

[emphasis in the original] In sum, genes affect culture by priming us for certain capacities and behaviours via the evolutionary blueprint of the "social suite".

[4] Christakis (2019, pp. 411–3) considers a number of other examples of how cultural norms or practices may affect genes, from monogamous marriage to religion and state institutions. But it is interesting to note that these examples are suggestive rather than definitive; they are all qualified by "likely", "may" or "can".

shows that traits of the social suite such as friendship and identification with one's own group are universal tendencies, and they have become such as they confer evolutionary advantages to humans. This is because such feelings and traits predispose humans towards cooperation, which has enabled our ancestors to survive and (eventually) thrive in hostile and volatile surroundings. Friendship and group identification pose a greater puzzle than love towards a mate or towards kin. This is because the latter feelings involve relationships in which reciprocation is more assured; instead, friendship and group identification involve unconditional attachment. As such, they are stronger indicators of the cooperative tendencies of the human species. In any case, as they confer evolutionary advantages, all these features have been built into the human genome—such may be the position of a socio-biologist like Christakis (2019).

The question of cooperation prevails, and the ways by which the tension between conflict and cooperation is resolved, is central for understanding a wide range of issues: from the development of institutions, including the welfare state and democracy, war (which involves not only conflict but also coordinated effort in the face of grave risk); to climate change and the responses to it, formal and informal (institutional); to how society responds to (e.g.) pandemics and similar risks. At a more context-specific level, cooperation (or lack of it) is critical about how tragedy-of-the-commons, free-rider and prisoner's-dilemma type of situations are resolved. At a level more familiar to macroeconomists, cooperation and sociality may affect consumption out of a given set of lifetime resources, the fiscal multipliers, the response to shocks, etc.

Evolutionary biology offers one line of explanation for cooperation based on kin-relation and repeated interactions (which fosters reciprocal altruism and conditional cooperation—I cooperate if others do so as well). But a powerful case has been put forward in a strand of the literature (e.g. Bowles and Gintis 2003) that these features are arguably not enough to explain cooperation among humans. This is not to say that relatedness and reciprocity are irrelevant; rather, it is arguably not adequate in explaining human cooperation, which is more extensive and complex than cooperation among non-humans. The cooperation that arises in repeated games played in laboratory experiments requires rather implausibly strong assumptions in order to be sustained: the gist is that individuals must be sufficiently forward-looking in order for defection and punishment to be sufficiently costly; informational and other requirements such as costs of contract enforcement are very strong; and the complexity of the coordination and incentive mechanisms required for the same purpose so as to make cooperation profitable increases very rapidly with group size (anything above n > 4 is really unwieldy, see Bowles and Gintis 2003, 2009). In other words, the selfishly-minded homo economicus, who decides whether to cooperate or free-ride based on a narrow cost–benefit calculation, will find it beneficial to free-ride; cooperation cannot be sustained based on narrow self-interest alone nor on conditional reciprocity (I cooperate if others return the favour).

Cognitive, linguistic and physical traits allow humans to communicate more effectively and in more nuanced ways, to construct norms, to internalise them and to create institutions (morality, polity, law) that support cooperation and punish any defectors. Decision-making at group level coupled with the existence of norms and punishment for free-riders and deviants may induce cooperation. Institutions and social norms that protect the cooperatively-minded from the free-riders and promote the sharing of resources ensure that the benefits of cooperation are shared widely at individual level. Thus, the benefits of cooperation are divulged down to the individual level. Successful individuals then proliferate either because they command more resources and are therefore more reproductively successful, or by being emulated. The capacities to sustain these features in human societies have evolved together with genetically transmitted individual behaviour. Such "gene-culture coevolution" is said to be the key supporting factor behind cooperation, a sense of fairness, and a taste for virtues such as honesty, courage, hard work, trustworthiness, and loyalty (Gintis 2012, 2017).

The elements that account for cooperation may be social emotions such as love, altruism and empathy but also shame, guilt and remorse, that induce us to accept morality and other social norms and make it acceptable or indeed imperative to punish the deviants from the norms. Cooperation at group level (with resource- and risk-sharing, consensus decision-making, even hostility towards "outsiders") may be conducive towards but is arguably not enough to sustain cooperation on its own (Bowles and Gintis 2003). A virtuous circle of few deviants from the norm leading on to low total cost of punishment for the group sustains a cooperative equilibrium. At the same time, a cooperation breaks down if there is a vicious circle of many deviants–high cost and therefore imperfect punishment. Thus, these traits (or their absence) give rise to multiple ranked equilibria (predominantly cooperative with heterogeneity, allowing both for self-regarding and conformists to the norm or generalised self-regarding behaviour) and persistent differences between groups as some will gravitate towards one and others towards the other equilibrium. Groups that are characterised by cooperation may have an evolutionary advantage if they can win in-group rivalries and conflicts. Furthermore, institutional and cultural environments that limit the within-group variation of behaviours are beneficial as they foster cooperation. Thus, social norms and institutional environments co-evolve with the transmission of individual behaviour and with the group characteristics that foster cooperation (e.g. small size, relative homogeneity): another instance of gene-culture coevolution. As Gintis (2012) writes: "According to gene-culture coevolution, human preferences and beliefs are the product of a dynamic whereby genes affect cultural evolution and culture affects genetic evolution, the two being tightly intertwined in the evolution of our species. ... [T]he process of differential replication affects the frequency of both individual traits, generosity towards fellow group members, say, and group traits, a system of consensus decision-making or property rights". In the absence of institutions, the evolutionary success of cooperative behaviour is shown in experiments to be very difficult (see Bowles and Gintis 2003). The conclusion is that the evolutionary success of such behaviour in human history is due to a unique human capacity to build social institutions, including altruism and morality.

All this points to the fact that preferences are not entirely self-regarding; they include elements that concern "the other" (see Sobel 2005, for a review). Gintis (2017, p. 3) writes: "Human actors exhibit three types of motives in their daily lives: self-regarding, other-regarding, and universalist. Self-regarding motives include seeking wealth, consumption, leisure, social reputation, status, esteem, and other markers of personal advantage. Other-regarding motives involve a concern for fairness, and a compassionate interest in the well-being of others [i.e. altruism]. Universalist motives are those moral rules that are followed for their own sake rather than directly for their effects. Among these universalist goals, which we term character virtues, are honesty, loyalty, courage, trustworthiness, and considerateness".

All this suggests how other-regarding preferences may be beneficial. Reciprocal altruism (altruistic if others return the feeling) turns public goods games to coordination games and selects the "good" equilibrium (Rabin 1998, p. 21). Indeed, the strategic complementarity aspect of reciprocal altruism turns the public good game (including any game of the commons type) into a coordination game; and the universal altruism or morality aspect selects the efficient/"good" equilibrium. Thus, such norms of behaviour give societies and groups an evolutionary advantage.

Some Reflections

From the preceding discussion, two key results emerge. One result seems indisputable, namely the social conditioning of human behaviour, including the economic. The old political dictum that "there is no such thing as a society", typified in neoclassical economics by the concept of the "economic (hu)man", is now defunct. A second result however of much of the above literature of the evolutionarily built "goodness of (hu)man" should be debated more. Of course, societies, non-human as well as human, have a tendency for love, friendship, altruism, cooperation, contribution to the common good, and all the other nice features of the social suite. These features ensure evolutionary advantages such as food-gathering efficiency, defence against predators, care for vulnerable members of the group including pregnant women and nursing mothers, care for the young, information exchange, etc. (see Christakis 2019, for a range of examples from human societies and groups of apes, elephants and whales).

But the indisputable advantage and predominance of the "social suite" should not make us lose sight of the fact that human societies also experience widespread rivalry and conflict, in the form of war, crime, class strife and conflict, hate and persecution, and much else and equally bad.[5] Less dramatically, the breakdown in cooperation is evident in countless "prisoner-dilemmas" and "tragedy-of-the-commons" problems, of which climate change may be the culmination, problems about whom Christakis is well aware (e.g. 2019, Chapter 9). Closer to macroeconomics, rising inequalities within societies, persistent "poverty traps", and other problems (e.g. global imbalances, indebtedness) are continuing problems. One may argue that, while cooperation takes us closer to Pareto efficiency, conflict takes us away from it.

[5] Christakis (2019, Chapter 8) argues that animosity is essentially the dual of kindness among humans. In fact, a line of thought among evolutionary biologists holds that the tendency of cooperation towards a group or network (of unrelated individuals) has evolved together with animosity towards outsiders.

Unfortunately, both outright strife and inefficiencies due to limited cooperation are timeless features of almost all societies since at least the dawn of history. The fact that the "human morphospace" is to a large extent empty should not obscure the fact that the variation in characteristics, both within and between societies, is considerable. Thus, to go from the "there is no society" dictum to another of the form "there exists society and it is good" would be unwarranted.[6] But the literature quoted above is a refreshing antidote to the "Hobbesian" view of the world as a place where (to paraphrase slightly) "(hu)man is against every other (hu)man".

3 Social Preferences

Standard theory considers preferences to be innate (to the individual) and exogenous (to theory)—no theory can explain them. However, there is a large and growing literature that emphasises the social determination of preferences, via social norms and conventions, fads and fashions, and identity. The status-seeking motive and the related positional concerns are also part of socially minded preferences; as we have covered these issues extensively in Chapter 3, will not add much here.

[6] An arguably extreme form of the latter view is the Panglossian dictum that "all is good in the best of all possible worlds", sometimes argued as permeating New Classical Macroeconomics (Buiter, 1980). A more apt summary of the good-society view is the common saying that "we are all in this together". Ironically, a well-known multibillionaire is quoted on the jacket of Christakis (2019) as suggesting that the book shows that this saying is now evolutionarily proven. Well, yes in some respects (e.g., climate change, pandemics) and not in others (inequality, distributive justice—particularly from the point of view of someone low on the ladder). Thus, a more realistic view of the world would be that we are somewhere between the "no society" and the "good society" polar cases. Christakis is well aware of strife and conflict, as well as of love and cooperation, as illustrated by the concluding sentences of the book (pp. 471–2):

> 'Humans have always had both competitive and cooperative impulses, both violent and beneficent tendencies. ... We are primed for conflict and hatred, but also for love, friendship and cooperation. If anything, modern societies are just a patina of civilization on top of this evolutionary blueprint. ... The arc of our evolutionary history is long. But it bends towards goodness.'

We may conclude that, in human societies as much as in animals, conflict is much a feature of society as is cooperation (see West and Ghoul 2019).

Social Norms

According to Elster (1989), social norms are rules, shared by others, that impose constraints on individual preferences and behaviour—their violation causes, embarrassment, shame, guilt or anxiety. They are not outcome-oriented (Elster 1989, p. 99). There is a wide variety of norms (legal or moral norms, economic norms such as on work or consumption, norms on reciprocity, cooperation or fairness) as there are motives for their existence. Norms are not mechanical and do not negate rational choice. But they can be argued to negate the methodological individualism of neoclassical theory, as individual behaviour is determined by external influences as well as individual decision-making. Incorporating norms into individual decision-making is one important step in socio-economics. A further important step will be to endogenise norms, to show how they develop, get propagated and prevail as an equilibrium.

Norms are key in pinpointing many of the anchors, reference points, targets or "endowment" points that we saw in Chapter 2, therefore they are closely linked with behavioural psychology. Norms are socially constructed, what we consider as "normal" is shaped by common belief or practice, past or present. If so, it follows that the "social" and "behavioural" aspects of all behaviour, including economic, are interrelated, they influence and reinforce one another.[7]

Norms are also important in considering fairness. Kahneman (2012, Chapter 8) points out that fairness may not be about identifying ideal behaviour but about finding the line that separates acceptable from non-acceptable behaviour, about identifying behaviour that does not break norms. Thus, this is a notion of reference-dependent fairness. Evidence shows that when individuals perceive others as breaking norms, as pursuing own gains by inflicting losses on others, they may engage in "altruistic punishment", by punishing the perpetrators even at their own cost. Much experimental evidence also indicates that individuals contribute to public good games more than any notion of self-interest would dictate (see Rabin 1998; and the discussion below). Individuals are also more prepared to cooperate if they see others cooperating ("reciprocal or conditional altruism"). Norms are also a key part of our identity, an important new theme in socio-economics, to which we return below.

[7] This provides an important motivation for the title and substance of this book, as mentioned in Chapter 1.

Culture and Individual Decision-Making

Humans (and animals to some extent) are enculturated, they let past social experiences and structures affect preferences and cognition through learning and adaptation. Culture is much too broad a topic to be given any just treatment here; nor does it seem to have been incorporated into macroeconomics much. So, we shall only give a flavour of the topic by a brief review of Hoff and Stiglitz (2016). They stress that human behaviour is affected by the interplay between individual decision-making, endogenous preferences, social context, and perception and cognition which is affected by categories, identities, narratives and worldviews—the latter overlaps to a great extent with culture. Accordingly, perception and cognition are not genetically determined; rather those are refined and built up over time and process of cultural transmission. These perceptions and cognitions influence the mental models that are used to process and interpret information. For example, as an application, in a gender-biassed society, Hoff and Stiglitz (2016) argue that a reserved leadership position for a woman will affect the attitude towards women and will help to reduce gender bias. Similarly, different programs in media also affect the perception, cognition, and behaviour.

Culture, its transmission and adaptation can give rise to a variety of social dynamics. There can be multiple equilibria. With the existence of large enough disturbances, a society can move from one equilibrium to another. These equilibrium conditions can be affected by policies, legal codes, punishments mechanisms for deviants, etc. This is in fact both the strength and weakness of such analyses—the wide range of possibilities which can be fascinating but also an "embarrassment of riches". As a corollary, economics should have input from sociology, anthropology and psychology—and vice versa.

Identity

"Identity" is a concept with a long history in social sciences (see, e.g. Hornsey 2008). Identity introduces a channel whereby non-market economic interactions exist among individuals. The starting point is that, as casual observation suggests, individuals take into account norms, referencing standards, "what others do". These referencing standards differ across people; furthermore, each individual pays more (in the limit: exclusive) attention to the arguments of their peers (once they have decided which is their peer group) in constructing the referencing standards that inform their behaviour. By affecting individual behaviour, these referencing standards interact with societal outcomes. This line of thinking applies to many aspects of behaviour, like our dress code, choice of private or public education, or crime.

In a series of papers, Akerlof and Kranton (2000, 2002, 2010) have introduced the notion into economics. They take "identity" to be the choice of a peer group with the adoption of its norms and highlight its importance as an economic decision. Choice of group constrains an individual to behave according to the chosen norms or beliefs or referencing standards, but it confers the benefit of a membership of a group. Thus, individual behaviour is affected by the endogenous choice of a peer group (that may be only a subset of society) and adoption of the norms, aspirations or referencing standards of that group.[8] The endogeneity of the reference standards has been recognised in a few contributions such as Falk and Knell (2004) and Tournemaine and Tsoukis (2015a, 2015b), and the other contributions discussed in Chapter 3. The new element of identity economics is that those referencing standards are adopted by individuals after they identify themselves with certain peer groups.[9] Akerlof (2007) intuitively shows how identity and group-related norms can be central to an explanation of well-known puzzles in macroeconomics.[10] The relation between identity and sociality (cooperation or not) is explored in Snower and Lindbeck (2019). Tournemaine and Tsoukis (2015a, 2015b) have explored the implications of individuals forming

[8] The Oxford Living Dictionary defines identity as: "The fact of being who or what a person or thing is; the characteristics determining who or what a person or thing is". Social psychologist Baumeister (1986) elaborates: "An identity is a definition, an interpretation, of the self ... defining the self [implies] the establishing of long-term goals, major affiliations, and basic values".

[9] The resulting equilibria are essentially Nash equilibria, as agents optimise taking the response of others as given. See Shayo (2009, 2020) and Pradelski (2015) for game-theoretic analyses: In the former, the individual identifies with a group (of fixed size) which features (an endogenously determined) "prototypical behaviour" with status effects. In the latter, social influence on potential innovators derives from reference standards that may vary (based on current adoption of practices or cumulative usage). In other words, these contributions are political-economy approaches (as are those of Bonomi et al. 2020; and Snower, and Lindbeck, 2019.

[10] See his discussion in Section V of his 2007 paper on the sociology of consumption, emphasising norms and the reference standards of different social classes.

two groups: those attending state education and the more motivated ones who attend private education.

These ideas received empirical support from experimental evidence: Mechtel et al. (2014) confirm all these aspects of identity: individuals value their membership of groups; furthermore, group choice is endogenous (optimally made); it is correlated positively with the status enjoyed by each group and negatively with their distance from the key characteristics of the individual from those of that group; and finally, this choice affects subsequent behaviour. Self-selection into groups based on the gain to be had from membership of each group receives confirmation from the experimental evidence of Cicala et al. (2018).[11] Shayo (2020) reviews a wealth of further evidence supporting identity, group selection and adoption of norms. Relatedly, selective norm-taking is emphasised by Senik (2009), Clark and Senik (2010) and Goerke and Pannenberg (2015) who find support for localised consumption comparisons (one compares oneself with their social milieu); and briefly in Genicot and Ray (2017), as mentioned.

Moreover, Benjamin, Choi and Strickland (2010) find that ethnic identity affects attitudes to risk and time; gender identity also affects outcomes via identification with norms. Using experimental evidence from rural India, Hoff and Pandey (2006) find that membership in groups that are discriminated against is invested with social meaning and affects economic behaviour. Other effects of identity on behaviour include residential segregation (Schelling 1978); and choices over school or neighbourhood or job (Akerlof and Kranton 2000, 2010). Benabou and Tirole (2011) highlight the interplay of identity and morality.

In unpublished work, Tsoukis and Tournemaine (2016) develop a simple macroeconomic model with endogenous group formation and identity.[12] Heterogeneous individuals choose one of two groups of endogenous size and adopt its corresponding group-specific consumption reference benchmark. The specification of preferences incorporates

[11] More experimental evidence on the psychological value of belonging to groups is offered by Hargreaves et al. (2009). In that contribution, the overall welfare effects of the existence of groups are unclear as there is discrimination towards outsiders; several elements of that paper corroborate our framework. Related to our work is also the finding of Chen and Chen (2011) that identification with groups affects the work effort; see also Charness, Rigotti and Rustichini (2007).

[12] Cf. Pinker (2021, p. 296): "... humans are keen to divide themselves into competitive teams....".

a variant of the status motive that involves loss of utility from falling short of a reference standard, something akin to loss aversion (Tversky and Kahneman 1991). Specifically, recalling the discussion in Chapter 3, utility takes the form:

$$U_i = U\left(c_i, \frac{c_i}{\overline{c}}^{\varphi_0+\frac{\varphi_1}{2}\ln\left(\frac{c_i}{\overline{c}}\right)}\right), \quad \varphi_0 > 0, \quad \varphi_1 < 0$$

As mentioned, following Tournemaine and Tsoukis (2009, 2010a) and Tsoukis and Tournemaine (2013), the assumption of $\varphi_1 < 0$ is made on both empirical and intuitive grounds. It is nicknamed "pains from the loss of status", as it implies that an individual loses utility faster from falling short of the reference standard than from exceeding it. So, the assumption is akin to loss aversion (see Chapter 2). It implies strategic complementarity in consumption (Cooper and John 1988), i.e. a positive reaction function of individual consumption to the reference one, or "conformist" behaviour in the terminology of Clark and Oswald (1998) and Bratsiotis and Peng (2008). Genicot and Ray (2017, 2020) simply call the case of $\varphi_i < 0$ "disappointment" (e.g. see Fig. 2 and associated discussion in their 2020 paper).

The status motive, in its "pains" variant ($\varphi_1 < 0$), generates two conflicting motives: motivation versus disappointment and the need to feel better (self-achievement); see also Falk and Knell (2004). The result is the choice of one of two groups ("high-fliers" and "low fliers"), guided by exogenous ability, with endogenous group size and reference standards.[13] In general socio-economic equilibrium, reference benchmarks, aggregate output, and group choice are jointly determined. A stronger sense of identity is shown to lead to less aggregate activity, less polarisation, a higher "social multiplier" (see below), and it also decreases inequality. It also exacerbates the impact of other factors on output. A key implication of identity is that changes that impact individuals uniformly will have distributional implications as they cause a re-allocation between groups. The endogenous group formation shapes the distribution of macroeconomic outcomes in a different way than the underlying exogenous

[13] "Low achievers" will not compare themselves with "high achievers" as this will reduce their self-esteem, while "high achievers" always choose to aim to keep up with other high achievers.

fundamentals (which is a skill in the paper). Thus, as a corollary, identity is an important determinant of macroeconomic outcomes. The paper reconciles individual decision-making with the endogenous determination of groups and their norms or reference standards.

The recent contributions of Genicot and Ray (2017, 2020) merit a mention here. They term a broad class of consumption reference standards "aspirations" and discuss their features and effects. However, they do not discuss group-based aspirations, i.e. identity. The closest they come to that is in Example 6 in their 2017 paper, when they discuss "local income windows", what may alternatively be termed neighbourhood effects in determining the reference benchmark. But the size of the window is arbitrarily fixed and there are no distinct groups, as "identity" implicitly presupposes.

The endogenous formation of groups is emphasised in Schelling's (1978, Chapter 3) and Granovetter's (1978) analyses of the thresholds that determine the boundaries of groups. Akerlof and Kranton (2010) give numerous examples of how social divisions, groups and norms interact with (cause and are caused by) economic inequality. Levitt and Dubner (2014) discuss how members of racial groups in the US identify themselves with their groups by "living out" the norms of their groups (in terms of, e.g. choice of names, school performance, patterns of behaviour, etc.). This identification comes about because it is costly (in psychic terms) for individuals to deviate from the norms of the groups they see themselves as belonging to (Akerlof and Kranton 2000)—but these psychic costs of deviating from the group norm are assumed exogenous.

There are also informal but credible narratives of the key ideas underpinning identity. Kelly (2021) argues that the choice of position in a debate may have to do more with the belief system of an already chosen political or ideological camp (a "tribe") rather than a rational assessment of evidence. This is happening both because of social processes and because of cognitive limitations. It is further argued that the internet age, with its focus on algorithmic selection of information will enhance the "tribal" way of thinking. Koike (2015) gives anecdotal evidence on the interplay between the intensity of the status motive and inequality - both arguably low in her native Japan. She presents informal evidence that the reference benchmarks of even the rich do not deviate much from societal averages—hence the lack of very ostentatious lifestyles. In other words, the extent to which each group uses peer group versus societal-average comparisons varies across countries; we parameterise it here.

Identity, group selection, and endogenous referencing also have political implications. Bonomi, Gennaioli and Tabellini (2021) emphasise the effect of identity on political conflict and policy selection: Their political-economy setup assumes that income is exogenous and groups are effectively fixed as the distributions of decisive features and the thresholds that divide groups are fixed. Along broadly similar lines, Grossman and Helpman (2018) show that identity has important implications for the choice of trade policy. In relation to former President Trump's election in 2016, Munz (2018) provides evidence that a key driver of the Trump vote was the perceived status threat among high-status groups due to increasing racial diversity and globalisation. Runciman (1966) found that English workers compare themselves not to the rich, or even the wide societal average, but to those near them in the income pecking order. Mann (2013, p. 340) argues that this may well be one of the leading reasons why individuals do not seem to mind the growing inequality around them so that there is no great demand for redistribution.[14] An open question is whether identity promotes or hinders Pareto efficiency and cooperation (see Snower and Lindbeck 2019). Hornsey (2008) reviews the theory of social identity from a wider social theory perspective.

4 Social Capital and the Social Multiplier

The concept of "social capital" has a long history in the social sciences and a rapidly expanding presence in the economics literature. In varying, it has been shown to affect positively growth and development (Knack and Keefer 1997; Knack and Zak 1999; Dasgupta and Serageldin 2000; Grootaert and van Bastelear 2002; Putnam et al. 1993), institutional design and performance (Djankov et al. 2003) and financial development (Guiso et al. 2004). In his seminal early contribution, Putnam (1993) found a correlation between measures of civic engagement and governmental quality across Italian regions. Similarly, Guiso et al. (2004) find a correlation between civic engagement and financial development, again for Italy. La Porta et al. (1999) find cross-country correlation between a measure of trust and judicial efficiency (positive) and government corruption (negative). Very useful surveys on social capital include

[14] See DeLong (2013) on rising inequality and relative deprivation and the curious absence of a political backlash.

Dasgupta (2003), Durlauf and Fafchamps (2005) and Guiso et al. (2012). The various contributions have used diverse definitions of the concept. The resulting lack of conceptual clarity hampers both further formal analysis and empirical measurement (see Durlauf 2002). Arriving at a clear-cut definition is not trivial, as our critical review below shows. At a minimum, a definition should satisfy Solow's (1995) four essential criteria for a concept of capital: (i) distinctiveness (particularly from human capital), (ii) measurability (in principle), (iii) costly accumulation and (iv) depreciation.

Landmark contributions in sociology such as Coleman (1990), Putnam (1993, 2000) and Fukuyama (1999) place shared norms, beliefs and trust that facilitate economic (and wider) activity and promote efficiency, at the heart of social capital. Putnam et al. (1993), Bowles and Gintis (2002) and Routledge and von Amsberg (2002) define social capital as the social or governance structures that facilitate cooperation. However, this defines social capital through its supposed effect (cooperation) rather than providing a clear definition first followed by an investigation of its effects. Additionally, in some of these analyses, social capital is a by-product of exchange, social interaction, or other decision such as location; there is no associated investment decision and therefore the definition does not satisfy Solow's (1995) criteria.

In an attempt to define the concept more precisely, Guiso et al. (2012) define social capital as "[...] shared beliefs and values that help a group overcome the free-rider problem in the pursuit of socially valuable activities". To distinguish from other approaches, they call this "civic capital". This is plausible but perhaps slightly restrictive, because there exist other inefficient externalities in addition to free-riding such as (e.g.) the status-related "rat races". In the same spirit, Durlauf and Fafchamps (2005) suggest that: (a) social capital generates positive externalities for members of a group; (b) these externalities are achieved through shared trust, norms, and values and their consequent effects on expectations and behaviour; (c) shared trust, norms, and values arise from informal forms of organisations based on social networks and associations. The first two aspects of this definition are virtually identical to the Guiso et al. (2012) definition; requirement (c), however, appears a little restrictive in that beneficial collective action, even informal and unintended, may happen in the wider community, outside of such associations.

A further point that requires clarification is the distinction between a pure social capital and socially related but privately owned capital. Social capital is often defined in such a way that it entails a private as well as a social benefit via various externalities. E.g. Glaeser et al. (2002, p. F439) define social capital as "social characteristics that yield a market as well as non-market yield"; as they themselves acknowledge however, such social skills (to use the everyday term) include those of "[...] the stereotypical used car salesman who has lots of individual social capital (i.e. he's good at selling lemons to naïve consumers), but who generates little net social capital because of his negative social capital externalities". Thus, this type of skill should more appropriately be considered as a socially related, private skill or form of human capital; social capital properly defined should be closer to what Glaeser et al. (2002) call "aggregate" social capital, which nets out all the externalities from individual capital; and which (Glaeser et al. 2002) treat as exogenous. Likewise, membership in an organisation or network, a common definition of social capital, that confers a private benefit and perhaps positive externalities among the group but little or no wider social benefit, should also be excluded from a proper definition of social capital for the same reasons.

Itaya and Tsoukis (2022) argue that one should start from the words themselves: "social" and "capital": Social capital involves costly (in an opportunity-cost sense) investment (as per Solow 1995), e.g. education; but it may well be intangible, such as shared norms, beliefs, networks and institutions; and social, contributed to by many but not owned by anyone in particular. A further point that needs clarification concerns the exact nature of the benefit that accrues at the societal level. Activities such as communal policing and cleaning of streets, while socially beneficial, are arguably more in the nature of public services arising from voluntary contributions (of time and effort). Hence, Itaya and Tsoukis (2022) define social capital to be all community-related formal and informal engagement, beliefs, values, norms and practices that help society achieve Pareto-superior outcomes and that require resources to build. Examples may include contributing to charity, ethical behaviour and norms such as politeness and mutual help, environmentally friendly norms and practices, quality of governance and institutions (Tabellini 2008), etc. In order to be sustained, all these types of behaviour require "something", a stock variable that is built through investment such as formal and informal education and/or personal involvement and time. All such capital also involves depreciation, in that, if it is not maintained in a conscious and costly way, it wears out. Thus, all Solow's (1995) four minimum criteria for a successful definition of (any type of) "capital" are satisfied.

More concretely, social capital alleviates the social inefficiencies associated with negative externalities. Such inefficiencies include those discussed in Chapter 3 and are related to status-seeking, conspicuous, corrupt or aggressive behaviour, other rat races, free-riding, etc. Additionally, social capital may confer utility directly: Helliwell et al. (2017) find that a higher social capital is associated with a greater subjective well-being. This is an effect akin to the "warm glow" type of benefit from giving (Andreoni 1990) except that it stems from the level of social capital rather than the individual contribution to it. Indeed, one may think of plausible reasons why there may be utility derived directly from social capital in the form of a lower crime rate or greater social ties, mutual trust and cooperation, reducing monitoring costs, reducing contractual costs, and so on, in addition to the mitigation of the negative externalities.

Formal treatment of the concept of social capital is rather sparse. In an elegant early contribution, Glaeser et al. (2002) model the investment-into-social capital decision in an explicitly optimising way; a clear progress over earlier analyses. However, as alluded to above, their interface between individual and aggregate social capital fails to clearly delineate the externalities. Routledge and von Amsberg (2002) offer a careful game-theoretic analysis of social capital-as-cooperation. In a model where growth arises from productivity changes that require labour re-allocation, social capital has welfare effects. Without social capital, maximum growth arises from frictionless re-allocation, yet this re-allocation will involve less likelihood of stable (repeated) trade relationships and therefore cooperation is harder to sustain. Since social capital is defined as the sustenance of cooperation, welfare may be higher with less labour mobility. Without calling it social capital, Tabellini (2008) models the willingness to cooperate which develops from the costly education by parents to their children in order for the latter to acquire more cooperative values. In other words, there is "something" that is sustained by costly investment and that helps society achieve more efficient outcomes; Tabellini (2008) calls it cooperation, but it much akin to social capital. Varvarigos and Xin (2015) present a formal framework which is focused more on the theme of trust, which may arguably be a component of social capital. One question that is open in relation to both trust and social capital is reciprocity, and this is perhaps where the two concepts may diverge. One may argue that trust is more likely to be reciprocal, either shared widely or not; whereas one may think of examples of social capital in such a way that one person may contribute to it while another may not, thus, reciprocity is not a necessary feature.

In Itaya and Tsoukis (2022), social capital is an aggregate state variable that alleviates the status motive and its concomitant suboptimal effects. The focus on the status motive is made for analytical convenience; the concept is taken as a parable for all inefficient antagonistic behaviour and associated negative externalities. Analytically, the model uses dynamic non-cooperative game theory and models the formation of social capital as a Markov Nash equilibrium. It incorporates private optimising behaviour and accounts for the strategic interaction between non-atomistic individuals and their private decisions to invest towards social capital. This allows the endogenization of aggregate social capital—which is said to be an improvement to such analyses as (e.g.) Glaeser et al. (2002) that take the aggregate social capital as exogenously given. In a similar spirit, Chou (2006) presents a model in which social capital facilitates standard human capital formation. Interestingly, this paper shows that there is a possibility of a poverty trap with little social capital and development. Poverty traps is a wide-ranging theme in macroeconomics and growth where lots of avenues have been explored but where rather little convergence has been reached.

Thus, the various contributions take different approaches to the tension between the traditional individual-optimising approach of economics and more sociological analyses that view the community level as the appropriate decision-making unit for social capital (see Glaeser et al. 2002). Game-theoretic approaches such as that of Itaya and Tsoukis (2022) and others may be best placed to combine both conscious individual behaviour and social interactions and processes.

Related to social capital is the concept of the "social multiplier" (Scheinkman 2008; Glaeser et al. 2003). A social multiplier is said to arise when social interactions of various types of agents give rise to a total effect of fundamentals that is greater than if such social interactions did not exist. Social capital may be said to be an embodiment of social interactions both directly (as it is communally built) and indirectly (as it alleviates the effects of externalities) (for more discussion, see Itaya and Tsoukis 2022).

5 Social Structure and Macroeconomic Outcomes

Granovetter (2005) offers various examples of how social influences shape economic outcomes. E.g. (p. 36), social networks are important in labour markets (both workers and employers learn about jobs from one another, social capital and trust at place). Price formation is affected by interpersonal relations (p. 38): "Customer markets" (a theme highlighted by the post-WWII macroeconomist Arthur Okun) and clientelisation create informational asymmetries and fragmentation of markets; networks are also important in assessing creditworthiness; market participation, demand and prices are affected by all the above. Social relations also affect productivity (p. 41) as various tasks involve interaction, cooperation and learning from others; in all these, the quality of interactions is others key. Group norms and culture also play a role. Trust and loyalty also play a role, as theories of efficiency wages have emphasised (see Chapter 1 and below). All the above traits also play a role in innovation and its diffusion.

One point that can be made on all this is that it is micro in nature; it is not related to the aggregate level and therefore to macroeconomics. The analysis of Granovetter (1985) on the problem of "embeddedness" (i.e. to what extent individual behaviour is determined by social relations and structures) also is not macro in nature as Granovetter (1985, p. 506) himself acknowledges. Yet, the argument is, understanding the problem of embeddedness at the micro level is a prerequisite for understanding the same issue at the macro level and for understanding the relations between the micro and macro level.

Two invaluable sources for understanding "embeddedness" at the macro level are Akerlof and Shiller (2009) and Schelling (2006). Schelling (2006), a book that deserves to be read more widely and its central messages to be incorporated into macroeconomics, first appeared in 1978. As the title suggests, the book builds a theory of macro(economic) behaviour from individual motives, that however are far removed from the standard micro-foundations (though not incompatible with them). The gist of the book is to show how the individual motives are not independent, but constrained or shaped in various ways by the aggregate outcomes, that they themselves give rise to. In this way, and in endogenizing the aggregate behaviour, he manages a theory of micro–macro interactions that "embeds" social behaviour at the appropriate extent, as per Granovetter (1985), neither “under-socialising” nor “over-socialising” it.

Schelling (2006) motivates his analyses with two examples: In one of his lectures, he talked to an audience of 800 people in an auditorium where all rows up to no, 12 were empty and from the thirteenth onwards they were absolutely packed. Schelling felt, he says like “[...] addressing a crowd at the opposite bank of a river” (Schelling 2006, p. 12). Obviously, as the audience suggested, no-one had arranged this seating plan. Social interactions that were implicit (as the audience did not know one another), through peer effects, and reverse status (no-one wanted to be conspicuous) gave rise to this aggregate structure. This structure is obviously a Nash equilibrium, as is (whether stated or not) much of the analysis of Chapters 3 and 4 concerning status and relative position, and the analyses on identity and social capital mentioned in Chapter 8. The key point is that the aggregate outcome is unintentional from the point of view of any individual. In important policy corollary, mentioned also in Chapter 1 in another context, is that a welfare evaluation of the aggregate outcome becomes conceptually difficult for this very reason (Schelling 2006, p. 19).

Another example that brings about the difference between individual aims and aggregate configurations, but also the multiplicity and fragility of equilibria is the example of the standing ovation (Schelling 2006, Chapter 2). Imagine a distribution of concertgoers such that, after a very good performance, one person is enthusiastic enough to stand up to applaud, a second one will do so if another one has done that before them, a third one wants to see two people standing before s/he stands, a fourth wants to see three people, and so on. Now, imagine another distribution that is virtually the same except no-one is willing to stand up first, there are two people who want to see someone else before them, a third person who wants to see two, etc. The two distributions, though virtually identical, will produce very different outcomes: The first one will produce a standing ovation occasionally, the second one will never do.

Schelling (2006) offers a typology of mechanisms whereby individual and aggregate variables interact: accounting identities, stock-flow interactions, adding-up constraints, and transition matrices, all imply that individual actions are interrelated. In addition, explicit social interactions (peer effects, status-seeking or relative position motives, strategic complementarities—Cooper and John 1988) add depth and complexity to resulting mechanisms. Many types of behaviour are subject to (formal or informal) coordination: Driving on the same side of the street for each direction, or synchronisation of clocks, the established "QWERTY" keyboard, are examples of coordinated actions. We will not dwell more on these well-known effects except to say that various social interactions are at play (as well as institutional and formal coordination). The well known "toilet paper disappearance effect" during the Covid-19 pandemic is another coordination effect where social influences played an important role. Apart from peer effects and pressure (on how critical toilet paper may or may not be in times of crisis), there is also a "self-fulfilling expectations" effect: Everybody rushes to buy toilet paper thinking that other will do so as well and that the supermarkets will run out. Many of these effects are also at work in financial markets, as we shall see below.

Thresholds, tipping points and critical mass features can have important effects (see Granovetter 1978). For instance, "thermostats" (a nickname for such thresholds) may give rise to cyclical patterns and Goodwin cycles: If the temperature on the thermostat is set to X degrees, the boiler will switch off when the temperature reaches that point; but the hot water in the system will continue to raise the temperature. Then, when the temperature falls back to X, the boiler will switch on again, but the temperature will fall below X before the water warms up. Such patterns in inventories or in housebuilding (for instance) can give rise to Goodwin cycles (see also Tsoukis 2020, Chapter 11).

Sigmoid functions are often used to capture formally such threshold and critical-mass arguments. An example, inspired by Schelling (2006, Chapter 3), is the following (the simple analytics is shown in Fig. 1 below). Let us imagine an activity where people are more encouraged to participate if others also do so; e.g. more people attend a rally, or a lecture, or a social function if they expect others to do so (see Schelling 2006, p. 104). In Fig. 1, the vertical axis has those attending and the horizontal those expected to attend. For simplicity, the total mass of people is 1. The sigmoid solid line displays two key features: The positive slope shows strategic complementarity—people are more likely to do something if more others do so as well. Secondly, there is a critical mass shown by the steeper slope in the middle, so that below a certain level of expected attendance, the enthusiasm and willingness to attend is low, but above that, enthusiasm picks up considerably.[15] The broken line is the celebrated 45^0 line, which shows equality between the actual and expected attendees; this must be the case in equilibrium, at least on average. (If expected and actual do not equal each other, that would indicate permanent over- or under-estimation, which would be a case not of bounded rationality but of sheer stupidity.) Fig. 1

There are three possible (Nash) equilibria. Standard dynamical methods (e.g. Tsoukis 2020, Chapter 5) show that the middle one is unstable whereas the two on the sides are stable. Ignoring the unstable equilibrium, the question which of the two stable ones will be selected may depend on history,[16] or on any case-dependent circumstances that make one of the equilibria more likely (in the language of game theory: a "focal" equilibrium), or on psychology (confidence, trust), or on culture, or perhaps on simple chance.

The model is more general than it seems at first sight. Apart from models of social participation through strategic complementarity as

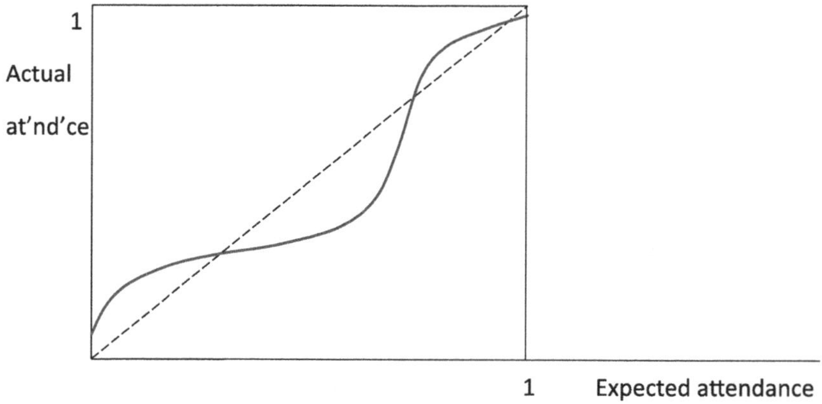

Fig. 1 Peer effects and equilibria

[15] Strictly speaking, a strict threshold or critical mass should be shown by a vertical middle section; the steeper (but not vertical) segment indicates a "softer" threshold.

[16] If history matters, then we get "path dependence" or "hysteresis"—how you progress helps select the arrival point, i.e. the equilibrium, in contrast to standard models which predict that the equilibrium will depend on preferences, endowment or technology, irrespective of history.

discussed above, coordination games also fit in here. Re-interpret the sigmoid function as "the fraction of people who will drive on the right depending on others driving on the right" (for instance) and (with only minor amendment in the setup), we get the two equilibria whereby all drive on the right or all on the left. Or we can cast the culture-society nexus in these terms. For instance, re-interpret the sigmoid to mean "fraction of people driving aggressively on the road depending on others doing so". There are then two equilibria, where the vast majority either drives aggressively or not aggressively—not half and half. Which equilibrium each society gravitates to depends on history, institutions, even climate, and much else besides. In all these situations, the social effects are apparent.

All such models give rise to multiple equilibria and fragile equilibria: A small change in the setup, may result in a radical alteration of the aggregate result; e.g. we may move from one equilibrium to the other, or equilibria may emerge or disappear, see also Granovetter (1978). A weakening or strengthening of peer effects can be crucial. For instance, re-interpret the sigmoid to be "people who are prepared to give a standing ovation depending on how many stand up before them". As shown above, the sigmoid assumes that a couple of people are prepared to stand up without anyone else having preceded them. The result is two equilibria, with a few people and almost everyone standing up. Now, imagine the curve moving to the right a little (to start from the origin, showing that everyone requires someone else to move first), and then we get two equilibria—no-one and almost everyone standing up. The 0 equilibrium may then be the outcome most of the time. Language may be another application: Re-interpret the sigmoid to mean "language preferred by a certain fraction of the population depending on how many other people speak that language". Closer to macroeconomics, the celebrated "efficiency wage model" (e.g. Akerlof and Yellen 1985; see also Chapter 1) may also be interpreted in those terms, with a slight adaptation, if the sigmoid curve can be interpreted as "the wage the typical employer is prepared to offer given the average wage". Then, the wage of the typical employer is the average wage, and (possibly multiple) equilibrium(a) ensue(s). Moving from one equilibrium to another will entail (social) multipliers (as defined above), acceleration effects and big changes in welfare. Specifically, the various (Nash) equilibria are often Pareto-ranked, with one being better than the other for all parties ("efficient"). If we are stuck at an inefficient equilibrium (e.g. everybody drives aggressively on the road and as a result everybody loses out, but no-one has a private incentive to change) then institutional or societal intervention is being called for (e.g. Schelling 2006, p. 225).

Congestion, "prisoners' dilemmas" and "tragedies of the commons" may be seen as variations of the above themes (Schelling 2006, Chapter 7). The key feature in these cases is of course the suboptimality of the resulting equilibria. For our purposes, it is important to note how social interactions may shape these setups in critical ways.

Segregation and neighbourhood models are also prominent in the book, e.g. in Chapter 4. They are an important instance when the identities, adding-up and other aggregate constraints emphasised above, produce aggregate outcomes that may be at odds with individual aims. One famous instance is the two communities of "whites" and "blacks" who both wish to live in cosmopolitan neighbourhoods but everybody wishes to be in a local majority. The result is total segregation (Schelling 2006, p. 141; see also p. 37 for a similar example involving men and women in a social function). The difference between individual aims (cosmopolitanism) and end result (segregation) makes a welfare evaluation of the aggregate result problematic, as mentioned above.

The analyses in Schelling (2006) encompass a wide range of phenomena, applicable in diverse spheres, from demographics, to marriage patterns, to population distributions, to epidemics. The results of coordination and strategic complementarities give rise to spontaneous organisation (with ant colonies having been used as parables of such, see e.g. Schelling 2006, p. 21, and in socio-biology see also Kirman and Serletis 2016). Using analyses from a variety of disciplines, Krugman (1996) also shows perspectives on the "self-organising economy"—another text that needs to be read more.

A direct application of behavioural economics to macroeconomics is Akerlof and Shiller (2009). The overarching theme of the book, as its title suggests, is "animal spirits", Keynes' byword for the irrational impulses of market participants (see Chapter 1). Perhaps one should say more precisely rational-irrational impulses, in the sense that rational calculation is surely part of economic behaviour, as is however impulsive thinking, sentiment (and all the heuristics and biases we saw in Chapter 2), and peer pressure (status-seeking, panic, contagion, herding). Thus, "animal spirits" encapsulates all the behaviouristic and bounded-rationality traits we saw in earlier Chapters. Akerlof and Shiller's (2009) view is that such animal spirits are the main culprits of the malfunctioning of the market system; and such was, arguably, one of the main messages of the *General Theory*. With the gradual purging of all things Keynesian from macroeconomic theory, the argument continues, the intellectual climate became too permissive of market excesses; one implication is that "Wall Street got drunk" (former US President G.W. Bush's phrase, Akerlof and Shiller 2009, p. x) and the crisis and recession of 2007–9 ensued. The corollary is that macroeconomics theory, properly constructed, should consider "animal spirits" and should therefore lead to policy proposals that limit their worst effects.

Important elements of "animal spirits" are confidence—which can help select a good equilibrium among the various possible, according to the analysis related to Fig. 1. Bad faith is in a way the opposite of confidence and may be related to corruption (Akerlof and Shiller 2009, Chapter 3). Again, the framework of Fig. 1 may be useful. Re-interpret the sigmoid function to indicate "the frequency of corruption of the typical individual depending on how much corruption exists in society". Then, the two stable (Nash) equilibria are one of low corruption (no-one is corrupt because no-one else is) and that with high corruption. Culture and mass psychology, including good or bad faith, help select one of the two equilibria. In general, good or bad faith, trust or lack of it, a sense of fairness are elements of social norms and culture; therefore, once again, norms and culture have important implications for aggregate economic behaviour.

In their totality, "animal spirits" may be at the root of various macroeconomic phenomena. We mentioned efficiency wages above and in Chapter 1, on which loyalty and trust, but also peer pressure ("what others do") is very important. An essential extension and implication of efficiency wages concern involuntary unemployment, as Shapiro and Stiglitz (1984) have pointed out[17]; see also Akerlof and Shiller (2009, Chapter 8). One key motivation for the firm to offer an "efficiency" (i.e. above-market) wage is to elicit effort and raise productivity via the worker feeling more valued; another motive is to make shirking less attractive, as the possibility of losing a good wage (if caught and fired) is now more costly. But when the typical employer tries to offer a wage above the market average, the result is that the average wage rises, and unemployment ensues. The prospect of this very unemployment is what

[17] See again—where else—Tsoukis (2020, Chapter 4).

prevents workers from shirking. Thus, as the title of the article suggests, the efficiency wage (and concomitant unemployment) jointly is a discipline device.[18] What is important for our purposes, is the prominence of social elements in the efficiency wage theory.

Special mention should be made of De Grauwe and Ji (2018, 2019), which are among the few attempts to incorporate behavioural elements into macroeconomic models. Specifically, they use a rather narrow conception of "animal spirits" to indicate idiosyncratic individual actions unjustified by fundamentals; e.g. an agent may adjust their spending more or less than optimal, considering developments exogenous to the individual (e.g. the wage). They also combine this with learning, which however, while deviating from full rationality, is not among the cognitive limitations that behavioural psychology emphasises. De Grauwe and Ji (2018, 2019) show that such "animal spirits" can be the source of business cycles (in addition to other exogenous shocks); models that incorporate such animal spirits can account better for the synchronisation of cycles across countries. They also analyse the implications of this idea for monetary policy. De Grauwe and Ji's (2018, 2019) ideas and analyses are innovative and deserve attention. On the downside, one may argue that the notion of "animal spirits", as they use it, is rather limited, resembling exogenous idiosyncratic shocks like those investigated in "sunspot" models. The literatures and analyses with which this book is preoccupied should help shed more light on the nature of these "animal spirits"; are they due to cognitive limitations, peer pressures, present-bias, or something else? Are they to some extent endogenous or purely exogenous and random? Such understanding may help the analysis of their effects and of why they (possibly) do not average out to zero. But such advances are the next step; De Grauwe and Ji (2018, 2019) represent important first steps in introducing behavioural elements in macroeconomics.

Further manifestations of the effects of animal spirits (broadly understood) include "money illusion", again mentioned in Chapter 1 (see Akerlof and Shiller 2009, Chapter 4). The inability of the average person to distinguish nominal and real values, in various ways, is a well-known phenomenon (see e.g. Tsoukis 2020, Chapter 3, for a review). Various

[18] This theory goes some way towards the Marxian notion of the "reserve army of unemployment", except that in the Marxian theory, unemployment works towards depressing the wage, while in the Shapiro-Stiglitz story, unemployment is correlated with a high (efficiency) wage.

biases and cognitive limitations such as mental accounting are at work here. It plays an important role in the dynamics of inflation and the shape of the Phillips Curve. Furthermore, social pressures ("keeping up with the Joneses"), norms (fairness, confidence), and all manner of animal spirits, Akerlof and Shiller (2009, Chapter 6) argue, are crucial in understanding various prominent (or notorious) recessionary episodes in the US in the last 150 years. Saving (Akerlof and Shiller 2009, Chapter 10) is also affected by behavioural elements, key of which is perhaps the present-bias we have discussed in Chapters 2, 5 and 6. Peer pressures, status quo bias, and financial (il)literacy, are some other key elements at work, as emphasised by both Thaler (2016) and Shiller (2005). The susceptibility to selecting the default position is the key motivating factor in the policy proposals of Thaler and Sunstein (2009) based on the idea of "nudge". Finally, we should also mention private indebtedness, which is rising at alarming levels. This may be related to the rising inequality. The "keeping up with the Joneses" theory, combined perhaps with present-bias and the motive for immediate gratification, imply that those lower down the ladder may borrow excessively to "keep up".

Both Schelling (2006) and Akerlof and Shiller (2009), with their apparent differences but fairly similar core message, deserve to be read more widely, as mentioned. Their analyses and models have far-reaching implications for aggregate behaviour. The ideas deserve to be worked out more in more detail and unified, so that their implications for macroeconomics can be fully appreciated. But one thing is clear, namely how important such socio-behavioural elements are for the macroeconomy.

At the very time of writing these pages, early August 2024, world stock markets have been in wild turmoil, with a drop of the order of 2.5% in a day on the 5th (a Monday) and an almost equally spectacular rebound on the 6th.[19] All this may have come against a background of nervousness and anxiety, whether because of geopolitical uncertainty, or because of fears that the US economy is on the verge of a recession and the Fed is slow or reluctant to act to stave it off, or because of high government indebtedness, or because the high-tech companies have failed to produce financial results in accordance with the wildly exaggerated expectations. But it is also clear that nothing so specific or dramatic happened on Monday; rather, impulsive behaviour, panic and herding behaviour,

[19] The Japanese Topix index lost 12% during the day.

loss aversion, etcetera, "animal spirits" in short, have combined to create a dramatic overreaction to exogenous developments; see Thaler (2016, p. 223) on investor sentiment and overreaction. Beauty contests and social comparisons are also key for such episodes—surely investors and fund managers are not only interested in having or engendering profits, but in doing so more than the person next door. All these elements are emphasised in Chapter 11 of Akerlof and Shiller (2009) and in Shiller (2005), to whom we turn next.

6 Financial Markets: Socio-Behavioural Traits and "Narratives"

Shiller (2005) is a treatise on the sociology and psychology of financial markets, with an application to the stock and real estate markets, primarily of the US. Its title, "irrational exuberance", refers to a quote used back in 1996 by then Fed Chairman Alan Greenspan. A book that deserves to be core reading in all courses of behavioural finance, it details how all the socio-behavioural elements we have seen (and more) play a role in the wild gyrations of financial markets. Such exuberance is exacerbated by the media and the internet. The media, in seeking attention in a competitive news marketplace, add emphasis, embellish, over-dramatise and exaggerate. They are prone to highlighting unpleasant information (e.g. crime, financial disasters), and thereby stoke fear, anxiety and nervousness. At other times, they promote false expectations and over-optimism (see Shiller 2005, Chapter 5).[20] "Expert" opinion through books or op-eds does all the above plus it propagates fads and rumours.

The role of the internet, email and the "social media" merit a note here, as their use has sky-rocketed over the last couple of decades (in a way that could not be predicted in, say, 2005). Several characteristics can be mentioned. These media have the advantage that they make communication fast and technically accurate (e.g. much more accurate than speech over the telephone and much faster than mail or even fax). They allow any individual to have a voice (whereas before, to be put in the public domain,

[20] The math of epidemics is argued to shed useful light on the transmission of information and thereby on the dynamics of financial markets; see Shiller (2005, p. 165, 2017) and below. This is related to the socio-biological studies of ant colonies as parables for the dynamics of financial markets mentioned above; see Kirman (1992) and Kirman and Serletis (2016).

an opinion would have needed to go through a medium with editorial control like a newspaper); has this new freedom improved the quality of communication, or has it allowed deeper instincts to be aired, or both? Even worse, the internet, once supposed to allow everything to come to light, is now as much a source of misinformation as information. So, both (proper) information and "fake news" are at our fingertips. Finally, social media can also exacerbate the beauty contest effects and herd phenomena (e.g. stories that "go viral" and people being famous for being famous—the "influencers"). All these effects have implications in many domains, e.g. politics, but also in financial markets.

Ambiguity is one big factor in assessing and reacting to a fast-changing reality: Often, the line between "true" information and misinformation is fuzzy, even when it is promoted by "expert" opinion. In reviewing the most dramatic episodes of financial market revaluations (up or down), Shiller (2005, Chapter 7) shows the dramatic interplay of true underlying economic reasons for revaluation together with the fuzzy understanding or interpretation of those by public opinion. Often, it is not easily discernible what may be "rational" market reaction and what be "irrational exuberance". As a result, many of the dramatic revaluations were reversed in a five-year horizon (though not in a 12-month horizon).

In general, in its various manifestations, "irrational exuberance" (and the closely related "animal spirits") leads to market prices at odds with fundamentals. The Efficient Market Hypothesis (EFH) tells us that, the various financial instruments are correctly priced according to the available information. It is of course a contested proposition: For instance, Thaler (2016) argues at length that the EFH applies to an economy populated by Econs but not Humans. The Human economies are prone to "Ponzi Games", "bubbles" and "excess volatility" that produce substantial and prolonged misalignment between prices and fundamentals (see Shiller 2014). All the social and behavioural traits play a role in the generation and propagation of such bubbles. To begin with, it may be argued that anyone who is in financial markets for short-run gains (as opposed to the long-term gains that the fundamentals will produce, i.e. profits and dividends) suffer from overconfidence, one of the behavioural traits we saw in Chapter 2. This is because, in the short run, the game is zero-sum. Anyone aiming to beat the market and make a gain implicitly (and sometimes explicitly) believes that they are smarter than "the market"; but that cannot be true on average. (Apart from overconfidence, we also have a failure to consider adding-up constraints and the like, as Schelling 2006, has emphasised).[21]

Manifestations of boundedly rational behaviour abound in Shiller (2005). Eg., in Chapter 8, the role of the various psychological anchors for the market is analysed. Quantitative anchors may include previous levels of the market (particularly if experience shows reversals)—but there is also the subjective and fictitious "anchoring effect" of Tversky and Kahneman (i.e. on completely irrelevant "information"). Anchoring may explain (e.g.) why the location of a company's headquarters may explain its performance better than its sector or industry (p. 149). Moral or psychological anchors involve vivid storytelling and (ultimately arbitrary) justification, the representativeness heuristic (looking at seemingly familiar patterns that are not really there), overconfidence, magical thinking (wishful or illogical, but an innermost belief that someone would not repeat to others), or gut feeling/common sense unsupported by facts. "Psychological anchors ... [are situated] ... at the muddy bottom of our consciousness" (Shiller 2005, p. 156). Those anchors are often very fragile (changeable), trivial or barely perceptible. Tuckett (2009) offers an analysis of the effects of psychology on financial markets, informed by a psychoanalytic perspective.

Chapter 9 on "Herd Behavior and Epidemics" discusses the social basis of thinking: Individual errors or biases will likely cancel out if they are random and independent of one another. It is only because there is some coordination that such errors translate into sizeable movements in markets. Coordination may happen because of various mechanisms, including peer pressure, inability to deviate from the group ("identity"—see above), respect to authority ("someone says so") and informational cascades. The latter is illustrated by the two restaurants, the busy and the empty one—people go to the busy which keeps being busy, and no-one goes to the empty one, which continues to be empty. This highlights the fact that such informational cascades may propagate both valuable and fake information.

[21] Associated with "animal spirits" is noise trading (see e.g. Thaler, 2016, p. 231-33). "Noise" refers to signals that are (seemingly) unrelated to the "fundamentals" which (according to the Efficient Markets Hypothesis) drive financial market prices. Noise traders are said to act on sentiment, impulsively or based on rumour and hear-say. As noise is orthogonal to valuable information, noise traders should not make any profits, but that is a contested matter. See also Shiller (2017).

As mentioned, the role of the media is critical in communicating information. The type and quality of communication matters. Uniquely among the rest of nature, humans are able to communicate through language and that allows our species to cooperate and thereby gain an advantage. Communication is most effective by word-of-mouth, when facial expression, tone of voice etc. can convey emotions with vividness. Artificial communication is less effective than direct interpersonal communication, and at best, it approaches it "from below" so to speak. The telephone, invented in 1876 but only broadly used in the 1920s, cannot be an effective medium of communication for news related to financial markets. The TV and the most recent internet are much more effective as they convey images and can emulate human communication better.

But then, however effective, personal communication suffers from ambiguity and subjectivity. Storytelling helps in promoting certain facts or phenomena in the public consciousness (e.g. Shiller 2005, p. 167, discusses the example of Mona Lisa, whose enigmatic smile translates an average painting into a viewing sensation). The transmission of ideas facilitated by the media can focus attention on something. The human mind seems capable of focusing on something that appears the most salient effect, as behavioural psychology has pointed out (see Chapter 2); other facts tend to be forgotten. And the focus equally easily switches, no doubt again helped by media; often people do not remember why. And conflicting ideas can co-exist in the human mind (Shiller 2005, p. 169). All this implies (once again) that the social and the behavioural traits get intertwined; media, social interactions and cognitive limitations produce a complex cocktail.

Stories are closely related to "narratives" which have been receiving some attention recently as determinants of economic behaviour, including the behaviour in financial markets (Shiller 2005, Chapter 5; 2017). Narratives are simple stories or easily expressed explanations that people use to communicate their thoughts about events to others. They often appeal to human emotions, or they have some human interest, so as to become vivid and effective. The concept has received a lot of attention (says Shiller 2017) in several social science and humanities disciplines. However, a precise and widely accepted definition seems elusive. As explanations, they are imperfect "human constructs that are mixtures of fact and emotion and human interest and other extraneous detail that form an impression on the human mind" (Shiller 2017, p. 973). They involve lots of the heuristics that behavioural psychology has highlighted (framing, the affect and representativeness heuristics, the salience effect, groupthink, wishful thinking—see Chapter 2) and they often involve distortions of facts, wishful thinking, even peddling conspiracies or stereotyping of others; all this against a backdrop of a reality complex and fuzzy at best (see above).

In any case, Shiller's (2017) big point is that narratives play a powerful role in propagating business cycles; quite convincingly, he argues that various narratives have played a role in the inter-war years in the US (during the 1920s and the Great Depression) and also during the Great Recession of 2007–9.[22] Shiller argues that the dynamics of narratives (how they emerge or gather strength) can be usefully modelled along the lines of the models of epidemics, and he presents evidence to back this claim. It may be argued (and this is not against Shiller's perspective) that actual, "hard" developments (in economies, policies, resources, geopolitics) drive business cycles and financial market fluctuations in association with the dominant narratives that concern them. A richer macroeconomics (Shiller's argument) would account for the two-way interaction between "hard" developments and narratives.

Against this sense of use of the word "narrative" by Shiller (2017), we have a different use of the "Conviction Narrative Theory" (CNT—e.g. Johnson et al. 2023; Fenton-O'Creevy and Tuckett 2022). Though the differences are to some extent a matter of emphasis, Shiller refers to public narratives, stories that are being communicated; and importantly, they are caricatures (though this is our interpretation, Shiller does not use that word), more distortion than likeness of a situation. In contrast, CNT thinks of narratives in a more benign way, as mental representations to make sense of situations or events by the individual. "[They are] the currency of thought that unifies our sense-making and decision-making faculties [...] arising from the interplay between individual cognition and the social environment, with reasoners adopting a narrative that feels 'right' to explain the available data [...]" (Johnson et al. 2023, p. 1). Finite and imperfect minds, conditions of radical uncertainty with unquantifiable probabilities and fuzzy or ambiguous characteristics and implications, and social embeddedness of beliefs and values, are the building blocks; if so, CNT argues, narratives are important constructs that guide the interpretation of the external signals and ultimately human action. This is because a complex, fuzzy world cannot be

[22] We leave it to the reader to refer to the article for examples, as any venture into those would take us too far.

directly perceived but must be interpreted. The role of emotions is important in guiding both perception and action. Fenton-O'Creevy and Tuckett (2022) consider the role of narratives in association with ambivalence, doubt, and intuition, all relevant to actual decision-making as experience confirms.

Tuckett et al. (2020) investigate the relation of UK monetary policy to narratives, in the dual sense both of how actors understand the current circumstances and of narrative as a communication device by the Bank of England. Collier and Tuckett (2021) investigate the role of narratives in promulgating spatial disequilibria among UK regions (the north–south divide). In doing so, they emphasise two elements of narratives, firstly the fact that they are socially embedded, each affected by every other; and second, the fact that narratives and "hard reality" affect each other. A Nash equilibrium of narratives-reality then arises (which can be modelled along the lines of Fig. 1). Importantly, two equilibria arise, which we can label the optimistic and the pessimistic one. Collier and Tuckett's (2021) plausible point is that this framework can be useful in explaining UK regional disparities, with the north/south stuck at the pessimistic/optimistic equilibrium, respectively.

Tuckett (2011) offers an analysis of how narratives and emotions affect financial markets. It is perhaps too early to say where this exciting new field of "narratives" (in both Shiller's and the CNT sense) may lead; the concept deserves further attention and elaboration. But the general thrust is that it undermines the Efficient Market Hypothesis that maps (hard) fundamentals neatly into outcomes; things are way more complex than that. And they open the door for policy recommendations to stem the wild excesses of "animal spirits" and "irrational exuberance". Akerlof and Shiller (2009), Shiller (2005) and Tuckett (2011) all discuss policy implications, which, in general envisage less "laissez-faire" in financial markets.

7 Concluding Remarks

We have come a long way. This Chapter, as the book in its entirety, argues that there is compelling evidence for the practical relevance of many of the ideas that make up behavioural and sociological economics. Furthermore, we argue that such ideas deserve a natural place in macroeconomics, which has long suffered (in our view) from being based on stylised, but quite unrealistic assumptions. To use Thaler's (2016) amusing as well as informative terminology, macroeconomics is inhabited by Econs, fictitious creatures endowed with full rationality (or in plain English: unlimited cognitive powers) and living pretty much in a social vacuum. For good or bad, though, the world and the macroeconomy are inhabited by agents like us, Humans, with our (considerable but) finite cognitive abilities, and our many biases and heuristics, and inhabiting societies with their multi-faceted interactions and effects. We have surveyed at length the diverse literatures that can contribute useful ideas towards enhancing (macro)economics and imbuing it with more realism. As well as surveying work by others, in the more analytical parts of the book, we also suggest ways in which such advances could be made. We emphasise that such advances could help us understand better a wide range of macroeconomic phenomena, from growth to business cycles to inequality to financial market gyrations; implications for saving, the labour supply and factor shares are no less interesting. Such analyses will have important policy implications, concerning stabilisation policy (monetary and fiscal policy), taxation, pensions, saving plans, the regulation of financial markets, and much more. We have touched on those at various parts of the book.

Despite the growing introduction of behavioural and social elements into macroeconomics, it may be fair to say that such advances have not, on the whole, dislodged the dominant macroeconomic paradigm. The core idea of rational, atomistic behaviour exerts a firm grip on macroeconomics. The key reason seems to be that socio-behavioural macro models remain a rather disparate collection of interesting analyses—in the same way that models of bounded rationality have not converged to a dominant alternative to full rationality. Hence, a sufficiently coherent alternative has yet to emerge, to significantly alter or replace the status quo. This book has surveyed various possibilities. The priority for future research, we would argue, should be to forge a consensus on the key socio-behavioural characteristics of economic action. This direction of travel holds the biggest promise to replace the currently dominant paradigm with its many acknowledged shortcomings.

References

Akerlof, G.A. 2007. The Missing Motivation in Macroeconomics. *American Economic Review* 97 (1): 3–36.

Akerlof, G.A., and R. Kranton. 2000. Economics and Identity. *Quarterly Journal of Economics* 115 (3): 715–753.

Akerlof, G.A., and R. Kranton. 2002. Identity and Schooling: Some Lessons for the Economics of Education. *Journal of Economic Literature* 40 (4): 1167–1201.

Akerlof, G.A., and R. Kranton. 2010. *Identity Economics*. Princeton, N.J.: Princeton University Press.

Akerlof, G.A., and R.J. Shiller. 2009. *Animal Spirits: How Human Psychology Drives the Economy and Why it Matters for Global Capitalism*. Princeton University Press: Princeton.

Akerlof, G.A., and J. Yellen. 1985. A Near-Rational Model of the Business Cycle, with Wage and Price Inertia. *Quarterly Journal of Economics* 100 (Supplement): 823–838.

Andreoni, J. 1990. Impure Altruism and Donations to Public Goods: A Theory of Warm-Glow Giving. *Economic Journal* 100 (401): 464–477.

Apicella, C.L., and J.B. Silk. 2019. The Evolution of Human Cooperation. *Current Biology* 29 (11): R447–R450.

Backhouse, R.E., and P. Fontaine. 2018. Economics and Other Social Sciences: A Historical Perspective, Annals of the Fondazione Luigi Einaudi: An Interdisciplinary Journal of Economics, History and Political. *Science* 52 (2): 7–44.

Baumeister, R.F. 1986. *Identity: Cultural Change and the Struggle for Self*. Oxford: Oxford University Press.

Benabou, R., and J. Tirole. 2011. Identity, Morals, and Taboos: Beliefs as Assets. *Quarterly Journal of Economics* 126 (2): 805–855.

Benjamin, D.J., J.J. Choi, and A.J. Strickland. 2010. Social Identity and Preferences. *American Economic Review* 100 (4): 1913–1928.

Bonomi, G., N. Gennaioli, and G. Tabellini. 2021. Identity, Beliefs, and Political Conflict. *Quarterly Journal of Economics* 136 (4): 2371–2411.

Bowles, S. and H. Gintis. 2003. Origins of human cooperation. In P. Hammerstein (ed.). *Genetic and cultural evolution of cooperation* (pp. 429–444). Cambridge, MA: MIT Press.

Bowles, S. and H. Gintis. 2009. Beyond Enlightened Self-Interest: Social Norms, Other-Regarding Preferences, and Cooperative Behavior, Ch. 3 in S.A. Levin (ed.). *Games, Groups, and the Global Good*. New York: Springer (Series in Game Theory).

Bowles, S., and H. Gintis. 2006. Social Preferences, Homo Economicus, and Zoon Politikon. In *The Oxford Handbook of Contextual Political Analysis*. Edited by Robert Goodin, and Charles Tilly. Oxford: Oxford Academic.

Bowles, S., and H. Gintis. 2002. Social Capital and Community Governance. *Economic Journal* 112 (483): 419–436.

Bramoullé, Y., A. Galeotti, and B.W. Rogers. eds. 2016. *The Oxford Handbook of the Economics of Networks*. Oxford: Oxford Handbooks.

Bratsiotis, G.J., and B. Peng. 2008. Social Interaction and Effort in a Success-at-Work Augmented Utility Model. *The Journal of Socio-Economics* 37 (4): 1309–1318.

Buiter, W.H. 1980. The Macroeconomics of DR Pangloss: A Critical Survey of the New Classical Macroeconomics. *The Economic Journal 90* (357): 34–50.

Charness, G., L. Rigotti, and A. Rustichini. 2007. Individual Behavior and Group Membership. *American Economic Review* 97 (4): 1340–1352.

Chen, R., and Y. Chen. 2011. The Potential of Social Identity for Equilibrium Selection. *American Economic Review* 101 (6): 2562–2589.

Chou, Y.K. 2006. Three Simple Models of Social Capital and Economic Growth. *Journal of Socio-Economics* 35 (5): 889–912.

Christakis, N.A. 2019. *Blueprint: The Evolutionary Origins of a Good Society*. New York: Little, Brown Spark.

Cicala, S., R.G. Fryer, and J.L. Spenkuch. 2018. Self-Selection and Comparative Advantage in Social Interactions. *Journal of the European Economic Association* 16 (4): 983–1020.

Clark, A.E., and A.J. Oswald. 1998. Comparison-Concave Utility and Following Behaviour in Social and Economic Settings. *Journal of Public Economics* 70 (1): 133–155.

Clark, A.E., and C. Senik. 2010. Who Compares to Whom? *The Anatomy of Income Comparisons in Europe, Economic Journal* 120 (544): 573–594.

Coleman, J.S. 1990. *The Foundations of Social Theory*. Cambridge, Mass: Harvard University Press.

Collier, P., and D. Tuckett. 2021. Narratives as a Coordinating Device for Reversing Regional Disequilibrium. *Oxford Review of Economic Policy* 37 (1): 97–112.

Cooper, R., and A. John. 1988. Coordination Failures in Keynesian Models. *Quarterly Journal of Economics* 103 (3): 441–463.

Dasgupta, P. 2003. Social Capital and Economic Performance: Analytics. In *Foundations of Social Capital*, ed. E. Ostrom and T. Ahn, 309–339. Cheltenham: Edward Elgar.

Dasgupta, P., and I. Serageldin. 2000. *Social Capital: A Multifaceted Perspective*. Washington, DC: The World Bank.

De Grauwe, P., and Y. Ji. 2018. Behavioural Economics is Useful Also in Macroeconomics: The Role of Animal Spirits. *Comparative Economic Studies* 60 (2): 203–216.

De Grauwe, P., and Y. Ji. 2019. *Behavioural Macroeconomics: Theory and Policy*. Oxford: Oxford University Press.

DeLong, J.B. 2013. The Strange Case of American Inequality, Project Syndicate blog (31 December 2013). http://www.project-syndicate.org/commentary/j--bradford-delong-asks-why-americans-are-not-clamoring-for-polices-that-would-leave-90--of-them-better-off

Djankov, S., E. Glaeser, R. La Porta, F. Lopez-de-Silanes, and A. Shleifer. 2003. The New Comparative Economics. *Journal of Comparative Economics* 31 (4): 595–619.

Durlauf, S.N. 2002. On the Empirics of Social Capital. *Economic Journal* 112: 459–479.

Durlauf, S.N., and M. Fafchamps. 2005. Social Capital. In *Handbook of Economic Growth*, vol 1, North Holland, Amsterdam

Elster, J. 1989. Social Norms and Economic Theory. *Journal of Economic Perspectives* 3 (4): 99–117.

Falk, A., and M. Knell. 2004. Choosing the Joneses: Endogenous Goals and Reference Standards. *Scandinavian Journal of Economics* 106 (3): 417–435.

Fenton-O'Creevy, M., and D. Tuckett. 2022. Selecting Futures: The Role of Conviction, Narratives, Ambivalence, and Constructive Doubt. *Futures and Foresight Science* 4 (3–4): 1–16.

Fukuyama, F. 1999. Social Capital, Social Capital and Civil Society, Lecture Delivered at the IMF Conference on Second Generation Reforms.

Genicot, G., and D. Ray. 2017. Aspirations and Inequality. *Econometrica* 85 (2): 489–519.

Genicot, G., and D. Ray. 2020. Aspirations and Economic Behavior. *Annual Review of Economics* 12 (1): 715–746.

Gintis, H. 2012. The Evolution of Human Cooperation. *Cliodynamics: THe Journal of Quantitative History and Cultural Evolution* 3 (1): 172–190.

Gintis, H. 2017. A Typology of Human Morality', Ch. 7 in D.S. Wilson and A. Kirman (eds). *Complexity and Evolution: Toward a New Synthesis for Economics*. Cambridge, MA, MIT Press.

Glaeser, E.L., D. Laibson, and B. Sacerdote. 2002. An Economic Approach to Social Capital. *Economic Journal* 112 (483): 437–458.

Glaeser, E.L., B.I. Sacerdote, and J.A. Scheinkman. 2003. The Social Multiplier. *Journal of the European Economic Association* 1 (2–3): 345–530.

Goerke, L., and M. Pannenberg. 2015. Direct Evidence for Income Comparisons and Subjective Well-Being Across Reference Groups. *Economics Letters* 137 (C): 95–101.

Granovetter, M. 1978. Threshold Models of Collective Behavior. *American Journal of Sociology* 83 (6): 1420–1443.

Granovetter, M. 1985. Economic Action and Social Structure: The Problem of Embeddedness. *American Journal of Sociology* 91 (3): 481–510.

Granovetter, M. 2005. The Impact of Social Structure on Economic Outcomes. *Journal of Economic Perspectives* 19 (1): 33–50.

Grossman, G.M., and E. Helpman. 2018. Identity Politics and Trade Policy. *The Review of Economic Studies* 88 (3): 1101–1126.

Grootaert, C., and T. van Bastelear, eds. 2002. *The Role of Social Capital in Development: An Empirical Assessment*. Cambridge: Cambridge University Press.

Guiso, L., P. Sapienza, and L. Zingales. 2004. The Role of Social Capital in Financial Development. *American Economic Review* 94 (3): 526–556.

Guiso, L., P. Sapienza, and L. Zingales. 2012. Is social capital the missing link? In *Handbook of Social Economics*, ed. J. Benhabib, A. Bisin, and M. Jackson, 417–480. Amsterdam: Elsevier.

Hargreaves Heap, S.P., and D.J. Zizzo. 2009. The Value of Groups. *American Economic Review* 99 (1): 295–323.

Helliwell, J.F., L.B. Aknin, H. Shiplett, H. Huang, and S. Wang. 2017. Social Capital and Prosocial Behaviour as Sources of Well-Being, NBER Working Paper, No. 23761

Hoff, K., and P. Pandey. 2006. Discrimination, Social Identity, and Durable Inequalities. *American Economic Review* 96 (2): 206–211.

Hoff, K. and J.E. Stiglitz. 2016. Striving for balance in economics: Towards a theory of the social determination of behavior. *Journal of Economic Behavior & Organization* 126 (Part B): 25–57.

Hornsey, M.J. 2008. Social Identity Theory and Self-categorization Theory: A Historical Review. *Social and Personality Psychology Compass* 2 (1): 204–222.

Itaya, J.-i, and C. Tsoukis. 2022. Social Capital and the Status Externality. *International Journal of Economic Theory* 18 (2): 154–181.

Johnson, S.G.B., A. Bilovich and D. Tuckett. 2023. Conviction Narrative Theory: A theory of choice under radical uncertainty. *The Behavioral and brain sciences* 46: Article e82.

Kahneman, D. 2012. *Thinking, Fast and Slow*. London: Penguin.

Kelly, J. 2021. Sometimes We Need to 'Unbelieve' Our Tribe. *Financial Times*, 25/11/2021

Kirman, A.P. 1992. Whom or What Does the Representative Individual Represent? *The Journal of Economic Perspectives* 6 (2): 117–136.

Kirman, A.P., and A. Serletis. 2016. Ants and Nonoptimal Self-Organization: Lessons For Macroeconomics. *Macroeconomic Dynamics* 20 (2): 601–621.

Knack, S., and Zak, P. 1999. Trust and Growth. Claremont University Working Paper.

Knack, S., and P. Keefer. 1997. Does Social Capital Have an Economic Payoff: A Cross Country Investigation. *Quarterly Journal of Economics* 112 (4): 1251–1288.

Koike, Y. 2015. Thomas Piketty's Japanese Tour, Project Syndicate, 1/3/2015 http://www.project-syndicate.org/commentary/japanese-income-inequality-by-yuriko-koike-2015-03

Krugman, P.A. 1996. *The Self Organizing Economy (The Mitsui Lectures in Economics)*. Hoboken: Wiley-Blackwell.

La Porta, R., F. Lopez-de-Silanes, A. Shleifer, and R. Vishny. 1999. The Quality of Government. *Journal of Law, Economics and Organization* 15 (1): 222–279.

Levitt, S.D., and S.J. Dubner. 2014. *A Rogue Economist Explores the Hidden Side of Everything*. London: Penguin.

Lewin, S.B. 1996. Economics and Psychology: Lessons for Our Own Day from the Early Twentieth Century. *Journal of Economic Literature* 34 (3): 1293–1323.

Mann, M. 2013. *The Sources of Social Power*, Vol. 4: Globalizations, 1945–2011, Cambridge UP.

Manski, C.F. 2000. Economic Analysis of Social Interactions. *Journal of Economic Perspectives* 14 (3): 115–136.

Mechtel, M., F. Hett, and M. Kröll. 2014. Endogenous Social Identity and Group Choice, Beiträge zur Jahrestagung des Vereins für Socialpolitik 2014: Evidenzbasierte Wirtschaftspolitik - Session: Culture and Social Background, No. E16-V2. http://econstor.eu/bitstream/10419/100307/1/VfS_2014_pid_467.pdf

Munz, D.C. 2018. Status Threat, Not Economic Hardship, Explains the 2016 Presidential Vote. *PNAS (Proceedings of the National Academy of Science of the USA)* 115 (19): E4330–E4339.

Pinker, S. 2021. Rationality: What It Is, Why It Seems Scarce, Why It Matters. Toronto, Ontario: Allen Lane Schelling, T.C. (2001–6). *Micromotives and Macrobehavior*. New York: WW Norton & Company.

Pradelski, B.S.R. (2015): The dynamics of social influence, *Oxford Dept. of Economics DP No. 742* , February. http://www.economics.ox.ac.uk/materials/papers/13857/paper742.pdf

Putnam, R.D. 1993. The prosperous community: Social Capital and Public Life. *The American Prospect 4* (13): 35–42.

Putnam, R.D., R. Leonardi and R. Nanetti. 1993. *Making Democracy Work: Civic Traditions in Modern Italy*. Princeton, NJ: Princeton University Press.

Putnam, R.D. 2000. *Bowling Alone: The Collapse and Revival of American Community*. New York: Simon and Schuster.

Rabin, M. 1998. Psychology and Economics, *Journal of Economic Literature 36* (1): 11-46.

Routledge, B.R., and J. von Amsberg. 2002. Social Capital and Growth. *Journal of Monetary Economics* 50 (1): 167–193.

Runciman, W.G. 1966. *(1966): Relative Deprivation and Social Justice*. Berkeley: University of California Press.

Scheinkman, J.A. 2008. Social Interactions. In *The New Palgrave Dictionary of Economics*. Edited by S. Durlauf and L. Blume, 2nd ed. London: Palgrave Macmillan.

Schelling, T.C. 1978. *Micro Motives and Macro Behavior*. New York: W.W. Norton.

Schelling, T.C. 2016. Micromotives and Macrobehavior. New York: WW Norton &Company

Senik, C. 2009. Direct Evidence on Income Comparisons and Their Welfare Effects. *Journal of Economic Behavior and Organization* 72 (1): 408–424.

Shapiro, C., and J.E. Stiglitz. 1984. Equilibrium Unemployment as a Worker Discipline Device. *American Economic Review* 74 (3): 433–444.

Shayo, M. 2009. A Model of Social Identity with an Application to Political Economy: Nation. *Class, and Redistribution, American Political Science Review* 103 (2): 147–174.

Shayo, M. 2020. Social Identity and Economic Policy. *Annual Review of Economics* 12 (1): 355–389.

Shiller, R.J. 2017. Narrative Economics. *American Economic Review* 107 (4): 967–1004.

Shiller, R.J. 2005. *Irrational Exuberance*, 2nd ed. Princeton: Princeton University Press.

Shiller, R.J. 2014. Speculative Asset Prices. *American Economic Review* 104 (6): 1486–1517.

Smith, V.L. 1991. Rational Choice: The Contrast between Economics and Psychology. *Journal of Political Economy* 99 (4): 877–897.

Snower, D., and A. Lindbeck. 2019. Cooperation and Identity, Social Macroeconomics Working Paper sm-wp-2019–06 (June).

Sobel, J. 2005. Interdependent Preferences and Reciprocity. *Journal of Economic Literature* 43 (2): 392–436.

Solow, R. 1995. Trust: The Social Virtues and the Creation of Prosperity (Book Review). *New Republic* 213 (1): 36–40.

Steuer, M. 2003. *The Scientific Study of Society*. Dordrecht: Kluwer Academic Publishers.

Swedberg, R. 1991. Major Traditions of Economic Sociology. *Annual Review of Sociology* 17 (1): 251–276.

Tabellini, G. 2008. The Scope of Cooperation: Values and Incentives. *Quarterly Journal of Economics* 123 (3): 905–950.

Thaler, R.H. 2016. *Misbehaving*. London: Penguin.

Thaler, R.H., and C. Sunstein. 2009. *(Updated Edition): Nudge: Improving Decisions About Health, Wealth, and Happiness*. New York: Penguin.

Tournemaine, F., and C. Tsoukis. 2015b. The Growth-Distribution Nexus in a Mixed Regime of Education with a Status Motive: On the Macroeconomic of the Welfare State. *Economic Modelling* 47 (C): 235–243.

Tournemaine, F., and C. Tsoukis. 2009. Status Jobs, Human Capital and Growth: The Effects of Heterogeneity. *Oxford Economic Papers* 61 (3): 467–493.

Tournemaine, F., and C. Tsoukis. 2010a. Gain Versus Pain From Status and Ambition: Effects on Growth and Inequality. *The Journal of Socio-Economics* 39 (2): 286–294.

Tournemaine, F., and C. Tsoukis. 2015. Public Expenditures, Growth and Distribution in a Mixed Regime of Education with a Status Motive. *Journal of Public Economic Theory* 17 (5): 673–701.

Tsoukis, C. and F. Tournemaine. 2013. Status in a canonical macro model: Status, growth, and inequality. *The Manchester School* 81 (S2): 65–92.

Tsoukis, C. and F. Tournemaine. 2016. *Status, identity and the macroeconomy*. Mimeo: https://www.researchgate.net/publication/311102042_Status_identity_and_the_macroeconomy

Tsoukis, C. 2020. *Theory of Macroeconomic Policy*. Oxford: Oxford University Press.

Tuckett, D., Holmes, D., Pearson, A., and Chaplin, G. 2020. Monetary Policy and the Management of Uncertainty: A Narrative Approach, Bank of England Staff Working Paper No. 870.

Tuckett, D. 2009. Addressing the Psychology of Financial Markets, Economics. *The Open-Access, Open-Assessment E-Journal* 12 (3) (2009–40): 1–22.

Tuckett, D. 2011. *Minding the Markets*. London: Palgrave Macmillan.

Tversky, A., and D. Kahneman. 1991. Loss Aversion in Riskless Choice: A Reference-Dependent Model. *Journal of Economic Literature* 106 (4): 1039–1061.

Varvarigos, D., and G. Xin. 2015. Social Interactions, the Evolution of Trust, and Economic Growth. Working Paper No. 15/05, University of Leicester.

West, S.A. and M. Ghoul. 2019. *Conflict within cooperation. Current Biology* 29 (11): 425–426.

Zafirovski, M. 2016. Toward Economic Sociology/Socio-Economics? *Sociological Components in Contemporary Economics and Implications for Sociology, American Sociologist* 47 (1): 56–58.

References

Abel, A. 1990. Asset Pricing under Habit Formation and Catching up with the Joneses. *American Economic Review* 80 (2): 38–42.

Abel, A.B. 2005. Optimal Taxation when Consumers Have Endogenous Benchmark Levels of Consumption. *Review of Economic Studies* 72 (1): 21–42.

Acemoglu, D., and J.A. Robinson. 2013. *Why Nations Fail: The Origins of Power, Prosperity, and Poverty*. New York: Profile Books.

Aghion, P., and P. Howitt. 1992. A Model of Growth through Creative Destruction. *Econometrica* 60 (2): 323–351.

Aghion, P., U. Akcigit, A. Bergeaud, R. Blundell and D. Hémous (2015): Innovation and Top Income Inequality, NBER working paper No. 21247

Ainslie, G.W. 1992. *Picoeconomics*. Cambridge, UK: Cambridge UP.

Akerlof, G.A. 1976. The Economics of the Caste and of the Rat Race and Other Woeful Tales. *Quarterly Journal of Economics* 90 (4): 599–617.

Akerlof, G.A. 2002. Behavioral Macroeconomics and Macroeconomic Behavior. *American Economic Review* 92 (3): 411–433.

Akerlof, G.A. 2007. The Missing Motivation in Macroeconomics. *American Economic Review* 97 (1): 3–36.

Akerlof, G.A. 2009. How Human Psychology Drives the Economy and Why It Matters. *American Journal of Agricultural Economics* 91 (5): 1175–1175.

Akerlof, G.A. 2020. Sins of Omission and the Practice of Economics. *Journal of Economic Literature* 58 (2): 405–418.

Akerlof, G.A., and J. Yellen. 1985. A Near-Rational Model of the Business Cycle, with Wage and Price Inertia. *Quarterly Journal of Economics* 100 (Supplement): 823–838.

C. Tsoukis et al., *Social and Behavioural Macroeconomics*,
https://doi.org/10.1007/978-3-031-77748-6

Akerlof, G.A., and P. Michaillat. 2018. Persistence of False Paradigms in Low-Power Sciences. *Proceedings of the National Academy of Sciences of the United States of America* 115 (52): 13228–13233.

Akerlof, G.A., and R. Kranton. 2000. Economics and Identity. *Quarterly Journal of Economics* 115 (3): 715–753.

Akerlof, G.A., and R. Kranton. 2002. Identity and Schooling: Some Lessons for the Economics of Education. *Journal of Economic Literature* 40 (4): 1167–1201.

Akerlof, G.A., and R. Kranton. 2010. *Identity Economics*. Princeton, N.J.: Princeton University Press.

Akerlof, G.A., W.T. Dickens, and G. Perry. 2000. *Brookings Papers on Economic Activity* 31 (1): 1–60.

Akerlof, G.A., and R.J. Schiller. 2009. *Animal Spirits: How Human Psychology Drives the Economy and Why it Matters for Global Capitalism*. Princeton University Press: Princeton.

Alesina, A., and D. Rodrik. 1994. Distributive Politics and Economic Growth. *Quarterly Journal of Economics* 109 (2): 465–490.

Allegretto S.A. 2012. The State of Working America's Wealth, 2012: Through Volatility and Turmoil, the Gap Widens, Economic Policy Institute Briefing Paper #292. http://epi.3cdn.net/2a7ccb3e9e618f0bbc_3nm6idnax.pdf

Al-Nowaihi, A., and S. Dhami. 2006. A Note on the Loewenstein-Prelec Theory of Intertemporal Choice. *Mathematical Social Sciences* 52 (1): 99–108.

Al-Nowaihi, A., and S. Dhami. 2008. A Note on the Loewenstein-Prelec Theory of Intertemporal Choice. *Mathematical Social Sciences* 52 (1): 99–108.

Aloi, M., J. Poyago-Theotoki, and F. Tournemaine. 2022. The Geography of Knowledge and R&D-led Growth. *Journal of Economic Geography* 22 (6): 1149–1190.

Alonso-Carrera, J. 2001. More on the Dynamics in the Endogenous Growth Model with Human Capital. *Investigaciones Economicas* 25 (3): 561–583.

Alonso-Carrera, J., J. Caballé, and X. Raurich. 2004. Consumption Externalities, Habit Formation and Equilibrium Efficiency. *Scandinavian Journal of Economics* 106 (2): 231–251.

Alstadsaeter, A. 2011. Measuring the Consumption Value of Higher Education. *Cesifo Economic Studies* 57 (3): 458–479.

Alvarez-Cuadrado, F., G. Monteiro, and S. Turnovsky. 2004. Habit Formation, Catching Up with the Joneses, and Economic Growth. *Journal of Economic Growth* 9 (1): 47–80.

Anderson, D.S. 1988. Values, Religion, Social Class and the Choice of Private School in Australia. *International Journal of Educational Research* 12 (4): 351–373.

Andreoni, J. 1990. Impure Altruism and Donations to Public Goods: A Theory of Warm-Glow Giving. *Economic Journal* 100 (401): 464–477.

Angeletos, G.-M., D. Laibson, A. Repetto, J. Tobacman, and S. Weinberg. 2001. The Hyperbolic Consumption Model: Calibration, Simulation, and Empirical Evaluation. *The Journal of Economic Perspectives* 15 (3): 47–68.

Antoninis, M., and P. Tsakloglou. 2001. Who Benefits from Public Education in Greece? *Evidence and Policy Implications, Education Economics* 9 (2): 197–222.

Apicella, C.L., and J.B. Silk. 2019. The Evolution of Human Cooperation. *Current Biology* 29 (11): R447–R450.

Aronson, E., T.D. Wilson, and R.M. Akert. 1994. *Social Psychology: The Heart and the Mind*. New York: Harper Collins.

Arrow, K.J. 1971. Political and Economic Evaluation of Social Effects and Externalities. In *Frontier of Quantitative Economics*. Edited by M. Intriligator. Amsterdam: North-Holland.

Arrow, K.J. 1991. Economic Theory and the Hypothesis of Rationality. In The New Palgrave: The World of Economics. Edited by J. Eatwell, M. Millgate, and P. Newman. New Yok: Macmillan.

Arrow, K.J. 1962. The Economic Implication of Learning by Doing. *Review of Economic Studies* 29 (3): 55–173.

Artinger, F.M., G. Gigerenzer, and P. Jacobs. 2022. Satisficing: Integrating Two Traditions. *Journal of Economic Literature* 60 (2): 598–635.

Attanasio, O.P., and G. Weber. 2010. Consumption and Saving: Models of Intertemporal Allocation and Their Implications for Public Policy. *Journal of Economic Literature* 48 (3): 693–751.

Axtell, G. S. 1993. *Review of "The Rational and the Social" by J.R. Brown, Noûs*, vol. 27, 2nd ed., 276–278.

Backhouse, R.E., and P. Fontaine. 2010. Introduction: History of Economics as History of Social Science. *History of Political Economy* 42 (1)(Supplement): 1–21.

Backhouse, R.E., and P. Fontaine. 2018. Economics and Other Social Sciences: A Historical Perspective, Annals of the Fondazione Luigi Einaudi: An Interdisciplinary Journal of Economics, History and Political. *Science* 52 (2): 7–44.

Baddeley, M.C. 2016. Behavioural Macroeconomics: Time, Optimism and Animal Spirits. In *Routledge Handbook of Behavioral Economics*, 266–279. Abingdon: Routledge.

Balestrino, A., and C. Ciardi. 2008. Social Norms, Cognitive Dissonance and the Timing of Marriage. *Journal of Socio-Economics* 37 (6): 2399–2410.

Ball, S.J. 1993. Education Markets, Choice and Social Class: The Market as a Class Strategy in the UK and the USA. *British Journal of Sociology of Education* 14 (1): 3–19.

Ball, S.J. 1997. On the Cusp: Parents Choosing Between State and Private Schools in the UK: Action within an Economy of Symbolic Goods. *International Journal of Inclusive Education* 1 (1): 1–17.

Ball, S.J., R. Bower, and S. Gewirtz. 1995. Circuits of Schooling: A Sociological Exploration of Parental Choice of School in Social Class Contexts. *Sociological Review* 43 (1): 52–78.

Banerjee, A.V., and E. Duflo. 2012. *Poor Economics*. London: Penguin Books.

Banerjee, A.V., S. Cole, E. Duflo, and L. Linden. 2007. Remedying Education: Evidence from Two Randomized Experiments in India. *Quarterly Journal of Economics* 122 (3): 1235–1264.

Banks, J., R. Blundell, and J. Smith. 2004. Wealth Portfolios in the United Kingdom and the United States, Chapter 5. In *Perspectives on the Economics of Aging*. Edited by D.A. Wise. Chicago: University of Chicago Press.

Barnett, R.C., J. Bhattacharya, and H. Bunzel. 2010. Choosing to Keep up with the Joneses and Income Inequality. *Economic Theory* 45 (3): 469–496.

Barro, R,J., and X. Sala-i-Martin. 2004. *Economic Growth*. The MIT Press: Cambridge.

Barro, R.J. 1990. Government Spending in a Simple Model of Endogenous Growth. *Journal of Political Economy* 98 (5): S103–S125.

Barro, R.J. 1991. Economic Growth in a Cross Section of Countries. *Quarterly Journal of Economics* 106 (2): 407–443.

Barro, R.J. 1999. Ramsey Meets Laibson in the Neoclassical Growth Model. *Quarterly Journal of Economics* 114 (4): 1125–1152.

Baumeister, R.F. 1986. *Identity: Cultural Change and the Struggle for Self*. Oxford: Oxford University Press.

Becchetti, L., S. Castriota, L. Corrado, and E.G. Ricca. 2013. Beyond the Joneses: Inter-Country Income Comparisons and Happiness. *Journal of Socioeconomics* 45: 187–195.

Becker, G.S. 1991. *A Treatise on the Family*. Cambridge, MA: Harvard University Press.

Becker, G.S., K.M. Murphy, and R. Tamura. 1990. Human Capital, Fertility, and Economic Growth. *Journal of Political Economy* 98 (5): S12–S37.

Benabou, R. 1996. Heterogeneity, Stratification, and Growth: Macroeconomic Implications of Community Structure and School Finance. *American Economic Review* 86 (3): 584–609.

Benabou, R., and J. Tirole. 2003. Intrinsic and Extrinsic Motivation. *Review of Economic Studies* 70 (3): 489–520.

Benabou, R., and J. Tirole. 2011. Identity, Morals, and Taboos: Beliefs as Assets. *Quarterly Journal of Economics* 126 (2): 805–855.

Benhabib, J.A., and A. Schotter. Bisin. 2010. Present-Bias, Quasi-Hyperbolic Discounting, and Fixed Costs. *Games and Economic Behavior* 69 (2): 205–223.

Benjamin, D.J., J.J. Choi, and A.J. Strickland. 2010. Social Identity and Preferences. *American Economic Review* 100 (4): 1913–1928.

Bertola, G. 1993. Factor Shares and Savings in Endogenous Growth. *American Economic Review* 83 (5): 1184–1198.

Birdsall, N., D. Ross, and R. Sabot. 1995. Inequality and Growth Reconsidered: Lessons from East Asia. *The World Bank Economic Review* 9 (3): 477–508.

Black, S.E., and C. Juhn. 2000. The Rise of Female Professionals: Are Women Responding to Skill Demand? *American Economic Review* 90 (2): 450–455.

Blanchard, O.J. 2017. Do DSGE Models Have a Future? Chapter 9. In *DSGE Models in the Conduct of Policy: Use as intended*. Edited by R. Gürkaynak, and C. Tille. Paris and London: CEPR Press.

Blankenau, W.F., and N.B. Simpson. 2004. Public Education Expenditures and Growth. *Journal of Development Economics* 73 (2): 583–605.

Blaug, M. 1992. *The Methodology of Economics, or How Economists Explain*, 2nd ed. Cambridge: Cambridge University Press.

Bloom, D.E., and J.D. Sachs. 1998. Geography. *Demography, and Economic Growth in Africa* 1998 (2): 207–295.

Blume, L., and D. Easley. 2007. *Rationality, New Palgrave Dictionary of Economics*. Edited by S. Durlauf, and L. Blume, 2nd ed.

Bonomi, G., N. Gennaioli, and G. Tabellini. 2021. Identity, Beliefs, and Political Conflict. *Quarterly Journal of Economics* 136 (4): 2371–2411.

Boonprakaikawe, J., and F. Tournemaine. 2006. Production and Consumption of Education in a R&D-Based Growth Model. *Scottish Journal of Political Economy* 53 (5): 565–585.

Boserup, E. 1965. *The Conditions of Agricultural Growth: The Economics of Agrarian Change under Population Pressure*. London: George Allen and Unwin Ltd.

Boskin, M.J., and E. Sheshinki. 1978. Optimal Redistributive Taxation when Individual Welfare Depends upon Relative Income. *Quarterly Journal of Economics* 92 (4): 589–601.

Bowles, S., and T. Park. 2005. Emulation, Inequality, and Work Hours: Was Thorsten Veblen Right? *Economic Journal* 115 (507): 397–412.

Bowles, S., and H. Gintis. 2000. Walrasian Economics in Retrospect. *Quarterly Journal of Economics* 115 (4): 1411–1439.

Bowles, S., and H. Gintis. 2002. Social Capital and Community Governance. *Economic Journal* 112 (483): 419–436.

Bowles, S. and H. Gintis. 2003. Origins of human cooperation. In P. Hammerstein (ed.). *Genetic and cultural evolution of cooperation* (pp. 429–444). Cambridge, MA: MIT Press.

Bowles, S., and H. Gintis. 2006. Social Preferences, Homo Economicus, and Zoon Politikon'. In *The Oxford Handbook of Contextual Political Analysis*. Edited by Robert Goodin, and Charles Tilly. Oxford: Oxford Academic.

Bowles, S. and H. Gintis. 2009. Beyond Enlightened Self-Interest: Social Norms, Other-Regarding Preferences, and Cooperative Behavior, Ch. 3 in S.A. Levin (ed.). *Games, Groups, and the Global Good*. New York: Springer (Series in Game Theory).

Bowles, S., and S. Polania-Reyes. 2012. Economic Incentives and Social Preferences: Substitutes or Complements? *Journal of Economic Literature* 50 (2): 368–425.

Bowles, S., and W. Carlin. 2020. What Students Learn in Economics 101: Time for a Change. *Journal of Economic Literature* 58 (1): 176–214.

Bramoullé, Y., A. Galeotti, and B.W. Rogers. eds. 2016. *The Oxford Handbook of the Economics of Networks*. Oxford: Oxford Handbooks.

Bratsiotis, G.J., and B. Peng. 2008. Social Interaction and Effort in a Success-at-Work Augmented Utility Model. *The Journal of Socio-Economics* 37 (4): 1309–1318.

Buiter, W.H. 1980. The Macroeconomics of DR Pangloss: A Critical Survey of the New Classical Macroeconomics. *The Economic Journal 90* (357): 34–50.

Caballero, R.J. 2010. Macroeconomics after the Crisis: Time to Deal with the Pretense-of-Knowledge Syndrome. *Journal of Economic Perspectives* 24 (4): 85–102.

Cabo, F., G. Martín-Herrán, and M.P. Martínez-García. 2015. Non-constant Discounting and AK-Type Growth Models. *Economics Letters* 131 (C): 54–58.

Cabo, F., G. Martín-Herrán, and M.P. Martínez-García. 2016. Unbounded Growth in the Neoclassical Growth Model with Non-constant Discounting. *Mathematical Social Sciences* 84 (C): 93–104.

Cagetti, M., and M. De Nardi. 2008. Wealth Inequality: Data and Models. *Macroeconomic Dynamics* 12 (52): 285–313.

Caldwell, B.J. 1982. *Beyond Positivism: Economic Methodology in the Twentieth Century*. London: Routledge.

Caliendo, F.N., and D. Aadland. 2007. Short-Term Planning and the Life-Cycle Consumption Puzzle. *Journal of Economic Dynamics and Control* 31 (4): 1392–1415.

Carroll, C.D. 2000. Why Do the Rich Save So Much? In *Does Atlas shrug? The Economic Consequences of Taxing the Rich*. Edited by J.B. Slemrod. Cambridge: Harvard University Press.

Carroll, C.D., J. Overland, and D. Weil. 1997. Comparison Utility in a Growth Model. *Journal of Economic Growth* 2 (4): 339–367.

Carroll, C.D., J. Overland, and D. Weil. 2000. Saving and Growth with Habit Formation. *American Economic Review* 3 (90): 341–355.

Caselli, F., and J. Ventura. 2000. A Representative Consumer Theory of Distribution. *American Economic Review* 90 (4): 909–926.

Cerra, V., R. Lama, and N. Loayza. 2021. Links Between Growth, Inequality, and Poverty: A Survey, International Monetary Fund, Working Paper No. 2021/068.

Chakraborty, S. 2004. Endogenous Lifetime and Economic Growth. *Journal of Economic Theory* 116 (1): 119–137.

Charness, G., and M. Rabin. 1999. Understanding Social Preferences with Simple Tests. *Quarterly Journal of Economics* 117 (3): 817–869.

Charness, G., and M. Sutter. 2012. Groups Make Better Self-Interested Decisions. *Journal of Economic Perspectives* 26 (3): 157–176.

Charness, G., L. Rigotti, and A. Rustichini. 2007. Individual Behavior and Group Membership. *American Economic Review* 97 (4): 1340–1352.

Chatterjee, S. 1994. Transitional Dynamics and the Distribution of Wealth in a Neoclassical Growth Model. *Journal of Public Economics* 54 (1): 97–119.

Chen, H.J. 2005. Educational Systems, Growth and Income Distribution: A Quantitative Study. *Journal of Development Economics* 76 (2): 325–353.

Chen, R., and Y. Chen. 2011. The Potential of Social Identity for Equilibrium Selection. *American Economic Review* 101 (6): 2562–2589.

Chou, Y.K. 2006. Three Simple Models of Social Capital and Economic Growth. *Journal of Socio-Economics* 35 (5): 889–912.

Choudhary, A., P. Levine, P. McAdam, and P. Welz. 2007. *Relative Preferences, Happiness and Corrective Taxation*. Mimeo: University of Surrey.

Choudhary, M.A., and P. Levine. 2006. The 24/7 Society and Multiple Habits, Department of Economics, University of Surrey, Discussion Paper no. 0506.

Christakis, N.A. 2019. *Blueprint: The Evolutionary Origins of a Good Society*. New York: Little, Brown Spark.

Cicala, S., R.G. Fryer, and J.L. Spenkuch. 2018. Self-Selection and Comparative Advantage in Social Interactions. *Journal of the European Economic Association* 16 (4): 983–1020.

Clark, A.E., and A.J. Oswald. 1996. Satisfaction and Comparison Income. *Journal of Public Economics* 3 (61): 359–381.

Clark, A.E., and A.J. Oswald. 1998. Comparison-Concave Utility and Following Behaviour in Social and Economic Settings. *Journal of Public Economics* 70 (1): 133–155.

Clark, A.E., and C. Senik. 2010. Who Compares to Whom? *The Anatomy of Income Comparisons in Europe, Economic Journal* 120 (544): 573–594.

Clark, A.E., P. Frijters, and M.A. Shields. 2008. Relative Income, Happiness, and Utility: An Explanation for the Easterlin Paradox and Other Puzzles. *Journal of Economic Literature* 46 (1): 95–144.

Colander, D., ed. 2006. *Post Walrasian Macroeconomics: Beyond the Dynamic Stochastic General Equilibrium Model*. Cambridge: Cambridge University Press.

Colander, D. 2005. The Making of an Economist Redux. *Journal of Economic Perspectives* 19 (1): 175–198.

Colander, D. 2016. Liberal Arts Macro Economists are Becoming an Endangered Species. *Eastern Economic Journal* 42 (1): 1–6.

Colander, D., H. Foellmer, A. Haas, M. Goldberg, K. Juselius, A. Kirman, T. Lux, and B. Sloth. 2014. The Financial Crisis and the Systemic Failure of Academic Economics, Chapter 13. In *The Economics of Economists Institutional Setting, Individual Incentives, and Future Prospects*, 344–360. Cambridge: Cambridge University Press.

Coleman, J.S. 1990. *The Foundations of Social Theory*. Cambridge, Mass: Harvard University Press.

Collier, P., and D. Tuckett. 2021. Narratives as a Coordinating Device for Reversing Regional Disequilibrium. *Oxford Review of Economic Policy* 37 (1): 97–112.

Commendatore, P., Kubin, S. Bougheas, A. Kirman, M. Kopel, and G.I. Bischi. eds. 2018. *The Economy as a Complex Spatial System, Macro, Meso and Micro Perspectives*. Springer: Berlin.

Conlisk, J. 1996. Why Bounded Rationality? *Journal of Economic Literature* 34 (2): 669–700.

Cooper, R., and A. John. 1988. Coordination Failures in Keynesian Models. *Quarterly Journal of Economics* 103 (3): 441–463.

Corneo, G., and O. Jeanne. 1997. On Relative Wealth Effects and the Optimality of Growth. *Economics Letters* 54 (1): 87–92.

Corneo, G., and O. Jeanne. 1998. Social Organization, Status and Saving Behaviour. *Journal of Public Economics* 70 (1): 37–52.

Corneo, G., and O. Jeanne. 1999. Pecuniary Emulation, Inequality and Growth. *European Economic Review* 43 (9): 1665–1678.

Corneo, G., and O. Jeanne. 2001. Status, the Distribution of Wealth, and Growth. *Scandinavian Journal of Economics* 103 (2): 283–293.

Cowen, T. 2017. *The Complacent Class: The Self-Defeating Quest for the American Dream*. New York City: St Martin's Press.

Crenshaw, E., A. Ameen, and M. Christenson. 1997. Population Dynamics and Economic Development: Age Specific Population Growth and Economic Growth in Developing Countries, 1965 to 1990. *American Sociological Review* 62 (6): 974–984.

Croix (de la), D., and M. Doepke. 2004. Public versus private education when differential fertility matters. *Journal of Development Economics* 73 (2): 607–629.

Dai, D., W. Gao, and G. Tian. 2020. Relativity, Mobility, and Optimal Nonlinear Income Taxation in an Open Economy. *Journal of Economic Behavior and Organization* 172: 57–82.

Dang, H.A., and F.H. Rogers. 2008. The Growing Phenomenon of Private Tutoring: Does It Deepen Human Capital, Widen Inequalities, or Waste Resources? *The World Bank Research Observer* 23 (2): 161–200.

Dang, H.A. 2007. The Determinants and Impact of Private Tutoring Classes in Vietnam. *Economics of Education Review* 26 (6): 683–698.

Dasgupta, P. 2003. Social Capital and Economic Performance: Analytics. In *Foundations of Social Capital*, ed. E. Ostrom and T. Ahn, 309–339. Cheltenham: Edward Elgar.

Dasgupta, P., and I. Serageldin. 2000. *Social Capital: A Multifaceted Perspective.* Washington, DC: The World Bank.

Davies, S. 2004. School Choice by Default? Understanding the Demand for Private Tutoring in Canada. *American Journal of Education* 110 (3): 233–255.

De Grauwe, P., and Y. Ji. 2018. Behavioural Economics is Useful Also in Macroeconomics: The Role of Animal Spirits. *Comparative Economic Studies* 60 (2): 203–216.

De Grauwe, P., and Y. Ji. 2019. *Behavioural Macroeconomics: Theory and Policy.* Oxford: Oxford University Press.

De Nardi, M. 2004. Wealth Inequality and Intergenerational Links. *Review of Economic Studies* 71 (3): 743–768.

DellaVigna, S. 2009. Psychology and Economics: Evidence from the Field. *Journal of Economic Literature* 47 (2): 315–372.

DellaVigna, S., and U. Malmendier. 2006. Paying not to Go to the Gym. *American Economic Review* 96 (3): 694–719.

DeLong, J.B. 2013. The Strange Case of American Inequality, Project Syndicate blog (31 December 2013). http://www.project-syndicate.org/commentary/j--bradford-delong-asks-why-americans-are-not-clamoring-for-polices-that-would-leave-90--of-them-better-off

Dhami, S. 2016. *The Foundations of Behavioral Economic Analysis*. Oxford: Oxford University Press.

Díaz-Giménez, J., V. Quadrini, and J.-V. Ríos-Rull. 1997. Dimensions of Inequality: Facts on the U.S. Distributions of Earnings, Income, and Wealth. *Quarterly Review, Federal Reserve Bank of Minneapolis* 21: 3–21.

Diener, E., and F. Fujita. 1997. Social comparison and subjective well-being. In *Health, Coping and Well-being: Perspectives from Social Comparison Theory.* Edited by B.P. Buunk, and R. Gibbons. Lawrence Erlbaum Associates: Mahwah.

Djankov, S., E. Glaeser, R. La Porta, F. Lopez-de-Silanes, and A. Shleifer. 2003. The New Comparative Economics. *Journal of Comparative Economics* 31 (4): 595–619.

Dodge, D.A., and D.A.A. Stager. 1972. Economic Returns to Graduate Study in Science, Engineering and Business. *Canadian Journal of Economics* 5 (2): 182–198.

Doepke, M. 2004. Accounting for Fertility Decline During the Transition to Growth. *Journal of Economic Growth* 9 (3): 347–383.

Dolado, J., F. Felgueroso, and J.F. Jimeno. 2001. Female employment and occupational changes in the 1990s: How is the EU performing relative to the US? *European Economic Review* 45 (4–6): 875–879.

Dold, M., and P. Lewis. 2022. F.A. Hayek on the Political Economy of Endogenous Preferences: An Historical Overview and Contemporary Assessment. *Journal of Economic Behaviour and Organization* 196 (3): 104–119.

D'Orlando, F., and E. Sanfilippo. 2010. Behavioral foundations for the Keynesian Consumption Function. *Journal of Economic Psychology* 31 (6): 1035–1046.

Drouhin, N. 2009. Hyperbolic Discounting May Be Time Consistent. *Economics Bulletin* 29 (4): 2549–2555.

Duesenberry, J.S. 1949. *Income, Saving and the Theory of Consumer Behaviour*. Cambridge: Harvard University Press.

Durlauf, S.N. 2002. On the Empirics of Social Capital. *Economic Journal* 112: 459–479.

Durlauf, S.N., and M. Fafchamps. 2005. Social Capital. In *Handbook of Economic Growth*, vol. 1. North Holland, Amsterdam.

Durlauf, S.N., and Y.M. Ioannides. 2010. Social Interactions. *Annual Review of Economics* 2 (1): 451–478.

Dynan, K.E., J. Skinner, and S.P. Zeldes. 2004. Do the Rich Save More? *Journal of Political Economy* 112 (2): 397–444.

Easterlin, R.A. 1974. Does Economic Growth Improve the Human Lot? Some Empirical Evidence. In *Nations and Households in Economic Growth: Essays in Honor of Moses Abramowitz*. Edited by P.A. David, and M.W. Reder. New York: Academic Press.

Easterlin, R.A. 2001. Income and Happiness: Towards a Unified Theory. *Economic Journal* 111 (473): 465–484.

Ehrlich, I., and F. Lui. 1997. The Problem of Population and Growth: A Review of the Literature from Malthus to Contemporary Models of Endogenous Population and Endogenous Growth. *Journal of Economic Dynamics and Control* 21 (1): 205–242.

Elster, J. 1989. Social Norms and Economic Theory. *Journal of Economic Perspectives* 3 (4): 99–117.

Epper, T., E. Fehr, H. Fehr-Duda, C. Thustrup Kreiner, D. Dreyer Lassen, S. Leth-Petersen, and G. Nytoft Rasmussen. 2020. Time Discounting and Wealth Inequality. *American Economic Review* 110 (4): 1177–1205.

Ermini, L. 1991. Hierarchical Decomposition in Economic Analysis. In *Behavioral Decision Making: Handbook of Behavioral Economics,* vol. 2B, 547–62. Edited by R. Frantz, H. Singh, and J. Gerber. Greenwich, CT: JAI Press.

European Commission. 2011. The Challenge of Shadow Education: Private Tutoring and Its Implications for Policy Makers in the European Union, ISBN: 978-92-79-19986-8.

Falk, A., and M. Knell. 2004. Choosing the Joneses: Endogenous Goals and Reference Standards. *Scandinavian Journal of Economics* 106 (3): 417–435.

Farzin, Y.H., and R. Wendner. 2014. The Time Path of the Saving Rate: Hyperbolic Discounting and Short-Term Planning, FEEM WP No. 063.2014.

Fehr, E., and K.M. Schmidt. 1999. The Theory of Fairness, Competition, and Cooperation. *Quarterly Journal of Economics* 114 (3): 817–868.

Fenton-O'Creevy, M., and D. Tuckett. 2022. Selecting Futures: The Role of Conviction, Narratives, Ambivalence, and Constructive Doubt. *Futures and Foresight Science* 4 (3–4): 1–16.

Ferrer-i-Carbonnel, A. 2005. Income and Well-Being: An Empirical Analysis of the Comparison Income Effect. *Journal of Public Economics* 89 (5–6): 997–1019.

Fershtman, C., K.M. Murphy, and Y. Weiss. 1996. Social Status, Education and Growth. *Journal of Political Economy* 104 (1): 108–132.

Fershtman, C., K.M. Murphy, and Y. Weiss. 1993. Social Status, Culture and Economic Performance. *Economic Journal* 103 (419): 946–959.

Festinger, L. 1954. A Theory of Social Comparison Processes. *Human Relations* 7 (2): 117–140.

Festré, A. 2010. Incentives and Social Norms: A Motivation-Based Economic Analysis of Social Norms. *Journal of Economic Surveys* 24 (3): 511–538.

Findley, T.S., and F.N. Caliendo. 2014. Interacting Mechanisms of Time Inconsistency. *Journal of Economic Psychology* 41 (C): 68–76.

Fisher, W.H., and F.X. Hof. 2000. Relative Consumption, Economic Growth and Taxation. *Journal of Economics* 73 (3): 241–262.

Fisher, W.H., and F.X. Hof. 2005. Status Seeking in the Small Open Economy. *Journal of Macroeconomics* 27 (2): 209–232.

Flache, A., and J. Dijkstra. 2015. Rationality in Society. In *International Encyclopedia of the Social and Behavioral Sciences*, 2nd ed., ed. J.D. Wright, 907–912. Amsterdam: Elsevier.

Foley, D.K. 2004. Rationality and Ideology. *Social Research* 71 (2): 329–342.

Francis, J.L. 2009. Wealth and the Capitalist Spirit. *Journal of Macroeconomics* 31 (3): 394–408.

Frank, R. 1985. The Demand for Non-observable and other Non-positional Goods. *American Economic Review* 75 (1): 101–116.

Frankel, M. 1962. The Production Function in Allocation and Growth: A Synthesis. *American Economic Review* 52 (5): 995–1022.

Frederick, S., G. Loewenstein, and T. O'Donoghue. 2002. Time Discounting and Time Preference: A Critical Review. *Journal of Economic Literature* 40 (2): 351–401.

Frerichs, S. 2019. Bounded Sociality: Behavioural Economists' Truncated Understanding of the Social and Its Implications for Politics. *Journal of Economic Methodology* 26 (3): 243–258.

Frey, B.S., and A. Stutzer. 2002. What Can Economists Learn from Happiness Research? *Journal of Economic Literature* 40 (2): 402–435.

Frey, B.S., and R. Jegen. 2001. Motivational Interactions: Effects on Behaviour. *Annales D'économie Et De Statistique* 63 (64): 131–153.

Friedman, M. 1953. *The Methodology of Positive Economics, in His: Introduction: Essays In Positive Economics*, 3–16. Chicago: University of Chicago Press.

Fuchs, D., M. Sahakian, T. Gumbert, A. Di Giulio, M. Maniates, S. Lorek, and A. Graf. 2021. *Consumption Corridors: Living a Good Life within Sustainable Limits.* Routledge; Open Access.

Fuhrer, J.C. 2000. Habit Formation in Consumption and Its Implications for Monetary-Policy Models. *American Economic Review* 90 (3): 367–390.

Fukuyama, F. 1999. Social Capital, Social Capital and Civil Society, Lecture Delivered at the IMF Conference on Second Generation Reforms.

Futagami, K., and A. Shibata. 1998. Keeping One Step Ahead of the Joneses: Status, the Distribution of Wealth and Long Run Growth. *Journal of Economic Behavior and Organization* 36 (1): 109–126.

Gabaix, X. 2020. A Behavioral New Keynesian Model. *American Economic Review* 110 (8): 2271–2327.

Galbraith, J.K. 1958. *The Affluent Society.* Boston: Houghton Mifflin.

Gali, J. 1994. Keeping up with the Joneses: Consumption Externalities, Portfolio Choice, and Asset Prices. *Journal of Money, Credit and Banking* 26 (1): 1–8.

Gali, J. 2015. *Monetary Policy, Inflation, and the Business Cycle: An Introduction to the New Keynesian Framework and Its Applications*, 2nd ed. Princeton: Princeton University Press.

Galor, O., and D.N. Weil. 1999. From Malthusian Stagnation to Modern Growth. *American Economic Review* 89 (2): 150–154.

Galor, O., and Ö. Özak. 2016. The Agricultural Origins of Time Preference. *American Economic Review* 106 (10): 3064–3103.

García-Peñalosa, C., and S.J. Turnovsky. 2006. Growth and Income Inequality: A Canonical Model. *Economic Theory* 28 (1): 25–49.

García-Peñalosa, C., and S.J. Turnovsky. 2008. Distributional Dynamics in a Neoclassical Growth Model: The Role of Elastic Labor Supply. *Journal of Economic Dynamics and Control* 32 (5): 1399–1431.

Garcia-Penalosa, C., E. Caroli, and P. Aghion. 1999. Inequality and Economic Growth: The Perspective of the New Growth Theories. *Journal of Economic Literature* 37 (4): 1615–1660.

Gellner, E. 1992. *Reason and Culture*. Blackwell.

Genicot, G., and D. Ray. 2017. Aspirations and Inequality. *Econometrica* 85 (2): 489–519.

Genicot, G., and D. Ray. 2020. Aspirations and Economic Behavior. *Annual Review of Economics* 12 (1): 715–746.

Georgarakos, D., M. Haliassos, and G. Pasini. 2013. Household Debt and Social Interactions, SAFE Working Paper Series, No. 1.

Ghosh, S., and R. Wendner. 2017. Positional Preferences and Efficient Capital Accumulation when Households Exhibit a Preference for Wealth. *Oxford Economic Papers* 70 (1): 114–140.

Gigerenzer, G. 2010. Moral Satisficing: Rethinking Moral Behavior as Bounded Rationality. *Topics in Cognitive Science* 2 (3): 528–554.

Gigerenzer, G. 2021. Axiomatic Rationality and Ecological Rationality. *Synthese* 198 (4): 3547–3564.

Gigerenzer, G., and H. Brighton. 2009. Homo Heuristicus: Why Biased Minds Make Better Inferences. *Topics in Cognitive Science* 1 (1): 107–143.

Gintis, H. 2012. The Evolution of Human Cooperation. *Cliodynamics: THe Journal of Quantitative History and Cultural Evolution* 3 (1): 172–190.

Gintis, H. 2017. A Typology of Human Morality', Ch. 7 in D.S. Wilson and A. Kirman (eds). *Complexity and Evolution: Toward a New Synthesis for Economics*. Cambridge, MA, MIT Press.

Glaeser, E.L., D. Laibson, and B. Sacerdote. 2002. An Economic Approach to Social Capital. *Economic Journal* 112 (483): 437–458.

Glaeser, E.L., B.I. Sacerdote, and J.A. Scheinkman. 2003. The Social Multiplier. *Journal of the European Economic Association* 1 (2–3): 345–353.

Glewwe, P., and M. Kremer. 2006. School, Teachers, and Education Outcomes in Developing Countries. In *Handbook of the Economics of Education*. Edited by Eric A. Hanushek, and Finis Welch. Amsterdam: North-Holland.

Glomm, G., and B. Ravikumar. 1992. Public Versus Private Investment in Human Capital: Endogenous Growth and Income Inequality. *Journal of Political Economy* 100 (4): 818–834.

Goerke, L., and M. Pannenberg. 2015. Direct Evidence for Income Comparisons and Subjective Well-Being Across Reference Groups. *Economics Letters* 137 (C): 95–101.

Gomes, P. 2021. *Friday is the New Saturday: How a Four-Day Working Week Will Save the Economy*. London: Flint.

Gomez, M.A. 2008. Convergence Speed in the AK Endogenous Growth Model with Habit Formation. *Economics Letters* 100 (1): 16–21.

Gowdy, J., J.B. Rosser, and L. Roy. 2013. The Evolution of Hyperbolic Discounting: Implications for Truly Social Valuation of the Future. *Journal of Economic Behavior and Organization* 90 (Supplement): S94–S104.

Graham, L., and D.J. Snower. 2010. Hyperbolic Discounting and the Phillips Curve. *Journal of Money, Credit and Banking* 40 (2–3): 427–448.

Granovetter, M. 1978. Threshold Models of Collective Behavior. *American Journal of Sociology* 83 (6): 1420–1443.

Granovetter, M. 1985. Economic Action and Social Structure: The Problem of Embeddedness. *American Journal of Sociology* 91 (3): 481–510.

Granovetter, M. 2005. The Impact of Social Structure on Economic Outcomes. *Journal of Economic Perspectives* 19 (1): 33–50.

Grootaert, C., and T. van Bastelear, eds. 2002. *The Role of Social Capital in Development: An Empirical Assessment*. Cambridge: Cambridge University Press.

Grossman, G.M., and E. Helpman. 1991. Quality Ladders in the Theory of Growth. *Review of Economic Studies* 58 (1): 557–586.

Grossman, G.M., and E. Helpman. 2018. Identity Politics and Trade Policy. *The Review of Economic Studies* 88 (3): 1101–1126.

Guiso, L., P. Sapienza, and L. Zingales. 2004. The Role of Social Capital in Financial Development. *American Economic Review* 94 (3): 526–556.

Guiso, L., P. Sapienza, and L. Zingales. 2012. Is social capital the missing link? In *Handbook of Social Economics*, ed. J. Benhabib, A. Bisin, and M. Jackson, 417–480. Amsterdam: Elsevier.

Gullason, E.T. 1989. The Consumption Value of Schooling. An Empirical Estimate of One Aspect. *Journal of Human Resources* 24 (2): 287–298.

Gürkaynak, R., and C. Tille. eds. 2017. *DSGE Models in the Conduct of Policy: Use as Intended*. CEPR Press: Paris & London.

Guvenen, F. 2016. *Quantitative Economics With Heterogeneity: An A-to-Z Guidebook*. Princeton: Princeton University Press.

Hall, R.E. 1988. Intertemporal Substitution in Consumption. *Journal of Political Economy* 96 (2): 339–357.

Hamermesh, D.S., and J.B. Slemrod. 2008. The Economics of Workaholism: We Should Not Have Worked on This Paper. *The B.E. Journal of Economic Analysis and Policy* 8 (1): 1793–1793.

Hammond, P.J. 1997. Rationality in Economics. *Rivista Internazionale di Scienze Sociali* 105 (3): 247–288.

Hardin, R. 2015. Rational Choice Explanation: Philosophical Aspects. In *The International Encyclopedia of the Social and Behavioral Sciences*. Edited by J.D. Wright, 2nd ed., 896–900. Amsterdam: Elsevier.

Hargreaves Heap, S.P., and D.J. Zizzo. 2009. The Value of Groups. *American Economic Review* 99 (1): 295–323.

Harris, C., and D. Laibson. 2001. Dynamic Choices of Hyperbolic Consumers. *Econometrica* 69 (4): 935–957.

Haveman, R.H., and B.L. Wolfe. 1984. Schooling and Economic Well-Being: The Role of Nonmarket Effects. *The Journal of Human Resources* 9 (3): 377–407.

He, Q., Y. Luo, J. Nie, and H.-F. Zou. 2023. Money, Growth, and Welfare in a Schumpeterian Model with the Spirit of Capitalism. *Review of Economic Dynamics* 47: 346–372.

Heathcote, J., K. Storesletten, and G.L. Violante. 2009. Quantitative Macroeconomics with Heterogeneous Households. *Annual Review of Economics* 1: 319–354.

Helliwell, J.F., L.B. Aknin, H. Shiplett, H. Huang, and S. Wang. 2017. Social Capital and Prosocial Behaviour as Sources of Well-Being, NBER Working Paper, No. 23761.

Hendricks, L. 2007. How Important is Discount Rate Heterogeneity for Wealth Inequality? *Journal of Economic Dynamics and Control* 3 (9): 3042–3068.

Hiraguchi, R. 2011. A Two-Sector Endogenous Growth Model with Habit Formation. *Journal of Economic Dynamics and Control* 35 (4): 430–441.

Hirsch, F. 1976. *Social Limits to Growth*. Cambridge: Harvard University Press.

Hirshleifer, D. 2020. Presidential Address: Social Transmission Bias in Economics and Finance. *The Journal of Finance* 75 (4): 1779–1831.

Hoff, K., and P. Pandey. 2006. Discrimination, Social Identity, and Durable Inequalities. *American Economic Review* 96 (2): 206–211.

Hoff, K. and J.E Stiglitz. 2016. Striving for balance in economics: Towards a theory of the social determination of behavior. *Journal of Economic Behavior & Organization* 126 (Part B): 25–57.

Hoover, K.D. 2016. The Crisis in Economic Theory: A Review Essay. *Journal of Economic Literature* 54 (4): 1350–1361.

Hoover, K.D., and A. Svorenčík. 2023. Who Runs the AEA? *Journal of Economic Literature* 61 (3): 1127–1171.

Hopkins, E., and T. Kornienko. 2004. Running to Keep in the Same Place: Consumer Choice as a Game of Status. *American Economic Review* 94 (4): 1085–1107.

Hornsey, M.J. 2008. Social Identity Theory and Self-categorization Theory: A Historical Review. *Social and Personality Psychology Compass* 2 (1): 204–222.

Ikeda, S., M.-I. Kang, and F. Ohtake. 2010. Hyperbolic Discounting, the Sign Effect, and the Body Mass Index. *Journal of Health Economics* 29 (2): 268–284.

Itaya, J.-i, and C. Tsoukis. 2022. Social Capital and the Status Externality. *International Journal of Economic Theory* 18 (2): 154–181.

Johnson, S.G.B., A. Bilovich, and D. Tuckett. 2023. Conviction Narrative Theory: A Theory of Choice Under Radical Uncertainty. *The Behavioral and Brain Sciences* 46 (Article e82).

Jones, C.I. 1995a. Time Series Tests of Endogenous Growth Models. *Quarterly Journal of Economics* 110 (2): 495–525.

Jones, C.I. 1995b. R&D-Based Models of Economic Growth. *Journal of Political Economy* 105 (4): 759–784.

Jones, C.I. 2003. Population and Ideas: A Theory of Endogenous Growth. In *Knowledge, Information, and Expectations in Modern Macroeconomics, in Honor of Edmund S Phelps*. Edited by P. Aghion, R. Frydman, J. Stiglitz, and M. Woodford. Princeton: Princeton University Press.

Kahneman, D. 2012. *Thinking, Fast and Slow*. London: Penguin.

Kahneman, D., and A. Tversky. 1979. Prospect Theory: An Analysis of Decision Under Risk. *Econometrica* 47 (2): 263–291.

Kaplan, G., B. Moll, and G.L. Violante. 2018. Monetary Policy According to HANK. *American Economic Review* 108 (3): 697–743.

Kapteyn, A., S. Van de Geer, H. Van de Stadt, and T. Wansbeek. 1997. Interdependent Preferences: An Econometric Analysis. *Journal of Applied Econometrics* 12 (6): 665–686.

Karnizova, L. 2010. The Spirit of Capitalism and Expectation-Driven Business Cycles. *Journal of Monetary Economics* 57 (6): 739–752.

Kay, J., and M. King. 2021. *Radical Uncertainty: Decision-Making Beyond the Numbers*. Norton.

Kazantzakis, N. 1965. *Report to Greco*. Translated by P.A. Bien. London: Faber and Faber.

Keane, M.P., and K.I. Wolpin. 1997. The Career Decisions of Young Men. *Journal of Political Economy* 105 (3): 473–522.

Kelley, A.C. 1988. Economic Consequences of Population Change in the Third World. *Journal of Economic Literature* 26 (4): 1685–1728.

Kelly, J. 2021. Sometimes We Need to 'Unbelieve' Our Tribe. *Financial Times*, 25/11/2021.

Kempf, H., and F. Moizeau. 2009. Inequality, Growth, and the Dynamics of Social Segmentation. *Journal of Public Economic Theory* 11 (4): 529–564.

Kennickell, A.B. 2009. Ponds and Streams: Wealth and Income in the U.S., 1989 to 2007, Finance and Economics D.P. 2009–13, Board of Governors of the Federal Reserve System.

Keynes, J.M. 1930. Economic Possibilities for our Grandchildren, in J.M. Keynes. 1963: *Essays in Persuasion*. New York: W.W.Norton & Co. (pp. 358–373).

Keynes, J.M. 1936. *The General Theory of Employment, Interest and Money*. London: Macmillan.

Kiesewetter, B., and A. Worsnip. 2023. Structural Rationality. In *The Stanford Encyclopedia of Philosophy (Fall 2023 Edition)*. Edited by E.N. Zalta, and U. Nodelman.

Kim, S., and J.H. Lee. 2010. Private Tutoring and Demand for Education in South Korea. *Journal Economic Development and Cultural Change* 58 (2): 259–296.

King, R.G., and S.T. Rebelo. 1999. Resuscitating Real Business Cycles. In *Handbook of Macroeconomics*. Edited by J.B. Taylor, and M. Woodford, vol. 1, Chap. 14, 927–1007. Amsterdam: Elsevier.

King, R.G., C.I. Plosser, and S.T. Rebelo. 1988. Production, Growth and Business Cycles I. The Basic Neoclassical Model. *Journal of Monetary Economics* 21 (2–3): 195–232.

Kirman, A.P. 1992. Whom or What Does the Representative Individual Represent? *The Journal of Economic Perspectives* 6 (2): 117–136.

Kirman, A.P. 2010. The Economic Crisis is a Crisis for Economic Theory. *Cesifo Economic Studies* 56 (4): 498–535.

Kirman, A.P. 2011. *Complex Economics: Individual and Collective Rationality*. Routledge.

Kirman, A.P. 2016. Complexity and Economic Policy: A Paradigm Shift or a Change in Perspective? *A Review Essay on David Colander and Roland Kupers's Complexity and the Art of Public Policy, Journal of Economic Literature* 54 (2): 534–572.

Kirman, A.P., and A. Serletis. 2016. Ants and Nonoptimal Self-Organization: Lessons For Macroeconomics. *Macroeconomic Dynamics* 20 (2): 601–621.

Knack, S., and P. Keefer. 1997. Does Social Capital Have an Economic Payoff: A Cross Country Investigation. *Quarterly Journal of Economics* 112 (4): 1251–1288.

Knack, S., and Zak, P. 1999. Trust and Growth. Claremont University Working Paper.

Knight, J., L. Song, and R. Gunatilaka. 2009. Subjective Well-Being and Its Determinants in Rural China. *China Economic Review* 20 (4): 635–649.

Knowles, S. 2010. Inequality and Economic Growth: The Empirical Relationship Reconsidered in the Light of Comparable Data. *Journal of Development Studies* 41 (1): 135–159.

Koike, Y. 2015. Thomas Piketty's Japanese Tour, Project Syndicate, 1/3/2015. http://www.project-syndicate.org/commentary/japanese-income-inequality-by-yuriko-koike-2015-03

Kolodny, N., and J. Brunero. 2023. Instrumental Rationality. In *The Stanford Encyclopedia of Philosophy (Summer 2023 Edition, Online)*. Edited by E.N. Zalta, and U. Nodelman.

Kotlikoff, L., and L. Summers. 1981. The Role of Intergenerational Transfers in Aggregate Capital Formation. *Journal of Political Economy* 89 (4): 706–732.

Koundouri, P., N. Pittis, and P. Samartzis. 2023. Conceptions of Rationality and Their Justifications, DEOS Working Paper 2322, Athens University of Economics and Business.

Kremer, M. 1993. Population Growth and Technological Change: One Million B.C. to 1990. *Quarterly Journal of Economics* 108 (3): 681–716.

Kroes, P., M. Franssen, and L. Bucciarelli. 2009. Rationality in Design. In *Handbook of the Philosophy of Science, Philosophy of Technology and Engineering Sciences*. Edited by A. Meijers, 565–600. North-Holland.

Krugman, P.A. 1996. *The Self Organizing Economy (The Mitsui Lectures in Economics)*. Hoboken: Wiley-Blackwell.

Krusell, P., and A. Smith. 1998. Income and Wealth Heterogeneity in the Macroeconomy. *Journal of Political Economy* 106 (5): 867–896.

Krusell, P.B., and A.A. Smith Jr. 2003. Consumption-Savings Decisions with Quasi-Geometric Discounting. *Econometrica* 71 (1): 365–375.

Kumhof, M., and R. Rancière. 2010. Inequality, Leverage and Crises, IMF Working Paper WP/10/268, November. http://www.imf.org/external/pubs/ft/wp/2010/wp10268.pdf

Kydland, F.E., and E.C. Prescott. 1982. Time to Build and Aggregate Fluctuations. *Econometrica* 50 (6): 1345–1370.

La Porta, R., F. Lopez-de-Silanes, A. Shleifer, and R. Vishny. 1999. The Quality of Government. *Journal of Law, Economics and Organization* 15 (1): 222–279.

Laibson, D. 2001. A Cue-Theory of Consumption. *Quarterly Journal of Economics* 116 (1): 81–119.

Laibson, D. 1997. Golden Eggs and Hyperbolic Discounting. *Quarterly Journal of Economics* 112 (2): 443–477.

Laibson, D. 2015. Why Don't Present-Biased Agents Make Commitments? *American Economic Review: Papers & Proceedings* 105 (5): 267–272.

Laibson, D., A. Repetto, and J. Tobacman, 2007. Estimating Discount Functions with Consumption Choices over the Lifecycle, NBER Working Paper No. 13314.

Lebaron, B., and L. Tesfatsion. 2008. Modeling Macroeconomies as Open-Ended Dynamic Systems of Interacting Agents. *American Economic Review* 98 (2): 246–250.

Lee, R.D. 1988. Induced Population Growth and Induced Technological Progress: Their Interaction in the Accelerating Stage. *Mathematical Population Studies* 1 (3): 265–288.

Leibenstein, H. 1966. Allocative Efficiency Versus "X-Efficiency". *American Economic Review* 56 (3): 392–415.

Levine, R., and Y. Rubinstein. 2017. Smart and Illicit: Who Becomes an Entrepreneur and Do They Earn More? *The Quarterly Journal of Economics* 132 (2): 963–1018.

Levitt, S.D., and S.J. Dubner. 2014. *A Rogue Economist Explores the Hidden Side of Everything*. London: Penguin.

Levy, D., A. Snir, A. Gotler, and H. Chen. 2020. Not All Price Endings Are Created Equal: Price Points and Asymmetric Price Rigidity. Journal of Monetary Economics 110 (C): 33–49.

Lewin, S.B. 1996. Economics and Psychology: Lessons for Our Own Day from the Early Twentieth Century. *Journal of Economic Literature* 34 (3): 1293–1323.

Li, D. 2002. Is the AK model still alive? The long-run relation between growth and investment re-examined. *Canadian Journal of Economics* 35: 93–113.

Li, T., S. Wang, and J. Yang. 2021. Robust Consumption and Portfolio Choices with Habit Formation. Economic Modelling 98 (C): 227–246.

Lindenberg, S. 1990. Homo Socio-Economicus: The Emergence of a General Model of Man in the Social Sciences. *Journal of Institutional and Theoretical Economics* 146 (4): 727–748.

Lindenberg, S. 2006. Social Rationality. In *International Rncyclopedia of Economic Sociology*. Edited by J. Beckert, and M. Zafirovski, 618–620. London: Routledge.

Lindenberg, S. 2013. Social Rationality, Self-Regulation and Well-Being: The Regulatory Significance of Needs, Goals, and the Self. In *Handbook of Rational Choice Social Research*. Edited by R. Wittek, T.A.B. Snijders, and V. Nee, 72–112, Stanford: Stanford University Press.

Linder, S.B. 1970. *The Harried Leisure Class*. New York: Columbia University Press.

Ljungqvist, L., and H. Uhlig. 2000. Tax Policy and Aggregate Demand Management Under Catching Up with the Joneses. *American Economic Review* 90 (3): 356–366.

Loewenstein, G., and D. Prelec. 1992. Anomalies in Intertemporal Choice: Evidence and an Interpretation. *Quarterly Journal of Economics* 107 (2): 573–598.

Lucas, R.E. 1988. On the Mechanics of Economic Development. *Journal of Monetary Economics* 22 (1): 3–42.

Maddison, A. 2001. *The World Economy: A Millennial Perspective OECD*. Paris.

Malthus, T.R. 1798. *An Essay on the Principle of Population*. London: W. Pickering.

Mankiw, N.G., and R. Reis. 2002. Sticky Information Versus Sticky Prices: A Proposal To Replace The New Keynesian Phillips Curve. *Quarterly Journal of Economics* 117 (4): 1295–1328.

Mankiw, N.G., D. Romer, and D.N. Weil. 1992. A Contribution to the Empirics of Economic Growth. *Quarterly Journal of Economics* 107 (2): 407–437.

Mann, M. 2013. *The Sources of Social Power*, Vol. 4: Globalizations, 1945–2011. Cambridge UP.

Manski, C.F. 2000. Economic Analysis of Social Interactions. *Journal of Economic Perspectives* 14 (3): 115–136.

Mankiw, N.G. and R. Reis. 2007. Sticky Information in General Equilibrium. *Journal of the European Economic Association*. 5: 603–613.

Maurer, J., and A. Meier. 2008. Smooth it Like the 'Joneses'? *Estimating Peer-Group Effects in Intertemporal Consumption Choice, Economic Journal* 118 (527): 454–476.

McBride, M. 2001. Relative Income Effects on Subjective Well-Being in the Cross-Section. *Journal of Economic Behavior and Organization* 45 (3): 251–278.

McDonald, R., and D. Siegel. 1986. The Value of Waiting to Invest. *Quarterly Journal of Economics* 101 (4): 707–727.

McGrattan, E.R. 1998. A defense of AK growth models. *Federal Reserve Bank of Minneapolis Quarterly Review* 22: 13–27.

Mearsheimer, J.J., and S. Rosato. 2023. *How States Think: The Rationality of Foreign Policy*. New Haven: Yale University Press.

Mechtel, M., F. Hett, and M. Kröll. 2014. Endogenous Social Identity and Group Choice, Beiträge zur Jahrestagung des Vereins für Socialpolitik 2014: Evidenzbasierte Wirtschaftspolitik - Session: Culture and Social Background, No. E16-V2. http://econstor.eu/bitstream/10419/100307/1/VfS_2014_pid_467.pdf

Munz, D.C. 2018. Status Threat, Not Economic Hardship, Explains the 2016 Presidential Vote. *PNAS (Proceedings of the National Academy of Science of the USA)* 115 (19): E4330–E4339.

Nelson, R.R., and S.G. Winter. 1995. Recent Evolutionary Theorizing About Economic Change. *Journal of Economic Literature* 33 (1): 48–90.

Ng, Y.-K., and J. Wang. 1993. Relative Income, Aspiration, Environmental Quality, Individual and Political Myopia: Why May the Rat-Race for Material Growth Be Welfare-Reducing. *Mathematical Social Sciences* 26 (1): 3–23.

Norman, N. 2023. Summary: Affluenza: The All-Consuming Epidemic by John de Graaf, David Wann and Thomas Naylor, Published Online: May 20, 2023 - Last Updated: October 27, 2023. https://paminy.com/summary-affluenza-consuming-epidemic/

O'Donoghue, T., and M. Rabin. 1999. Incentives for Procrastination. *Quarterly Journal of Economics* 114 (3): 769–816.

O'Donoghue, T., and M. Rabin. 2000. The Economics of Immediate Gratification. *Journal of Behavioral Decision Making* 13 (2): 233–250.

O'Donoghue, T., and M. Rabin. 2001a. Choice and Procrastination. *Quarterly Journal of Economics* 116 (1): 121–160.

O'Donoghue, T., and M. Rabin. 2001b. Self Awareness and Self Control. In *Chapter in Now or Later: Economic and Psychological Perspectives on Intertemporal Choice*. Edited by R. Baumeister, G. Loewenstein, and D. Read. Russell Sage.

O'Donoghue, T., and M. Rabin. 2015. Present Bias: Lessons Learned and to Be Learned. *American Economic Review: Papers and Proceedings* 105 (5): 273–279.

OECD. 2008. Education at a Glance, OECD Indicators.

Ogaki, M., and A. Atkeson. 1997. Rate of Time Preference, Intertemporal Elasticity of Substitution, and Level of Wealth. *Review of Economics and Statistics* 79 (4): 564–572.

Ok, E.A., and L. Koçkesen. 2000. Negatively Interdependent Preferences. *Social Choice and Welfare* 17 (3): 533–558.

Oosterbeek, H., and H.V. Ophem. 2000. Schooling Choices: Preferences, Discount Rates, and Rates of Return. *Empirical Economics* 25 (1): 15–34.

Oswald, A. 1997. Happiness and Economic Performance. *Economic Journal* 107 (445): 1815–1831.

Pham, T.K.C. 2005. Economic Growth and Status-Seeking Through Personal Wealth. *European Journal of Political Economy* 21 (2): 404–427.

Phelps, E.S., and R.A. Pollak. 1968. On Second-best National Saving and Game-Equilibrium Growth. *Review of Economics Studies* 35 (2): 185–199.

Phelps, E.S. 1968. Population Increase. *Canadian Journal of Economics* 1 (3): 497–518.

Picketty, T. 2014. *Capital in the Twenty-First Century*. Boston, MA: Belknap (Harvard) Press.

Picketty, T. 2015. Putting Distribution Back at the Center of Economics: Reflections on Capital in the Twenty-First Century. *Journal of Economic Perspectives* 29 (1): 67–88.

Pinker, S. 2021. Rationality: What It Is, Why It Seems Scarce, Why It Matters. Toronto, Ontario: Allen Lane Schelling, T.C. 20016. *Micromotives and Macrobehavior*. New York: WW Norton &Company

Pollak, R.A. 1976. Interdependent Preferences. *American Economic Review* 66 (3): 309–320.

Pradelski, B.S.R. (2015): The dynamics of social influence, *Oxford Dept. of Economics DP No. 742*, February. http://www.economics.ox.ac.uk/materials/papers/13857/paper742.pdf

Prescott, E.C. 2004. Why Do Americans Work So Much More than Europeans? Federal Reserve Bank of Minneapolis *Quarterly Review*. 28 (1): 2–14.

Putnam, R.D. 1993. The prosperous community: Social Capital and Public Life. *The American Prospect 4* (13): 35–42.

Putnam, R.D., R. Leonardi and R. Nanetti. 1993. *Making Democracy Work: Civic Traditions in Modern Italy*. Princeton, NJ: Princeton University Press.

Putnam, R.D. 2000. *Bowling Alone: The Collapse and Revival of American Community*. New York: Simon and Schuster.

Rabin, M. 1998. Psychology and Economics, *Journal of Economic Literature 36* (1): 11–46.

Rauscher, M. 1997. Conspicuous consumption, economic growth and taxation. *Journal of Economics* 66: 35–42.

Rodrik, D. 2014. *The Globalization Paradox: Democracy and the Future of the World Economy*. New York: W.W. Norton & Company.

Romer, P. 1986. Increasing Returns and Long-Run Growth. *Journal of Political Economy* 94 (5): 1002–1037.

Romer, P. 1990. Endogenous Technological Change. *Journal of Political Economy* 98 (5): S71–S102.

Romer, P. 2015. Mathiness in the Theory of Economic Growth. *American Economic Review: Papers and Proceedings* 105 (5): 89–93.

Romer, P. 2016. The Trouble with Macroeconomics, Update. https://paulromer.net/trouble-with-macroeconomics-update

Rose, D. 2006. Social Comparisons and Social Order: Issues Relating to a Possible Restudy of W.G. Runciman's Relative Deprivation and Social Justice, University of Essex ISER Wroking Paper No. 2006–48, (September).

Routledge, B.R., and J. von Amsberg. 2002. Social Capital and Growth. *Journal of Monetary Economics* 50 (1): 167–193.

Rubinstein, A. 2003. Economics and Psychology? *The Case of Hyperbolic Discounting, International Economic Review* 44 (4): 1207–1216.

Runciman, W.G. 1966. *Relative Deprivation and Social Justice*. Berkeley: University of California Press.

Russel, N.U. 1997. Lessons from Japanese Cram Schools. In *The Challenges of Eastern-Asian Education: Lessons from America*, 153–170. Albany, NY: University of New York Press.

Saint-Paul, G. 1993. Economic Reconstruction in France: 1945–58. In Postwar Economic Reconstruction and Lessons for the East Today. Edited by R. Dornbusch, W. Nolling, and R. Layard. Cambridge MA: MIT Press.

Saint-Paul, G. 2011. *The Tyranny of Utility: Behavioral Social Science and the Rise of Paternalism*. Princeton: Princeton University Press.

Saint-Paul, G., and T. Verdier. 1993. Education, Democracy and Growth. *Journal of Development Economics* 42 (2): 399–407.

Sandel, M.J. 2012. *What Money Can't Buy: The Moral Limits of Markets*. London: Allen Lane.

Schaafsma, J. 1976. The Consumption and Investment Aspects of the Demand for Education. *Journal of Human Resources* 11 (2): 233–242.

Schade, C.D., and A. Snir. 2020. A Lab Test on the Decision not to Decide. *Business Research* 13 (3): 1253–2129.

Schafer, A., and S. Valente. 2011. Habit Formation, Dynamic Altruism, and Population Dynamics. *Macroeconomics Dynamics* 15 (3): 365–397.

Scheinkman, J.A. 2008. Social Interactions. In *The New Palgrave Dictionary of Economics*. Edited by S. Durlauf, and L. Blume, 2nd ed. London: Palgrave Macmillan.

Schelling, T.C. 1978. *Micro Motives and Macro Behavior*. New York: W.W. Norton.

Schultz, T.W. 1963. *The Economic Value of Education*. New York: Columbia University Press.

Schumpeter, Joseph. 1954. *History of Economic Analysis*. London: George Allen and Unwin.

Selten, R. 2001. What is Bounded Rationality? In *Bounded Rationality: The Adaptive Toolbox*, ed. G. Gigerenzer and R. Selten, 13–36. Boston: The MIT Press.

Senik, C. 2009. Direct Evidence on Income Comparisons and Their Welfare Effects. *Journal of Economic Behavior and Organization* 72 (1): 408–424.

Shapiro, C., and J.E. Stiglitz. 1984. Equilibrium Unemployment as a Worker Discipline Device. *American Economic Review* 74 (3): 433–444.

Shayo, M. 2009. A Model of Social Identity with an Application to Political Economy: Nation. *Class, and Redistribution, American Political Science Review* 103 (2): 147–174.

Shayo, M. 2020. Social Identity and Economic Policy. *Annual Review of Economics* 12 (1): 355–389.

Shiller, R.J. 2005. *Irrational Exuberance*, 2nd ed. Princeton: Princeton University Press.

Shiller, R.J. 2014. Speculative Asset Prices. *American Economic Review* 104 (6): 1486–1517.

Shiller, R.J. 2017. Narrative Economics. *American Economic Review* 107 (4): 967–1004.

Siegel, H. 2004. Rationality and Judgment. *Metaphilosophy* 35 (5): 597–613.

Simon, H.A. 1955. A Behavioral Model of Rational Choice. *The Quarterly Journal of Economics* 69 (1): 99–118.

Simon, H.A. 1978. Rationality as Process and as Product of Thought. *American Economic Review* 68 (2): 1–16.

Simon, H.A. 1981. Information-Processing Models of Cognition. *Journal of the American Society of Information Science* 32 (5): 364–377.

Simon, H.A. 1993. Altruism and Economics. *American Economic Review* 83 (2): 156–161.

Simon, H.A. 2001. Rationality in Society. In *International Encyclopedia of the Social and Behavioral Sciences*, ed. N.J. Smelser and P.B. Baltes, 12782–12786. Oxford: Pergamon Press.

Simon, H.A. 2018. Rationality, Bounded. In The New Palgrave Dictionary of Economics. Edited by Macmillan Publishers Ltd. 3rd ed., 11288–11290. London: Palgrave Macmillan.

Simon, J.L. 1977. *The Economics of Population Growth*. Princeton: Princeton University Press.

Simon, J.L. 1981. The Ultimate Resource. Princeton: Princeton University Press.

Sims, C.A. 2003. Implications of Rational Inattention. *Journal of Monetary Economics* 50 (3): 665–690.

Six, M., and F. Wirl. 2015. Optimal Pollution Management When Discount Rates Are Endogenous. *Resource and Energy Economics* 42: 53–70.

Skidelsky, R. 2021. *What's Wrong with Economics? A Primer for the Perplexed*. New Haven: Yale University Press.

Smith, R. 2022. Do Emotions Help or Hinder Rational Thinking? More Rational Individuals Show Greater Emotional Awareness, Psychology Today (Online), August. https://www.psychologytoday.com/us/blog/the-neuroscience-emotion-and-decisionmaking/202208/do-emotions-help-or-hinder-rational-thinking

Smith, V.L. 1991. Rational Choice: The Contrast between Economics and Psychology. *Journal of Political Economy* 99 (4): 877–897.

Smith, V.L. 2003. Constructivist and Ecological Rationality in Economics. *American Economic Review* 93 (3): 465–508.

Snir, A., D. Levy, and H. Chen. 2017. End of 9-Endings, Price Recall, and Price Perceptions. *Economics Letters* 155 (C): 157–163.

Snower, D., and A. Lindbeck. 2019. Cooperation and Identity, Social Macroeconomics Working Paper sm-wp-2019–06 (June).

Smith, A. 1759, 1982. *The theory of moral sentiments*. Liberty Fund: Indianapolis.

Smith, A. 1776. *The Wealth of Nations*. W. Strahan and T. Cadell: London.

Sobel, J. 2005. Interdependent Preferences and Reciprocity. *Journal of Economic Literature* 43 (2): 392–436.

Solow, R. 1995. Trust: The Social Virtues and the Creation of Prosperity (Book Review). *New Republic* 213 (1): 36–40.

Spear, Stephen E. 1991. Growth, Externalities, and Sunspots. *Journal of Economic Theory* 54 (1): 215–223.

Sprenger, C. 2015. Judging Experimental Evidence on Dynamic Inconsistency. *American Economic Review: Papers and Proceedings* 105 (5): 280–285.

Startz, R., and K.-P. Tsang. 2012. Nonexponential Discounting: A Direct Test and Perhaps A New Puzzle. *The B.E. Journal of Macroeconomics* 12 (1): 1–35.

Steele, G.R. 2004. Understanding Economic Man: Psychology, Rationality, and Values. *The American Journal of Economics and Sociology* 63 (5): 1021–1055.

Steuer, M. 2003. *The Scientific Study of Society*. Dordrecht: Kluwer Academic Publishers.

Stiglitz, J.E. 2023. Keynote Address in the Festschrift for Professor Alan Kirman, Bank of England, 16–17th March 2023. https://www.rebuildingmacroeconomics.ac.uk/_files/ugd/1a4a52_1f851a5b627d4719b59275c615c8d7c8.pdf

Stiglitz, J.E. 2012. *The Price of Inequality*. London: Penguin.

Stiglitz, J.E. 2015. Reconstructing Macroeconomic Theory to Manage Economic Policy, in Laurent, E. and J. Cacheux (Eds). 2015. *Fruitful Economics: Papers in honor of and by Jean-Paul Fitoussi*, Palgrave Macmillan. Ch. 1 (pp. 20–56).

Stiglitz. J.E. 2018: Where Modern Macroeconomics Went Wrong. *Oxford Review of Economic Policy* 34 (1-2): 70–106.

Storr, V.H. 2014. Why Culture in Economics? *Review of Austrian Economics* 27 (4): 495–503.

Strotz, R.H. 1956. Myopia and Inconsistency in dynamic Utility Maximization. *Review of Economic Studies* 23 (3): 165–180.

Strulik, H. 2015. Hyperbolic Discounting and Endogenous Growth. *Economics Letters* 126 (C), 131–134.

Strulik, H. 2021. Hyperbolic Discounting and the Time-Consistent Solution of Three Canonical Environmental Problems. *Journal of Public Economic Theory* 23: 462–486.

Swedberg, R. 1991. Major Traditions of Economic Sociology. *Annual Review of Sociology* 17 (1): 251–276.

Swedberg, R. 2005. Towards an Economic Sociology of Capitalism. *L'année Sociologique* 55 (2): 419–449.

Sylwester, K. 2002. Can Education Expenditures Reduce Income Inequality? *Economic Education Review* 21 (1): 43–52.

Tabellini, G. 2008. The Scope of Cooperation: Values and Incentives. *Quarterly Journal of Economics* 123 (3): 905–950.

Taleb, N.N. 2008. *The Black Swan: The Impact of the Highly Improbable*. London: Penguin.

Tamura, R. 1991. Income Convergence in an Endogenous Growth Model. *Journal of Political Economy* 99 (3): 522–540.

Tansel, A., and F. Bircan. 2006. Demand for Education in Turkey: A Tobit Analysis of Private Tutoring Expenditures. *Economics of Education Review* 25 (3): 303–313.

Taylor, J.B. 1993. Discretion Versus Policy Rules in Practice. *Carnegie-Rochester Conference Series on Public Policy* 39 (1): 195–214.

Tesfatsion, L. 2006. Agent-Based Computational Economics: A Constructive Approach to Economic Theory, Chapter 16. In *Handbook of Computational Economics*. Edited by L. Tesfatsion, and K.L Judd, vol. 2, Part 2. Amsterdam: North-Holland.

Thaler, R.H. 1981. Some Empirical Evidence on Dynamic Inconsistency. *Economic Letters* 8 (3): 201–207.

Thaler, R.H. 2016. *Misbehaving*. London: Penguin.

Thaler, R.H., and C. Sunstein. 2009. *(Updated Edition): Nudge: Improving Decisions About Health, Wealth, and Happiness*. New York: Penguin.

Thaler, R.H., and H.M. Shefrin. 1981. An Economic Theory of Self-Control. *Journal of Political Economy* 89 (2): 392–406.

Trentmann, F. 2016. *Empire Of Things: How We Became a World of Consumers, from the Fifteenth Century to the Twenty-First*. Toronto, Ontario: Allen Lane.

Tsoukis, C. and F. Tournemaine. 2016. *Status, identity and the macroeconomy*. Mimeo:https://www.researchgate.net/publication/311102042_Status_identity_and_the_macroeconomy

Tournemaine, F., and C. Tsoukis. 2008. Relative Consumption, Relative Wealth and Growth. *Economics Letters* 100 (2): 314–316.

Tournemaine, F., and C. Tsoukis. 2009. Status Jobs, Human Capital and Growth: The Effects of Heterogeneity. *Oxford Economic Papers* 61 (3): 467–493.

Tournemaine, F. and C. Tsoukis. 2010. Gain versus pain from status and ambition: Effects on growth and inequality. *The Journal of Socio-Economics* 39 (2): 286–294.

Tournemaine, F. 2007. Can Population Promote Income Per-Capita Growth? *A Balanced Perspective, Economics Bulletin* 15 (8): 1–7.

Tournemaine, F. 2008. Social Aspirations and Choice of Fertility: Why Can Status Motive Reduce Per-Capita Growth? *Journal of Population Economics* 21 (1): 49–66.

Tournemaine, F., and C. Tsoukis. 2010a. Gain Versus Pain From Status and Ambition: Effects on Growth and Inequality. *The Journal of Socio-Economics* 39 (2): 286–294.

Tournemaine, F., and C. Tsoukis. 2010b. Status, Fertility, Growth and the Great Transition. *The Singapore Economic Review* 55 (3): 553–574.

Tournemaine, F., and C. Tsoukis. 2015. Public Expenditures, Growth and Distribution in a Mixed Regime of Education with a Status Motive. *Journal of Public Economic Theory* 17 (5): 673–701.

Tournemaine, F., and C. Tsoukis. 2015b. The Growth-Distribution Nexus in a Mixed Regime of Education with a Status Motive: On the Macroeconomic of the Welfare State. *Economic Modelling* 47 (C), 235–243.

Tournemaine, F., and C. Tsoukis. 2018. The Great Transition: Implication from Environmental Policy for the Quality-Quantity Trade-Off in Children-Rearing. *The Singapore Economic Review* 63 (5): 1155–1174.

Tournemaine, F., and P. Luangaram. 2012. R&D, Human Capital, Fertility, and Growth. *Journal of Population Economics* 25 (3): 923–953.

Tsoukis, C. 2007. Keeping up with the Joneses, Growth, and Distribution. *Scottish Journal of Political Economy* 54 (4): 575–600.

Tsoukis, C. 2014. *Status, Hyperbolic Discounting, Growth, and Distribution*. New York: Mimeo.

Tsoukis, C. 2020. *Theory of Macroeconomic Policy*. Oxford: Oxford University Press.

Tsoukis, C., and F. Tournemaine. 2013. Status in a Canonical Macro Model: Status, Growth, and Inequality. *The Manchester School* 81 (S2): 65–92.

Tsoukis, C., and F. Tournemaine. 2016. *Status, Identity and the Macroeconomy*. New York: Mimeo.

Tsoukis, C., and F. Tournemaine. 2024. *Hyperbolic Discounting, Labour Supply and Growth*. New York: Mimeo.

Tuckett, D. 2009. Addressing the Psychology of Financial Markets, Economics. *The Open-Access, Open-Assessment E-Journal* 12 (3) (2009–40): 1–22.

Tuckett, D., Holmes, D., Pearson, A., and Chaplin, G. 2020. Monetary Policy and the Management of Uncertainty: A Narrative Approach, Bank of England Staff Working Paper No. 870.

Turnovsky, S.J. 1996. *Methods of Macroeconomic Dynamics*. Boston, MA: MIT Press.

Tversky, A., and D. Kahneman. 1991. Loss Aversion in Riskless Choice: A Reference-Dependent Model. *Journal of Economic Literature* 106 (4): 1039–1061.

Uzawa, H. 1965. Optimal Technical Change in an Aggregative Model of Economic Growth. *International Economic Review* 6 (1): 18–31.

Varvarigos, D., and G. Xin. 2015. Social Interactions, the Evolution of Trust, and Economic Growth. Working Paper No. 15/05, University of Leicester.

Veblen, T. 1899. *The Theory of the Leisure Class: An Economic Study of Institutions*. Macmillan.

Vedder, R.K., and L.E. Gallaway. 1997. *Out of Work: Unemployment and Government in Twentieth-Century America*. New York: New York University Press.

de Vries, J. 2008. *The Industrious Revolution: Consumer Behavior and the Household Economy, 1650 to the Present*. Cambridge: Cambridge University Press.

Weber, M. 1958. The Protestant Ethic and the Spirit of Capitalism, English Translation, Charles Scribners' and Sons [from the Original 1905 German Edition].

West, S.A. and M. Ghoul. 2019. *Conflict within cooperation. Current Biology* 29 (11): 425–426.

Weiss, Y., and C. Fershtman. 1998. Social Status and Economic Performance: A Survey. *European Economic Review* 42 (3–5): 801–820.

Wiener, M. 1981. *English Culture and the Decline of the Industrial Spirit, 1850–1980*. Cambridge: Cambridge University Press.

Wilkinson, R.G., and K.E. Pickett. 2009a. Income Inequality and Social Dysfunction. *Annual Review of Sociology* 35 (1): 493–511.

Wilkinson, R.G., and K.E. Pickett. 2009b. *The Level Spirit*. London: Allen Lane.

Williamson, O.E. 2000. The New Institutional Economics: Taking Stock, Looking Ahead. *Journal of Economic Literature* 38 (3): 595–613.

Witztum, A. 2019a. *The Betrayal of Liberal Economics: Volume I: How Economics Betrayed Us*. London: Palgrave Macmillan.

Witztum, A. 2019b. *The Betrayal of Liberal Economics: Volume II: How We Betrayed Economics*. London: Palgrave Macmillan.

Wolf, H. 1993. The Lucky Miracle: Germany 1945–1951. In *Postwar Economic Reconstruction and Lessons for the East Today*. Edited by R. Dornbusch, W. Nolling, and R. Layard. Cambridge MA: MIT Press.

Wolff, E.N. 2010. Recent Trends in Household Wealth in the United States: Rising Debt and the Middle-Class Squeeze—an Update to 2007, WP No. 589, March 2010, Levy Institute. http://www.levyinstitute.org/publications/?docid=1235

Woodford, M. 2003. *Interest and Prices: Foundations of a Theory of Monetary Policy*. Princeton: Princeton University Press.

Yand, Z., and R. Zhang. 2018. On the Diversity of Growth Patterns with Habit Formation. *Economics Letters* 170 (C): 155–158.

Zafirovski, M. 2016. Toward Economic Sociology/Socio-Economics? *Sociological Components in Contemporary Economics and Implications for Sociology, American Sociologist* 47 (1): 56–80.

Zhang, J. 1996. Optimal Public Investments in Education and Endogenous Growth. *Scandinavian Journal of Economics* 98 (3): 387–404.

Zhang, L. 2008. Political Economy of Income Distribution Dynamics. *Journal of Development Economics* 87 (1): 119–139.

Zhou, G. 2016. The Spirit of Capitalism and Rational Bubbles. *Macroeconomic Dynamics* 20 (6): 1432–1457.

Zou, H.-F. 1994. The Spirit of Capitalism' and Long-Run Growth. *European Journal of Political Economy* 10 (2): 279–293.

Zou, Z., S. Chen, and W. Lei. 2014. Finite Horizon Consumption and Portfolio Decisions with Stochastic Hyperbolic Discounting. *Journal of Mathematical Economics* 52 (C): 70–80.

Index

C. Tsoukis et al., *Social and Behavioural Macroeconomics*, https://doi.org/10.1007/978-3-031-77748-6

O

P

Q

R

W

The manufacturer's authorised representative in the EU is Springer Nature Customer Service Centre GmbH, Europaplatz 3, 69115 Heidelberg, Germany. If you have any concerns regarding our products, please contact ProductSafety@springernature.com

Printed and bound by CPI Group (UK) Ltd, Croydon, CR0 4YY

01/10/2026

02225967-0016